Electronic Media and Indigenous Peoples

A Voice of Our Own?

A Voice

Electronic Media and Indigenous Peoples

of Our Own?

DONALD R. BROWNE

Iowa State University Press / Ames

Donald R. Browne is professor and chair of the Department of Speech-Communication at the University of Minnesota.

© 1996 Iowa State University Press, Ames, Iowa 50014

∞ Printed on acid-free paper in the United States of America

First edition, 1996

Library of Congress Cataloging-in-Publication Data

Browne, Donald R.
    Electronic media and indigenous peoples: a voice of our own? /
Donald R. Browne. — 1st ed.
        p.   cm.
    Includes bibliographical references (p.   ) and index.
    ISBN 0-8138-2316-1 (alk. paper)
        1. Ethnic mass media—Australia. 2. Mass media and minorities—Australia. 3. Mass media
    and language—Australia. I. Title.
P94.5.M552A83   1996
302.23'0994—dc20   96-17865

Last digit is the print number: 9 8 7 6 5 4 3 2 1

Cover illustration: adaptation of traditional Maori depiction of messenger bird, to serve as symbol of the modern Maori messenger—radio. Used by permission of Radio Tumeke, Whakatane, Aotearoa/New Zealand.

To my family

AND TO THE INDIGENOUS PEOPLES OF THIS WORLD

C O N T E N T S

PREFACE

The question mark following the subtitle of this book is something of a chameleon. "A Voice of Our Own?" can be interpreted in several ways; I've chosen three. The first, and most prominent, is the question of *whose* own, within a given indigenous community, local or national. Who seems to control programming, for whom is it intended, and to what ends? The second interpretation is less obvious. It involves the question of whether, and, if so, to what extent, indigenous peoples can develop their own approaches to the electronic media, as opposed to consciously or unconsciously aping the approaches of the majority culture media that have monopolized the media landscape until recently.

The third is the least obvious of all, and yet I very much hope that it will become clearer through what I set forth here. I've experienced real joy whenever I hear a language spoken, sung, or chanted for hundreds or even thousands of years by the oldest still-present inhabitants of the countries in which I've conducted my research. That joy has come in many forms: hearing a group of high school students singing and drumming Lakota songs over KILI-FM as I neared the station, and thinking that the surrounding South Dakota Badlands once again resounded to the music they echoed long before radio; watching a rock video with a group of young Aborigines in Alice Springs and learning from them how the conventions of MTV were transformed to present an infectiously rhythmic tribute to their extended family in Arnhem Land; driving through Norway's far north with the manager of NRK Sami Radio, discussing how the ancient *joik* (originally a herder's song) now covered a wide range of modern activities, thanks in part to its frequent appearance on Sami radio, then hearing him sing his personal joik and explain how its creator (a close friend) had woven into its wordless melody most of his quirks, foibles, and finer points.

While it's clear that the indigenous peoples themselves are the primary beneficiaries of their various electronic media outlets, it seems to me equally clear that majority culture peoples also can benefit enormously from this media's presence. Indigenous peoples once dominated the lands where majority cultures now rule and, through the media, can deepen the majority peoples' (as well as their own) appreciation and respect for those lands. They can help to remind majority cultures that there are many ways of thinking, feeling, and expressing, not a few of which could increase the majority's sense of interdependency, compassion, and mutual respect. They can promote understanding of their frustrations over injustice, prejudice, and neglect—frustrations that majority culture media often have fueled. And, through their manifold uses of the electronic media, they can provide a sense of discovery, of freshness, for eyes and ears jaded by the sameness of so much of majority culture media. In those respects, then, the indigenous electronic media can be a voice of our own for *all* of us.

The organization of this book is somewhat unconventional, at least for works about the electronic media. I open with a consideration of the term *indigenous,* as well as what it might mean in the context of the electronic media, and then complete the first chapter by discussing several media theories that might assist readers in understanding and assessing what follows. Chapter Two outlines the historical development of indigenous uses of electronic media. Chapter Three highlights programming purposes and practices. Chapter Four explores the supporting structure, such as the management, training, sources of influence on decision making, and financing and publicizing of indigenous operations.

Those general chapters are followed by three subject-specific chapters, each in my view crucial to an understanding of how the indigenous media operate: a detailed examination of how one indigenous people—the Maori—managed over time to establish themselves as a media presence; a consideration of issues related to language choice and usage—a somewhat controversial, even loaded, and certainly prominent subject of discussion among media practitioners; and a presentation of two political dimensions of indigenous electronic media: the political influences on this media and their own presentation of political material. The final chapter represents my attempt to pull the various threads together and then to explore future prospects for these media.

The research that informs this project has been a labor of love, but a costly labor. I've received strong financial support from various units at the University of Minnesota: the Department of Speech-Communication, the Graduate School, the Office of International Education, the Center for European Studies, and the College of Liberal Arts. I've also received intellectual advice and support from my academic colleagues at the University of Minnesota; Doug Boyd at the University of Kentucky; Tapio Varis at the University of Technology (Helsinki, Finland); and Carmin O'Leister at the Irish Studies Institute; Bruce Grundy at the University of Queensland; Ranginui Walker at the University of Auckland; Helen Molnar at the Royal Melbourne Institute of Technology; Helen Wilson at the New Zealand School of Broadcasting; Piripi Walker, a Maori educator; Samuli Aikio, a Sami educator; Brad Weiland, a Native American educator; and E. B. Eiselein, a Native American educator and researcher.

Most of all, I owe a tremendous debt to all of the indigenous electronic media staff members, and especially those whose names appear below, who so readily opened their doors to me, answered my questions, made observations and furnished data that I wouldn't otherwise have considered, and displayed a real curiosity to learn more about what their counterparts elsewhere were up to.

Australia: Tiga Bayles, Frieda Glynn, Graham Steele, Tony Walker, Dot West, Wayne Wharton

Canada: Bruce Girard, Conway Jocks

France: Roger Bordeu

Ireland: Aogan o Muircheartaigh, Brendan Feiritear, Tom Hardiman, Bobby Collins

New Zealand: Taura Eruera, David Harcourt, Ken Hippolite, Dinny Jaram, Chris Prowse, Henare Te Ua

Scandinavia: Nils Johan Héatta, Juhani Nousuniemi

United Kingdom: Alun Evans, Elwyn Jones, Lyn Jones

United States: Tom Casey, Phoebe Nez, Donovin Sprague, Frank Tyro

I told them that I hoped that my book would satisfy that curiosity and, to some extent, underscore the importance of their common endeavor. Now that the book has been completed, I hope that it does.

G L O S S A R Y

ABC—Australian Broadcasting Corporation.

Aboriginal—The indigenous peoples of Australia. While the term often is applied to indigenous peoples in other countries, Canada in particular, I limit its application to Australia in the present text.

ATSIC—Aboriginal and Torres Strait Islander Commission. The Australian federal government department in charge of Aboriginal affairs.

CPB—Corporation for Public Broadcasting. Administers budget for those public radio and television services receiving financial support through Congress' annual appropriation for public broadcasting.

DAA—Department of Aboriginal Affairs. The predecessor to ATSIC.

Iwi—Maori term for tribe.

Joik—Traditional Sami singing, usually wordless and somewhat chantlike.

Mana—Maori term for one's standing or reputation.

Narradio—localized radio service in Norway, Sweden, and Denmark, featuring the sharing of transmission time by many groups.

NRK—Norsk Rikskringkasting. The Norwegian Broadcasting Corporation.

Pakeha—Maori term for white persons. Not derogatory.

PSB—Public service broadcaster. Usually a noncommercial broadcast service and often one that has been (or still is) a nationwide monopoly, such as Great Britain's BBC.

RAI—Radio Audizioni Italia. The Italian Broadcasting Corporation.

Rangatiritanga—Maori term for trustee/trusteeship.

RNG—Raidio na Gaeltachta. The all-Irish language radio service of RTE.

RTE—Raidio Telefis Eirann. The Irish Broadcasting Corporation.

SBS—Special Broadcasting Services. The Australian public service broadcasting organization that is responsible for broadcasting to "nonmainstream" Australians: émigrés from Europe, Asia, and elsewhere, with a very small amount of programming for Aborigines in English.

SR—Sveriges Radio. The Swedish Broadcasting Corporation.

Taonga—Maori term for highly valued object.

TMP—Te Mangai Paho. The Maori-run funding agency for Maori broadcasting.

USAID—United States Agency for International Development. An associated agency of the U.S. Department of State, USAID is responsible for disbursing U.S. foreign aid to assist foreign nations with scientific, educational, agricultural, and other projects aimed at improving standards of living.

YLE—Yleisradio. The Finnish Broadcasting Corporation.

Electronic Media and Indigenous Peoples

A Voice of Our Own?

An Introduction and Some Theories

The term *indigenous* poses more than a few problems of definition. Its basic meaning is "one who is native to an area." But how large is an "area"? And how far back in time must one go to determine whether an individual or group is "native" to it? In our genealogically conscious era, we sometimes seem to feel that we can go back as far in time as we wish when we choose to search out our roots. The tracing of lineage has become something of a cottage industry in North America and in much of Europe. Once put to the test, however, the task may prove much more difficult, and the trail may disappear before we've even reached the nineteenth century. Non-Western population groups, especially if they lack written records, may resort more often to oral tradition, but the controversy over the accuracy of African-American author Alex Haley's efforts to determine his African lineage shows that that tradition, too, has its shortcomings.

Here, I take a more pragmatic approach: I attempt to determine which population groups presently living in a given area were first on the scene, according to available records. Cave dwellers inhabited much of Europe for millennia, but we have no evidence to indicate that an identifiable body of them is anywhere to be found now. Some population groups can establish that they inhabited a certain area before certain of its present-day tenants arrived and drove them out (e.g., the Cherokee of the United States). For my purposes, those who can establish that they have been in the area for the longest time, and continue to live there, would be the indigenous peoples of that area. And finally, all of the indigenous peoples whose experiences I present here are, or have been, in the minority in their lands, at least with respect to the development and administration of national or regional institutions: social, cultural, religious, military, economic, and political.

I do not attempt the difficult task of sorting out who is indigenous in most parts of postcolonial Africa and Asia. Most African and Asian nations are made up of a host of peoples, many of whom have lived in roughly the same area for centuries or millennia. While they were under colonial rule, they would have qualified as indigenous under the above definition, not only because of their long residency, but also because they were minorities in terms of holding power.* I refer to some of their experiences with the electronic media during the colonial period but supply few postcolonial examples, even though many indigenous groups in those nations enjoy the rights of citizenship yet have little access to the institutions mentioned above.

The preceding has some bearing on the uses made of the electronic media in any given society, because the media are closely linked with a society's institutions. As I observe time and again, the electronic media are dominated by the majority culture in virtually every nation or region, whether that culture is a numerical majority or not. As such, the media reflect the history, values, and institutional structures of that culture.

In that respect, the neglect of indigenous history, values, and institutions generally has been no worse than it has for minorities in general. But that observation itself helps to explain the lack of specific visibility for indigenous media: they tend to be treated as just another form of ethnic minority activity. In many ways, they are. I very much hope that what I present here also will be regarded as applicable to ethnic minority uses of, for example, broadcasting or tape.

Still, there are differences between indigenous peoples and other mi-

---

*The so-called Bantu peoples of South Africa pose a problem in that regard, since some of them were moving south into parts of present-day South Africa as white settlers were moving north, making it more difficult to establish who were the original settlers. However, I have chosen to treat South African Blacks, "Bantu" and otherwise, as indigenous peoples in the present account, since they certainly did not hold power during most of the years that electronic media have been present in South Africa.

norities, and I would argue that they are important differences. First, the most readily apparent difference is that indigenous peoples inhabited a particular region centuries or even millennia before someone else did. If others preceded them, we generally know little or nothing about their ways of life. While the indigenous peoples may not have been the original settlers of a given area—although the Maori in New Zealand, the Aborigines in Australia, and Native Americans and Inuit of North America seem to have been—they're the closest to holding that status in the eyes of present-day majority cultures.

Because they were there first, they were on hand to assist and/or resist succeeding settlers, who often eventually became the present-day majority. The assistance or resistance they provided is a part of a nation's history, culinary and religious practices, recreation, and much else, even if the majority fails to acknowledge or distorts what it has received from its indigenous forerunners.

Second, the indigenous peoples were at one time sovereign in their lands. They no longer are nor is it likely that they ever will be again, at least to the same extent. They lost those lands through warfare, through negotiation, through treason, through neglect, through intermarriage, through depopulation (often brought about by diseases introduced by more recent immigrants), through religious conversion, through enslavement, and through a host of other causes and acts. Where Western societies are concerned, most settlement by other than indigenous peoples came about by choice on the part of the settlers. The great exceptions are the shipment of slaves to the Americas and convict transportation to Australia. The former involved a non-Western population that has remained a minority (except in Haiti); the latter, a Western population that eventually became a substantial part of the majority culture.

Certainly one may argue about whether any or all of that gives indigenous peoples a special claim on the resources of the lands that once were theirs, but recent court decisions in Australia (the *Mabo* case), New Zealand (various Maori land rights cases), Canada (cases establishing Native American rights to self-government), and the United States (cases involving fishing and hunting rights for Native Americans) would indicate that there *is* a special claim.

The differences between indigenous peoples and other minorities have relevance to the electronic media. First, it seems quite clear that majority culture media generally have neglected the place and contributions of indigenous peoples in and to society. It also seems quite clear that those media have contributed to the perpetuation of negative stereotypes about indigenous peoples. While many minorities have suffered in those ways, this particular minority has suffered longer, yet indigenous peoples are more fundamental to a sense of history for any given country than any other minority could be, by having been there first and thus, willingly or not, shaping the nation that was to evolve. The present-day majority owes much to, and has much to learn from, indigenous peoples. The indigenous media can help that educational process. They can also help present generations of indigenous peoples to rediscover their pasts, as well as to learn of their present-day achievements. In the process, some indigenous listeners or viewers may become angrier about past or present injustices. That may pose a threat to the tranquillity of society as a whole, but it is unlikely to lead to anything so radical as independence movements. In any event, society as a whole can only become healthier when it addresses injustices.

The second point bears particularly on one of the most difficult issues where indigenous media are concerned: do indigenous peoples have a special right to access to the media? If they do, what forms should that right take? Full ownership and operation of media outlets? Guarantees of space or time on existing media outlets? And who will pay the substantial costs involved for reasonably professional production and transmission facilities so that indigenous media aren't ghettoized by virtue of their poor self-presentation or substandard media distribution systems? Court decisions on land and water usage and on ownership rights may or may not be applicable to rights of access to media outlets, but they surely are worth considering. In fact, Maori land rights cases, argued under the 1840 Treaty of Waitangi, have also helped Maori to establish their right to a share of the frequency spectrum and governmental assistance for Maori stations broadcasting over it.[1]

There is another important consideration that has little to do with history per se, or with judicial decisions. Rather, it is cultural. It has to do with different ways of seeing and hearing. Might majority cultures be able to learn something useful about alternative approaches to aural and visual portrayal through the electronic media by being exposed to indigenous media? And this leads to another question: are the indigenous media all that different in *how* they present their messages? These questions arise more than once in the chapters that follow, and the answers are neither clear nor unambiguous. There is evidence to indicate that there are some differences, and that they can help to introduce fresh and potentially valuable perspectives regarding the forms and substance of majority culture media presentation.

There is no doubt that, measured in strictly economic terms, indigenous electronic media are not economically efficient,[2] particularly when they prepare and present messages in indigenous languages spoken by as few as several hundred individuals. Furthermore, many speakers of indigenous languages are quite capable of speaking majority culture languages with roughly equal fluency. But the life of a culture has much about it that transcends economic efficiency. It is fundamental to the continued enrichment of the larger society because it is a continual reminder of alternatives. And nothing is more fundamental to a culture than its language.

The preservation or restoration of a language, and a culture in a larger sense, is not the task of the media alone. Schools, religious organizations, and other societal institutions all have roles to play. These roles are not the subjects of this book, although there are references to them. But it's worth emphasizing that this is not the task of the indigenous media alone, either: majority culture media also have roles to play in dispelling prejudice, in avoiding stereotypes, and in redressing neglect.

Still, the indigenous media clearly will play a leading role in preserving, restoring, and expanding the languages. Esekia Solofa, vice chancellor of the University of the South Pacific, expresses it very well: "Through the newspapers, radio, television and other audiovisual devices, they [media personnel] can set standards of language usage, coin new words, even set directions for development that can enliven and empower indigenous languages to carry the ever-changing information of technological change and development."[3]

Another important consideration is this: along with the power to affect the future of an indigenous language comes the issue of how to use that power responsibly. All media operations face that issue, although many don't acknowledge it. But indigenous electronic media operations really must do so. In many instances, they are the first channels through which the indigenous peoples have been able to enter the public sphere and there represent themselves in their own voices, under their own control. If those operations exclude some segments of the indigenous community from representation, they risk replicating the very thing that indigenous groups have resented in the majority culture's media portrayal of them. The line running between social responsibility and censorship can be a very fine one, and the manner in which the indigenous electronic media deal with it should be instructive (in a positive way, one hopes) for majority culture media.

I should make it clear at the outset that I do not see myself as speaking *for* indigenous peoples and their experiences with the electronic media. Rather, I speak *about* them in the hope that this book might enable them to learn from one another's experiences, and that still others, in majority and minority cultures, might learn from and through them.

Theory
and
Indigenous
Media

Very few indigenous media staff whom I've met think of their work in theoretical terms.

However, when I begin to discuss such subjects as the influence that majority electronic media "models" may have on indigenous media practices, and relate this to theories such as cultural imperialism or dependency, they often begin to see the subject in a new light, particularly in terms of being able to consider it with greater detachment. That certainly should be one of the uses for any good theory, or even a bad one.

The theories that have been most helpful to me in my studies of indigenous media are not among the classics in the field of communication research.* Most have been around for 20 or fewer years, and the studies that serve as their underpinnings and purportedly validate them often seem to me to lack rigor, both methodologically and with respect to quality of data. Still, they do serve a useful *suggestive* role, and it is in that spirit that I offer them here.

POLITICAL ECONOMY

Political economy has enjoyed some popularity with mass communications researchers (e.g., Babe, Bagdikian, Garnham, Pendakur, Smythe, Murdock, and Golding).[4] As applied by them, this theory treats politics and economics as interdependent factors or forces that influence such things as the relative strength of a nation's motion picture industry through legislation encouraging or discouraging that industry, such as surtaxes, import restrictions, and funding agencies (e.g., Canada's National Film Board). Its

---

*I am fully in agreement with Klaus Krippendorff when he admonishes us to remember that theories of human communication are not objective; rather, they are constructed out of our own cultural, social, linguistic, and perceptual systems. This has particular relevance for claims regarding their cross-cultural applicability. Krippendorff, Klaus, "Conversation or Intellectual Imperialism in Comparing Communication (Theories)," *Communication Theory,* 3, 3 (1993), 252–266.

supporters also regard *class* as key to understanding patterns of domination in the media and, therefore, predominant influences on media production.

Political economy has always struck me as more a perspective than a theory, but it certainly could be applied to indigenous media, particularly if a comparative examination of indigenous media in different countries were to reveal the presence of certain economically based political policies in some countries, but not in others, and a strong correlation between the presence or absence of those policies and the relative strength or weakness of the indigenous media. That relative strength or weakness could be assessed in part through the degree to which indigenous media productions resembled dominant culture productions in, for example, themes or production values. John Downing certainly applies it in a comparative fashion when he discusses comparative media resources available to ethnic minorities and to majority culture in the United States.[5]

HEGEMONY

Hegemony has been a popular theory for mass media scholars over the past 20 years or so. Drawing upon the work (not media-related) of Antonio Gramsci, its proponents consider media products as transmitting the values of one (often small, usually powerful) portion of society to society in general. Society in general, drawing much of its value system from the media, unconsciously and perhaps uncritically absorbs the values of that "elite" segment of society, making it difficult for alternative approaches to gain any toehold. It even may be that the elite itself is unaware, largely because it's held those values for years, decades, even centuries, that it *is* imposing them on the larger society. That element of unconscious transmission and reception strikes some media scholars as the most insidious aspect of hegemony, but such lack of awareness also reduces the likelihood of detecting hegemony's presence.

Todd Gitlin applies hegemony to the examination of U.S. commercial television programming, both by analyzing program content and by studying the process of developing programs. The quality of his evidence is uneven: not only is the analysis of program content quite subjective but there also is the problem of obtaining information on all of the major steps involved in program decision making, since much of the action takes place in private meetings and may or may not arise from conscious deliberation.[6] Carlos Lins da Silva applies hegemony to media development in Brazil and makes a quite convincing, if not very detailed, case for the position that the nature and agents of hegemony change over time.[7] Celeste Condit makes a quite compelling case for the consideration of hegemony as evolutionary social change, brought about through the interaction of numerous "contesting groups.''[8] That interpretation comes closest to helping to explain the evolution of at least some of the indigenous experiences I describe in succeeding chapters.

CULTURAL (MEDIA) IMPERIALISM

In many ways, hegemony is related to cultural (media) imperialism. Authors such as Herbert Schiller, Alan Wells, Oliver Boyd-Barrett, Kaarle Nordenstreng, Luis Beltran, C. C. Lee, Thomas McPhail, and several others have written works based on, or dealing with, cultural imperialism.[9] The gist of the theory is that certain nations are major exporters of their own cultures and that the ideological aspects of such exports are semipurposeful: individuals and companies (and, sometimes, governments) engaged in the act of exporting movies, radio and television programs, and other media do so not only for economic reasons but also in the belief that such exports will help to introduce audiences in other countries to different, and probably "superior," values and lifestyles—or, in the case of news services, a "North-dominated" picture of world events.

Evidence to support the theory of cultural imperialism is circumstantial, for the most part. Most of the scholars mentioned above have made a leap of faith in their reasoning along the following lines: U.S., British, Australian, Japanese, Mexican, and other countries' television entertainment is being exported to many countries that cannot afford to produce much TV entertainment of their own. The exporting countries' programs reflect their particular cultures. The exported material is so inexpensive and so well produced that it comes to dominate the TV schedules of those other countries, weakening or obliterating their own cultural values.

To be sure, there are certain nations that export a great deal of television programming, as well as movies. *Some* of that material does represent dominant national values. It certainly is inexpensive, and sometimes it's more "professionally" produced than what the receiving country can manage, at least for certain genres of programming (e.g., action-adventure shows). But there is very little hard (survey- or laboratory-based) evidence to support the contention that such shows displace or erode other country's cultures,[10] and such evidence as we have is inconclusive. Furthermore, many more countries are now producing more of their own entertainment programming.

CULTURAL DEPENDENCY

It is with respect to that last statement of the preceding section that cultural dependency may come into play.[11] The specific aspect of that theory that enters into my own work is based on the premise that receivers of imported material may not be aware of their dependency and may feel, or come to feel, that it is quite natural for their cars to come from Japan, their powdered milk from France, their movies and TV programs from Great Britain or the United States. Where cultural products in particular are concerned, a given country's broadcasters actually may seek to produce more of their own programs, but it is quite possible that they will have been so influenced by the "models" furnished through a heavy diet of imported material over the years that the new self-produced material will embody the cultural characteristics of the imported material that it replaces. What's more, the program producers and audiences may not even be aware that such a transfer is occurring.

Hard evidence to support cultural dependency as it may apply to the electronic media is scarce, as well. Omar Souk Oliveira's study of Brazilian soap operas makes the case that U.S. soaps and Brazilian soaps exist for the same purpose—to sell products—and exhibit a number of features in common,[12] but there's little clear indication of dependency in terms of Brazilian soaps being modeled after their U.S. counterparts. Still, my personal observation of TV sitcoms and game shows in several dozen Western and non-Western countries over nearly 40 years leads me to conclude that there is good reason to think that this aspect of the theory is supportable. The level of support differs: more in some countries than in others, more for some genres than for others, and perhaps to a greater degree now than earlier, with the combination of a spreading "free enterprise" approach and the increasing amounts of channel choice made possible by satellites, cable, and VCRs. The greater number of channels seems to have tempted more program producers to work for broader levels of acceptability so that their productions can find niches in wider markets. That in turn seems to be leading to greater levels of sameness in sitcoms, game shows, and perhaps news and action-adventure series.

The decision to round off or eliminate the sharp edges—the elements of a program that mirror most closely the producing country's culture—is conscious. But there is another aspect of dependency that has received little systematic exploration. Two studies, both conducted in Africa in the mid-1970s, raise the basic issue I take up here: how have majority culture (colonial or otherwise) models of professional conduct by broadcast staff influenced indigenous staff members? The studies, by Rita Cruise O'Brien (Algeria and Senegal) and Peter Golding (Nigeria),[13] both indicate some quite evident modeling behaviors, although they aren't universal.

The lack of exploration of this aspect of the electronic media may be due to the behavior's manifesting itself *un*consciously, which makes it more difficult to detect. It has particular application to the situations faced by indigenous electronic media staff. Recall the historical sequence of electronic media development outlined earlier. Indigenous electronic media operations were real rarities before the 1970s by which time the chief majority culture electronic media—radio and television—were well established. Most indigenous viewers and listeners, even some of the elderly, had never heard or seen anything else. Is it possible that they have become so dependent on the model of media performance exhibited by the majority culture media that it's difficult for them to conceive of alternative approaches? Might indigenous media staff (who, if they have prior experience with media operations, almost certainly would have attained it by working with majority culture media, at least until quite recently) face similar difficulties in conceiving of alternative approaches? Or, even if they can see other ways to communicate, might they assume, rightly or wrongly, that the indigenous audience would reject or question such approaches?

Finally, the concept of public sphere, as set forth by Jurgen Habermas,[14] but particularly as interpreted by James Curran,[15] intrigues me. Clearly the indigenous peoples have had little opportunity to gain prominence within the sort of public sphere Curran has extrapolated from Habermas: "a neutral zone where access to relevant information affecting the public good is widely available, where discussion is free of domination by the state, and where all those participating in public debate do so on an equal basis."[16] Now that indigenous peoples *are* gaining some degree of access to such a sphere, might this affect the quality of discussion and debate?

If any theory guides my work in indigenous media, it is cultural dependency theory—or, at least, the two aspects I have just noted. I am reluctant to call the material that appears in this book a test of that theory, simply because I have yet to develop a sufficiently systematic set of criteria through which to carry out such a test. I can hope that I may succeed in guiding or encouraging others. My tentative conclusions appear in the final chapter of this book. While they will not encourage anyone who is uncomfortable with ambiguity, they should encourage anyone who thinks of humans as adaptable.

A Brief History of Indigenous Electronic Media

There is some dispute as to which nation was the first to license an electronic media service intended for the general public. Canada (1919) and the United States (1920) are the most frequently cited claimants to the title, but there are several others. There is no dispute that the medium grew rapidly over the next 10 years, to the point where virtually all industrialized nations had licensed radio services by the end of the 1920s. Some of those services were publicly "owned," some were private, and some were units of government, but they had one thing in common: they were established by, operated by, and reflected the majority culture of each nation.

The 1920s were not characterized by sensitivity toward ethnic or linguistic minorities. In schools, religious institutions, business, and government, majority cultures dominated, usually to the point of passively ignoring or actively excluding consideration of minorities. The general expectation was that minorities would wish to become like the majority in dress, language, and even, if possible, skin color and hair style. So equipped, they would be in a better position to enjoy the benefits of majority society membership.

That expectation already existed in many countries before radio came on the scene. As public education, mass circulation newspapers, entrepreneurship, and popularly elected governments developed during the nineteenth century, they took forms congenial to majority cultures. While minorities might not have been excluded from participation (although quite often they were), they were expected to play the game according to majority culture rules and usually under majority culture leadership.

A large share of the world had come under colonial rule during the period stretching from the seventeenth to the nineteenth century, and much of it remained so through the first half of the twentieth century. But most of the colonizing nations—Great Britain, France, Russia, Spain, Portugal, Italy, Germany, the Netherlands—already had various minorities within their own borders well before they extended their domains to more distant lands. Most of those minorities were religious, but some were linguistic, and a few of them were remnants of the indigenous peoples who had once ruled the lands now governed by larger or more powerful forces. If they continued to speak their sometimes ancient languages—Basque, Breton, Catalan, Frisian, Irish, Provençal, Welsh, or any of a number of others—it wasn't because the ruling majority encouraged it. It most certainly wasn't helpful in dealing with members of the majority society, most of whom regarded such languages as quaint at best or as crude, barbaric, or even subversive at worst.

It isn't surprising that the colonial powers tended to follow similar practices when they occupied foreign soil. Rarely did those who represented secular interests bother to learn indigenous languages, but it soon became clear that "locals" who learned colonial languages could profit greatly thereby. The same held true to some extent for representatives of Christianity, although more of them at least attempted to learn indigenous languages. In any event, locals by and large remained in a state of submission from which they could escape through assimilation, linguistic and otherwise, with the new majority (in power, if not in number) represented by the colonists.

By the turn of the twentieth century, the process of assimilation had taken a considerable toll on indigenous languages, although some of them probably would have died out in any case. A few groups were attempting to reclaim their linguistic heritage before their tongues, too, vanished from this earth. Prosper Mérimée and other late nineteenth-century writers struggled to save Provençal through their novels, plays, and poetry in the language; the first Sami language newspaper commenced publication in 1922 but lasted less than two years.[1] The preservation of indigenous languages through the medium of print was proving difficult.

Radio's Initial Decades: 1920–1939

Radio should have been a more congenial medium for indigenous languages, based as it was on oral communication. As such, it could enable users of those languages to communicate without recourse to the printed word, which sometimes didn't exist for given languages, and when it did, the considerable expense of printing made it impractical to prepare and distribute newspapers, magazines, and books to an often minuscule readership. Also, certain indigenous peoples seemed to attribute greater authority to the spoken word than to its written counterpart.

However, the government authorities in charge of licensing radio stations, much like the larger societies of which they were a part, saw radio as a reflection of those societies. Minority groups, indigenous or not, went largely unacknowledged on the airwaves, aside from live performances or recordings of Basque dances, Sami *joiks*, Maori hymn singing, or other forms of music. The groups themselves usually lacked the financial and/or political power to seek radio licenses, and many probably never entertained the hope of receiving them, anyway—and, thus, never tried.

Countries that featured reasonably distinctive regional variations, or which were made up of states, provinces, principalities, or other political units, sometimes were willing to accommodate indigenous voices on a small scale through regional or provincial stations that functioned as part of national (usually monopoly) systems. The British developed specific British Broadcasting Corporation (BBC) broadcast units for Scotland (1932), Northern Ireland (1934), and Wales (1937), as well as parts of England. Norway's monopoly broadcast service, Norsk Rikskringskasting (NRK), experimented irregularly with programs in Sami (Lapp) starting in 1934 and developed a regularly scheduled Sami service in 1946 for the northernmost region of the country; Finland followed suit a year later. Iraq introduced a Kurdish language service in 1939.

Such stations had a few minutes to a few dozen hours weekly of program time to themselves, but their indigenous minority programming was limited: for example, the BBC's service for Wales contained sporadic programming in Welsh starting in 1923, but Welsh language broadcasts over the next four decades fluctuated and failed to be so much as a dozen hours per week.[2] The BBC service for Scotland introduced Scots Gaelic in 1923, but it was sporadic until 1935, when a Gaelic department was created and began to produce 35 minutes of programming—per *week!*[3] The NRK's regularly scheduled Sami service initially ran for 20 minutes a week, but for only 17 weeks out of the year; a yearlong weekly service did not come about until 1957.[4]

Such minuscule amounts of airtime for indigenous languages hardly were surprising in view of the attitude of a number of the corporate decision makers. When the BBC's regional director for Scotland wrote to the BBC's director of programs in London, requesting consideration of airtime for broadcast lessons in speaking Scots Gaelic, the latter replied, "I personally disagree with the idea, as I should have thought that it was better not to do anything which would stimulate the spread of 'native' languages at a time when we are doing all we can for the English language."[5]

What the BBC was doing—and what many of the public service monopoly broadcasters in Europe did in those days—involved the establishment and maintenance of a standard of language usage. The broadcast services were expected to lead the nation in and into the "correct" use of English, French, or whatever the majority language was. Michael Shapiro sees this as political, in part, in that other than "pure" languages were (and sometimes still are) regarded as a potential challenge to central authority.[6]

The Spain of Generalissimo Francisco Franco was even less well disposed toward its indigenous minorities and their languages. The Basques of northeastern Spain had fought on the Republican side during the Spanish Civil War (1936–1939), and a number of prominent Basques fled the country as Franco's forces took power. Just after World War II, they established a radio station (Radio Euzkadi, or Basque Radio) in southwestern France and began broadcasting back into Spain. Their broadcasts included Basque language lessons—of vital importance because the Franco government had outlawed even the speaking of Basque in public—but most of their programming was in Spanish. Spain pressured the French government to withdraw that privilege in 1954, and the station didn't resume broadcasting until 1965, when it was moved to Venezuela. From there it broadcast back to Spain (via shortwave) until 1977, when it went off the air as a result of the restoration of democracy (including the initiation of a Basque radio and TV service) in Spain following Franco's death.[7]

Broadcast practices in the African colonies and protectorates of the four major colonial powers—France, Great Britain, Belgium, and Portugal—generally favored broadcasts in the colonial languages in those few colonies where broadcasting was available at all. (Even Nigeria, the largest and most populous of all African colonies, had only a wired radio service, largely rebroadcasting material relayed from London, until 1949.)

The Soviet Union had broadcast in some of the languages of its many national groups starting in the mid-1920s. Most of those languages were the majority languages of the various republics (e.g., Ukrainian in the Ukrainian republic), but others were the minority groups', such as Yakut (Siberia). A low level of literacy in any language was a major reason for providing radio services in a variety of languages, since that presumably would assist in the more rapid dissemination of the Communist doctrine. But Russian was the predominant broadcast language, and as Ellen Mickiewicz points out, Russian received the lion's share of the resources.[8]

World War II and Its Aftermath: 1940–1964

World War II proved to be a turning point of sorts: indigenous minorities served as members of national armed forces and as factory workers in defense industries and often became more visible within national life. They were interviewed and otherwise depicted not only through newspaper and magazine articles but also through radio. New Zealand, for instance, introduced Maori language newscasts in 1942 (five minutes, once per week), primarily to carry news about Maori military personnel overseas to their kinfolk back home. The service continued after the war, but it was not until the late 1980s that full-fledged Maori radio stations began to be licensed. The British colonial government in Kenya also began to broadcast in several Asian and African languages shortly after the beginning of World War II, perhaps fearing renewed German interest in Tanganyika—its former colony and Kenya's next-door neighbor.

Strangely enough, there was almost no broadcasting in indigenous languages by international radio services during World War II. One might have thought that the major combatants, especially the Axis Powers, would have attempted to reach such audiences in the enemies' home countries or colonies: France and Great Britain should have been especially vulnerable, thanks to their large colonial empires. Nazi Germany did broadcast in Hindi (then called *Hindustani*) to British-ruled India, and Japan broadcast to south Asia in Hindi, Urdu, Bengali, and Tamil. Italy's Radio Bari broadcast in Arabic to British-ruled (under League of Nations mandate) Palestine, and Germany offered the African Service, which included programs in Afrikaans. But international services in languages spoken by Black Africans or by the indigenous peoples of North America, Australia, New Zealand, France, or Scandinavia were absent. Perhaps Radio Roma, Radio Tokyo, and Deutschlandsender lacked access to speakers of languages such as Swahili, Maori, Basque, Anishinabe, and Inuktitut. Perhaps their governmental masters doubted that the target populations would possess international radio receivers. Or perhaps they just weren't all that important in the list of priorities.

Once the war had ended, certain countries, most of them in the western hemisphere, expanded the licensing of radio stations. However, any newfound access to the airwaves rarely translated into major shares of airtime for indigenous languages, let alone indigenous ownership or operation of any of the electronic media. The few qualified exceptions to that rule came about in some unusual locations; none was perhaps more unusual than the Union (later, Republic) of South Africa.

The Nationalist party (largely Afrikaaner) election victory in the union in 1948 saw *apartheid,* or "separateness" (of races), develop into a full-fledged policy. Yet in 1952 the government licensed a British firm to set up a wired radio system for Black South Africans living just outside of Johannesburg, and later in other locales. The government-run South African Broadcasting Corporation (SABC) took over the service in 1957. During the early 1960s, the government introduced FM service for much of the country and in 1964 created "Radio Bantu," an FM-only service in seven tribal languages, as well as English and Afrikaans.[9]

The choice of FM was dictated in part by a scarcity of spectrum space in the medium- and shortwave bands, but it had another advantage: FM receivers couldn't pick up the broadcasts that were beginning to emanate from some of the newly independent Black African nations to the north, as well as from Egypt, China, and the Soviet Union. Those broadcasts, whether in Zulu, Xhosa, N'debele, Sotho, or other languages spoken by Blacks living in or near the republic, were strongly anti-apartheid and generally anti-Afrikaaner. Radio Bantu's programming featured progovernment news, much religious broadcasting, and many cultural features in one or more of the seven tribal languages; the features sometimes took the form of folk tales or original plays by Zulu, Sotho, or other writers and also included such works as translations of Shakespeare's plays and Afrikaaner short stories.

While the vast majority of Radio Bantu staff were members of the tribal groups, the operation was strictly supervised by SABC senior management.[10] Major racial confrontations (such as Sharpesville and Soweto) received highly biased, prowhite government coverage; smaller confrontations generally went unreported. All of that changed with the advent of majority rule in 1994, and in 1995, the country's Independent Broadcasting Authority began to license community radio stations. The first of those, Radio Maritzburg, broadcasts in both English and Zulu.[11]

The Union of South Africa was not the only nation to find itself on the receiving end of indigenous language broadcasts from abroad. As the so-called cold war between communist and capitalist nations ripened during the 1950s and 1960s, and as independence movements blossomed in much of Africa, several international broadcasters—Radio Moscow and Radio Peace and Progress in the Soviet Union, Radio Peking in the People's Republic of China, and Radio Cairo in Egypt—began to broadcast in several indigenous languages. They included Quechua and Guarani to South America; Swahili, Hausa, Zulu, N'debele, Shona, Sesuto, Njanja, Somali, and Dankali to sub-Saharan Africa; Kurdish to western Asia; and many Indian languages, such as Marathi, Malayalam, Telugu, Kannada, and Assamese.[12]

In most cases, the broadcasters hoped to appeal to a disaffected indigenous minority in a particular country, not so much in expectation of a declaration of independence by the group, but rather with the intention of weakening existing pro-Western governments. Egypt's broadcasts to sub-Saharan Africa over Radio Cairo seemed designed to portray Egypt as an African power. As the transmission signals often were weak, the broadcasts brief (sometimes as little as 15 minutes a day), and program cancellations frequent (often the station had only one individual available who could speak the indigenous language), it's doubtful that those services were very effective, but they did sometimes prompt governments in the target countries to develop or expand their own domestic indigenous language broadcasts. Some Western international broadcasters also began indigenous services (e.g., the BBC External Services), which added Hausa, Swahili, and Somali in 1957, "in response to the growing radio propaganda effort from Cairo."[13]

The addition of indigenous services in colonial Africa also was influenced by two further factors: the overall colonial policy of the "mother country" and the presence or absence of large numbers of colonists. Great Britain tended to encourage the development of indigenous language broadcasting in its African colonies, especially starting in the 1950s: anthropologist Hortense Powdermaker comments favorably on the sense of partnership she perceived between Africans and Europeans at the Central

African Broadcasting Station in Lusaka, Zambia (then Northern Rhodesia).[14]

The French were generally less favorable toward the introduction of
such services, in part because broadcasting in French was part of *la mission civilisatrice,* or "the civilizing mission," of France. The Portuguese
permitted the development of largely private "radio clubs" in Angola,
Mozambique, and the Cape Verde Islands, but they were almost all operated by Portuguese colonists; only those few in the hands of Catholic missionaries broadcast anything in indigenous languages. The Belgians were
relatively laissez-faire in permitting stations to develop in Belgian Congo
but did carry many indigenous languages on the regional radio services established by the colonial government in 1958. But virtually all of the stations in colonial Africa, whatever the identity of the colonizing power, carried substantial amounts of programming in the languages of the
colonizers.[15]

The reasons for creation of indigenous services within the colonies
varied, and some are noted above, but some scholars (e.g., Zahir Ihaddaden) believe that the policy sometimes was along the lines of "divide and
conquer"; at least that is Ihaddaden's claim in the case of France's 1948 decision to create a radio service in Kabyle (a Berber language spoken in Algeria). There, he feels, "[i]ts object was nothing other than exacerbating the
uniqueness of the Kabyles to create antagonism between them and the
other Algerian populations." He adds the observation that this also was a
way for the French to practice "a policy of cultural deprivation because 90
percent of the population in this area was maintained in total illiteracy."[16]

As the colonies became independent, starting in the late 1950s, the
balance in languages began to tilt more heavily in the direction of the indigenous tongues. However, various forms of dependency continued. In
the former French colonies, French "advisers" often continued to play important roles in managing stations.[17] In nearly all of the former colonies—
even those such as Guinea, which had parted company with the "mother
country" on less than friendly terms—the European languages remained an
important part of the broadcast schedule, and programs imported from the
mother country were an important part of such services.[18] Two of the colonizing powers, Great Britain and France, stepped up their training programs for broadcasters from abroad, helping to ensure reasonably good relations between former colonizers and their erstwhile charges.[19] And
various technical assistance programs aided the newly independent nations
in expanding their radio facilities and also in adding television.[20] None of
those aspects of dependency was necessarily bad, but each had at least the
potential to hold back the development of more truly indigenous approaches to broadcasting.[21]

The People's Republic of China, created in 1949, quickly encouraged the creation of minority (some of them indigenous) language services. The Central People's Broadcasting Station developed a service in Tibetan by 1950. (But of course that isn't a minority language for residents of Tibet, especially for those who consider themselves to be under Chinese occupation.) Mongolian, Uighur, Korean, and Kazak services followed shortly after. By late 1983, there were 29 stations carrying minority language broadcasts, and some of those language services (e.g., Zhuang and Dai) include two or three dialects.[22]

The government also encouraged rural communities to develop their own radio stations to receive and rebroadcast programs from urban centers, with little or no assistance from those centers. By 1955, some of the stations had begun to originate their own programs in their own regional or local languages. The Cultural Revolution of the late 1960s saw a number of the rural stations damaged or put off the air, but the broadcast system began to recover by the end of the decade. It had one unusual feature: the peasants themselves usually built the stations, using such indigenous materials as rocks for transmitting and receiving towers![23]

Most other indigenous radio operations were the result of initiatives undertaken by religious organizations; the motivation for them, however, sometimes included the fear that indigenous groups would fall prey to the "siren songs of communism." In Bolivia, the Catholic church (initially through the Maryknoll order) established Radio San Gabriel in 1956. Initially intended to make the Aymara Indians fluent in Spanish, and therefore "civilized and modern" (as well as less receptive to communism), it soon began to broadcast in Aymara since its audience was by and large incapable of following its all-Spanish literacy lessons. But it was not until the 1960s, and then only gradually, that its broadcasts began to acknowledge the authenticity of Aymaran culture.[24]

The Jesuit missionaries to the Tarahumara (northwestern Mexico) established radio schools in 1955. They were designed to educate both Tarahumara and whites living in the Sierra Tarahumara, but they soon turned out to be almost completely white in their structure and approach. Only Spanish was used in broadcasts, and Tarahumara pupils did considerably less well than their white counterparts on most subjects—but did about as well in mathematics, where language was not such a barrier. Understaffing, uncertain financial support, and radio sets frequently out of repair all contributed to a less than satisfactory overall experience, and the use of radio for the schools ceased in 1974.[25]

The Mexican Catholic church-sponsored Patrimonio Indigena del Valle del Mezquital (PIVM) received government permission to establish a station for the Mezquital area in 1963. Its chief purpose was to make its indigenous listeners literate in Spanish; one Mexican observer contends that it did little to help them to free themselves from a dependency mentality.[26] However, broadcasts in the indigenous language increased over time, and in 1976, PIVM established a second indigenous station, in Ixmiquilpan. Both stations carried commercials, which helped to reduce PIVM's financial burden; they also moved more and more in the direction of supporting the validity of the indigenous cultures.[27]

The Bolivian and Mexican stations both featured supervision by non-indigenous staff—Catholic missionaries for Radio San Gabriel and experienced majority culture broadcasters, for the most part, at the PIVM stations. Radio Bantu's African language services ordinarily had indigenous supervisors, but they were carefully chosen for their political correctness. Thus, the indigenous stations coming on the air during this period hardly could be said to operate with any real independence.

There was one great exception to that rule: the clandestine radio stations operated at various times by various Kurdish political groups. The Kurds, an ancient central Asian people, inhabit an area stretching from eastern Turkey through Iraq and Iran, and including a small portion of Azerbaijan and Syria. They constitute a minority in each country, and their language is distinct from the official languages of all five of those nations. Their struggle for an independent Kurdistan began centuries ago, but modern weaponry has enabled them to put up more of a battle for their independence. In modern times, the five nations hosting them have variously ignored, cultivated, or used them. Iran under the Shah supported them in their guerilla war against Iraq; there was no love lost between Iraq and Iran, and the two nations were involved in a border dispute, so it was advantageous for Iran to make Iraq's life more difficult. When the dispute was settled in 1975, Iranian aid to the Kurds ended.

That was only one example of Kurdish activity in the region. There have been many more. And that helps to explain why Kurdish-operated broadcast services have gone on and off the air so frequently since the Kurdish Democratic party first came on the air in 1965. Kurdish language broadcasts go back to 1939, when Iraq introduced them over its national service,[28] but with the exception of Iraq, the other countries have been inconsistent in maintaining a Kurdish language service. Such a service became a bargaining chip of sorts in the 1995 Turkish military attack on the Kurdish Workers party. Turkish Prime Minister Tançu Ciller promised that, once the party was crushed, the Turkish government would permit broadcasts in Kurdish.[29]

Even within the Kurdish population, splits have developed that have given rise to opposing Kurdish services, sometimes "sponsored" by Iran or Iraq, sometimes independent of both.[30] It's doubtful that any of the Kurdish stations has ever spoken for more than one segment of Kurdish society and thus made any substantial contribution to Kurdish unity.

Indigenous television stations hadn't yet appeared by 1965, but "access" TV through cable and public television in the United States and through public service broadcasting in Europe (both the BBC and Independent Television Authority in Great Britain developed such services) began to appear in the mid-1960s. That gave some minorities, including indigenous groups, the chance to try their wings in the video world. The broadcasters and cable operators themselves furnished the facilities free of charge, so the groups faced no financial barrier to participation. However, the access programs often were a weekly (or less frequent) offering, and airtime on them had to be divided among many would-be users, so none of the indigenous groups could broadcast with the frequency or regularity needed to gain solid experience and audience loyalty. Also, many of those groups lived far enough from the TV stations to make it difficult for them to come in for training and actual use of equipment.

The subsequent development of portapak recording gear lessened that problem, and many minority groups (e.g., African-Americans in the United States) have become more involved in programming over access channels on cable TV. Indigenous groups have lagged behind, in part because many of them live in rural areas, where cable penetration is low. Also, the cost of cable service is too high for many indigenous households. However, some have been quite active in producing and distributing videocassettes (discussed later in the chapter).

The activities of the 1940s, 1950s, and early 1960s did constitute a beginning. But most indigenous peoples had to wait until the latter half of yet another war to have their turns behind the microphones or the cameras, speaking in their own languages, and (sometimes) making independent decisions as to what to broadcast.

Vietnam and After: 1965–1979

The Vietnam War provoked widespread antiwar demonstrations not only in the United States but also in several European nations, as well as in Australia and New Zealand. It also appears to have served as catalyst for several other social movements: antiracism, feminist, homosexual, anti- and pro-abortion rights. In some cases, those movements had

begun their activist phases well before the outbreak of the Vietnam War—
the U.S. civil rights movement is one prominent example—but they also
profited from the spirit of citizen activism that arose in many different nations. Individuals associated with the movements found themselves enjoying the attention of the mass media, and some of them became quite adept
at manipulating the media for their own purposes.[31]

Those and other individuals also began to develop their own media
outlets, such as mimeographed newsletters, wall posters, and audiotaped
statements. Eventually, where licensing rules permitted it and where
money was available, groups began to establish radio stations or find outlets through stations run by organizations sympathetic to their interests. A
few took to the airwaves as "pirates" (unlicensed stations), particularly in
Great Britain, the Netherlands, Italy, and France.[32]

But most ethnic and linguistic minorities, including indigenous peoples, lacked the capital necessary to acquire their own stations and as a result worked through the community-based public radio stations that began
to appear in Australia, Canada, Italy, and the United States during the
1970s. Although airtime usually was free or inexpensive, it was rare that
there would be more than a few hours available per week for any one
group.

There were exceptions to that general rule. The U.S. and Canadian
governments both began to provide financial support for Native American
radio stations in the two nations through grants for the acquisition of buildings, equipment, supplies, and training. Almost all of the stations were located in reservations, where poverty and the emigration of young people to
urban centers made it difficult to sustain those operations. There are hundreds of reservations in the two nations, but growth in their station numbers has been modest in the United States. The first U.S. Native American
stations, KYUK in Bethel, Alaska, and WYRU in Red Springs, North Carolina, came on the air in 1971;* by 1991, there were 22 Native American-
and Inuit-operated radio stations in the United States, with relatively
steady annual growth across the two decades.[33] The first Canadian Native
American station, CKQN in Baker Lake, Northwest Territories, came on
the air in 1972; by 1991, there were 158 Inuit- and Native American–op-

---

*A pirate radio service was active during the Native American occupation of Alcatraz Is-
land prison (1969–1971). A Santee Sioux, John Trudell, hosted a daily program, "Radio Free
Alcatraz." Kasee, Cynthia, "John Trudell," *Notable Native Americans,* Detroit, Mich.: Gale
Research, 1994, 439. A U.S. noncommercial station, WNAD (University of Oklahoma, Norman), began Native American programming as early as 1941. The weekly program's host, a
Sauk/Fox, presented (largely in English) such items as the deeds of Native American soldiers
in World War II and also provided Native American versions of historical confrontations with
whites. "Indians for Indians," *Time,* 41 (May 31, 1943), 40.

erated stations in Canada. Growth accelerated at the end of the 1970s, and the period 1988–1991 saw 30 new stations come on the air.[34]

Why were the figures so much more impressive for Canada? In part because the 1980s were a decade of massive and sometimes painful reassessment of Canada as a political, social, and cultural entity. Although Quebec's threats to seek independence were more widely publicized, Native Americans and Inuit also worked for a clearer and fairer allocation of resources and rights where they were concerned. The Canadian government adopted a Northern Broadcasting Policy (discussed later in the chapter) in 1983, a year after the Canadian Broadcasting Corporation (CBC) began to share television facilities with Inuit broadcasters and CBC Quebec began to share shortwave and satellite radio transmission facilities with Atikamekw- and Montagnais-speaking peoples; in 1984, the CBC announced a formal native access policy with goals of five hours a week for TV and 20 for radio; and, in a move that made Native Americans and Inuit furious (but also strengthened their commitment to obtain their own broadcast outlets), the CBC canceled (because of low ratings) its 25-year-old series "Our Native Land"—the only national program specifically oriented to Native American and Inuit concerns.[35]

The vast majority of Native American stations were, and still are, located far from urban areas. However, some of the stations already referred to were located in or near larger cities, where linguistic minorities often faced the difficult choice of whether to broadcast in their own languages or in the majority culture's languages. The former would help to perpetuate the use of a given language, but many of the urban listeners for whom it should have been the native language couldn't speak it. That was especially true for indigenous language groups, where rural dwellers (older ones in particular) had preserved their native tongues, while urban dwellers had lost most or all of their command of them. Not surprisingly, most linguistic minorities opted for broadcasts in majority culture languages, which had the added benefit of making their programs accessible to members of the mainstream cultures. But that did nothing to help rescue disappearing languages.

The climate of change reached some mainstream broadcasters, as well. In the United States, ethnic and other groups dissatisfied with their portrayals or absences from broadcast programming and/or station staffing took advantage of a U.S. Circuit Court of Appeals reversal of a 1965 Federal Communications Commission (FCC) decision limiting the ability of citizen groups to protest station license renewals.[36] The court held that the FCC could not refuse to take citizen protests into account when relicensing stations just because the groups didn't wish to claim a given station's license for themselves. That opened the floodgates to hundreds of petitions to deny renewal of licenses, introduced by African-American, Hispanic, classical music–loving, and assorted other groups, chiefly during the period 1969–1975.

Less than 10 percent of those petitions led to FCC hearings, and only 16 led to a loss of license, but many broadcasters made accommodations with groups through improvement of hiring practices, deletion or modification of programs the groups found offensive, and addition of programs that would reflect their interests.* The three major networks for that period—ABC, CBS, and NBC—already were working through an Urban League–sponsored Broadcast Skills Bank that helped to train ethnic minority production and performance staff.[37] The networks also began to broadcast television entertainment programs with identifiable ethnic minorities such as Bill Cosby and Diahann Carroll, both African-American, in major and nonstereotyped roles, although that commitment waxed and waned along with the program ratings.[38] None of those actions on the part of stations or networks guaranteed the groups any role in the decision-making process. Furthermore, U.S. indigenous minorities—Native Americans and Inuit—remained inaudible, and certainly invisible, until the early 1970s, when "reservation radio" began to take hold. And Hawaiians had to wait until 1994 for regularly scheduled news broadcasts in the Hawaiian language.

The Republic of Ireland's approach was quite different, as were its circumstances. Raidio Telefis Eirann (RTE) had broadcast in Irish Gaelic from the time of its inauguration in 1926. However, those broadcasts were few in number and often were irregularly scheduled—this despite the fact that the Irish constitution had designated Gaelic as the nation's first official language ever since 1937.

That designation didn't do much to rescue a language in decline. Only 5 percent or so of the population used it on an everyday basis,[39] despite the fact that all schoolchildren had to learn it.** A combination of protests

---

*A good example is a series that was initiated by TV station WTCN in Minneapolis-St. Paul in 1973, in response to protests by Native Americans that they were virtually invisible people where WTCN's programming was concerned. The series, an interview-discussion program entitled "Madagimo" ("The Messenger"), ran from 1973 to 1981 and was hosted by an Ojibwe, Emily Peake. However, its time slot wasn't particularly favorable: Saturday morning, when the three other commercial channels, all network affiliates (WTCN was independent at the time), ran children's cartoons.

**The learning wasn't particularly pleasant in that very few of the teachers knew the language all that well themselves or were skilled as instructors. Once schools were required to offer instruction in Irish, however, they quickly had to recruit teachers for it and in many cases ended up with little more than "warm bodies" to fill the need. O'Fiannachta, Padraig, MA, MRIA, expert in the Irish language and its instruction, personal interview, Dingle, Ireland, August 1994.

from pro-Gaelic groups, and a feeling of need on the part of some senior RTE staff for a separate Gaelic service, led to the creation of Raidio na Gaeltachta ([RNG] Radio of the Gaelic Speakers) in 1972. RNG was part of RTE and financed by the latter through a portion of the annual household license fee. It began as a five-days-a-week, 2.5-hours-a-day service but soon expanded and by 1990 was broadcasting 11.5 hours per weekday and roughly 8 hours on Saturdays and Sundays. It offers a full news service, quiz shows, music, current affairs, and a host of other formats, all in Gaelic. Music is included: it cannot contain any lyrics in English, which means no Irish artists performing in English, such as U-2 or Sinead O'-Connor, which in turn severely limits the station's attractiveness for younger listeners.[40]

Norway, Sweden, and Denmark all followed yet another path. Each modified its broadcast system in the late 1970s and early 1980s in order to accommodate those interested in broadcasting their own points of view. *Närradio,* which could be translated as "neighborhood radio," as "personal radio," or as both, took the approach of setting aside certain broadcast frequencies (all FM) and transmitters and invited groups to apply for airtime on them, rather than for full- or part-time stations (for which there would not have been enough frequencies, anyway). Each licensed group would have to guarantee that it would broadcast throughout the year, at least once a week, for a minimum of 15 minutes, obtain and equip its own studio, and pay for a land line connection to the transmitter. Furthermore, there could be no commercial advertising. Hundreds of political, religious, ethnic minority, social, and other groups have used närradio since its inception, some of them receiving license renewals year after year.[41]

Norway's indigenous population, the Sami—and particularly those Sami speakers living in the lower half of the country—developed several närradio services in Oslo, Bergen, and other cities. The service in Oslo, Radio Ofelas, was off the air briefly in the early 1990s, due to lack of volunteers and management problems, and again in 1995, due to a dispute over an altered time slot for the service (very late at night). Local government and some trade unions have provided some modest financial support, and a national agency, the Statensmedieforwaltung (State Media Administration) furnishes 15,000 Norwegian *kroner* (about U.S. $2,400) a year, as of 1995. (Studio rental for the weekly one-hour broadcast is 400 kroner per session.) Because many of the Sami living in Oslo do not speak Sami well, if at all, and also because there are several Sami dialects (and some unwillingness to even try to understand a dialect other than one's own!), the station broadcasts most program material in Norwegian.[42]

As noted earlier, some groups operated outside the law, as "pirates" (unauthorized broadcasters). They were especially numerous in Italy, in the

Netherlands, in Great Britain, and, to a lesser extent, in France. In the first two, government officials were quite tolerant of the stations, so long as they operated at very low power for brief periods and didn't attack the beliefs and practices of others. A 1975 decision on Italy's broadcast law by the Italian Constitutional Court made it possible for the pirates to seek licenses, and most did so. In Great Britain, and particularly after the Conservative party came to power in 1979, government officials were of two minds as to how to deal with the stations. Some favored toleration, on the grounds that such stations were a good example of the entrepreneurial spirit favored by the party, especially under Prime Minister Margaret Thatcher (1979–1991). Others saw them as a threat to law and order and sought to close them down. That sentiment applied particularly to stations broadcasting in foreign languages, such as Hindi: the fear was that authorities wouldn't know whether such stations were preaching subversion or insurrection.*

That was not easy: many of the pirates, especially those run by and for ethnic minorities and located in areas where such minorities were prevalent (West Indians and South Asians living in metropolitan areas), had elaborate warning systems to alert them to the presence of law enforcement officials, and their equipment was portable enough to be disassembled and hidden or removed within a matter of minutes. And when the authorities managed to confiscate the equipment, the groups usually could raise enough money (e.g., $300 for a small transmitter) to purchase replacements and come back on the air, sometimes within a week or two.[43]

France began to license previously illegal radio stations in 1982, following the election of a Socialist government (whose leaders themselves had broadcast over pirate stations while in the opposition).[44] Changes in broadcast laws at the end of the 1980s for the Netherlands and the United

---

*Such fears were not confined to Great Britain. In 1977, the U.S. FCC brought a case against New York City ethnic station WHBI, which the city felt was not supervising, and indeed was unable to supervise, broadcasting in a number of the languages employed by groups using its facilities; therefore, it could not carry out its duties as a "responsible" (to the public) broadcast operation. The station ultimately retained its license. See Grame, Theodore, *Ethnic Broadcasting in the United States,* Washington, D.C.: American Folklife Center, Library of Congress, Publication No. 4, 1980, 27–28. Grame also notes that the FCC had developed a policy statement in 1942 on "Foreign Language Radio Wartime Control." It urged station managers to insist upon English language translations of foreign language scripts, and to conduct on-air checks of the latter, to ensure that no changes would be made (18–19)! Just after World War II, rumors began to circulate that some members of Congress were considering introduction of legislation that would abolish foreign language radio and newspapers. While no such legislation ever appeared, the 79th Congress (1946) did receive a congressional committee report that recommended that all foreign language newspapers be required to provide parallel columns with English translations; if they did not, they would lose their second class mailing privileges (125–126).

Kingdom made it possible for many pirates to obtain broadcast licenses in those countries, as well, and many have done so, although some have chosen to remain outside the law.

Where indigenous groups were concerned, the changes in France saw the licensing of various Provençal, Breton, Basque, and other minority language private radio stations,[45] including Paris-based Radio Pays, with programming in six French minority languages. Other indigenous groups— the Germans in northeastern Italy, the Frisians in the Netherlands, and the Scots and Irish Gaelic speakers and the Welsh in the United Kingdom— hadn't been heavily involved in pirate broadcasting, perhaps in part because all but the Irish Gaelic speakers in Northern Ireland had broadcast outlets through the public service broadcasting systems. And Irish Gaelic broadcasts from Ireland's Raidio na Gaeltachta were easy to receive in Northern Ireland.

However, while Welsh speakers may have appreciated the increasing hours devoted to broadcasts in Welsh over BBC Radio Cymru, they did not appreciate the meager supply of Welsh language television available through the BBC and the two commercial TV stations serving parts of Wales. The leader of the Welsh National party, Dr. Gwynfor Evans, threatened in 1980 to starve himself to death if the newly authorized commercial TV service, Channel 4, was not made an all-Welsh service within Wales.[46] He and others won their point, and Sianel Pedwar Cymru (Channel 4 Wales) came on the air in 1983. It has developed a wide range of programming, from national and world news through situation comedy and soap opera, and has commissioned much original drama.[47] A large share of drama in Welsh comes from BBC Wales.*

Access to airtime for indigenous groups varied a great deal. Italy had long since committed itself to major radio services in German and in Slovene for its German- and Slovene-speaking minorities living in areas acquired by Italy after World War I and added a television service in German in the 1960s. Both media operate under the auspices of Radio Audizioni Italia (RAI), the Italian public broadcasting service, but enjoy considerable independence. Frisian broadcasting began in the northern Netherlands in the mid-1970s, as a regional service of the Dutch public broadcasting system, and broadcasts for slightly under three hours a day in the language (closely related to Dutch). Radio Fryslan features news, music, weather, and Frisian music.[48]

---

*Davies, John, *Broadcasting and the BBC in Wales,* Cardiff: University of Wales Press, 1994, 376–386. Davies also notes that BBC Wales, established as such in 1964, produced several hours per week in Welsh from the beginning. Granada, Independent TV's licensee in Manchester, began to produce two hours a week in Welsh in 1957, shortly after its foundation, whereas the BBC provided only 30 minutes a week in Welsh at the time (213, 274–275).

Scots Gaelic radio broadcasts had taken place on a modest scale since 1923; the effort to increase airtime, aided by protests from Gaelic activists, moved into high gear with the creation of BBC Radio Highland in 1976— the same year in which the BBC inaugurated a Gaelic Advisory Council. More important yet was the designation of a specific BBC Gaelic service, Raidio nan Eilann (Radio of the Islands) in 1979. It was reorganized as Raidio nan Gaidheal (Radio of the Gaels) in 1985 and currently broadcasts up to 4.5 hours a day in Gaelic, although only the heaviest Gaelic-speaking regions of Scotland—the northwest coast and the western islands—receive that much. Television in Gaelic is in much shorter supply, although both BBC TV and two of the commercial stations—Grampian and Scottish—broadcast in it, each with a few regularly scheduled weekly programs (news, music, children's, and educational) as well as series (on fashion, gardening, current affairs, and learning Gaelic). Some of the TV programs have prime-time slots, and certain programs are subtitled in English.[49]

The Australian government began to license community and educational radio services in 1974, partly in response to public pressure, partly because the Labor party then in power was favorable to the idea of opening the airwaves to a wider range of societal groups. The groups were expected to share airtime and facilities, and a number of Aboriginals began to come on the air, generally in larger cities at first and spreading to smaller population centers as community radio itself spread through the country. Certain Aboriginal operations—Radio Redfern in Sydney and Koori Radio in Brisbane—soon claimed 20–30 hours of airtime per week and, in the case of Redfern, furnished their own facilities.[50]

All of those European and Australian initiatives have drawn one common criticism,[51] although its intensity has varied from nation to nation and has appeared to lose steam over time: wasn't it a waste of resources (annual license fee revenue or government subsidy in particular) to develop such services when so few people (sometimes less than 1 percent of a nation's population) could understand them? What the critics often didn't realize was that (1) the services didn't cost all that much, (2) the 1970s were marked by a general increase in public sentiment favoring attempts to "return to one's roots," and (3) music, which dominated the schedules of most of the new services, was understood and enjoyed by a far larger number of people than could speak the languages themselves.

Third World nations generally followed one of two "models" for broadcasting during the 1970s. Most of Central and South America featured a high degree of commercial station competition, somewhat along the lines of U.S. practice. Africa and Asia generally operated through a structure that many of the nations had inherited from their former colonial rulers: a monopoly broadcasting through a single station, usually located in the capital city. There were a few attempts at establishing local stations for indigenous groups—two notable examples were a Quiche language service in the Guatemalan highlands, starting in 1974, and a Mapuche language station in southern Chile in 1968, and both of those were financed by "outsiders": a Dutch Catholic group for the Chilean station, the U.S. Agency for International Development (USAID) in Guatemala. In both cases, the outsiders discovered that the indigenous groups had their own agendas and their own means of resisting imposition of an outside model.[52]

Mexico took a somewhat different approach. The government's Instituto Nacional Indigenista (INI) began to finance the construction and operation of indigenous radio stations in 1979, when La Voz de la Montana (Tlapa de Comonfort, State of Guerrero) came on the air, broadcasting in Nahua, Mixtec, and Tlapaneca. More stations followed: within 10 years, there were seven INI-supported stations, broadcasting variously in Chontal, Mixtec, Triqui, Tepehuano, and several other languages. While the primary goal of the stations was to increase self-reliance and pride on the part of Aztec, Mayan, and other Native American groups, literacy training was aimed at making listeners literate in Spanish, and listeners were encouraged to consider themselves as one part of the national, European-flavored culture.[53]

Several of the larger countries, such as India and Nigeria, developed regional services, and most stations in Africa added (if they weren't already present) African language services to the French, Spanish, English, or Portuguese broadcasts that were a part of their colonial inheritance, but they remained under close supervision by the national governments, which were not anxious to encourage anything resembling separatist movements on the part of indigenous or other minority populations. Those fears weren't baseless: nations such as Guinea served as bases for many dissident groups from nearby countries, the groups broadcasting back to their homelands in indigenous languages.

The United Nations Educational, Scientific, and Cultural Organization (UNESCO) was the major source of support for Senegal's Radio Educative Rurale (RER), founded in 1968. RER encouraged rural dwellers, using their own languages, to tape-record their problems and concerns for government officials; RER staff would play the tapes for the officials, record their replies, and then edit and broadcast the material nationwide. This served to empower the rural population, and here, when UNESCO terminated its support in 1974, the government continued to finance it, which is something of a rarity: many such services supported largely by external funding sources die a sudden death when external financing stops. However, the lower level of financial support that followed did weaken the quality of programming, chiefly because RER staff based in Dakar sharply reduced their visits to the rural areas.[54]

Television also began to appear in many Third World nations, a few of which had had TV since the 1950s. But TV presented some special problems where indigenous languages were concerned. Whereas it was relatively easy to initiate radio broadcasting in languages lacking written form, that proved much more difficult over television for one simple reason: due to the relative economic poverty of so many of those nations, and given the expense of original TV production, much of the program schedule contained imported material. Dubbing was costly, and subtitling was out of the question for nonwritten languages, so viewers speaking only those languages (a minority of the TV audience in many countries, to be sure) were limited to making what sense they could out of the visual images and those French, Spanish, English, German, or other words they might understand. Also, the selection of one indigenous language in preference to others when producing, dubbing, or subtitling a program could be rife with political implications, especially if there was no single national indigenous language.

Australia's Special Broadcasting Service (SBS), founded in 1978, provides an example of one possible line of approach, even though it broadcasts very little in indigenous languages—occasional Aboriginal language programs, a bit of Frisian, and a few hours weekly of Maori. (It does broadcast English language radio and TV programming made by Aboriginals, some primarily for Aboriginal audiences, some for all viewers.) It presents a mixed schedule of programming in a number of European and Asian languages spoken by émigré populations in Australia, such as Greek, German, Italian, Arabic, Mandarin, and Indonesian.

Most of the TV material comes from countries where those are the majority languages, and most of it is then subtitled in English. Newscasts run 30 minutes per language, aren't subtitled, and contain a mixture of imported and SBS-produced items. Radio programs more often are produced by émigrés themselves, including journalistic reports originating in SBS stations in each of Australia's states. SBS is funded by the federal government, at a cost of about AUS $60 million per year (1994–1995 budget).[55]

Growth
in the
1980s

In some ways, the 1980s represented an expansion of the sorts of activities just noted.
However, more countries also became com-
fortable with the notion of letting groups speak in their own rights. A few,
such as France and Norway, joined Australia, Canada, and the United
States in making government subsidies available to noncommercial community stations, including those broadcasting in Basque, Breton,
Provençal, and Sami, as well as Aboriginal, Inuit, and Native American
languages. New Zealand began in 1989 to earmark a share of audience license fees to help support radio stations broadcasting to Maori, Samoan,
and assorted South Pacific islander listeners, resulting in an expansion
from two Maori stations at the beginning of 1989 to 25 stations (not all of
them receiving license fee money) in 1994.

Indigenous television, a scarce commodity in earlier decades, received greater support in the 1980s. New Zealand set aside a small portion
of license fee money for the support of Maori video work, most of it to appear on one of the country's three television services; also, TVNZ began in
1983 to carry a daily Maori news program, "Te Karere." Australia licensed
an Aboriginal commercial TV service, Imparja, in 1985.

The U.S. Federal Communications Commission developed a new licensing category for low-powered television stations (LPTV) in 1983. Minority groups applying for LPTV licenses (issued by lottery) were given
two "chances" per lottery drawing, and by the late 1980s, Native American
LPTV stations began to appear: in 1987, Navajos in Rock Point, New
Mexico, initiated service with Channel 56 ("Purple Cow"), and in 1988,
the Confederated Salish and Kootenai tribes, on Montana's Flathead
Reservation, came on the air with SKC-TV.[56] Neither operation provides
more than a few hours per week of its own programming but instead relies
heavily on public television material provided through the U.S. Public
Broadcasting Service (PBS).

Third World nations began to move away from the "models" noted
above. Some appeared to follow the lead of the People's Republic of
China, particularly in terms of self-development of stations in rural areas.
When the Sandinista government came to power in Nicaragua in 1979, it

implemented a rural reform program in which a rural radio system (CORADEP) was organized along somewhat similar lines, in that rural residents had to provide a great deal for themselves. Most of the broadcast staff had never handled radio equipment, and few of them had ever been interviewed, much less conducted one. But they took to the task with zeal and, at most stations, prodded listeners to become involved in broadcasting themselves. The station at Puerto Cabezas, on the coast of the Gulf of Mexico, broadcast in the regional Indian language Miskito and had a Miskito woman as its director. Most of the stations diminished or disappeared when the Sandinistas were voted out of power in 1989.[57] Clemencia Rodriguez contends that the Sandinista government made a real effort to train reporters to fully and honestly reflect their communities but that bureaucracy and centralization eventually discouraged honest reporting of news the government didn't want to hear.[58]

The generally higher level of activity in Third World nations during the 1980s appears to have been prompted in part by the release through UNESCO of three reports, two by Francis Berrigan, one by Jeremiah O'-Sullivan-Ryan and Mario Kaplun, on broadcasting and community involvement and empowerment. All had stemmed from UNESCO-sponsored meetings and research projects during the 1970s. Hans Enzensberger's 1972 essay "Constituents of a Theory of the Media" also may have inspired that effort.[59] The reports encouraged broad participation by community members, in part through the demystification of media: people without media experience could and should learn that it was fairly easy to record and edit material for broadcast. From this, so the authors claim, could arise a fresh or revitalized sense of community.[60]

The term *participatory media* now began to enter the vocabulary of media consultants and scholars. The basic idea was to encourage existing stations to involve the audience in program making as much as possible and to develop new stations that would build their schedules on such a basis. The O'Sullivan-Ryan and Kaplun report points out that "participation" itself hadn't been clearly defined and that there were very few analyses of participatory approaches, in part because projects containing such approaches were simply assumed to be "good";[61] therefore, it wasn't necessary to conduct empirical research. The report also provides summaries of a number of participatory projects but points out that few lasted more than a year or two, thanks to withdrawal of funding, governmental dissatisfaction or suspicion, or the perception of the local population that participation was severely limited.[62]

Very few of the projects noted in that report involved indigenous peoples, at least as separately identified groups. However, one station not noted in the report already had begun to operate on a participatory basis—in theory, if not in practice. And it was indigenous.

The Baha'i faith operates without clergy and with maximum participation from its members. It wasn't surprising that a Baha'i radio station would exhibit such a feature; it may have been surprising that the station was established in Otavalo, Ecuador, and that its primary purpose was to assist a heavily Quechua-speaking rural population in the task of development. However, from the station's founding in late 1977 until 1980, there were a number of problems with the participatory approach, not least of all the amounts of time eaten up in meetings where everyone had the opportunity to speak up, and did. By 1981, things had stabilized (partly because of the appointment of a manager who was adept at time management), and the station—still on-air—appears to have captured the loyalties of its intended audience.[63]

Still, as Josiane Jouet observes in a 1978 analytical report, experiments featuring participatory approaches to media use generally were short-term, underfinanced, and poorly conceptualized; thus, when they were implemented, the participants tended to become frustrated because of too little time to get the job done, too few facilities, and too vague a sense of goals and procedures and ended up either spending too much time in discussion of how to accomplish the seemingly impossible or simply quitting.[64] Those observations seemed to fit a number of more-or-less participatory projects that developed during the 1980s, as well.

The Sri Lankan government, with the financial assistance of the Danish International Development Agency, established Mahaweli Community Radio in 1981. MCR was to serve a newly settled region with programming that might help to develop some sense of community where no community had existed previously.[65] The station also was to be a source of information on agricultural practices. It has regularly broadcast programs that note developments in specific communities within the region, and it uses local dialects and idioms in some of its broadcasts—a rarity in Sri Lanka. The program producers were to involve the villagers directly with the production process, and a number of the latter have contributed songs, poems, comic sketches with development themes, and, on occasion, drama. Even so, a 1984 study shows that over 80 percent of those surveyed ($N = 450$) were familiar with MCR, but only 17 percent listened to it regularly.[66]

Kenya established a local radio station, Homa Bay Community Radio, in 1982. UNESCO financed the construction and equipping of the station; it wished to see whether community radio might be useful in aiding community development. At the time (as remains largely true today), broadcasting in little spoken local languages, and even in more widely used ones such as Luo, received little airtime over the government-run Voice of Kenya. Nor were there any local stations—only the headquarters operation in Kenya's capital, Nairobi, and three smaller regional stations. Homa Bay not only was 300 miles west of the capital but also had to broadcast in the local language (Luo) in order to have any hope of reaching its audience with its programs about topics such as family planning, better agricultural practices, and women's rights.

The station functioned reasonably well in terms of working with the local population but had one enormous handicap: it broadcast on FM, and very few local residents owned FM receivers. Also, the Voice of Kenya was responsible for staffing and maintaining the station, but staff turnover in Nairobi saw the departure of the key individuals who had supported the idea of such an experiment in the first place. It also didn't help matters that the Luo often have been at political odds with the Kikuyu, the predominant tribe in Kenya. Within two years, the station went off the air (with 24 hours' notice to staff), and its programming was absorbed within the regional station of the Kenya Broadcasting Corporation (KBC) at Kisumu, where it lost most of its local flavor.[67]

Radio Onda Azul in Puno, Peru, had been broadcasting since 1963 but began to feature a participative approach in 1981. Supported (very modestly) by the Catholic church diocese of Puna, it began to train listeners in villages throughout the area to serve as correspondents. It developed a staff of five promoters, or extension workers, to go out to communities and stimulate interest in becoming involved with broadcasts. The promoters encountered a good deal of suspicion at first—why did outsiders want to know about the communities? But gradually, some of the communities began to exhibit interest and bought their own rudimentary recording equipment so that they could participate.[68]

The government of Mali authorized a rural station at Kayes in 1988, in part because the community felt that its self-identity went largely unrecognized by Radiodiffusion-Television Malienne's headquarters (and, at the time, sole) station in Bamako. However, the financial support came not from RTM but from an Italian nongovernmental organization, and the unevenness and uncertainty of that support have meant that the station often has been in danger of closing. Also, the strategy of involving local residents in the broadcasts seems to have been unsuccessful, due in part to a long-standing perception of the "locals" that "messages are sent from the center to the periphery."[69]

Support through the International Program for the Development of Communication (IPDC) of the United Nations has led to the establishment or revitalization of similar operations in Benin, Laos, and the Philippines; IPDC also supported a rural television project at Oued Madani, Sudan, in the early 1980s.[70] Religious groups such as the Catholic church and the Baha'i, as noted earlier, have supported rural stations in Chile and Ecuador, not without some eventual misgivings: indigenous station staff at times have bitten the hand that feeds them by criticizing the religions them-selves.[71]

The Liberian Rural Communications Network, founded in 1986, is an example of how a well-conceived, carefully executed media project for mi-norities can come to grief for reasons other than funding. LRCN worked to involve the people of three northern counties in the broadcasts of its three rural stations, all of them broadcasting exclusively in the languages of their regions. Farmers spoke about their agricultural techniques, and mothers described their approaches to infant care. The network attracted a broad and sizable audience, and funding from the Liberian government and from the U.S. Agency for International Development remained strong.[72] How-ever, the outbreak of the Liberian civil war in 1989 made the stations prime targets for the warring forces, and all three eventually were destroyed or taken over by those forces.

While most activities along the lines noted above required the bless-ing of national governments, there were a few examples of state govern-ment involvement, as well. The Mexican state of Hidalgo began to develop Radio Estatal in December 1985 in part on the initiative of a progressive state governor, in part thanks to the example of a group noted above, PIVM. The latter had added "y Huasteca Hidalguense" to its title and had established two indigenous radio stations in Hidalgo earlier in the year. Ra-dio Estatal started with one station, added two more, and merged with PIVMHH, and by 1989 there were seven stations in the system, broadcast-ing in such languages as Nahuatl and Hnahnu and drawing their financial support from a combination of state government appropriations, PIVMHH assistance, and advertising. However, Spanish dominated the daily sched-ule, both in music broadcasts and in other formats. Some programs fea-tured bilingual speakers. The assumption appears to have been that the in-digenous listeners were to think of themselves as Mexicans first and foremost but with a greater sense of pride in their own cultures.[73]

Indigenous communities sometimes took the initiative to become in-volved with electronic media before any outside assistance was available and before they had received any authorization to do so. In other words, they were "pirate" broadcasters, although they generally weren't aware of existing European activities along those lines. Yuendumu and Ernabella, Aboriginal communities in Australia's Northern Territory, set up their own (unauthorized, although permission had been sought in the case of Yuen-dumu) satellite reception systems in 1985. Members of each community had begun two years earlier to make videotapes about community activi-ties such as ceremonies, so they had at least some experience with televi-sion production. Yet even they made mistakes in terms of what was ac-ceptable video material for the entire community to see—understandable, perhaps, given that the earlier videocassettes had been made and viewed largely within kinship groups rather than by and for the community as a whole.[74]

During roughly the same time period, the Central Australian Aboriginal Media Association (CAAMA), based in Alice Springs, Northern Territory, was preparing for the launch of what would be the first full-time Aboriginal radio station in the country. Individual Aborigines had begun in 1980 to gain experience with radio through access to bits and pieces of airtime over the three Alice Springs radio stations, which is when and why CAAMA was organized. All three stations identified Europeans as their primary audience, so most of the Aboriginal broadcasting was in English. But a full-time station, particularly if it had a powerful signal, could accommodate several languages spoken in central Australia. Government authorization came through in 1985, and by the end of the year, station 8KIN was on-air from Alice Springs, with a 50-kilowatt FM signal, and access to a 50-kilowatt shortwave (high-frequency) transmitter operated by the Australian Broadcasting Corporation (ABC). It soon was broadcasting in six Aboriginal languages, as well as in English.[75]

Even as the radio station was taking form, CAAMA was planning for the introduction of Australia's first Aboriginal-owned and -operated television station. It had started a video training program in 1984 and was producing video material by 1986. It applied for a remote commercial television service (RCTS) license at the very end of 1984 and was awarded one in January 1987, after more than two years of often bizarre competition with a Darwin, Northern Territory–based, white Australian applicant.

The station is called *Imparja,* a European corruption of the Arrente term *impatye,* meaning "tracks" or "footprint"—apt because the TV signal is delivered by satellite to a few dozen widely scattered ground retransmission sites. Since the license is commercial, and since the numbers of white Australian owners of TV sets in the satellite footprint area (Northern Territory and South Australia) far outnumber Aboriginal owners, the program schedule is heavily tilted in favor of European-oriented programs. Still, newscasts, coverage of special events (Aboriginal music festivals, for example), and video recordings (usually documentaries) made by Aboriginals do lend something of an Aboriginal flavor to Imparja's offerings.[76]

Economics played various roles in the development of indigenous electronic media during the 1980s. On the one hand, there was the push by U.S. President Ronald Reagan, British Prime Minister Margaret Thatcher, and other Western leaders, to "rationalize" the economic environment in favor of a more heavily free market approach. By that token, the electronic media should move away from dependency on the national government, where that existed, and toward greater self-support. That condition made it harder for the new indigenous media enterprises to obtain the needed financing.[77] On the other hand, a number of philanthropic groups (e.g., Germany's Friedrich Ebert Stiftung), plus one new United Nations program—the International Program for the Development of Communication (IPDC)—brought fresh sources of financial help to industrially developing nations for various electronic media projects. However, those groups generally dealt with national governments, who rarely gave top priority to their indigenous minorities. So the supply of money for indigenous media ventures actually may have diminished during the decade, at least in relation to the increased activity in that realm.

Audio- and Videocassettes: Alternative Approaches

When conventional broadcast outlets either aren't available, or become unavailable as a result of war, change in government policy, or lack of funding for daily operations, indigenous groups sometimes have arranged for their own distribution networks. That became much more feasible starting in the 1970s, thanks to the development of relatively inexpensive audiotape-duplication machines and the increasing availability of audiocassette playback systems. People often have been encouraged to pass tapes along to other potentially interested individuals. Video profited from similar developments with VCRs and portapaks in the 1980s.[78]

Religious "fundamentalists" in Iran and in Saudi Arabia have achieved widespread audiocassette distribution of sermons by their leading clerics,[79] while in Egypt some of the more popular fundamentalist clerics have rented or sold large quantities of videotapes of their own sermons.[80] The Pan American Health Organization financed the Pila (Fountain) Project in Guatemala during the mid-1970s; here, village women coming to wash their clothing at the communal fountain would hear tape-recorded 30-minute programs containing information on health and other subjects.[81] Kaplun directed a project in Uruguay during the late 1970s, in which members of rural co-ops could both hear a tape of a development-oriented program and then record their own comments on the subject; the comments then were edited and included in a subsequent program.[82] And, just before the Mexican presidential election in 1994, the partly indigenous Zapatista National Liberation Army in the state of Chiapas sold a nine-videotape collection of Zapatista declarations; also, audiocassettes of "songs inspired by the hooded Zapatista leader Subcomandante Marcos" were for sale. Some months later, the group distributed a quite professionally produced videocassette about its National Democratic Convention in Aguascalientes.[83]

As the Yuendumu experience cited earlier indicates, some taped material is not meant to be shared. However, several central Australian Aboriginal groups (e.g., women's groups) exchanged videos with one another or used them as "message sticks" to transmit information to other like groups.[84] Journalists seeking to present something other than officially sanctioned coverage (or noncoverage) of controversial events prepared and distributed videocassette "magazines" in then-communist Hungary and in India.[85] A few Ainu, the indigenous peoples of Japan, have begun production of a videocassette series aimed at resurrecting the nearly extinct Ainu language.[86] CAAMA has a large catalogue of video documentaries depicting local crafts such as woodcarving and sells them to tourists, teachers, and others.[87]

The Kayapo Indians of Brazil prepare video recordings as a means of preserving their cultural traditions and of pressing for political rights. But they also see video cameras as visually symbolic of power and sometimes have shown up at public meetings with them, not so much to record the event but to *be* recorded by other reporters so that others would see them as powerful.[88] And the Mille Lacs band of Ojibwe (Anishinabe) have produced a video about their history that they distribute free of charge to schools and to libraries in hopes of increasing public understanding of them.[89]

The period of the *intifada* (uprising) in the Israeli-occupied Gaza strip also saw an interesting use of video, here in the form of video diaries recorded by Palestinians so as to show a Palestinian perspective on daily life at the time (late 1980s to early 1990s). The diaries subsequently were edited into a documentary, which has appeared over several European TV services, has been distributed within the occupied territories, and has been shown in Israel itself. The technical quality of the diaries sometimes was poor, but that may have contributed to a perception by Palestinian viewers that they were an honest, accurate representation of events.[90]

The idea of video diaries has taken slightly different forms in other countries. Brazil's Centro de Trabalho Indigenista coordinates a video as a tribal project through which tribal members learn to make videos about such topics as their culture and their interactions with whites. That and other projects, many of them with labor unions, women's organizations, and other groups, have brought about the creation of a coordinating organization, ABVP, through which video project participants can do such things as receive training and exchange ideas and tapes with one another. However, little of their work comes to the attention of the larger public, since Brazilian TV stations aren't required, or even encouraged, to make airtime available for such offerings.[91]

Video equipment had become widely enough available among Blacks in South Africa by the mid-1980s to encourage the formation of small video production units, such as Video News Services (VNS) and Dynamic Images (DI). Those units attempted to collect video footage that would show Black perspectives on strikes and demonstrations. Sometimes the government confiscated equipment, but there was enough material to permit production of "video pamphlets" of about 15 minutes' duration. These were copied and circulated among Black South Africans through the Congress of South African Trade Unions (COSATU), plus assorted church, civic, student, and other organizations. Those "networks" also served to circulate material that had been shown on British, U.S., and other foreign TV systems, especially anything portraying the activities of the African National Congress, which in essence was banned from appearing in programs transmitted by the South African Broadcasting Corporation.[92]

While many of the indigenous video production groups receive financial and technical support from such groups as religious organizations, professional broadcasters, labor unions, and political parties, some depend solely upon their own resources. A small group of young Zapotecs (an indigenous people in the Mexican state of Oaxaca) earn money as migrant workers in the United States and use some of it to produce videos about themselves, which they hope will increase Zapotecan self-esteem, and possibly help to correct majority culture impressions of "dumb Indians." One of their projects, a 10-minute video entitled "Nuestro Tequio," shows one community's resurrection of the Zapotecan custom of working together one day a week on a community project, in this case the restoration of the old town hall.[93]

As Music Television (MTV) has spread to more parts of the world, the notion of creating music videos has taken hold with many young people, including indigenous youth. When the Australian government provided video equipment to some of the BRACS communities in the late 1980s (discussed later in the chapter), there were no restrictions (other than those imposed by the community itself, where in fact some small groups of individuals did exercise tight control) on how it was to be used. Youth groups began to experiment with music video formats and have produced a number of videos emphasizing such messages as the importance of kinship, pride in tribal arts such as dancing, and the negative effects of alcohol. Some of the videos have been broadcast over Imparja.[94]

Indigenous youth groups have become involved in other forms of programming. As one example, a primary school class in the Hopi Second Mesa Day School (Arizona) produced a "News and Views" program, complete with sports, fictional advertising (one ad was for Desert Pizza, with toppings of bobcat toenails and tarantula legs!), and a class survey on the guilt or innocence of accused murderer O. J. Simpson. The project seemed to encourage students to feel that video making wasn't beyond their reach.[95]

Some of the more interesting uses of videocassette recordings have not involved broadcasting, selling, or even widespread distribution of free cassettes. Instead, some groups have regarded videocassettes as a means of raising their intragroup self-esteem. One example would be the work of SEWA—the Self-Employed Women's Association of the Indian state of Gujerat. This association—there are others in other Indian states—consists of some 25,000 self-employed poor women engaged in piecework or in vending. A subgroup—Video SEWA, formed in 1984—has made over a hundred recordings, ranging from how to organize for self-protection to how to carry out a given work-related task. They are shown to new or incipient SEWA members and also, where appropriate, to policy makers. The members themselves make the recordings, play them back immediately, evaluate them, and eventually develop a finished product that will represent them clearly and honestly. And, although it was not the original intent of Video SEWA, some of the recordings have been broadcast and have been sold in India and abroad.[96] (Several other video production experiences involving women are covered in Chapter Seven.)

Satellites and Indigenous Communication

Communication by satellite also is playing an increasingly significant role in the development of indigenous electronic media, both as an aid to distribution of programming *to* indigenous stations and to the exchange of programming *among* them. Canada and Alaska, both with considerable Native American and Inuit populations scattered across vast, inhospitable territories, have led the way in satellite usage, with Australia not far behind.

The Canadian Broadcasting Corporation began development of its Northern Service in 1958, acquiring community radio stations in Dawson, Whitehorse, Yukon, and Yellowknife, Northwest Territories. The service expanded its reach in 1960 by initiating shortwave service to the High Arctic. However, most of the program material originated in southern Canada, and much of it was irrelevant to Inuit and Native Americans. In any event, it wasn't in their native languages. Nor was it possible for them to pool their resources through a network.

The Northern Pilot Project (NPP), a Canadian Department of Communications venture that ran from 1972 to 1974, provided financial and technical assistance for the operation of radio services in remote communities in northwestern Ontario and the Northwest Territories. Station CKQN, in Baker Lake, Northwest Territories, came on the air in 1972, broadcasting in Inuktitut and in English (especially music). However, the spoken word programming in Inuktitut increased from 60 percent to 80 percent within the first year of operation.[97] Also, the community itself took over full responsibility—financial, managerial, and programming—for the station within about 18 months.

Simultaneously, the NPP established a high-frequency (shortwave) radio two-way service for some 24 Native American communities in the area around Sioux Lookout in northwestern Ontario. It was heavily used and helped lead to the foundation of the Wawatay (Northern Lights) Native Communication Society, which began to produce a bilingual monthly newspaper.[98] However, the two-way service didn't function as a radio station any more than the Baker Lake station functioned as a two-way service. (A local experimental radio station in the region, at Big Trout Lake, came on the air in 1973 and helped lead to the establishment of other community stations in the area.)[99] The satellite technology of the times was not especially well-suited to meet the needs of either type of operation.

Television faced even greater obstacles, given the enormous cost that would be involved in serving the north's vast but thinly populated reaches. During the 1970s, "package" TV stations, consisting of a uniform set of low-power transmitters and modest studio equipment, enabled a few dozen Canadian indigenous communities to originate their own programs, but the system served far more heavily as a collection of relay points for taped broadcast material from the south. Again, there was no networking capability.

In 1972, the Canadian national government began to make use of satellites to supply the northern stations with broadcasts through the Canadian-built Anik (Inuktitut for "friend") series. However, that did little to aid the broader regional development of indigenous broadcasting. In 1980, the Therrien Committee reported to the Canadian Parliament on the need to extend broadcast services (including program origination) to northern and other underserved areas.[100] In 1982, the Canadian government developed the Northern Broadcasting Policy, which sought to provide broadcast outlets for native cultures and languages.[101]

In that same year, the Inuit Broadcasting Corporation began regularly scheduled, satellite-delivered TV service (it had conducted experiments since 1978) across the north. It included 5.5 hours per week of news, current affairs, entertainment, and children's programming in Inuktitut. Funding for that programming, as well as for Native American language programming, began to flow through the Northern Native Broadcast Access Program, funded through the secretary of state. Within a few years, there were satellite downlinks to nearly 400 Native American and Inuit communities, and production studios in a dozen or so of them.[102]

Television Northern Canada began transmission through satellite in January 1992. Funded by the national government and the provincial government of the Northwest Territories,[103] and administered through a consortium of six Native American and Inuit broadcasting societies, the provincial government, and educational institutions, TVNC produces a northern version of "Sesame Street," with Johnny the Lemming and Tulu the Raven as stars. Transmissions are in 12 native languages and English and are downlinked by over 100 communities.[104] By 1994, the network was carrying about 100 hours a week of children's, educational, cultural, and phone-in shows.[105]

The U.S. state government of Alaska began funding public broadcasting in 1970, establishing the Alaska Educational Broadcasting Commission as the agency through which funding for equipment and station operation would flow. In 1971, the first station to receive support through the AEBC came on the air in Bethel (southwestern Alaska). The Bethel station broadcast primarily in English but also in Yupik Eskimo (Inuit). Others soon followed, in Kotzebue, Barrow, Wrangell, Ketchikan, Sitka, and several other small remote communities, many with Native American or Inuit populations that sooner or later received programs in their own languages.[106]

Initially, those stations operated independently of one another, with no satellite linkage. However, in 1971, the U.S. National Library of Medicine sponsored an experiment in two-way communication through the *ATS-1* satellite of the National Aeronautics and Space Administration (NASA). It allowed physicians to conduct diagnoses and offer care through two-way radio service to and from a remote region surrounding Athabascan, in central Alaska. There was considerable "dead" airtime, so other experiments took place, including a three-credit University of Alaska course in coronary care and "enrichment" programs for elementary schools; some of the latter included programs about different sorts of Inuit and Native American traditions.[107] There also was a regular Wednesday night program slot for

Inuit, containing interview- and feature-based shows on village activities, teenager issues, and Inuit stories. Within a year, there was Inuit programming almost daily.[108]

Alaska began experimentation with satellite television for Native American and Inuit peoples in 1974 as part of a larger experiment involving NASA's ATS (Applications Technology Satellite) program. According to the Alaskan Public Broadcasting Commission, it had begun tests of 10-watt VHF TV transmitters for rural sites in 1971 and, through grants from the U.S. Corporation for Public Broadcasting, established stations in St. Paul, Unalaska, and Fort Yukon. The stations received the bulk of their programming through mail-delivered videocassettes.[109]

NASA's launch of the *ATS-6* satellite in 1974 provided the Appalachians, the Rocky Mountain states, and Alaska with their first opportunities to use satellites for televised delivery of health information, much as the *ATS-1* satellite had done for Alaska through radio starting in 1971. Alaskan educational authorities arranged to use some of the available transponder time to conduct trials of educational television, including broadcasts in Inuit and Native American languages. The University of Alaska, with funding from NASA, the U.S. Department of Health, Education, and Welfare, the National Institute of Education, and the Corporation for Public Broadcasting, developed several satellite-delivered programs, including "Alaska Native Magazine," with material in English, Athapascan, Tlingit, and Yupik.[110]

In 1975, NASA moved the *ATS-6* to serve India, but the availability of other satellites prompted the state legislature, after considerable debate, to provide funding for lease of a satellite transponder to permit satellite delivery on a continuing basis, both for educational programming and for the material going out to the 10-watt stations.[111] That commitment has continued but has not reached the scale of similar operations for Inuit and Native Americans in northern Canada. Satellites have assisted the roughly one dozen radio stations serving partially or fully Native American and Inuit communities in Alaska,[112] but Patrick Daley and Beverly James criticize the project itself for featuring a level of technological complexity that discouraged meaningful community involvement.[113]

Alaska also serves as home base for two other satellite-distributed indigenous media services. National Native News, founded in early 1987 with the help of a substantial grant from a U.S. private foundation, provides a daily newscast about Native American activities to just under 200 radio stations in some 30 U.S. states. Its host until 1995, Gary Fife, has been especially active in promoting links with non-Native American stations that serve areas with fair numbers of Native American listeners; he has gotten some of them to increase their coverage of Native American issues, which they also share with National Native News for inclusion in its newscasts.[114] Fife now is involved with "Heartbeat Alaska," a weekly TV program of news and features about Native Americans and Inuit, with contributors from Alaska and the Lower Forty-eight. This program, too, is distributed through satellite.

Australia's size and population distribution, together with its widely distributed indigenous population, make it analogous to Canada and Alaska. Yet satellite technology in the service of Aboriginal peoples developed much later, in part because the country's relatively small population and remote location made it a less profitable venue for satellites. When an indigenous service did come along in 1987, it took a form far different from anything that had been attempted in either of its two predecessors.

Australia's BRACS (Broadcasting for Remote Aboriginal Communities Scheme) resulted in part from a study conducted for the Australian Department of Aboriginal Affairs in 1984. The study report, "Out of the Silent Land," recommends development of a system to supply broadcast programming to remote communities. (Interestingly, the committee had visited only one such community.) According to the study satellite delivery would be ideal; however, given the underdeveloped state of satellite technology in Australia, a shortwave (high-frequency) radio delivery system might be the best bet in the short run. Much like Canada, remote communities would have high-quality receivers to pull in the signals and, if community size warranted it, modest studio equipment for local program production.[115]

The Department of Aboriginal Affairs (DAA) considered the report and, by late 1987, began to act on its recommendations. It decided to equip 74 remote communities (later increased to 82) with radio and TV reception, transmission (for a three- to five-kilometer radius), and production equipment, at a cost of about AUS $35,000 per installation. Initially, the DAA planned to install receivers capable of picking up only ABC radio and television, but it ultimately purchased models that could also receive commercial stations and CAAMA's new Alice Springs television station, Imparja. Installation of the equipment was slow, but by June 1989, 26 communities in western Australia and in the Northern Territory had it in place.[116]

What the communities were able to do with it was another matter. The equipment was rudimentary (e.g., there were no editing suites or special effects generators), and communities had to supply their own tape, building, air-conditioning, and maintenance, as well as funding for equipment repair and replacement and salaries for staffing the BRACS studios. Training of staff might or might not be covered by the ABC. Given that the communities *were* remotely located (that was the purpose of the project, after all), not to mention economically deprived, those were tremendous handicaps, and it was not surprising to learn that few of the operations were still functioning after the first year. Some hadn't even come on the air in the first place, since they hadn't known that they were to establish BRACS studios, had no idea what to do with the equipment when it arrived, and received little or no guidance in its assembly and operation.[117]

The Aboriginal and Torres Strait Islander Commission (ATSIC), which had replaced the DAA in 1989, reconsidered the BRACS project in 1992 and took a new approach to it—one that would include guidance in installation, furnishing of repair services, and training programs for BRACS operators to be run partly at designated training centers (Batchelor, Northern Territory; Townsville, Queensland) and partly in the communities themselves. As many as 200 communities eventually may receive studios, and the original equipment already is being replaced in some of the existing studios. But Australian indigenous media scholars Michael Meadows and Helen Molnar remain skeptical that the government will provide the financial support necessary for the meaningful involvement of Aboriginals in the development of their own programming.[118]

In recent years, Australia has been using satellite-delivered television to win friends, influence people, and expand the market for distribution of its domestic TV programs throughout Asia and beyond.[119] As it does so, it fuels controversy over the issue of whether or not it should be investing more time, energy, and money in the further development of Aboriginal electronic media. At an ATSIC-sponsored conference on indigenous media held in Brisbane, Queensland, in 1993, Aboriginal journalists pointed out that the BRACS network received AUS $1.1 million in 1992, whereas the government gave ABC AUS $3.5 million to launch the satellite-delivered overseas television service.[120]

Cost is an issue in almost every situation involving indigenous use of satellites. American Indian Radio on Satellite (AIROS) has been available since 1982, but it took several years for the cost of using it to drop to a level affordable by most Native American stations. Launching the service itself would have been far beyond the capabilities of those stations; fortunately, the Corporation for Public Broadcasting provided a seed money grant and an over $450,000 three-year development grant for the project.[121] As of mid-1995, AIROS transmitted two Monday-through-Friday radio programs to 29 subscribers, not all of whom are Native American. There's a newscast, "National Native News," and a discussion program with call-ins, "Native America Calling."[122]

There's one minor, but growing, category of satellite usage by indigenous groups. Raidio na Gaeltachta began in 1994 to rebroadcast some of its programs to the Irish-speaking *diaspora* in Europe through weekly satellite transmissions. One Irish entrepreneur bought the rights to broadcast, via satellite, the 1994 World Cup Football (soccer) matches involving the Irish team, but in Irish only (English language rights would have been prohibitively expensive). He then sold his service to roughly 200 Irish bars in the United States.[123] Maori broadcasters have experimented with the same sort of service to the Maori diaspora living in cities along the east coast of Australia, although in that instance the hope is that Australian community radio stations and/or SBS will relay the programming. Since direct reception from satellite requires additional equipment and, therefore, expense, relays through existing stations would seem to be a more effective way to reach that particular audience.

Other electronic media services have been slower to spread through the indigenous populations. Electronic bulletin boards perhaps show the most promise and already have been used by minority communities. Turkish students studying at U.S. universities exchanged messages with one another in the early stages of Operation Desert Storm in 1992. There were some lively clashes of opinion, bits and pieces of information from home, and speculation on possible outcomes of the conflict.[124] Because of the specialized and moderately expensive equipment required to both send and receive messages (and that would include a fairly sophisticated telephone system), and because of the need for literacy, such bulletin boards are likely to remain peripheral to the overall development of indigenous media for some time to come. E-mail exchanges between indigenous media personnel are another matter, and some indigenous stations (e.g., Maori) already use them.

Electronic systems also can serve as distribution channels for news about groups that have few other ways to reach the larger world. Supporters of the Zapatistas (see earlier discussion) have used the Internet to bring news about the group to audiences abroad, especially in North America. A rural development organization in Mexico City, Equipo Pueblo, receives the news, translates it, and sends it out over the Internet, which offers four separate bulletins on Chiapas.[125]

Interactive electronic conferencing also is beginning to take its place in indigenous communication, primarily as a means of enabling people with common concerns but living in remote locations to interchange questions, ideas, and even skills and lore. Four Aboriginal communities in the Tanami region of the Northern Territory established the Tanami Network in 1991; that followed a test videoconference involving two of the communities and Sydney in 1990, and a subsequent workshop for the assessment of needs, uses, and funding of the system. The communities and the provider company, AAP Communications, signed a three-year contract, with a price tag of AUS $2 million, in 1992. The communities pledged to cover a fourth of the sum from the start—no small undertaking, given their modest resources. Other governmental and nongovernmental users make up most of the balance.

The network has made it much easier for kinfolk to maintain contact, but it also has been used to share ideas on preservation of Warlpiri and Pintubi tribal lore, to discuss government plans and proposals, to set sales strategies for Aboriginal arts and crafts, and to provide evidence for trials taking place in distant locations. It is already directly connected with Alice Springs and Darwin and can be connected with more distant cities when needed. The four directors of the network come from the four communities and ensure that the system functions to help Aboriginals—not to bring in more of the outside (white) world. The conferences themselves follow Aboriginal practices of deliberation, which means that there often are silent pauses of several minutes' duration and even times when most people leave their meeting rooms for longer, unspecified intervals. Yet cameras remain on, waiting for people to filter back in.[126]

Native American groups in the U.S. Great Lakes region have been able to take advantage of an existing computer network (CICNET) operated by several midwestern universities. Several tribes founded GLAIN (Great Lakes American Indian Network) in March 1995 for the exchange of information among them—something that would have been out of the question if CICNET hadn't subsidized their participation.[127]

Finally, cable television has served as an outlet for a few indigenous media ventures. Channel 5, operated by the Navajo nation out of Window Rock, Arizona, was established in 1988, after receiving a grant from the National Telecommunications Information Administration. The few full-time staff members must be prepared to appear in front of or behind cameras. They have televised basketball games (the sport is very popular on many U.S. reservations), news, and coverage of Navajo nation council meetings, with much of the programming in Navajo. However, many reservation residents are so poor or so remotely located that they can't afford cable, and the station is setting up a translator (relay) based system to extend its reach.[128]

Governmental Policies and Commitments

The overall history of the development of indigenous electronic media up until the past decade has been largely one of individual indigenous stations, portions of airtime (not always stable) on majority culture outlets, and scattered uses of videotape by indigenous groups. None of those activities arose from the long-term commitment of any government to the development of indigenous electronic media. There were commitments by national broadcast services—BBC, CBC, ABC, Sveriges Radio, Norway's Norsk Rikskringskasting, and Finland's Yleisradio (YLE)—to radio and television broadcasts for, and usually by, indigenous groups, but those could be reduced or withdrawn if budgets became tight, and occasionally were.

In 1983, the Canadian government's Department of Communications released its Broadcasting Strategy for Canada. Following consultation, the ministers of communication and of northern affairs, along with the secretary of state, announced that there would be a specific Northern Broadcasting Policy, which would increase the availability of electronic technologies for residents of the north (Inuit, Native American, and Métis). They said indigenous groups living there should have the opportunity to work with the Canadian Radio-Television and Telecommunications Commission (CRTC), the CBC, and other agencies and operations to develop programming appropriate to their needs and to reject inappropriate programming.[129]

A policy is a policy, and nothing more. But this one soon was supported through a funding program—the Northern Native Broadcast Access Program (NNBAP)—which made roughly CAN $40 million available, over a four-year period (1983–1987), to northern indigenous communication societies for production of regional radio and TV programs in indigenous languages. (There was to be a similar funding program for southern indigenous groups, but budgetary stringency intervened.) Funding *was* limited to production, and the groups still had to rely on existing broadcast outlets (CBC and Cancom). Still, the groups managed to produce an average of over 90 hours a week for radio and 6.5 a week for TV before the NNBAP was three years old.[130]

That was easily the largest governmental investment in indigenous electronic media activity, for Canada or elsewhere, up until the mid-1980s. It was accompanied by increased efforts through the CBC to assist indigenous groups with their production efforts and in the development of their stations, to increase radio airtime for indigenous languages, and to make more time available through communications satellites for the delivery of programming to the north. As one example, CBC's French language service in Montreal supplies several hours of daily broadcasts in Cree and in various Inuit languages to the northern region east of Hudson Bay; the Cree service has a staff of 12, two-thirds of whom are Cree.[131]

The CRTC also stepped up its efforts, first by forming a Northern Native Broadcasting Committee in late 1984 and then by developing a comprehensive policy on northern indigenous broadcasting (1985–1987) through public hearings, written testimony, and field trips to the region. The NNBAP program was and remains independent of the CRTC but takes into account some of its recommendations, particularly along the lines of increasing broadcast and distribution outlets. The NNBAP funds communications societies in each of 13 northern cultural and linguistic regions. Some produce radio only, others television only, and still others work with both media.[132]

The Australian government, as noted earlier, had formed a commission to study the potential role of electronic communication for Aboriginal peoples. The commission's report, "Out of the Silent Land" (1984), suggests a number of concrete steps, government financing among them, that could improve the Aboriginal's situation. The report designates the Department of Aboriginal Affairs as the unit chiefly responsible for assisting Aboriginal electronic media activities, and the DAA began to support specific electronic media projects in 1985, as CAAMA prepared to go on-air with 8KIN. The DAA also encouraged formation of more Aboriginal media associations, although, with an initial (FY 1984–1985) budget of less than AUS $1 million, the encouragement was more in word than in deed.[133]

Aboriginal groups, stung by the discrepancy between government funding for the Special Broadcasting Services (providing radio and TV broadcasts in European and Asian languages other than English) at roughly AUS $45 million and DAA's AUS $1.5 million (both for FY 1986–1987),[134] began to press for more substantial support. The reorganization of DAA in 1989, and its emergence as the Aboriginal and Torres Strait Islander Commission, were accompanied by an attempt to develop a comprehensive policy for Aboriginal electronic media. ATSIC circulated a draft discussion paper on policy in 1989, received comments from interested parties, and, after two redrafts, released to the public the *Aboriginal and Torres Strait Islander Broadcasting Policy Discussion Paper* (October 1991). Several public meetings and conferences followed: time and again, participants stressed the need for more and better training, a variety of media outlets, a national association that would help to coordinate Aboriginal media efforts and perhaps disburse ATSIC funding of media activities, and, of course, more money to disburse. ATSIC then circulated a draft policy paper reflecting that input in January 1993.[135]

Despite the absence of a firm policy, the various discussions and drafts did help to call attention to two things: the strong desire of Aboriginal peoples to be involved in media activities and the inadequacy of resources, technical and human, that were needed to fulfill that desire. ATSIC increased its annual funding of electronic media throughout the period and by FY 1992–1993 was spending over AUS $10 million on the activity—substantially below SBS's allocation of AUS $60 million for the same year but at least slightly closer to parity. However, the discussions and drafts stimulated still more Aboriginal media activities—for example, roughly 40 Aboriginal and Torres Strait Islander groups were producing programming for broadcast over non-Aboriginal public radio stations by 1992—so average increases per activity were negligible.*,[136]

The policy-making process seems clearly to have encouraged an increase in indigenous media activity in both Canada and Australia, perhaps more spectacularly in the latter, where such activity developed much later. It also encouraged an increase in government spending on the activity—in Canada, more but ending sooner, in Australia, less but lasting longer. However, the fact remains that neither government has fully committed itself to both a firm policy and continuing financial support. Australia's decision to license community television stations starting in 1993 was criticized by Aboriginal groups because it made no special provision, financial or otherwise, for Aboriginal groups. An association of Aboriginal organizations with interests in television, Perleeka Television, has campaigned for such measures as the inclusion of mandatory access for Aboriginal and Pacific islander peoples in the constitutions of *all* community (sixth-channel) license holders.[137]

Norway began consideration of an electronic media policy for its Sami population in 1987. Both the national broadcasting service, Norsk Rikskringkasting and narradio, were already involved with Sami radio (and, for NRK, occasional TV) programming. A well-equipped NRK studio complex for the production of Sami radio programs already existed in Karasjok, more or less in the heart of the Norwegian portion of Sapme (the largely Sami-populated region stretching across northern Scandinavia). Einar Forde, the head of NRK, announced in December 1989 that there would be a major revision in NRK's Sami broadcast policy and structure and appointed a working committee to come up with a set of recommendations. These emerged in 1992 in a report entitled *Sami Radio toward the Year 2000*.[138] The Karasjok studio complex was to become the centerpiece for the development of a separate (but still within NRK) Sami radio service, which eventually would have dedicated transmitters, expanded studios, considerably increased broadcast hours, a larger budget, and a head

---

*In 1995, the government created a separate Torres Strait Islander Commission and endowed it with a portion of the funding that had gone to ATSIC. However, there was no specific provision for radio in the new TSIC budget; thus, the financing of the Torres Strait Islander Media Association, previously covered through ATSIC, was no longer assured. *NIMAA News* (newsletter of the National Indigenous Media Association of Australia), 3, 7 (March 1995), 3.

of operations who would report directly to the head of NRK. In 1995, construction was finished on a fully equipped radio-television newsroom, where most staff members are working through *both* media.

The move toward a stronger NRK Sami service was helped greatly by the commitment of Forde and by the lobbying of NRK Sami Radio manager Nils Johan Héatta. The result is a plan that, *if* fully implemented, would bring Sami radio, and a small amount of television (one hour a week of original programming) to *all* of Norway by the year 2000. That is the most unusual characteristic of the plan. The Australian and Canadian policy initiatives clearly aimed to improve the electronic media situation for rural dwellers but did very little for indigenous city dwellers. Norway's plan recognizes that there are probably about as many Sami living in and near its larger cities (Bergen, Oslo, Trondheim) as there are in the Norwegian portion of Sapme, a few hundred miles north. The programs they receive will be in Norwegian more often than they are in Sami, given the fact that many of them cannot understand Sami. (That's already true for the Sami närradio services available in Oslo and in Alta.) A related intent is that the wider Norwegian public will be able to learn more about its first people. The report also stresses the need for high-quality equipment and good training programs so that program quality will be first-rate.[139]

Even as of the mid-1990s, however, few broadcast laws provided indigenous stations with the fundamental security of a legal guarantee of their existence. One that does is Finland's Act on Yleisradio 1994, where several sections of the act make specific commitments to supporting Sami broadcasting, legally and financially. Section 7.4, for example, states that YLE shall "ensure equal treatment in programme policy for both Finnish and Swedish-speaking citizens, and provide services in the Lappish language (Sami)."[140]

When the initial draft of the act was circulated, Sami staff at YLE's Sami radio service in Ivalo noticed that there was *no* mention of Sami broadcasting in the document. The station manager, Juhani Nousuniemi, lobbied certain well-placed contacts in YLE and in key ministries, and the final act emerged with specific guarantees, such as the clause cited above, in place.[141]

Australia, Canada, and Norway all make a commitment to indigenous media that is strong on paper; financing may or may not follow. The first two nations are going through economic recessions at the moment. There are government officials and figures in private industry who doubt the wisdom, and perhaps the justice, of spending tens of millions of dollars or kronor to develop a healthy infrastructure for indigenous electronic media, let alone similar or greater sums over time to support those media. After all, none of the indigenous peoples amounts to more than 1 or 2 percent of the overall population. But the process that led up to the policies in each of the three cases just covered (the process followed for Maori media is presented in Chapter Five) made clear both the need for such services and the need and justification for government support, through whatever agency or broadcast organization. Continuing and substantial support will be the next step in establishing the importance and viability of indigenous electronic media in those nations and in others. Time will tell whether that step is taken.

The Lessons of the Past

There are few instances in history where governments have taken the initiative to assist in the development of indigenous electronic media. Rather, their involvement usually stems from the desire to influence indigenous peoples in other countries, the perceived need to counter such attempts at influence, the pressure of widespread public opinion (as in the "power to the people" movements in the early 1970s), and major instances of clashes between indigenous groups and law enforcement officials. The responses of governments often have been slow, modest in scope, and uneven in long-term commitment. Chapter Five, on the development of Maori broadcasting, presents a detailed example of just how slow, modest, and uneven.

Religious organizations were somewhat readier to initiate, although their earlier reasons for involvement often had more to do with the perceived need to combat possible Communist influence on indigenous peoples, or to bring (Christian) enlightenment to them, than they did with the intention of strengthening indigenous self-esteem or pride in the indigenous heritage. "Liberation theology" and other movements in Christianity led to increased willingness to recognize and strengthen indigenous cultures,[142] to the point where some of the indigenous media efforts the movements sponsored caused national governments to close them down, as did Ecuador in June 1994 in the case of Radio Latacunga—the station of the Cotapaxi provincial diocese of the Catholic church. The station had been supporting the protests of indigenous groups against the government's introduction of a new law on land usage.[143]

International aid organizations, whether run by individual nations (USAID), international organizations (World Bank and UNESCO), or nongovernmental groups (Germany's Friedrich Ebert Stiftung), have become involved with indigenous media from time to time but always at the invitation of the host (majority culture) government. Rarely did any of those organizations establish stations—the USAID support for a Guatemalan indigenous radio station (discussed earlier) is one of the few exceptions—and, when they did, the short- or medium-term financial support they offered generally came without any matching support by the host government. (That isn't surprising when, as in Guatemala or Homa Bay, the outside agency dictated the nature of the project that it was willing to fund.) When the foreign support ended, the station or specific program service (such as literacy or nutrition) usually did as well. Senegal's continuing support for RER again is an exception to the rule, but that support itself dwindled over time.

The Australian, New Zealand, Canadian, and U.S. governmental support for Aboriginal, Maori, Native American, and Inuit media in the 1980s was a refreshing change from much that had taken place earlier—refreshing because there appears to have been some recognition on the part of those governments that indigenous electronic media truly deserved support. Furthermore, that recognition didn't seem to be driven as much by protests (although there were some) as it was by the feeling of at least some majority culture officials that society in general might profit by the presence of such media. That would be a good omen, but it was qualified by the almost total withdrawal of Canadian government support starting in 1990.

Throughout the formative years of indigenous media, it was the indigenous peoples themselves who bore the greatest burdens and exerted the greatest effort. As you'll see in the chapters that follow, very often they were few in number, and those few often had had the experience of working in majority culture media operations. Sometimes they encountered indifference or opposition from within indigenous groups. And where they succeeded, it was usually after years of attempts to break down barriers, among which was the belief in many indigenous communities that they weren't capable of operating their own media.

Indigenous groups have been in the forefront of minorities seeking to use the electronic media. From the few thousand Ainu to the several hundred thousand Maori and few million Kurds, their media activities now span the globe. The United Nations proclamation of an International Year of the Indigenous Peoples in 1993 drew even more attention to their efforts to gain fairer treatment in their respective societies. The European Community also has begun to address the rights and privileges of various minority communities in the EC, although, as Carmelo Garitaonandia points out, there's a real question as to whether the EC's economically, competitively driven policies will meld with the realities of those minority groups—often small in population and weak in economic power.[144] On the whole, commercially supported systems haven't been very supportive of indigenous media efforts; as such systems spread, and as the notion of government support for electronic media activities of all types declines, which appears to be the case, the indigenous electronic media will face further challenges.

The media activities themselves now represent virtually every facet of all types of minority-operated electronic media—ethnic, cultural, linguistic, religious, political, economic. Furthermore, the indigenous language minorities exhibit a universal concern with language—its preservation, its modernization, its symbolic value. The ways in which they have addressed that concern, and others, should be of interest to any member of any group, minority or majority, who regards the electronic media as powerful agents in the shaping of society in general.

3

The Building Blocks of Indigenous Media: 1, Programming

Indigenous electronic media can be examined from a wide variety of perspectives: how they came into being, how they've evolved, how they're controlled and by whom, who pays for them, how they influence and/or mirror society for good and for ill, whose interests they chiefly serve, and how society can influence them. For each perspective, there are a number of common concerns: programming, financing, training, administration, and internal and external sources of control and influence.

Those concerns form the general subject matter for this chapter and the next, as well as the specific material for the case studies that follow. I see them as a set of interdependent building blocks, and not just for indigenous electronic media: my exploration of local and regional radio and television over a nearly 30-year period assures me that those concerns are widely shared by minority, and sometimes majority, broadcasters of all sorts. While the order of importance will vary according to time and situation, all become important sooner or later.

The central subject of Chapter Three is programming: its purposes, its practices, the "target" and other audiences it does and doesn't attract, and the concept of professionalism. After all, financing, regulation, and influence are important only with respect to the ultimate effect they have on programming, even though the top-heavy administrative structures of certain of the more traditional public service monopoly broadcast organizations in Europe might convey the opposite impression.

Programming Purposes

During the first half of the 1920s, radio broadcasting in most countries was developing a sense of purpose at a time when many in the audience thought of it strictly as another form of entertainment. In fact, entertainment has proven to be one of electronic media's major purposes over time, although more often on the basis of what it brings back to the media in the form of advertising revenue, listener and viewer monetary contributions, public good will (especially helpful in license fee–based systems, where audience satisfaction can make occasional increases in fees more palatable), and direct sales of program material both to other media outlets and as individual sales or rentals to the public.

But many broadcast operations developed other senses of purpose because of their social consciences; their perceived need to be something more than "just entertainers"; their excitement about ways in which broadcasting could enhance education, increase political participation, and promote civic responsibility; their concern over the declining quality (as they saw it) of language usage; their feeling that society would be far better if programs would challenge and assist them in elevating their tastes; or various other noble-sounding hopes. Quite often, those purposes became enshrined in the broadcast law of the nation: to inform, to educate, to entertain. In certain instances, the law required broadcasters to offer specified quantities of each category, although more often the broadcasters themselves, perhaps with the pressure of the government, citizen advisory boards, or print media criticism, saw to the provision of a reasonably balanced schedule in that regard.

By the time indigenous electronic media outlets began to appear in any considerable number, many majority culture stations, especially if they were advertiser-supported, had dropped whatever educational programming (formal instruction, at least) they once offered, and some had abolished their newsrooms in favor of total reliance on wire service copy. Thus, there was no legal expectation, at least in the form of licensing conditions, that stations fulfill certain specified purposes for certain amounts of the broadcast day. Furthermore, in countries where there were many different types of stations already on the air, with as many as 30, 40, or more in some metropolitan markets, the public was already accustomed to stations that were all music, all news, and all talk and would probably have had no expectation that the new indigenous stations would serve a variety of purposes.

As things have turned out, most of the indigenous media do so, anyway. Most of them were established by individuals with a strong sense of purpose—or, rather, a number of purposes. They can be represented by the following list:

1. To "rescue" the language, chiefly by using it in daily broadcasts but also perhaps by direct language instruction.

2. To increase a sense of self-esteem on the part of the indigenous population, both in their historical traditions and in their achievements in contemporary society.

3. To combat the negative images of indigenous peoples held by the majority population.

4. To work for a greater degree of cohesiveness among indigenous peoples, often so as to develop greater political influence in local, regional, and national life.

5. To provide a visible and audible symbol of indigenous society so that both indigenous and majority cultures would be aware that the former "counted for something" in the form of possession and operation of modern technology.

6. To provide an outlet for the creative production of, for example, indigenous singers, instrumentalists, and poets.

7. To provide another source of employment for the indigenous community, where, given frequently high unemployment, even the addition of 10 or 20 jobs can help.

Of the above list, the first three purposes stand out: to preserve and restore an indigenous language, to improve the self-image of the minority, and to change the negative impressions of the minority that are held by members of the majority culture. Virtually all indigenous media administrators, program staff members, and independent producers have that much in common.

PRESERVATION AND RESTORATION
OF AN INDIGENOUS LANGUAGE

Preservation and restoration of an indigenous language could be regarded as two separate purposes, but in the case of indigenous media, they become coterminous.[1] Preservation, in the sense of ensuring that the language not disappear but remain in an unchanged state and available through radio in much the way that paintings are available in a museum, makes no sense to indigenous language media staff. Almost without exception, they want to see the language restored to everyday use by increasing numbers of individuals.

But restoration brings with it some important questions. If there are dialects, which one, if any, will predominate? If the language had not developed much past the preindustrial stage, how will the media develop the terminology necessary to deal with science, technology, medicine, and other fields? Given the predominance of majority culture media, is it even possible to develop separate terminology for such things as space technology or biotechnology? Yet, if the indigenous language media resort to "indigenization" of majority language terminology, is there the risk that, at some point in the future, the indigenous language itself will have become little more than a version of the majority language?

Most indigenous languages have adapted to changing circumstances over time yet have managed to maintain their integrity. But the rapid rise of the electronic media during the twentieth century, along with their dominance by the majority culture, have posed a tremendous challenge to the continuing integrity, and even the very existence, of indigenous minority languages for several reasons.

First, those media diffuse information immediately, and that information includes the use of new terminology. Consider one all-too-familiar subject. As the media began to cover acquired immune deficiency syndrome in the early 1980s, the full terminology was rapidly replaced by the acronym *AIDS*. It became a household word in a matter of days or weeks. It usually takes longer to devise the appropriate terminology in an indigenous language, partly because certain words may not exist and will have to be developed by compounding or modifying other words. And when the process is complete, the resulting terminology might be awkward to use, particularly if it contains more and/or longer individual words. Acronyms, too, might not be "user-friendly," especially when compared with the acronyms already in general use in the media.

Second, electronic media structures in many countries have been heavily monopolistic during most of the century, although that is changing quite rapidly in the industrialized world as the century nears its end. As monopolies, they became important transmission points for acceptable language usage: the French government during the 1920s made it a condition of licensing any radio station that only "proper" French could be used on-air—no slang or regional dialects.[2] The language in question always was the majority language, and there was little or no consideration of indigenous languages. The sheer pervasiveness of the monopolies—the BBC's John Reith once called it their "brute force"—meant that indigenous peoples had no effective means of fighting back, unless they could convince the monopoly services to allow access for indigenous language broadcasts. Access rarely was granted, so indigenous language speakers had still another all-pervasive institution, along with schools, that promoted use of the majority language to the virtual exclusion of indigenous languages. Furthermore, as with schools, broadcasting was an early and important point of contact with the larger society for their children.

Third, the electronic media are readily accessible to illiterates. Given the limited economic and educational opportunities available to many of the indigenous minority populations throughout the world, illiteracy or limited literacy has been quite common among such populations. In that light, it isn't surprising that many indigenous minorities are heavy consumers of the electronic media and may be influenced more profoundly than they realize in terms of their language usage. Breda Luther contends that even audience participation shows can bring viewers to lose some of their "natural" ways of presenting themselves because of the controls on presentational styles exercised by the host of the program.[3]

Fourth, the electronic media use time in somewhat the same fashion as the print media use space. It would seem odd if newspapers and magazines were to employ large amounts of blank space to indicate pauses of various lengths in the thoughts of reporters writing their articles or to attempt to mirror in quotations the vocal mannerisms of an interviewee or speaker. Likewise, if print media were to replicate a speech by including vocalized pauses (*aaaah, errr, ummm*), we would be quite surprised. Although the electronic media can easily include pauses, vocalized or not, those elements usually are removed when the material is recorded for later broadcast, partly in the interests of time.

However, many indigenous languages employ pauses as signs, for example, of deliberation, of careful consideration of another point of view, of respect, and of politeness. In Aboriginal, Maori, Native American, and many other indigenous societies, it is not unusual for group deliberations to feature pauses of several minutes' duration. If the electronic media remove pauses, they remove an essential element of the language; still, it's rare to find an electronic media reporter or interviewer who doesn't regard pauses as time wasted and as an indication of lack of professionalism.

Therefore, they are to be avoided or removed whenever possible.

Fifth, with the advent of television, there was further reinforcement of certain majority culture visual conventions, such as direct eye contact between characters or eye contact between TV performers (e.g., news readers) and the audience. A number of indigenous cultures feature different visual languages, such as *not* looking directly at another individual in many circumstances. If an indigenous TV production with majority culture viewership was true to indigenous conventions, it could be misunderstood, which then could push indigenous productions to use majority culture visual languages.

For any or all of several reasons, some indigenous minority stations have chosen not to broadcast in indigenous languages. Certain of those languages are spoken by so few individuals that it seems almost hopeless to attempt to "rescue" them, at least by means of radio or television stations. Individuals seeking to rescue Ainu, spoken by perhaps a few hundred individuals, have chosen to work through videocassette recordings, although they would be happy to have broadcast licenses, if any were available. They have requested that the Japanese government consider licensing stations in the Kurile Islands and setting the islands aside for the Ainu. First, however, the islands would have to be returned to Japan by their current occupier, the Russian Republic.

As costs of satellite transmission for radio have dropped, a few indigenous language operations are beginning to export some of their broadcasts to the *diaspora*—those members of the indigenous group now living abroad who might appreciate having regular access to their home language. In September 1994, Ireland's Raidio na Gaeltachta (RNG) began to relay a portion of its schedule to Gaelic-speaking listeners in western Europe, through the *Astra* satellite. While the service is available only on Saturdays, RNG staff hope that listener response warrants extending it to other days of the week.

RESTORATION OF PRIDE AND
DEVELOPMENT OF A BETTER SELF-IMAGE

The second programming purpose of indigenous media—restoration of pride and development of a better self-image—certainly can be accomplished in part through broadcasts in indigenous languages. Simply hearing the language of one's people through the electronic media can help to restore a sense of self-worth, whether one speaks the language or not. But much more is needed, particularly in view of the common tendency of majority culture media to ignore and/or stereotype minorities of all sorts. An indigenous media operation usually finds it easier to combat ignorance than it does stereotyping, since the latter requires redefinition of existing images and beliefs, many of them conveyed by the media for decades or even a few centuries and accepted as more or less true not only by members of the majority culture but also by indigenous peoples themselves.

Most of the indigenous media devote a major share of their time and effort to attempts to portray the variety and diversity of indigenous life. While indigenous peoples often live together in communities, they are at least as likely to live in relative isolation from one another, especially in urban areas. The former probably have a good sense of each other's accomplishments within the community but relatively little sense of indigenous activity in the outside world—and perhaps relatively little interest in knowing more about it. The latter may know very little about any other indigenous activity, although religious institutions and, if they exist, nonofficial schools, may make them aware of what's happening locally. Still, it remains very difficult to discover much about the deeds of indigenous individuals and groups in other parts of the country, whether in contemporary life or historically.

Indigenous media can function to transform individual acts into societal acts by highlighting, through news items, interviews, quiz shows, soap operas, or a host of other program formats, the accomplishments of Native American automotive engineers, Maori international investment bankers, Aboriginal lawyers, Sami biologists, Basque politicians, and Welsh sportspersons. The hope is that those listening and viewing will be inspired to emulate the examples of individuals of their own ethnic group.

The media perform much the same function when providing historical material, whether through narratives, interviews with elders (good archival material, as well), documentaries, dramatizations, contests (game and quiz shows), tales and legends, and music, most often in the form of songs. Ideally, that would enhance a sense of pride in past accomplishments, which in turn would lead to a feeling that "we can do it again."

It may or may not work out that way in practice, especially if the material emphasizes *individual,* rather than *collective,* efforts. Indigenous societies often have a strong sense of collective identity, even to the point of sometimes discouraging individual initiative. In 1993, a Maori author argued strongly, in a book and in interviews about it,[4] that Maori wouldn't improve their lot in life until they shed what he regarded as their predominantly "collectivist" ways and exercised more individual initiative. This became the subject of intense discussion on most Maori radio stations, with some applauding him, and some condemning him. On the other hand, individual initiative in overcoming obstacles created largely by or through the majority culture can be a very positive stimulus.

Many indigenous societies feature rituals and specific forms of language that are not for the eyes and ears of the broader public, whether indigenous or not. There are rites of passage, birth, burial, and other activities and occasions that are to be known and used only by a relative handful of individuals of one or the other gender, of a certain age or standing, or of a specific family lineage. The concept of ownership of a story is especially complex. In some tribes, the question of who owns a story, and thus possesses the right to narrate it, is narrowly defined, while in others it is not. When there are different stories concerning the same phenomenon, establishing "truth" or "accuracy" is nearly impossible.

A group of anthropologist-historians discovered as much in 1990, when they sought to establish the traditional travel routes taken by the Hopi in the Salt River area. Groups in each village had their own versions, which some villagers would share in part, others fully, others not at all.[5] If the skills and patience of anthropologist-historians met roadblocks, one can imagine how broadcasters, lacking such skills and pressed for time, would fare in preparing a news story or feature on the subject.

There also are public rituals that last for days but cannot be edited for broadcast because that would compromise their very nature and purpose. And, while there is storytelling that is appropriate at any time, other stories may be told only in certain seasons or on certain days, in connection with certain events. It would be a real error in judgment for a family planning advisor, for instance, to take a story known to a tribe only in connection with a certain festival and then attempt to use it to illustrate some aspect of family planning, with no regard for the timing of the broadcast.[6]

Broadcasters face yet another problem with rites and rituals, which may appear in the same basic form in two adjoining, and even closely related, tribal groups. However, they may be regarded as public by one and private by the other, as the Aboriginal rock group Yotho Yindi discovered when it performed a kangaroo hunt dance, which one tribe regarded as public, before another tribe, which regarded it as private and showed its deep displeasure.[7]

For those reasons, some stations employ consultants who can advise them on what can be shared through the media and what cannot. However, because indigenous use of the electronic media is of recent vintage, many keepers of lore and ritual and many traditional singers and dancers are only now discovering just how widespread the sharing of material may become when the media diffuse it. They find it difficult to imagine how the making of a recording, and its subsequent distribution, may bring that material to audiences hundreds, and even thousands, of miles away. Ethical broadcasters should make that clear when working with such groups, even when those producing the recording are of the same tribe; views on sharing are apt to be governed by specific circumstance and can show enormous variation.

CHANGING THE MAJORITY CULTURE'S NEGATIVE
IMPRESSIONS OF THE INDIGENOUS MEDIA

The preceding leads logically to the third common purpose of indigenous media: changing the majority culture's negative impressions of the indigenous minority.[8] This may be the most controversial of all purposes, for several reasons. First, the minority may feel that, due to decades or centuries of misrepresentation by the media, by religious and educational institutions, and by public officials, the task of "image modification" is impossible, so why attempt it? A second and related reason would be along the lines of "They (majority culture) have their own media, which symbolize their own values. Now we have ours, so let's treat it as ours and let them be happy with theirs." Third, and especially if there is a heavy or even total devotion to use of the indigenous language, is the idea that "the language is *our* property and perhaps our very essence; why should we wish to attract outsiders or to explain ourselves to them?" Fourth, there may be a perception of the overwhelming need to restore use of the language, pride in accomplishments, and other cultural necessities to the point where there isn't the time, the staff, or the money to also attempt to reach majority culture audiences. And finally, there may be the feeling on the part of indigenous media staff themselves that, in order to reach the majority successfully, the indigenous media would have to become more like their majority culture counterparts than they'd wish, losing much of their indigenous character in the process.

If, in spite of any or all of those reasons, an indigenous media operation does attempt to attract majority culture audiences (and the vast majority of indigenously operated media outlets do so), the program formats already noted are likely to serve perfectly well. In fact, most station staff with whom I've spoken regard much of their programming as intended for both audiences. However, balance and approach might be quite different, sometimes to the point where it's doubtful that the two audiences would find the material equally appealing, and it's possible that neither would find it appealing at all.

Take as one example the programming of music, which is the predominant form of raw material for most indigenous radio stations. A majority culture audience might have some interest in hearing indigenous music (much of it heavily influenced by majority culture forms) but probably not for more than half of the program's duration, if even that much, and especially not if there were to be lots of vocal music and/or disc jockey chat in the indigenous language. A minority culture audience might enjoy the occasional majority culture selection, and might or might not object to the use of indigenous language by a DJ, but probably wouldn't be concerned about songs in the native tongue. The majority audience might welcome explanations of the context of traditional music; the indigenous audience might not need them and might even resent the implication that it did.

Newscasts can pose a similar problem. Majority culture listeners and viewers might welcome learning something more about indigenous activities and concerns but not to the exclusion of coverage of the majority culture. Indigenous audiences might relegate news about the majority to a very distant second place in the overall newscast time budget. The majority might resent a seeming overemphasis on the positive accomplishments of the indigenous minority, while the minority might welcome large numbers of such items as an antidote to the largely negative treatment it receives through majority media.

Of course, things aren't quite that black and white, so to speak. Most minorities, indigenous and otherwise, have grown up and continue to function in a larger society dominated by the majority and its media. They have a genuine interest in remaining aware of the majority culture. For their part, majority cultures with access to indigenous media—young people in particular—are discovering fresh insights (new perspectives on values, different forms of creative expression, and unimagined examples of injustice and need) through the news items, stories, songs, and other programming that they now hear and see. And if the nation is "media-rich," as is the case in most industrialized societies, and as is becoming more common in some Third World nations, there is freedom of choice. Still, considered on a program-by-program basis, it can be difficult to attempt to reach two quite different audiences with the selfsame program.

WORKING FOR A GREATER DEGREE
OF COHESIVENESS

Although they may not be common to all indigenous stations, the four remaining purposes in the list of programming purposes of indigenous media certainly deserve consideration, particularly number 4, working for a greater degree of (political) cohesiveness.

A tactic frequently employed by the great, as well as not-so-great, colonial powers in the sixteenth through nineteenth centuries was to divide and conquer. In many cases, the colonial powers came into lands where there was no larger "nation" in any Western political sense but, rather, an assortment of tribes, clans, families, or other groups in various states of conflict and cooperation with one another. If the colonizer hoped to rule over a large tract of land, it was easier to do so if its peoples were less, rather than more, unified. Sometimes disunity was encouraged by playing groups off against one another, stirring up old animosities, and favoring one against another when that suited colonial purposes. Treaties were made and broken readily. Christianity sometimes played its part, as well, bringing a new way of life that also included deep respect for the superior talents of the colonizers themselves and the cultures from which they came.

Most of Africa and Asia, and virtually all of Latin America, received such treatment, but so did North America, Australia and New Zealand, and parts of Europe (e.g., northern Scandinavia). By the time radio broadcasting came into being, the original inhabitants of those lands were sufficiently disunited, disenfranchised, and economically powerless that the new medium developed according to the needs of the colonizers and their descendants, with little or, far more often, no attention paid to the possibility that those needs might not coincide with the needs of the indigenous peoples and might even prove antithetical to them.

As indigenous radio began to appear, many stations—but certainly not all—considered what might be done to develop a greater sense of cohesiveness or to rebuild a unity that had once existed but had vanished in the wake of colonization. To the extent that any indigenous political movement might demand full restoration of sovereignty, radio would be an unlikely vehicle, unless it operated from outside the country in question: the very governments that license stations are unlikely to tolerate program material that advocates their overthrow. In fact, few such movements operate among the indigenous peoples, although the Basque "terrorist" group Euskadi ta Askatasuna (ETA), a group of Corsican nationalists, and, to a much lesser extent, the Sons of Glyndywr (Wales), come to public attention from time to time through their demands for independence, underscored by destruction of property and, on occasion, killings and kidnappings.[9] Certain individual writers, educators, politicians, and others call for indigenous sovereignty, but their numbers appear small, their tactics are usually nonviolent, and they sometimes are tolerated (in moderate doses) on the airwaves.

But there are a number of movements working to develop the national unity of indigenous peoples so that, with a better show of strength, they might improve their collective economic, cultural, societal, and political lots. Indeed, there were such movements in the past, but they often were ignored or misportrayed by the majority media. Their contemporary equivalents—the Maori Congress, the Sami Parliament, the National Aboriginal Conference, the Assembly of First Nations (Canada), and others—have the potential benefit of coverage by indigenous, and perhaps majority culture, media.

Whether they actually receive such coverage, or whether they or the broader indigenous public even desires it, is another matter. The stations themselves may or may not wish to provide it. "Divide and conquer" has left some very deep marks, as have animosities that predate the colonial era. Not every tribe (or, perhaps, tribal leader) wishes to see itself as one part of a larger "nation," whether because it's satisfied with the status quo, distrusts or disrespects other tribes, doubts the feasibility of unity, or sees it as irrelevant. In any event, a number of stations that would like to assist a unity movement have discovered that, even within the movement, there are forces at work that fail to see the relevance of indigenous radio or television for that purpose (majority culture stations may be a quite different matter) or that fear the possibility that the movement might escape their control if more of the public becomes aware of it and wishes or demands to join in.

Many (perhaps most) of the unity movement activists, along with many (perhaps most) of the media staff themselves, seem to consider political broadcasting in quite narrow terms: news items; interview, discussion, and debate programs; public service announcements on voting and how one goes about it; political advertising (if allowed, which it usually is not); coverage of legislative sessions, nominating conventions, and presidential or other addresses by leading government officials; and possibly feature reports and documentaries.

Rarely does their definition extend to popular entertainment, including that most common of all forms where radio is concerned—music. Yet a careful examination of indigenous "entertainment" media output reveals a myriad of political messages—some favoring unity, some not, others calling implicitly or explicitly for justice, respect, and a host of other major needs through whatever political mechanisms will lead to their implementation.

PROVISION OF A VISUAL AND AUDIBLE
SYMBOL OF INDIGENOUS SOCIETY

As for the remaining purposes, the provision of a visual and audible symbol of indigenous society may seem of modest importance, particularly if the stations are low in power, poorly equipped, or lack other resources. However, quite aside from the actual uses to which they're put, they clearly have great symbolic power in that they represent the possession by indigenous peoples of a modern means of mass communication and a means that, up until recently, had been identified solely with majority culture.

OUTLETS FOR THE CREATIVE
PRODUCTIONS OF INDIGENOUS ARTISTS

The particular use of electronic media as outlets for the creative production of indigenous artists has had several sorts of impact. The media have helped to encourage growth of indigenous recording industries, they sometimes have led majority culture stations to pay more serious attention to indigenous artists, and they certainly have brought about the revival of often dead or dying cultural-societal acts, whether as poetry, mythology, dance, drama, crafts, or vocal and instrumental music. They also have fostered the development of new forms of cultural expression, particularly musical expression.

Not all indigenous people are happy with what the media have done along those lines. Some individuals feel that there's no purpose in reviving a "dead" practice, either on the grounds that it's impossible to recreate the atmosphere in which those practices lived or that such revivals only serve to ghettoize indigenous cultures by reinforcing the idea that those cultures live in the past and thus have no place in modern society.

Such criticisms are rare. However, that is decidedly not the case where the development of new forms of musical expression are concerned. The tremendous growth of indigenous musical groups—contemporary popular music in particular—has led to some quite marked differences of opinion over the appropriateness of the use of traditional indigenous forms of musical expression in rock, rap, and other "modern," majority culture–derived forms of popular music. That criticism sometimes has included the appropriateness of the very use of the indigenous language in those forms.

The criticism itself usually comes from older individuals, most often male, and frequently with a certain standing, at least within more traditional communities. It stems from a fear that the indigenous forms will be transformed beyond recognition, will lose power, meaning, and respectability. Furthermore, there is a perception that, if majority culture forms are "borrowed," it is in fact those forms that will predominate and thus represent one more triumph by the majority over the minority. Where the language is concerned, the fear is that indigenous musicians will be tempted to borrow majority culture terms in order to deliver messages in a modern (musically speaking) way. That will weaken the language. Some critics also hold that placing the language at the service of rock, rap, or other majority culture forms shows disrespect for what should be considered as a sacred object.

It's quite true that the messages and modes of expression appearing in majority culture popular music sometimes contain language that many in majority cultures may consider rude, disrespectful, tasteless, biased, or sacrilegious. Thus, it's hardly surprising that certain members of indigenous cultures may react negatively if their languages are employed along the same lines. Indigenous stations themselves usually are quite aware of the potential for such objections and are careful to prevent the sorts of language usage that are most likely to upset older listeners.

For example, the Maori language doesn't contain swear words, at least in the Western sense. (Insults in Maori, and in many other indigenous languages, are likely to find expression through subtly worded, sometimes witty, remarks.) Various Maori rock and rap groups have brought tapes to stations for possible airing, only to be turned down because of the use of "four-letter words." But the groups may continue to include such words in their public performances, which can result in increased audience pressure on the stations, especially from younger listeners, to permit their use over the air. The stations then must balance the need to show respect to the opinions of those older listeners who are at odds with the need to attract younger listeners who are, after all, the ones who will determine whether indigenous languages and cultures are to remain vital on into the next century. Older audience members may not learn to love such music but may come to understand why stations broadcast it.

No indigenous stations that I've visited have had to radically modify their program policies as a result of the criticisms just indicated. That's in part because station staff have attempted to explain to their audiences just why it's necessary to mirror the past, the present, and the future in the station's overall program schedule. Most also have been careful to schedule programs so that those who might be most dissatisfied with any one offering aren't all that likely to be listening or viewing then, anyway. As one example, most indigenous radio stations schedule the more traditional stories and music during the midmorning hours, when teenagers are apt to be in school, and most "modern" popular music in the late afternoon and later evening hours, when teenagers will be around the household and often listening to radio as they do homework or talk with their friends.

EMPLOYMENT FOR THE INDIGENOUS COMMUNITY

The use of indigenous media provision of employment for the indigenous community certainly isn't a major objective, or even a stated objective, of most operations. Still, many indigenous media founders do acknowledge it. There seem to be two reasons: first, many nations have governmentally supported employment programs (e.g., Australia's Department of Education, Employment, and Training [DEET]), especially for young people. Some of those programs are meant specifically for indigenous peoples, such as the Aboriginal Training and Development Program. Those funding sources allow many indigenous media outlets to employ larger staffs than would be possible within the station's own budget, while at the same time removing a number of individuals from the unemployment rolls.

More important is a second reason: to be able to attract young indigenous people into a media activity that not only provides them with something meaningful and gainful but also helps the stations to show that they're interested in working with young people and consider them to be important as talent and as audience members. Several young staff members at indigenous stations in Australia, New Zealand, the United States, and Canada have told me that they became involved with the electronic media because the media seemed to offer the prospect of bringing purpose and organization to their lives. In some cases, they already were becoming alcoholics or engaging in petty crimes. They spoke of their media work in terms of personal salvation and hoped to help others who were like their former selves.

Government-financed employment and training programs seem to be the most common mode of support for the unemployed. However, many indigenous stations, especially those not operating as part of a public service broadcast organization, also have stretched their operating budgets to include more staff by keeping levels of compensation low for everyone. Public service organizations such as BBC, Raidio Telefis Eirann (RTE, Ireland), and Norsk Rikskringskasting (NRK, Norway) usually have fixed rates of compensation for each category of staff member, indigenous or not. That has made some stations major employers for their small communities, but it also has made it more difficult for some stations to attract highly talented people or to retain them in the face of other offers of employment.

It should be quite clear by now that any or all of the programming purposes for indigenous media presented here will not apply equally to all stations. Also, the importance of any single purpose may shift over time, as audiences change and as the overall media climate changes. To the extent that majority culture media adapt their programming so as to reach indigenous audiences, the indigenous media themselves may consider program modifications that take such a shift into account. Before actually implementing modifications, however, those media should assess their likely effect on audience loyalty and should carefully evaluate the majority culture media's long-term commitment to indigenous programming. Many industrialized nations are experiencing rising levels of commercialization of the electronic media, and programming is increasingly subject to rapid change as media outlets seek to maximize their profits. Stability in scheduling and content may prove more and more attractive in the long run to audiences swept by change, and indigenous stations may do well to provide it.

"Professionalism"

When minorities of any sort have been served exclusively by majority-operated and -oriented electronic media for decades, it's understandable that they would have a limited view of how to function through those media themselves, if and when such an opportunity became available. The "model" available to them over time would have been almost exclusively a majority culture, professional one. It would have included such aspects as

1. The use of grammatically correct (in majority culture terms) speech, often pronounced according to a set standard.
2. The avoidance of dialects and slang, except for character portrayals.
3. Heavy reliance on "rich" male voices for announcing, news reading, reporting, hosting of music and game shows, sports coverage, and other forms of information and factual entertainment.
4. Economical use of airtime, with brief pauses only.
5. Frequent reminders of time of day or evening.
6. Programs of fixed duration, generally 15, 30, or 60 minutes.
7. Care in pronunciation of, for example, place names and names of prominent institutions and individuals but often less care if the names are of indigenous origin.

Some of those aspects arose from structural factors (e.g., to accommodate the needs of network-based systems, where individual stations would have to know when to opt out for local programs or insertion of advertising). Some may have had commercial origins (e.g., the need to conserve time so that there would be enough for the advertising that supported the broadcasts). Others had their origins in assumptions about the physical nature of radio (e.g., that women's voices were harsher than men's or did not carry as well over the airwaves). Yet others probably were societal, as in the carryover from telephony to radio that long pauses would cause the listener to wonder what had happened to the speaker. Still others probably were psychosociological, such as the feeling that women would not be perceived as sufficiently authoritative to read news or report on political or commercial developments.

Sociolinguistic aspects may have accounted for frequent mispronunciation of indigenous names: anything related to indigenous populations once was commonly regarded as having little relevance to mainstream society, and besides, the names sometimes can be difficult to pronounce, particularly when the mainstream and the indigenous languages don't share common roots. For example, the name of one of the largest Australian Aboriginal tribes—Pitjantjatjara—is pronounced *pitnJARuh.* However, thanks to greater efforts on the part of many electronic media outlets in recent years, there appears to be a growing sensitivity to correct pronunciation of indigenous names.

Other professional standards also have changed over time, although the degree of change has varied from country to country. In many countries, broadcast speech generally has become more informal, although newscasts have tended to retain their formality. Dialects have made their inroads not only in local broadcasting but in national newscasts, but rarely are they much more than slight variants on "mainstream" speech. Women have entered the once all-male domain of newscasting, both as reporters and as anchorpersons, on radio and on television.

The devotion to careful and proper use of time has been more resistant to change and not just because "time is money." In fact, there seems to be an increasing emphasis on sound bites in the coverage of politics and other fields: religious authorities, educators, businesspersons, and others often are requested by media staff to consider how they can reduce their views on important issues to a few sentences, preferably colorful and even sensational. Part of this perceived need for brevity seems to stem from the belief that most audience members have very short attention spans and need both variety and color in their news diets.

Indigenous electronic media staff generally assume that they are not under any particular obligation to follow those majority culture practices regarding professionalism, and some will favor any conflicting indigenous practices, in both verbal and nonverbal forms. However, if they seek to include such practices in a redefinition of professionalism, they may face two problems: their indigenous audiences may be so imbued with the majority model that they regard it as the only valid model, even for their own stations, and attempts to follow indigenous practices may confuse or discourage majority culture audiences if they're an important segment of the audience.

There's a possible third problem—that indigenous broadcasters want to be considered as the full equals of their majority counterparts, either for their own self-satisfaction or because they hope to gain employment with the majority media, which often pay better and may offer more comfortable and stable working conditions. Therefore, they may resist the notion that they should adopt indigenous cultural practices that, in their eyes and ears, would make them sound unprofessional to a potential mainstream employer.

Still, many indigenous stations do sound quite different from their majority culture counterparts, particularly in their freer use of time: length of pauses, beginnings and endings of programs, and less frequent time checks. There usually is a concerted effort to see that *all* names, indigenous and otherwise, are pronounced correctly. There often is a much greater variety of voice types, as well—not just male and female, whether for information or entertainment, but light and dark, rich and thin, large and small. That may be due in part to the staffing needs of many indigenous stations, where low or no pay may limit the degree to which administrators can insist upon "professional" standards, but it may have something to do with the collective spirit of many indigenous communities where all willing workers are welcome.

There are other aspects of professionalism that bear more specifically on practices of journalism, such as assumptions regarding the right of reporters to ask questions of those in positions in authority, or the right of indigenous authorities to limit the freedom of journalists through anything other than published majority culture law. Yet many indigenous cultures have elaborate unwritten codes governing the conferral and exercising of authority, as well as the status of individuals, which in turn determines one's right to speak in public at certain times, on certain subjects, and to certain individuals and groups.

For example, Maori, Aboriginal, and Native American tradition calls for turn taking in meetings, but one's rank (standing) within the community often (in some groups, always) determines the *order* in which participants speak; some groups or members (e.g., women) may not have the right to speak on certain issues. Also, the physical arrangements for meetings, which frequently take the form of a large circle (thus giving each member of the group the opportunity to see every other member), may prove awkward to record for presentation over radio or TV. But no journalist, whether majority culture or indigenous, should expect that those practices should be changed so as to conform with journalistic needs.

However, indigenous peoples have realized on their own that it can be to their advantage to make *some* accommodations to such needs. For example, a number of Native American, Maori, and Aboriginal tribes follow the practice of designating certain of their members as spokespersons on given subjects. Strict adherence to that practice would mean that a reporter requesting information on a tribe's position regarding a controversial topic (e.g., a court case involving the tribe's fishing and hunting rights) could be told to come back again when the tribe's spokesperson on that subject was present. But tribes have learned the value of seizing the opportune moment and usually would have other individuals on hand who could respond, even if that isn't regarded by them as ideal.

When indigenous groups do choose to follow their traditional ways, majority culture audiences probably find it difficult to understand them. Why should a reporter for an indigenous station allow an interview with a tribal elder to run on seemingly ad infinitum, or why might a disk jockey place a last-minute music request from a very distant cousin at the head of the line, when there already are twice as many requests as the time available can accommodate? The answer in both cases is superior authority or standing and the perceived need on the part of the media staffer to acknowledge that authority by not claiming a superior right to choose what to edit in the interview or whose music request to honor.

It may be even harder for majority culture media staff to understand why they can't ask questions during certain public meetings of indigenous groups, even though they've been invited to cover the event, or why they may not be invited back if their subsequent reports show disrespect, perhaps in such a seemingly insignificant way as referring to an individual known by a more public name through her or his more private family name—especially if the individual is recently deceased. Names of certain sorts can be among the most taboo (itself a variant of the Maori term *tapu*) of symbols in many cultures.

As one example, most Aboriginal families will not permit the utterance of a person's name for a period of time following her or his decease. The period of time may vary from a week or two to years or decades; during that time, it would be a grave insult to the family to speak the person's name, even if the reference is to another individual with the same name. The indigenous electronic media would be expected to observe silence where other individuals with the same name are concerned insofar as that's possible, to the point where an indigenous station in the deceased person's community may be expected to see to it that music recordings in which the name appears are not aired. If the person was very well-known, the station might carry a news item on the death, but with reference to "our dear brother/sister" in place of the name.

Seeming exceptions to that rule usually have underlying explanations. One example concerns Eddy Mabo, the Torres Strait Islander who had brought an extremely important Aboriginal land rights case before the Australian courts in the early 1990s. The case ultimately acquired his name. Upon his death in 1992 (just before the Australian High Court ruled in his favor), the Aboriginal (and some majority culture) media asked his family whether it would be permissible to use his name in future reference to the case. The family replied that it was perfectly permissible, since Eddy Mabo was his *public* name, and not the name by which he was known to his extended family.[10]

In the case of entertainers who are well-known in indigenous and majority cultures alike, indigenous stations throughout the country often are expected to refrain from playing recordings of her or his performances until there has been a suitable period of mourning. Majority culture stations may not be expected to follow suit, but they certainly can increase their status among indigenous audiences by doing so, as some in New Zealand did upon the death of the highly popular Maori comedian Billy T. James in 1991.

Lest all of this seem like one vast anthropological minefield, the media and indigenous peoples usually manage to reach some accommodation. The latter generally are more forgiving of majority culture media staff than they are of indigenous station staff members (who should, but often don't, know better), but there is a general recognition that media time is not exactly like majority or indigenous time. There is an understanding that interviews may have to be edited, that a reporter may ask an authority figure to clarify her or his explanation of something, that, as I've noted, the absence of the chief spokesperson on a certain subject may be reason enough to allow a lesser authority (in stature, if not knowledge) to give an interview on a time-sensitive issue. Media staff who work with both cultures, whether as reporters, disc jockeys, producers of children's programs, or whatever else, sometimes gain a degree of cross-cultural sensitivity that would seem to be among the most desirable facets of professionalism.[11]

Audiences

Audiences for indigenous electronic media are highly diverse. Much depends on the purposes of the operations themselves (whether a few or all from the list provided earlier in this chapter) in terms of the nature of the audience each media operation intends, or hopes, to reach: one of the chief characteristics of the mass media is that audiences frequently turn out to be quite different in size and composition from what media staff predict or desire. There is no single, predictable audience for indigenous media either.

It's considerably more difficult to draw an audience profile for indigenous media programming than it is for majority culture media, simply because the data usually aren't available to support any very firm conclusions. Audience research, which provides the foundation for so many majority (and occasional minority) audience profiles, is in short supply for indigenous audiences. Expense is part of the reason, but indigenous stations themselves sometimes hesitate to undertake it, perhaps because they regard it as too complex or too labor-intensive and also because they may come out looking as if they're not reaching the audiences they want to, or are supposed to, reach.

While that is exactly what stations should want to discover, if it's true, it isn't surprising that administrators of indigenous stations may fear such disclosure. Most indigenous stations are quite new and realize that there will be growing pains. However, they're often not so sure that their indigenous communities, the leaders in particular, will be aware of that and will tolerate the mistakes that go along with the growing pains. Many administrators have told me that they were very aware of the "fishbowl" effect, with the eyes and ears of their own indigenous communities as well as the majority culture audiences *and* mass media, trained on them. Why provide critics with further ammunition?

But some indigenous stations and other organizations have begun to conduct audience surveys, usually of radio listening only.[12] Those results, coupled with various forms of anecdotal data (such as letters, telephone calls, personal conversations, turnouts at events promoted by stations) allow us to draw some tentative conclusions.

Indigenous audiences appear to be more predominantly female than male, and older (40+) rather than younger. However, many indigenous radio stations attract sizable audiences of younger listeners in the mid- to late-afternoon hours and late in the evening. Where relative popularity of indigenous stations is concerned, most of the formal surveys have been conducted in and around towns and small cities, rather than larger urban areas, so there's no simple way to calculate how indigenous audiences in those two situations might compare in terms of their relative devotion to indigenous stations. Also, a 1992 survey of 11 Native American public radio stations, all of them located well away from large urban areas, indicated that all but three of them were more or as heavily listened to, when respondents compared them with other stations available.[13]

One Maori urban station, Mai-FM in Auckland, New Zealand, does attract a large audience: a 6.8 rating in a 1993 survey made it one of Auckland's top stations, and it had climbed to number 3 in the 30-station Auckland market by 1995.[14] However, as figures aren't broken down for Maori and non-Maori listeners, the station may or may not be especially popular among Maori, and in fact it attracts a good deal of criticism from older Maori because it features youth-oriented music, uses little Maori language, and doesn't particularly emphasize recordings by Maori performers. If there were figures on amounts of time spent listening to a given station, that would be helpful, but surveys of indigenous listeners seldom request such estimates. Estimates of reach are slightly more common; E. B. Eiselein's 1992 survey of Native American listening showed that all but one of 11 stations reached more than half of their target populations (Native Americans) in an average week, and one station—Apache radio KNNB in Whiteriver, Arizona—had a daily reach for its target population of 89 percent.[15]

There are reasons for assuming that the data on audience composition are fairly close to the mark. Most indigenous stations make a major effort to attract young listeners, especially through after-school programming (3:00–7:00 p.m. or so) containing popular music, often available by request, and hosted by their contemporaries. If the station has an overall policy of broadcasting largely in the indigenous language, it may relax that policy for the late afternoon program block, since many young people do not speak or understand the language well enough to follow broadcasts in it, although words and sentences here and there are acceptable and even welcome.

The predominance of older listeners during most of the broadcast day probably stems from several causes. Such listeners are more apt to be unemployed or retired, with more time available for listening. If stations stress indigenous language programming, older listeners (especially 65 or older) are more likely to be able to follow it. Also, nostalgia may bring such listeners to use the programs to rekindle memories, accurate or not, of a less problem-ridden, kinder, gentler time. Older listeners also may be more radio-oriented, since most of them were well into adulthood by the time television became available to them. And they may be more enamored of the oral tradition than are younger people, which gives broadcasts of the very voices of the living and the deceased a special significance.

Whether any of those same arguments can explain why women generally predominate (at a level of about 45 to 55 percent) as listeners is debatable, although I have heard indigenous people argue that women are especially drawn to the oral tradition. Women in indigenous households probably do spend more time in and around the home than do men, and at most age clusters: two-income households generally are less prevalent in indigenous society than they are in majority culture society. Even where the unemployment rate for men is high (which it often is in indigenous society, where rates of 30 or 40 percent are not at all uncommon, and 80 or 90 percent not unknown), unemployed men often congregate outside the home for large portions of the day.

Program preferences emerge through a combination of survey and anecdotal data. Music is very popular, although in a few cases it comes in second to news about indigenous peoples—usually local but sometimes national and even international. However, there are some quite sharp divisions in terms of music. It isn't surprising that young (ages 14–25) listeners favor contemporary popular music, indigenous and majority culture alike (often such listeners make little or no distinction here), while older (40+) listeners favor more "traditional" music, which can include truly indigenous forms such as Sami *yoiks* or Maori *karanga* and also choral singing derived from "traditions" instilled by missionaries in the eighteenth and nineteenth centuries—missionaries have been very active in indigenous communities throughout the world.*

In the very few surveys that ask listeners what they *least* like about a given indigenous station's music programming, or what they think occupies too much airtime, those two segments of the audience are apt to select each other's preferences for that dubious honor. A 1993 study of listening to the Christchurch-based Maori radio station Te Reo Iriraki ki Otautahi, for example, showed that alternative, black ethnic, heavy metal, rap, and reggae were named as preferred categories by far more 13–17 year olds than by listeners over 50, while country and classical claimed far higher preference figures among the 50 and older group than they did among the 13–17 group. However, Maori songs (traditional) did well among both groups.[16]

On occasion, older listeners object to the playing of traditional music on the grounds that it's connected with a particular activity and shouldn't serve as entertainment. A 1992 study of Sami radio showed that roughly a third of listeners who were 65 or older felt that the stations aired too many *juouiggos* (yoiks), while another 23 percent from the same age group were uncertain. Their primary argument concerned the inappropriateness of radio as a vehicle for a chant that was performed most often in open spaces.[17]

Interview-based shows, especially those dealing with set topics on a regularly scheduled basis, also get high marks from that small portion of the audience that listens to them, but they draw "never listen" from the considerable majority. That leaves us ignorant as to whether people don't listen because they're unaware of the programs, aware but not available at times of broadcast, or aware but uninterested. Most indigenous station staff with whom I've spoken feel that they lack the time or money to publicize specific programs, aside from varying degrees of on-air promotion. Certain programs—music, sports, and religion—may carry their own promotion in that the program hosts are already local personalities, and some of those programs receive publicity through churches, sports clubs, and music stores. But many indigenous stations don't even have printed program schedules available for distribution, although many have bumper stickers displaying station call numbers/letters and broadcast frequencies. It isn't surprising to discover that, in those few surveys where the question has been asked, substantial percentages (20–40) of the indigenous population may indicate that they aren't aware of the station's existence, months to a year or more after it came into being.[18]

Karanga is a term undergoing transformation through radio. Traditionally, it has meant a particular type of song, chanted or sung by women in welcome or in mourning. Now, many disk jockeys use it to refer to any song performed in Maori, usually by Maori of either sex, but sometimes songs performed by *pakeha* (whites), as well.

Formal surveys rarely attempt to discover anything about the size or composition, let alone program preferences, of the majority culture audience. Letters, telephone calls, and personal visits tell indigenous stations that they do have listeners among this group. Young people share their indigenous counterparts' love of popular music, and they are as likely to request indigenous bands and vocalists as majority culture performers. Older majority culture listeners, particularly women in the age range 30–55 (gender attribution usually represents a rough guess by the station staff member receiving the call or reading the letter), contact stations during or after broadcasts to ask further questions about specific topics (e.g., Aboriginal religious practices), with 5–10 such requests for information if the subject has been particularly unusual or controversial.

Surveys of indigenous audiences for indigenous television programs are even rarer than radio surveys, aside from the BBC and Channel 4 surveys for Welsh TV. A 1993 survey conducted by A. G. B. McNair for New Zealand on Air shows a somewhat flatter overall viewing curve for Maori, as contrasted with *pakeha* (white) viewers, with a somewhat greater tendency of Maori to view late evening (after 10:00 p.m.) programs. The survey report also indicates that Maori viewers were more attracted to comedy and drama than they were to factual programs, but that their viewing of New Zealand–made documentaries about themselves was high: two of them ranked among the top eight programs for their particular weeks. The one regularly and continuously scheduled "talk/discussion accompanied by visuals" program in Maori, "Marae" (Sunday mornings), and the daily 15-minute news program in Maori, "Te Karere" (5:45–6:00 p.m.), were less heavily viewed, although the former regularly appeared in the top 40 (out of 200) programs list for Maori viewers, while the latter usually finished much farther down the list.[19]

It shouldn't surprise anyone that a daily news program in Maori—and a brief one, at that—wouldn't attract many majority culture viewers. It would be interesting to know why it doesn't attract many Maori viewers. Maori media staff have given me several possible explanations: the newscast is too brief for Maori, as well; it's "underproduced," meaning that there isn't much visualization (and there *is* considerably less than one sees in the main newscasts of TV New Zealand); lots of Maori don't speak Maori well enough to follow "Te Karere"; and lots of Maori became accustomed to watching the TV New Zealand newscast when there were no Maori TV newscasts and find "Te Karere" comes on "too early."

Genres,
Styles,
and
Scheduling

If indigenous and majority culture audiences described in the preceding indeed predominate, they aren't necessarily the only ones that the indigenous electronic media hope or attempt to attract. And if they prefer those sorts of materials, that certainly is not all that these media provide.

Much of what the indigenous media do provide depends upon the ways in which they're organized. If videocassettes are produced and distributed through an organization such as the Central Australian Aboriginal Media Association (CAAMA), the tourist trade will dictate their nature, to some degree, and subjects such as folklore, dances, music, and crafts are likely to predominate. Religious and political organizations producing video- or audiocassettes might sometimes use forms of entertainment, especially music, to get their messages across, but on the whole, the material is likely to be presented factually and soberly.

Broadcast services also feature a wide variety of genres and presentational styles, and here much depends upon the organizational structure of a given service. As noted before, there are services that make up part of a national public service or national commercial broadcast operation, as well as services that exist more or less independently. Both categories can be subdivided. The first includes a few stations that enjoy several-hour to full broadcast days, sole or primary use of transmitters, and relative autonomy. Raidio na Gaeltachta, BBC Radio Cymru, Channel 4's Sianel Pedwar Cymru, Spain's regional radio and TV services in Catalan and Basque, and the German language radio service of Italy's Radio Audizioni Italia (RAI) fall into that category. But Sami Radio and TV, BBC Raidio nan Gaidheal in Scotland, the various Basque, Corsican, Provençal, Alsatian, and other language services carried by Radio France, Radio New Zealand's Te Reo o Aotearoa, TVNZ's Maori news and features, Aboriginal radio and TV material on the Australian Broadcasting Corporation (ABC) and Special Broadcasting Service (SBS), and the Canadian Broadcasting Corporation's

(CBC) Northern Service broadcasts for Native Americans and Inuit must be content with limited airtime, shared transmitters, and, in many cases, limited autonomy.

Independent services break down along the same lines. Almost all of them are local or regional, although Radio Aotearoa, a Maori commercial station in Auckland, covers much of the country. A large number have full broadcast days and their own transmitters: Native American radio stations in the United States and Canada, Maori and Aboriginal radio stations in New Zealand and Australia, and most of the church-supported indigenous radio stations in Latin America enjoy that status. But a fair number must share facilities, usually through community radio or TV stations or *narradio* services, as with some Aboriginal radio and television in Australia, certain Sami groups in Norway, and a few Maori groups in New Zealand, and occasionally through commercial stations (Independent Local Radio's Swansea Sound has a few hours in Welsh per week, and Moray Sound in Inverness carries roughly the same amount of Scots Gaelic, while Independent Television's Scottish Television and Grampian Television broadcast a few hours per week in Scots Gaelic).

The operating budgets available for those activities obviously affect both the variety and quality of programming. In general, the national public broadcaster-supported indigenous services, and the few national commercial broadcaster-supported services, have higher per-production budgets than do their independent counterparts, and if they have several hours to full days of airtime at their disposal, usually offer far more varied schedules than do independent media. They usually play less music (*far* less, in the case of Raidio na Gaeltachta),* and they often provide genres of programming such as quiz shows, dramas, soap operas, and variety that have largely disappeared from radio in much of the world. That may be because of their direct ties with majority culture services that provided such programming from the early days of broadcasting and continue to provide it today, alongside their pop music, news, and other specialized radio channels.

That same mixture of genres sometimes occurs in television, as well. As I note later in the chapter, Welsh television is quite varied. Scots Gaelic TV, even within its few hours per week, manages to present material for children and adults, drama and comedy, fact and fiction.[20] Basque TV in Spain—Euskal Telebista—puts a great deal of time, money, and effort in traveling through Spanish and French Basque regions and recording festivals, song, sports contests, and occasionally dramas, as well as stories, for the evening newscasts in Basque.

---

*Possibly a reflection of the Irish love of talk. As one Irishman told me, "I'd make a long story short, but that's impossible for an Irishman."

RADIO

There's a characteristic that distinguishes national radio services from independent: each type has a very different, and almost immediately recognizable, sound. National radio services tend to sound more like the majority culture national services; they're more "correct," often less spontaneous, and somewhat more mindful of time and tend to feature older male voices. When driving through regions where there are both national indigenous and independent indigenous radio stations, I usually can tell within a few minutes which is which, without knowing their broadcast frequencies and even if both are broadcasting in the indigenous language.

Where I've been able to analyze program content in some detail, for indigenous stations broadcasting in English or French, there's yet another seeming distinction. The public service–affiliated indigenous stations tend to place more emphasis on cultural programming of diverse sorts but often lack material of specific appeal to subteens and teenagers. The independent indigenous stations feature a less varied cultural menu, but the vast majority of them have late afternoon programming blocks for subteens and teenagers. Also, although both types of station broadcast talk shows with call-ins, the indigenous independent stations tend to deal with controversial issues more often than do their public service counterparts; the former also appear to attract more calls per program than the latter.

One more quite evident difference is the sheer amount of music. For most of independent radio, music commands the major share of airtime—usually 50 percent or more. A few independent stations, such as Aboriginal station 4AAA Murri Country in Brisbane, or Maori station Mai-FM in Auckland, are virtually all music, although each also furnishes news and occasional features. If an indigenous service is on-air for only a few hours per week, as often is the case with narradio or community radio, there might be a higher proportion of spoken word programming, although I've heard many such services (e.g., Radio Wayee, the one-hour per week Aboriginal program broadcast by Hobart's community radio station) in which music took up at least half of the available airtime. The existence of indigenous media outlets for music has strongly encouraged the growth of indigenous music groups and of commercial recordings of their work.

That growth is particularly evident if one considers the amounts and types of prerecorded indigenous music available before indigenous media outlets became more widely available. A staff announcer for BBC Radio Cymru told me that, when he came on the air with the first Welsh language pop music request program in 1968, the station had one Welsh folk song disc and an instrumental version of "Autumn Leaves," played by a Welsh group.[21] He was exaggerating, but not by much: recordings of Welsh male choruses, folk singers, and colliery brass bands would have made up much of the few dozen discs then available. During the 1970s and 1980s, a number of Welsh musicians turned to various forms of rock to express their views about such subjects as their fears that Wales would become one huge tourist resort and that Wales should strive for greater political independence.* By the early 1990s, the catalogue of the largest recording company in Wales, Canolfan Sian, had hundreds of entries for traditional and contemporary artists recording in Welsh; Sian's chief executive, Bob Delyn, felt that much of the increased availability of artists and of demand for their work had come about because of Welsh language radio.[22]

The same would hold true for several other indigenous populations. Basque, Maori, and Aboriginal radio stations have stimulated the creation of recordings by many contemporary indigenous musicians, particularly through various forms of rock. The Taped Aboriginal Program Exchange (TAPE) service in Australia launched a monthly "Aboriginal Top Ten" program in early 1994—something that would have been impossible, given the dearth of new recordings, until the early 1990s.[23] Some of the Maori station managers and music directors were considering a similar service for Maori radio in late 1993, now that the quality and quantity of Maori pop music recordings made it feasible. It was implemented through Mana Maori Media's Thursday night (music night) "Mana Hour" in 1994 and is compiled by a rotation of *iwi* stations, each station presenting its own top 10 each week.[24]

The remaining portion of the typical broadcast day for an independent indigenous station tends to be quite varied—more so in the morning and evening hours than in the afternoon. Perhaps the first thing that a majority culture listener would notice about an indigenous station is that it has a somewhat more relaxed sound than do most majority stations, local or national. This stems in part from the treatment of time and the differences in presentational styles noted earlier, but it also has to do with the number of programs built around speech: news, community calendars, interviews, discussions, religious talks, children's stories, and poetry and, in far fewer instances, dramas, satires, quiz shows, documentaries, language lessons, and preschool activities. Most of that speech either is, or closely resembles, normal human conversation, with pauses and other "natural" qualities that make it seem relaxed in tempo, if not in subject. Very little of it is prescripted.

---

*John Davies notes that "by 1970 they [protest songs] had taken over the entire Welsh language pop scene, and George Thomas [Labour MP, Cardiff West] accused the young people's program, *Disc a Dawn*, of being a weekly half-hour plug for *Plaid Cymru* [a strongly nationalist Welsh political party]. Davies, John, *Broadcasting and the BBC in Wales*, Cardiff: University of Wales Press, 1994, 287.

Volunteers make up a large proportion of the on-air staff for many independent indigenous stations, and this also may result in a station's having a rather different sound, at least when compared with most majority culture stations. Some are careless with microphone placement; others take up many seconds of airtime in searching for something they've misplaced. And still others may phrase oddly because they haven't yet learned the knack of reading copy but sounding natural. Most of those problems disappear in time and with further training (if available, which it isn't always), but staff turnover among volunteers tends to be high so that many of the stations have at least a few beginners on-air at any one time. Also, most indigenous station managers have found that volunteers aren't always reliable and have found themselves, or other staff, filling in an air shift at the last minute.

The subjects covered initially might seem quite narrow, but prolonged listening often reveals a richer array, as history (contemporary and ancient), mythology, current affairs, and other dimensions bring more variety to specific programs. Mythology, for example, often helps to explain attachment to the land in a land rights case. A radio portrait of an indigenous rock star may feature comparisons with a famous indigenous singer of the same tribe or family, but several generations earlier.

A few stations have worked to revive, revitalize, and/or expand certain forms of indigenous cultural expression that are well-suited to radio, particularly **poetry and storytelling**, which follow certain set forms (e.g., rhymed couplets, restricted numbers of lines, chains of synonyms or homonyms). Such traditions are especially rich in Ireland and Wales, and both RNG and BBC Radio Cymru broadcast competitions featuring them; Radio Cymru devotes a weekly program ("Talwrn y Beirdd") to the competitions, which it records throughout Wales.

The stories and poetry aren't always traditional. The loneliness of the city, the dangers of alcohol, the abuse of women, and the forced separation of indigenous children from their families are frequent subjects, as in the following excerpt from a program featuring an Aboriginal female storyteller-poet, broadcast over Radio Redfern in Sydney:

> I not see you long time.
> White fella bin take me from you. I don't know why.
> Give me to missionary to be God's child.
> Give me new language, give me new name.
> All time I cry. They say, "That's [a] shame.
> I go to city down south, real cold.
> I forget all the stories, my mother, you told.
> Gone is my spirit, my dreaming, my name.

Gone to these people, our country to claim.
They gave me white mother, she gave me new name.
All time I cry. She say, "That's [a] shame."

MAUREEN WATSON, "Spirit Belong My Mother"[25]

Music is a staple element for indigenous stations, and it often displays considerable variety, mixing in a single program an indigenous rock band, an indigenous singer of legends, an indigenous choir performing in nineteenth-century religious or secular tradition, "protest" songs from indigenous and other minority groups (especially Afro-Caribbean and African-American) in other countries, and majority culture popular and semiclassical music. Late afternoon music programs for and by young people are more unidimensional, although they usually are more varied than are their majority station counterparts. One Maori station, Radio Aotearoa, features a late night sing-along, where host Papa Ruru sings along with his callers and even accompanies them on various instruments.[26]

Some of the indigenous stations in Australia and New Zealand have introduced computer-generated playlists, in part to ensure greater variety (or at least less repetition of a selection that a particular DJ happens to love!), but often variety takes care of itself quite well, simply because most indigenous stations have small record, disc, and/or tape collections, and rely on DJs and listeners to supplement the diet, which also helps to broaden the range of choice. And indigenous stations of all sorts often have an overall music policy along the lines of "three out of every four songs by indigenous artists" or "two out of every five songs by Australians."

The morning hours contain the highest percentages of talk programs. **Older members** of the indigenous community frequently host morning shows and draw upon their own knowledge of their history and language and interviews with other individuals in the community to provide legends, the origins of words, children's stories, historical sketches, quizzes about the indigenous past and present, poetry, and religious material that ranges from reading Bible passages to offering personal reflections. (Religion, usually a denomination of Christianity, often has a large following in indigenous communities, especially among older audience members.)

Discussion programs, often featuring call-ins, also are popular morning fare and frequently cover problems that are quite characteristic of many indigenous groups: alcoholism, diabetes, emphysema, addictive behavior (such as gambling or drugs), child and/or wife abuse, access to public services, relations with law enforcement officials, high rates of incarceration, job retraining, and dealing with the majority culture justice system. Some of those topics may be taken up in national indigenous service programs, but they seem to be far more prevalent on independent stations.

The older program hosts often serve another purpose: they remain at the station after their air shifts and work with the teenage hosts of the midafternoon music shows, helping them to improve their command of the indigenous language and providing them with a better working knowledge of indigenous customs.

Weekend schedules are apt to feature **sports** programs, some of them live broadcasts of local teams in action at home or away. The Sami narradio service in Kautokeino, Norway, Guovdageainnu Lagas Radio (GLR), began to follow the fortunes of the local football team in 1993 and developed Sami terms to cover some aspects of play, often mixing Sami and Norwegian in its play-by-play coverage of games 100 or more miles from home. Those efforts won the station the praise of the local weekly newspaper, which remarked on the pride it felt in hearing games described in Sami.[27] Raidio na Gaeltachta regularly broadcasts Irish football, hurling, and other contests on Saturdays; those live transmissions are the only times in some 70 hours of listening to RNG that I've heard announcers demonstrate much emotion—sometimes enough to overload the system!

Some stations have experimented with Saturday morning broadcasts for **teenagers**. BBC Radio Cymru developed a news program, "Doctor Newyddion," for such an audience in 1992 and placed it just before a "Top of the Pops" program. Early indications are that it's drawing increasing numbers of its target audience, partly because the topics covered in the program have been suggested by teenagers. For example, when a Welsh cleric made a scathing attack on young people, several teenage listeners suggested that they'd like to have him defend his views before a small panel of young people on "Doctor Newyddion." He did and had to back down on a number of points.[28] This program, as well as "Hwyrach" ("Later," a six-night-a-week program featuring specific genres of popular music for younger listeners), seems to have helped Radio Cymru to improve its demographics for younger listeners: the 1992 Radio Authority Joint Audience Research (RAJAR) survey for the fourth quarter shows listeners aged 15–34 at 12 percent, while the 1993 fourth-quarter figures are 15 percent.[29]

Radio **dramas, documentaries, and satires** are relative rarities for indigenous stations, particularly those that aren't part of a national broadcasting system such as the BBC or don't receive assistance from one. Younger staff members usually have little familiarity with such genres, and equipment (including sound effects) may be inadequate for anything even slightly complex. Various training programs available to indigenous staff teach editing skills and recording techniques, but they may be forgotten if the stations don't encourage their use. Still, a drama troupe in Wales began to prepare an original soap opera (about life in a town in rural Wales much like their own) for community station Radio Ceredigion (Aberystwyth) in 1994; a few members of the troupe worked as volunteers for the station and decided that it would be good experience for them to try their hands at the genre.[30]

Indigenous broadcasters sometimes have used drama (radio and TV) as a vehicle for "messages" (such as family planning and nutrition), without necessarily considering two potential drawbacks: that the indigenous audience might regard that as trivializing the message or that it might regard drama as socially inappropriate, as a Navajo production team discovered when testing English and Navajo language versions of a radio drama dealing with proper care of large animals—the English version came across effectively, but the Navajo version was a failure. When asked why, the Navajo test group responded that, when listening in Navajo, the drama struck them as a form of eavesdropping and made them feel uncomfortable. Remounted in Navajo as a narrative story, it worked perfectly well![31]

There are other notable successes, especially with minidocumentaries. Staff at a few of the Aboriginal stations have produced 10- to 15-minute sound portraits. Umeewara Media (Port Augusta, South Australia) producer Welsley ("Woody") Smith prepared a portrait of two Aboriginal athletes—their training regimes, their motivations and hopes, their acceptance by white athletes—that skillfully interwove their own comments and his continuity with devices such as music and crowd noises. Two young women trainees who worked as volunteers at Radio Redfern (Sydney) created a powerful portrait of Aboriginal rage over deaths of Aboriginals while in police custody; they mixed speeches, interviews, music, sounds of demonstrations, and their own continuity in a well-paced production.[32]

A few indigenous stations try to function as **archivists**. Ireland's Raidio na Gaeltachta has a substantial tape collection of music, interviews, poetry readings, storytelling, and other material. Some of it was recorded directly off the air, but much was gathered by going to people's homes, to festivals, and to churches. The three RNG stations have made a particular effort to tape the voices of the elderly, the stations realizing that there's no way to recreate them once the individuals are dead. The archives are carefully indexed, and the stations reuse them quite often, as do researchers.

Radio New Zealand (RNZ) is helping to create a Maori sound archive from its large collection of tapes and discs, but much of the material suffers from deteriorating sound quality, lack of documentation, or even indications of whose voice has been recorded.[33] That's a good reason for starting a sound archive as soon as possible and maintaining a thorough indexing system. However, many indigenous stations, even if they coordinate their efforts, can't afford the staff time, the storage space, or the proper storage conditions for such material. Some may not even be able to afford the extra tape needed. RNG and RNZ both are parts of national broadcasting organizations and have more budgetary leeway. Yet the legacy represented by such material should be of value to the nation as a whole and worth the nation's support, whether through the national broadcast service, an appropriate ministry (such as culture or indigenous affairs), or the national archive.

Most indigenous stations provide little or nothing by way of **formal education**. A few of the Maori radio stations have offered language lessons, and one of them—Radio Kahungunu, affiliated with a polytechnic institute in Hastings—developed a set of workbooks to help guide language learners. New Zealand's educational television service, eTV, carried a 13-part situation comedy–based series for advanced Maori language learners in 1995; viewers could register for credit through the University of Waikato.[34] Channel 4's service in Wales, Sianel Pedwar Cymru, has offered televised lessons in learning Welsh—again, with workbooks available. The three Sami public service broadcaster stations have broadcast language lessons in the past, and the Sami station in Finland initiated a new "let's learn Sami" series for adults in 1995; it combined radio, workbooks, and teletext. Several of the Native American radio stations in Canada and the United States have carried "word (or phrase) of the day (or week)" inserts.

But formal instruction, whether in languages or in other subjects, requires expertise that most indigenous stations don't possess. Individuals who do possess it—particularly teachers of indigenous languages—often are exceptionally busy with their institutional teaching activities and either find it difficult to make additional time available for broadcasts (including preparation of study guides) or don't really see the value of teaching through the media. Many teacher training institutions still do very little to help future teachers discover how to use the broadcast media in the classroom.

Furthermore, where language instruction is concerned, very few stations provide indigenous language programming that a language learner can follow. One of the few to do so is Sianel Pedwar Cymru, of Wales, which broadcasts a 20-minute news roundup ("Saith ar y Sul") for Welsh learners on Sunday evenings. There would be the risk of alienating fluent speakers if many programs in simplified versions of the language came onto the schedule, but there should be room for a few. It also helps when stations use announcers and other program talent, including interviewees, who are less than fully fluent in the language because this can encourage language learners to carry on. A few stations—Raidio na Gaeltachta is one—broadcast contests featuring language learners. Most indigenous stations will work with less-than-fully-fluent interviewees by editing their remarks so that they'll sound as fluent as possible, and most stations develop more casual participation, especially through "open mike" or request programs, by encouraging callers to use as much of their Sami, Maori, Basque, or whatever and by praising them when they do.

It would help if the indigenous media operations were to **collaborate with educational institutions**. In fact, some of them do. Video production has become increasingly common, as well as popular, in secondary schools, and sometimes the productions themselves find their way to broadcast outlets, either through majority culture programs or through indigenous services, such as exist in North America. A few of the Aboriginal media associations have begun to work with students in various forms: making a period of broadcast time (usually late afternoons on weekdays) available to them, jointly producing programs for broadcast, or accepting prerecorded material made by them.

The Broome Aboriginal Media Association in Western Australia received a request from a group of Aboriginal secondary school students that it develop, produce, and broadcast a series of radio dramas on various problems common to adolescents, such as premarital sexual relations, parental abuse, and consumption of alcohol. The series, broadcast in 1993, provoked considerable discussion locally; many parents reacted along the lines of "I didn't know that the kids were thinking about that sort of stuff, in that way."[35] Raidio na Gaeltachta held a competition for secondary schools in 1993 in which groups of students could submit radio documentaries, which were then broadcast. RNG also broadcast (1993) a series of programs designed to help secondary students study for their comprehensive exams in the Irish language. But such efforts are rare.

A major reason for encouraging closer cooperation between stations and schools is this: one of the seeming keys to success in the revival of use of indigenous languages is the development of an educational system, as well as media services, that encourages, and even requires, their use. Sometimes that can be done within the existing, majority culture school system. More often, it has to start as an independent, ancillary system, thus requiring students to attend two schools. Occasionally, as in Wales and Ireland, the indigenous language schools receive full accreditation, making it possible to complete one's primary, and perhaps even secondary, education in them. Wales now has a fully accredited Welsh language university, and a Maori language university may be in place within the next few years.

But such schools also can start before formal schooling begins, and preschool systems exist in many indigenous settings: Maori New Zealand, Wales, Basque France, Aboriginal Australia, and others. In some of those places, it's widespread: there are roughly 700 *kohanga reo* (literally, "language nests") in New Zealand. In others, such schools are few and far between. Most of them operate primarily to reinforce use of the indigenous language, not as an abstract exercise, but as it applies to indigenous cultural, social, economic, and political practices. A few of the Maori radio stations have begun to work with the kohanga reo in their areas, sometimes broadcasting directly from them, sometimes having their staff members on-air to explain what's going on this week or day, even occasionally working with the children to produce documentaries. Still, many of the Maori stations have little or nothing to do with the kohanga reo, whether because either or both aren't interested or because they feel that it would take too much time. Yet the payoff, in terms of drawing upon preschoolers' natural curiosity and heightening their interest in indigenous media, not to mention sharpening their language skills, could be tremendous: it could help to increase listenership (the children may induce their parents to listen), and it might eventually help to increase the pool of potential media staff. It also might help to hold the children as listeners and viewers when they become adults—a decided advantage in the face of the rapidly increasing competition on the airwaves in our multichannel universe.[36]

Many indigenous stations broadcast programs about **religion**—music, certainly, but also religious services, short talks, and "thoughts for the day." The vast majority of programs are connected with Christianity, most often Protestantism in one or another form. While some indigenous listeners (mostly older) enjoy such programs, and while others may be indifferent to them, a number of listeners resent their presence; they identify (Western) religion as one of the chief sources of their subjugation and repression. Churches ran the mission schools that were to "depaganize" their children; churches sought to replace many of their traditional practices, religious and otherwise; churches sometimes bargained on their behalf with Europeans, bringing their people to sign agreements that were disadvantageous to them.

There is some truth to all of those accusations, and there are efforts on the part of some individuals to restore certain practices that churches had discouraged as "pagan," such as Native American sweat lodges and use of hallucinogens to commune with the spirit world. Radio programs can be and are being made about those practices. However, Christianity enjoys several advantages when it comes to radio: there's plenty of recorded Christian music, there's a long tradition of majority culture broadcasts of material associated with Christianity, and the religious services and talks themselves fit in well with radio as a medium, with its structured, timed nature (as contrasted with the often variable and less structured nature of indigenous religious practices). If indigenous religious practices are to gain a larger share of airtime, either those practices or the practices of indigenous radio, or both, probably will have to adapt, even as Christianity often has adapted to the electronic media.

A few indigenous radio services are operated by religious groups.

Certain Protestant groups (such as Baptist and Seventh Day Adventist), as well as Mormons and Catholics, prepare taped programs in English and in indigenous languages and place them on commercial and noncommercial stations, indigenous and majority culture alike.* Occasionally, such groups also attempt to counteract what they regard as antireligious programming on indigenous stations, as Mormons did in the case of Navajo station KGHR (Tuba City, Arizona): according to KGHR's manager, the Mormons claimed that the station broadcast programs designed to bring listeners to reject Mormonism and return to Native American religious practices, which weren't "truly" religious.[37]

Finally, and regrettably, there's one very specialized form of programming that has been developed by several indigenous stations, especially Aboriginal radio. The rates of incarceration for ethnic minorities, indigenous minorities among them, often are much higher than they are for members of the majority culture.** Several of the Aboriginal stations have developed programs for and about **prisoners**, and those programs usually feature tape recordings made by inmates, in addition to music requests. Those recordings often display a high level of talent on the part of the inmates, as singers, instrumentalists, and (rarely, since prison authorities are wary of them) reporters.

Ross Watson, program director of Aboriginal radio station 4AAA in Brisbane, attempted to secure financial support from the Aboriginal and Torres Straits Islander Commission (ATSIC) and other public organizations for a special project on prisoner radio. His idea was to purchase a large number of audiotape recorders, place them in prisons around Queensland, provide some basic instruction in their use, and let the prisoners determine what to record. The recordings would have to be inspected by the authorities before leaving the prisons, and the station would apply its own criteria (usually technical, and not on content) in deciding what to broadcast. He felt that such an approach would give inmates a meaningful and positive outlet—one that might actually help their rehabilitation. ATSIC and the other organizations weren't interested in supporting the effort, so Watson purchased a few recorders, placed them in the toughest prison in

---

*As Keith indicates, the practice of placing religious programs for Native Americans on commercial stations has been followed for many years. Keith, Michael, *Signals in the Air: Native Broadcasting in America,* Westport, Conn.: Praeger, 1995, 7–10.

**The Royal Commission into Aboriginal Deaths in Custody made a number of recommendations regarding media attention to that situation. It urged adequate funding for the Aboriginal media themselves; it recommended development of codes and policies regarding coverage of Aboriginal issues by all media; and it made several other statements about needed improvements in quality and quantity of media attention to Aboriginal cultures, organizations, and problems. Royal Commission, *National Report,* vol. 5 (by Commissioner Elliott Johnston, QC), Canberra, A.C.T.: Australian Government Publishing Service, 1993, 115–116.

the Brisbane area (one with a high percentage of Aboriginal inmates), provided a bit of training, and waited for results.

For the first several weeks, there were none, and he was about ready to agree with the statement made by one prison authority, to the effect that inmates had little interest in recording anything and lacked the self-confidence to do so. But then the recordings started to flow, and some of them were exceptional—especially songs reflecting the everyday realities of prison life. There continue to be enough recordings to keep the effort going.[38] There probably would be many more if Watson's project proposal had been funded. But a major lesson learned surely should be that, if one is attempting to launch something new, and particularly if it involves production effort on the part of amateurs (or, at least, nonbroadcasters), one should give it some time to develop before concluding that it wasn't such a great idea, and dropping it.

TELEVISION

Television programming by indigenous groups generally has been limited to small portions, rather than entire days, of broadcast time; even Imparja, the Aboriginal-owned and -operated television service in Alice Springs, obtains the vast majority (around 90 percent) of its program material from white Australian sources or abroad. Sianel Pedwar Cymru has the most extensive TV schedule, but it does little morning or afternoon programming, and roughly half of its evening fare is imported material, subtitled in Welsh. A separate Irish language TV channel should be on-air by 1996, but it is likely to limit itself to three hours of transmission daily for the first year or two.

News is a staple offering for the few indigenous TV services that exist, and it features reports about indigenous activities and majority culture–indigenous interactions. Interview- and discussion-based shows on subjects of interest to indigenous peoples also are common. Many groups present programs portraying aspects of indigenous life in the past, often using a combination of photographs, readings from letters and texts, and prerecorded or live reminiscences of those who experienced them. A few of the better financed indigenous groups (e.g., Welsh and Maori) have been able to produce sitcoms and dramas. Welsh Channel 4 (Sianel Pedwar Cymru) and BBC-TV have provided a wide range of regularly scheduled Welsh language material: dramas such as "Pobol y Cym" and "Dinas," sitcoms such as "Hafod Henri," pop music programs ("Roc Rol Te"), farming features, children's shows ("Bilidowcar"), quiz shows, national and international newscasts, sports magazines, and numerous specials.[39] Other program formats are much rarer, although there are occasional productions of individual dramas and documentaries, most often in the indigenous language.

Partly because of the sheer expense of television, indigenous TV productions often are made in the majority language so that the cost will be justified by the potential to appeal to a much larger audience. That may make financial sense, but it sometimes places the producers in a difficult position if they attempt to appeal more or less equally to both cultures. As observed earlier in the chapter about bicultural radio programs, when does explanation of an indigenous practice begin to aggravate the indigenous audience?

Might the broadcast of certain terms and depiction of acts of familiarity among indigenous peoples lead the majority culture to interact in similar fashion with their indigenous friends and acquaintances, even though that might be totally inappropriate?

There is an interesting example of one form of the latter in a pakeha newspaper columnist's reaction to an episode of a Maori-written and -produced TV situation comedy, "Radio Wha Waho," a 10-part series (in English) about a fictional Maori radio station. One Maori character, joking with another, mentions that there's going to be a Maori version of the movie "Silence of the Lambs"; it's to be called "Shut Up, Ewes." The columnist reproduces the quip but adds, "I think I'm allowed to tell that one, because it was featured on ... Radio Wha Waho."[40] The implication seems clear enough: if Maori have broadcast it, it's "politically correct" for pakeha to use it.

The issue of cost of programming, important enough for radio, has even greater importance for indigenous language television programs. Many of those programs, especially informational, can be readily distinguished from their majority language counterparts: the sets are plain, talking heads predominate, visualization through films and photographs is limited and repetitious, graphics are modest, and even production quality, especially camera work, often shows signs of limited camera availability and inexperienced production crews.

VIDEOCASSETTES

Many indigenous groups have tried their hands at producing videocassettes, sometimes with highly interesting results in terms of what they show about another culture's way of visualizing things. Sol Worth and John Adair's early experiments with filmmaking by the Navajo[41] helped to inspire similar efforts involving videotaping by Aborigines in Australia[42] and by scavengers in Djakarta, Indonesia.[43] Certain of those videocassettes have been broadcast, usually through majority culture television stations, but they also have been sold in stores catering to tourists, and some have been distributed to schools, both indigenous and majority culture. They may cover legends, traditional arts and crafts, music (including rock videos), and other more or less "safe" subjects; with the exception of a few of the rock videos, they aren't used to portray the usually high incarceration or infant mortality rates for many indigenous peoples nor have many of them served as vehicles for "revolutionary" political or social views.

Videos made for distribution within the indigenous group, and possibly for on-air use, but with little or no thought of sale to tourists, are a different matter. The BRACS program in Australia (see Chapter Two) has stimulated a great deal of video activity, and some of it deals with emotionally charged issues, such as the wrongful conviction of an Aboriginal man for murder, the tortuous battle required to win rehearings, and, eventually, his release. New Zealand on Air has funded the production of a limited number of music videos; one of them, "Akona te reo," features a Maori group, Moana and the Moa Hunters, urging viewers to learn the Maori language. (The audio track sold very well as a single tape.) A video produced by a group of Cree Indians in Canada portrays the destructive effects of alcohol as an agent in child abuse and helped to stimulate discussion among the Cree as to how to deal with the problem.[44]

While programming is of primary importance, the quality of management, training, facilities, community support, and levels and continuity of budgetary resources also have a profound effect on indigenous media. They form the subject of the next chapter.

The Building Blocks of Indigenous Media: 2, Operating the Enterprise

All nonprogramming aspects of electronic indigenous media operations have some impact, sooner or later, on programming. That is why the chapter on programming came first, as recognition of its priority. Yet nonprogramming elements can be even more complex, whether because of their elaborate interconnections or because so many of them involve direct human interaction.

While I make no attempt to assign priorities to those elements, I lead off with staffing and training, which have the most direct and obvious connection with programming.

Staffing and Training

Indigenous media face two major problems in assembling staff: lack of money and deeply ingrained majority culture perceptions. The first of those is apparent enough from one angle, and I have touched upon it earlier: most indigenous media operate on very modest budgets and cannot afford the salaries that experienced personnel demand. That situation affects media both when hiring and when attempting to retain staff, but it also affects unpaid volunteers; after they've gained experience and confidence, they often find themselves much more employable, and at jobs that pay decent wages. Consequently, there's a fairly high turnover rate at indigenous stations—a situation that causes no end of stress for program directors, editors, and station managers, most of whom also are volunteers or poorly paid.

Majority culture perceptions pose a quite different problem. Some potential indigenous media staff are attracted by the prospect of working at a station because they feel that, thanks to having listened to, watched, and possibly visited majority culture media, they have a good idea of what they'll do and how they'll do it. Although indigenous media have been influenced by majority media to varying degrees, they do follow their own paths in several respects. Still, veteran staff members often don't have the time to adjust the preconceptions of new staff who are quite sure that there's only one way to be a disk jockey, newscaster, or interviewer: the way they've learned from mainstream media. While that is not a common occurrence, it happens often enough to cause varying degrees of disruption in station operations.*

The indigenous stations that experience the fewest difficulties with re-

---

*Many indigenous radio station managers have told me that the most difficult problem they face in working with young people (and sometimes with older adults) is that most of them want to be disc jockeys and can't see any other possibilities in the medium. That seems in part to be the influence of majority culture, but it may also reflect the feeling that other positions either aren't very interesting or are far too visible in terms of the criticism one is likely to receive from within the community. The latter applies to journalism in particular but also may reflect the fear that their writing skills may not be good enough to escape public criticism.

cruitment of staff are those operating as part of the national public broadcast service, for example, Radio Cymru (Wales) as part of the BBC. Pay
scales for various positions are fixed, rates of pay are quite attractive, and,
most important, the indigenous services almost always have been able to
begin operation on a modest scale—often an hour or less per day—so that
staff are added gradually as the scale of operation increases. There is the
occasional criticism from indigenous critics that such stations "don't sound
sufficiently Welsh" (or Sami, Irish, or whatever), because they're hybrids
of majority culture institutional practices and indigenous cultures. However, those stations often have produced much of the indigenous talent that
has gone on to manage, advise, and train indigenous stations and their staff
members.

Increasing numbers of potential indigenous broadcasters are able to
receive training, thanks to the creation of short and long courses for them.
Some of the training is provided by the majority culture national public
service, either as part of a broader training program or as a program run
specifically for indigenous broadcasters. The Australian Broadcasting Corporation (ABC) has provided both opportunities for Aboriginal trainees
over the past decade, thanks in large part to the efforts of Graham Steele
and John Newsome, both white Australians. They, and others working with
them, have struggled to keep both trainers and trainees from taking an
overly Western approach to training, not always with success: one Torres
Strait Islander trainee returned to the Thursday Island station full of zeal to
provide frequent time checks, à la white Australian radio, for a community
that neither needed nor appreciated frequent reminders of the exact time![1]

A few of the indigenous broadcast services have developed training
programs, as well. However, their ability to offer them over the long haul
is usually dependent upon external financing, and that isn't always de-
pendable. The Central Australian Aboriginal Media Association
(CAAMA) in Alice Springs received a three-year AUS $3.2 million grant
from the federal government's Department of Education, Employment, and
Training (DEET) in 1987. Roughly 100 Aboriginal trainees came through
it, and in 1989, CAAMA applied for a renewal of the grant. The review
team's report on the program was mixed, with some praise offset by indications that CAAMA had expanded too quickly to maintain quality control. DEET did not renew the grant, even though it hadn't established very
precise criteria for evaluation in the first place and CAAMA lost a number
of staff (some of whom had done regular air shifts).[2]

Educational institutions also have mounted training programs for indigenous broadcasters. Some of the institutions are majority culture, such
as the Australian School of Film and Television, which provides a regularly
scheduled 20-week course in television production (field production in par-

ticular) for Aboriginal trainees. Its coordinator, Lester Bostock, is a veteran Aboriginal film and television producer and is one of the founders of an Aboriginal media production company, Kuri Productions. In 1993, he launched a three-year training program that would equip its students for a variety of production-related jobs, such as camera operator, writer, director, and lighting technician. Employment in the media industry was guaranteed for those who satisfactorily completed the course, and culture awareness studies were included to help familiarize urban Aboriginals with Aboriginal culture, to equip all of the students with a better understanding of other ethnic groups, and to sensitize students in ways of dealing with prejudice, usually by confronting them with situations they're likely to face in the "real world."[3]

There also are increasing numbers of indigenous colleges and other tertiary institutions that are including media production courses, as well as degree programs, in their curricula. In Australia, Batchelor College (Northern Territory) and James Cook University (Townsville, Queensland) both do so, and the latter has new (as of 1994) studio facilities. It also has plans for a three-year degree (associate diploma of arts) in video production techniques, to be offered in conjunction with the Townsville Aboriginal and Islander Media Association (TAIMA).[4]

Sami College in Kautokeino, Norway, has taken a somewhat different approach. Sami students with media interests take courses on Sami culture and language at the college but attend media training courses at colleges in their country of origin: Bodo for Norway, Sundsvall for Sweden, Jyvaskyla for Finland. The director of the media education program in Kautokeino, Magne Uve Varsi, visits the training courses to supervise student work and helps to place the students as summer interns in Sami media operations. That arrangement frees the Sami College of the need for equipment and studios, as well as specialized instructors.[5]

The Indigenous Broadcast Center (IBC), part of the Alaska Public Radio Network,* operates the annual Alaska Native Youth Media Institute, which exposes young Native Americans and Inuit to a range of print and broadcast media production experiences. The one-week session concludes with critiques of student productions; the productions themselves cover a wide range of subjects, including video reports on hospital construction by Native communities and audio reports on work opportunities for Native youth.[6]

---

*The IBC, along with National Native News, became part of a new indigenous-controlled corporation, Koahnic Public Broadcasting, in 1995. KPB also has a construction permit to build an indigenous-programmed public radio station in Anchorage—the first such station in a major Alaskan city.

The growth of indigenous media also has stimulated the creation of indigenous training programs that operate more or less independently. Some of them both produce programs and train broadcasters, while others concentrate on training alone—financially risky, since government grants often help to subsidize such training but are uncertain sources of revenue from one year to another. Those programs usually are run by experienced broadcasters, some of them indigenous and some majority culture. George Burdeau (Blackfoot and French-Canadian) was a member of the Directors Guild of America and an experienced producer of film and TV documentaries before he developed a film and video training program for Native Americans at the Institute of American Indian Arts in Santa Fe, New Mexico, in 1989.[7]

A frequent complaint voiced by indigenous station staff is that some training programs are too protracted, especially if stations are expected to send their most promising recruits to attend such programs in other locations. When they are "lost" from the station roster for two or three months, other less capable staff may have to fill in, to the detriment of the station's program quality. There also are complaints that the sorts of training provided aren't appropriate to the situations the stations face. A course that emphasizes documentary production won't be of much use to a trainee returning to a station that might prepare two or three documentaries a year. And trainees may return with even greater ambitions to "make it" in majority media terms.

Trainers have similar complaints: that stations don't send their better staff, don't have very clear ideas of what they want the trainee to learn, or don't have a commitment to the sort of programming that the trainee would produce upon returning to the station, thus making the training itself a waste of effort and possibly causing good trainees to look for media outlets better suited to their skills. In fact, trainers frequently insist that their ultimate task is to equip their trainees for jobs in any and all electronic media-related activities, indigenous and majority culture alike.

Faults, where they exist, may lie with both parties. Station administrators may not have very clear ideas as to what could or should be accomplished through training. Trainers may not have a very clear idea of working conditions in the stations and may produce trainees who aren't able to function very well with poor equipment or under the time constraints faced by most stations, much less when up against cultural restraints. Many training program staff members also appear to assume that a *national* agenda will be of primary importance for any given indigenous people. In any case, given the fact that trainees come from a wide assortment of communities, it would be impossible for the programs to cover in detail the different restraints, technical or cultural, faced by their students.

More frequent meetings between administrators and trainers, and on each other's home ground, might help to improve the experience. If more of the training could be done on-site, as some already is, that would help to address the very real concern over the long-term absence of trainees, since most indigenous stations are thin on ambitious, dedicated, able staff—just the sort who will benefit most from training.

However, there are certain skills—documentary production clearly seems to be one of them—that cannot be taught very successfully on-site, where there are bound to be job-related and family-related concerns that work against the concentrated study the skill requires. Also, there is great potential benefit to conducting training in a setting where individuals with a common overall goal but quite different backgrounds and work situations can come together. That may be especially important for indigenous peoples who have strong tribal or extended family orientations, if there is some possibility that the indigenous media will serve to make those peoples more aware of their nationwide goals and problems. But that remains a big "if."

Many of the training courses just mentioned do include units and exercises (e.g., role-playing where one student acts as reporter and another as a "traditional" tribal authority) which are designed to reinforce consideration of indigenous perspectives, sensitivities, and modes of behavior. Many of the individual stations also conduct informal training along those lines. Such training often includes ongoing language lessons (informal) and also guidance in acquiring sensitivity to customs. Trainees often enter broadcasting in part because it's so connected with contemporary life; if so, they also may be relatively ignorant of indigenous customs and mores. Stations with morning program blocks that feature, for example, older people hosting talk shows and telling traditional stories often use those staff members as guides for younger staff. A few stations even employ individuals who serve as both guides and reference sources for language usage and customs, as does Mai-FM—a Maori rock station in Auckland, New Zealand—where an individual advises staff, singly and collectively, on proper word usage, forms of respect, and matters touching on *kaupapa* (custom) of various sorts. As neither the staff nor the vast majority of its young audience are likely to have grown up with much understanding of kaupapa, manager Taura Eruera thinks it important that staff and audience learn together and, in the process, come to understand and value their Maori identity.[8]

There are two areas of training that receive little attention, even though they are in considerable demand: sales and management.[9] Not all stations sell airtime, but increasing numbers do. Yet there are very few indigenous staff who have had sales experience of any sort, let alone in broadcasting: very few of the indigenous media, print or electronic, have been around long enough for their staff to have worked in sales, and the majority culture media rarely have seen indigenous audiences as important "sales targets," given their small numbers and relatively low incomes.

If stations are fortunate enough to have an experienced salesperson on staff, they may place apprentices with her or him and make available a fairly generous commission as further inducement. However, those stations that have taken such an approach—Tainui-FM in Ngarawahia, New Zealand, for example—report only moderate success, due in part to a seeming reluctance on the part of indigenous staff to put themselves forward. And if their self-confidence is low, which it sometimes will be when attempting to persuade a member of the majority culture to advertise on an indigenous station, failure to book sales contracts may have an especially devastating effect.

Managerial training poses other sorts of problems. Most of the managers of indigenous stations who had not been employed by majority culture media came to their positions over nonmanagerial tracks. Many had been teachers, some had been journalists (but rarely editors), a few had been clerics, but virtually none had ever managed part or all of a media operation. Their enthusiasm for helping their people, as well as their persistence in fighting the lengthy battles that led up to the creation of indigenous media in their respective countries, landed them in managerial positions. Once there, they largely taught themselves, although some took courses in management at nearby colleges. Not surprisingly, there have been some disastrous experiences, and turnover in the managerial ranks has been high.* Under those circumstances, it's easy to see why an apprentice system wouldn't work very well: it often would be akin to the blind leading the blind.

Most of the indigenous stations that are linked with national broadcast operations—Sami Radio with Norsk Rikskringskasting (NRK), Sveriges Radio (SR), and Yleisradio (YLE); Radio Cymru and Raidio nan Gaidhael with BBC; Sianel Pedwar Cymru with Channel 4; Raidio na Gaeltachta with Raidio Telefis Eirann (RTE); and Te Reo o Aotearoa with Radio New

---

*When I discussed managerial burnout with a Torres Strait Islander who had been involved with Aboriginal broadcasting for several years, he asked me whether I had ever heard of the Charcoal Club, in Sydney. I hadn't, so he enlightened me. It was founded by a group of Aboriginals who had spent large amounts of their time, energy, and sometimes money on various worthy Aboriginal causes, including radio. It provided a gathering place where exhaustion, if not misery, could find plenty of company! To him, it illustrated just how few Aborigines were available to devote themselves to causes and why progress was often slow. Personal conversation with Monte Prior, chairman, Board of Management, Townsville Aboriginal and Islander Media Association, Townsville, Queensland, Australia, October 1993.

Zealand (RNZ)—had indigenous managers from their early days as semi-autonomous organizations. As independent community-based stations have sprung up in those countries, the older stations sometimes have provided assistance, usually equipment but occasionally volunteer staff (often working on their own time). Managerial training hasn't been offered, but that could be because most of the newer stations are in communities some distance away from the older ones. If the training were to take place at the latter, it's doubtful that a manager from the former could be absent for prolonged periods, although two- or three-day workshops may be a feasible compromise.*

There is a common cultural problem, as well. Most indigenous peoples, but perhaps especially those living in rural areas, have a strong collective spirit. When that's combined with a strong sense of hierarchy, one can see why it might be a large task to interest an indigenous individual in managing a station. She or he will find it difficult to act as individualistically as managers sometimes must. Holding staff members to their responsibilities, particularly the responsibility for turning up in plenty of time to prepare for one's air shift, can be a real trial when the collective spirit makes it difficult to discharge people from their positions. The issue of hierarchy can mean that several individuals in the community outrank the station manager and may be in a position to tell her or him what to do or what not to do.

There's a closely related issue here, as well: when a media operation is a novelty for an indigenous community, as it often is in many remote and/or small towns, that group may feel threatened by both the technology and the individual in charge of it. Sometimes it's possible for the manager to allay those fears by "privileging" those who are superior in rank, perhaps by bringing them in to hear or see pretaped programs before they air, as was done in the USAID-sponsored Indian village radio project in Guatemala.[10] But such steps may not be enough to overcome suspicions that the new technology, and its manager, are not to be trusted.

It may even be the case that an indigenous individual heading up what could be considered an "imported" enterprise (particularly if a station programs large amounts of majority culture material) will have little standing at all. As anthropologist Eric Michaels observes about Aborigines who were elected to Aboriginal community councils (a white Australian-de-

---

*Some of the Aboriginal media associations (e.g., the Townsville Aboriginal and Islander Media Association) have held workshops for managerial personnel. Here, the assistance of an Aboriginal organization, the Yalga-Binbi Institute (specializing in management consulting) was crucial. *Townsville Aboriginal and Islander Media Association Annual Report, 1992,* Townsville, Queensland, Australia, 1992, 3.

vised institution): "a primary qualification for Council membership seems to be a demonstrated ability in European interaction styles, good conversational English, and literacy. Thus, Councils tend to be comprised of younger men (and some women) who may have little authority in any traditional sense. To the extent that European skills are achieved at the expense of Aboriginal ones, Councillors are apt to be marginal people."[11]

While it isn't likely that managerial training, if it were more readily available, could resolve such problems, it might at least give candidates the confidence that they know their jobs well enough to be able to stand their ground more effectively when confronted by critics. Whether bringing managers in from outside the community would help is another question: they might be free of obligations to the local hierarchy, but their outsider status may cause the community to consider the station far less their own. It also may lead to needless and costly confrontation brought about by managerial ignorance of the local power structure and the way things are done. Radio Tweed, in Selkirk, Scotland, found itself virtually shut out of local political coverage because its outsider manager violated local political custom.[12]

Most countries with indigenous stations will have at least a few with good managers, so one approach to managerial training might be to have apprentices working with such managers. They would be paid for full-time work and given increasing responsibility for specific duties. The managers themselves might be given incentives, such as extra clerical or other assistance, to offset the additional effort required to train the apprentice manager. The white Australian pro tem (on loan from ABC's Darwin station) manager of Waringarri Media, in Kununurra, Western Australia, proposed such an approach to the Aboriginal and Torres Strait Islander Commission (ATSIC) in 1993 and received polite expressions of interest, but no funding.[13]

Decision Making

The possible influence of a collective viewpoint on station management raises a broader issue: to what extent, if at all, is decision making in an indigenous station influenced by such a viewpoint, for better and for worse? Arguments have raged for many years now over the question of the possible superiority of the Japanese collective decision-making approach to other styles of decision making, whether top-down, referral upwards, or something else. By its very nature, collective decision making within the organization requires meetings, whether face-to-face or electronic. Electronic media operate in something very akin to perpetual motion: programming, sales, and other activities go on continually, and the presence of on-air deadlines makes it difficult to meet often or for very long. Therefore, the electronic media would not seem to lend themselves well to collective decision making.

However, observations of a number of formal and informal meetings in indigenous stations lead me to believe that there is more apt to be a collective approach to decision making than one usually finds in Western media. If the particular indigenous society is quite rule-governed, as is the case for Maori society, there is a very good possibility that those rules will have some influence on the society's media organizations. The few Maori radio station meetings that I have attended as a guest were characterized by two things: a set procedure for turn taking by members of the group and a great deal of discussion within the group as to who was, is, or will be responsible for what and, if help is needed, who will furnish it. In those cases where something had gone wrong, the individuals responsible were expected to apologize to the group for any embarrassment, stress, inconvenience, or other distress that others had experienced as a result. I have witnessed roughly similar situations in Aboriginal, Sami, and Native American radio stations.

Such meetings are not the only way that decisions are made in indigenous media. My own observations reveal a mix of decision-making approaches at most indigenous stations, and some indigenous groups may not be guided by collective decision making at all. Where such meetings do exist, they do seem to have one particular virtue: their emphasis on collective responsibility for media output, with a consequent reinforcement of the notion of obligation to the wider community. They could have two potential drawbacks—the prolonging of the decision-making process to the point where it interferes with adherence to the program schedule and the failure to reach decisions because none of them will satisfy everyone, resulting in lack of action on important issues. I have not personally seen much evidence of either problem.

It's also important to note that indigenous electronic media staff don't appear to be all that enamored of meetings. More often, they're regarded as a necessary evil. The one major exception is the need for meetings to hammer out appropriate translations for new words appearing in the majority culture languages. I describe the process in Chapter Six, but it's worth noting here that such meetings usually are brief. They also quite often result in agreeing to disagree, particularly where the system features highly localized stations serving specific tribes or dialect groups, or where the indigenous audience is spread across different countries with different majority culture languages (such as Sami, Kurdish, or Basque). Even when there's a national news service in the indigenous language, emanating from one central source (e.g., Mana Maori Media), local stations choosing to cover national and international events in the indigenous language may utilize a number of different terms. Dialects can be a powerful counterforce where development of new indigenous terminology is concerned.

Self-Regulation

On the whole, indigenous electronic media don't follow formal self-regulatory practices of the sort one finds in a number of nations, such as those of the Canadian, Japanese, and U.S. National Associations of Broadcasters and the Australian Federation of Commercial Broadcasters.[14] The National Indigenous Media Association of Australia doesn't have industry self-regulation as one of its mandates, nor does the Maori Te Whakaruruhau (association of managers of Maori stations), nor does the Indigenous Communications Association (ICA), for U.S. Native American stations.[15] There are too few Welsh, Sami, Basque, or Irish stations so far to warrant such organizations in those cases. There are organizations of Native American journalists in the United States and Canada. The Native American Public Broadcasting Consortium, in Lincoln, Nebraska, produces programming for local placement; while it can provide advice on programming about Native Americans, that is a secondary function.

Individual stations can, and occasionally do, set standards for programming that go beyond quantitative stipulations (e.g., X percent of indigenous music per hour). Those standards may be as informal as a hand-painted message on a studio wall, listing terms of reference (e.g., for racial minorities or women) that one is *not* to use on-air; they may be as formal as a printed set of station rules (e.g., those for Radio CHRQ (Restigouche, Quebec—a Micmac community), where rule 16 reads, "Announcers must not make derogatory remarks concerning race, color, sex, national origin, age, political affiliation and religion of any group or organization."[16] But usually the standards are not very detailed, and often they deal principally with the need to operate the service in a professional manner (e.g., "show up in plenty of time to prepare for your air shift" and "don't allow your friends into the studio when you're on the air").

Majority culture media services often have codes of practice containing specific reference to indigenous peoples. The Australian Broadcasting Corporation's *Code of Practice* (June 1993), Section 3.3, states that "Program makers and journalists should respect Aboriginal and Torres Strait Islander culture. Particular care should be exercised in traditional matters such as the naming or depicting of Aboriginal and Torres Strait Islander people after death."[17] The Federation of Australian Radio Broadcasters' 1993 *Commercial Radio Codes of Practice,* "Guidelines on the Portrayal of Indigenous Australians," Sec. 4, states that "Care should be exercised in depicting problems encountered by Aboriginal and Torres Strait Islander communities to achieve a balanced approach which does not unduly emphasise [*sic*] negative aspects to the exclusion of positive developments (e.g., descriptions of problems could usefully include efforts being made by the people themselves to resolve them)."[18] The *Commercial Television Industry Codes of Practice* contains a similar provision and follows it with "To avoid misrepresenting Aboriginal circumstances and traditions, reporters should where practicable consult local Aboriginal groups when preparing news and current affairs. Program makers should encourage Aboriginal involvement in all relevant stages of production of programs relating to Aboriginal people."[19] Australia's Special Broadcasting Services *Codes of Practice,* Sec. 2.1, also encourages such involvement.[20]

Independent institutions and individuals have attempted to assist majority culture media in their efforts to improve the quality of portrayal of indigenous peoples. The Australian Centre for Independent Journalism (Sydney, New South Wales) has published a handbook by Kitty Eggerking and Diana Plater entitled "Signposts: A Guide to Reporting Aboriginal, Torres Strait Islander, and Ethnic Affairs"; it goes into considerable detail on sensitive issues, such as the treatment of death or the concept of family ownership of a story about past events. Roughly similar guides have been written by Lester Bostock ("The Greater Perspective") and by Marcia Langton ("Well, I Heard It on the Radio and I Saw It on the Television"), while Michael King's "Kawe Korero" plays much the same role for coverage of Maori activities in New Zealand.[21]

Guidelines and handbooks serve to advise media staff on proper protocols, procedures, and sensitivities, but they have no legal power. Regulatory agencies such as the British Broadcast Complaints Commission, the Australian Broadcasting Authority (ABA), and the U.S. FCC have or have had complaints procedures through which anyone, including indigenous peoples, can level complaints against, for example, wrongful portrayals and ethnic slurs. The Australian Broadcasting Tribunal, which preceded the ABA, received over 70 complaints concerning objectionable radio program material regarding Aboriginal people during the period 1986–1992,[22] and some of the stations received warnings, but nothing worse. In the final analysis, standards usually must be set and kept by the media themselves in most countries, since the law offers little protection to indigenous peoples where harmful, demeaning, or inaccurate depictions of them are concerned.[23]

External Sources of Influence

In theory, indigenous radio and television stations are subject to the same regulatory conditions as are majority culture stations: they are expected to apply for licenses to broadcast and for license renewals. Those licenses require them to broadcast on an assigned frequency and at a specified level of transmitter power. There probably will be programming requirements and restrictions.

In practice, indigenous stations usually abide by those conditions. Certainly the indigenous stations affiliated with the Public Service Broadcaster (PSB) do so, as part of the overall PSB structure. But a number of the independent indigenous stations, especially in North America, may abide by the conditions and yet not acknowledge the power of the government to enforce them. Native American tribes in Canada and the United States have fought for sovereign rights over the past several decades and have won some of those battles during the past two decades. Those tribes with stations often have claimed full jurisdiction in deciding upon their operating conditions. If it pleases the tribal authorities to follow the majority government's regulatory practices, that's *their* decision.

The Native American station managers—anonymous in this instance—with whom I've spoken about this issue feel very strongly about sovereignty. At the same time, they realize that there's a reason for setting limits on power and keeping stations on their assigned frequencies, just as they realize that only a single licensing authority could manage that task. They reserve the sovereignty argument chiefly for matters of program content but readily admit that (1) there aren't many restrictions on content and

(2) the Canadian Radio-Television and Telecommunications Commission (CRTC) and the U.S. FCC don't bother them about content issues, anyway.*

There are other sources of influence, however, and one of them is particularly important where many of the independent stations are concerned. Tribal authorities often have a number of formal and informal powers to exercise over stations, particularly those on reservations or in rural locations outside reservations. In the case of Maori radio, tribal authority power is formal, in that most Maori stations are licensed through *iwi* (tribes) and money from the license fees goes to the iwi council, rather than directly to the stations.

Several iwi station managers indicated that they had excellent working relationships with tribal authorities, and money from the license fees wasn't used as a weapon of compliance. However, a few had felt pressures from that direction. In one case, a manager who billed the tribal council for airtime purchased by it to broadcast certain meetings was told that the amount was too high (even though it had been agreed upon in advance) and that the council could always refuse to pay, since it controlled the purse strings, anyway.[24] In another case, which I cover in Chapter Seven, a station whose manager had been at odds with some of the tribal authorities over a variety of issues soon found himself managing an independent station: a majority of the tribal council had voted to start its own station. Since license fee funding came to the iwi, the original station now was deprived of its predominant source of income—unfairly, its manager felt.[25] However, it had enough support within the community to survive.

There are times when tribal authorities, and the broader tribal communities, are divided over major issues. In another case, which I treat in detail in Chapter Seven, one group within a U.S. Native American tribe was willing to consider projects that another part of the tribe regarded as placing tribal sovereignty at risk. The latter felt that the tribal station manager favored the first group. That, and other grievances, led to a blockade of the station.[26]

There also are times when facilities are taken over and monopolized by one group within the community. That group might lack formal authority but claims right of rule on another basis, such as gender. A few of the Broadcasting for Remote Aboriginal Communities Scheme (BRACS) fa-

---

*The U.S. Indigenous Communications Association's Ray Cook, in a 1994 interview with Michael Keith, argued for Native American control of licensing. ICA Secretary Joseph Orozco agreed with that view, but on condition that there be a Native communication commission that would supersede individual tribal jurisdiction so that Native American stations wouldn't be under undue pressure from tribal authorities. (Keith, Michael, *Signals in the Air: Native Broadcasting in America*, Westport, Conn.: Praeger, 1995, 26.)

cilities in Aboriginal communities quickly came under the control of small groups of males, who reportedly refused to share any of the equipment with females. As there was no higher source of authority to which females could appeal, they remained excluded.[27]

Groups within communities might not wish to monopolize media facilities but may wish to gain control over certain categories of programming. Religious groups in particular often are anxious to broadcast their particular messages and may attempt to dissuade station managers from carrying opposing religious viewpoints. Political groups may have similar interests, although, as I indicate in Chapter Seven, they've been slow to realize the potential advantages of the electronic media.

Finally, there's the possibility that majority culture electronic media will influence the indigenous media in either of two ways: (1) through policies developed by and for majority culture media and then imposed by fiat on indigenous media or (2) by the very example they provide of how electronic media should and should not be operated. There are numerous examples in this book of each form of influence, but it's worth noting that such influence can be particularly strong if those working in the indigenous media hope to join the ranks of their majority culture colleagues: following the majority may be a useful qualification for joining it.

Financing

Perhaps the most difficult problem faced by most indigenous electronic media is the procurement of funding. Even the national Public Service Broadcaster–linked indigenous radio stations in Wales, Ireland, and Scandinavia may face it from time to time, especially with the current financial pressures on PSBs. Audience license fees have been virtually frozen in many countries, and the drive to economize sometimes falls heavily on the services that attract the least public attention, such as indigenous radio. Sveriges Radio, for example, spent very little over the past several years on the development of Sami radio in Sweden—6 million *kronor* (roughly U.S. $850,000) in a 1993 Sveriges Radio budget of 1.7 billion—and was considering even further cuts in the service.[28] Staff at the NRK Sami radio station in Karasjok, Norway, were "sounded" in 1994 by Sveriges Radio officials, who wondered whether there might be interest on the part of NRK in taking over operation of the Sami station in Kiruna, Sweden. There was not. The Kiruna station remained on-air as of 1996, with some possibility of increased financial support, should NRK, SR, and

YLE finally agree to create a unified Sami radio service, proposed for 1998.[29]

Stations not supported through PSBs are likely to obtain revenue through one or more sources: annual subsidies from the national government, a designated share of the audience license fee, advertising, voluntary contributions by the audience, program sponsorship, and revenue from games of chance, such as bingo. A growing number of stations also earn money through lease of their studios and engineers to music groups wishing to record, and a few (e.g., the Central Australian Aboriginal Media Association) have developed retail sales operations through which they sell audiotapes of traditional and contemporary (rock, country, folk) music, videotapes of dances and crafts, and an assortment of handicrafts. BBC Radio Cymru's studios in Bangor now offer a two-day training program, in Welsh, for the improvement of media skills. That program, meant for people in business, public enterprises, and other occupations involving public contact and media exposure, allows idle studio space to generate some income.

While that list looks to be comprehensive, there are a few sources that are notable by their absence. Corporate support, common in public broadcasting in the United States, is quite rare. Support from indigenous organizations—tribal councils, businesses, religious institutions, and national associations—is just as rare. (Those organizations, if they own buildings, do sometimes furnish space for the media operations at low rental charges.) It may not be surprising that few corporate bodies would have much interest in assisting indigenous media, since their support usually goes to high-visibility projects that are likely to earn them the goodwill of the majority population. But indigenous organizations might be expected to place a high priority on media, which show so much promise in terms of helping to raise indigenous self-esteem, to correct negative images held by the majority population, to galvanize indigenous opinion, to increase employment, and to foster cultural activity.

There are several factors that seem to account for the generally low level of indigenous organization support. Chief among them would be the widespread economic deprivation of indigenous communities and peoples. If there is money to spare, it's most likely to go into education, which in fact has shown some impressive gains among Maori, Aboriginals, and Native Americans and, in somewhat more prosperous groups, among Sami, Welsh, and Basques. Indigenous nursery schools and primary schools are becoming increasingly common, and secondary schools and colleges are beginning to appear with some frequency. Schools are considered an investment in the future. The electronic media don't appear to have benefited from a similar perception.

Why they have not benefited isn't always easy to determine, but one frequent explanation offered by station staff is that tribal councils and national indigenous organizations tend to be dominated by people who either have attained (1) "standing" through hierarchical processes or (2) prominence through coverage by the majority media. The former may be suspicious of indigenous media organizations because they've had so little contact with media of any sort and really don't understand how to deal with them. They may fear that they will come off badly in their media appearances, inasmuch as Western-style communication skills weren't essential elements in their rise to power. The latter often seem to see the indigenous media as irrelevant to their purposes, since they've already earned the attention of majority culture media and can reach their target audiences through them. A news director at an Aboriginal station told me of her frustration in obtaining interviews with Aboriginal political figures, even those from the station's area, as soon as they learned that the station wasn't ABC or one of the large commercial systems.[30]

There are even signs of a growing perception of indigenous media as moneymakers for the indigenous population. In several countries— Canada, the United States, Australia, New Zealand, and Sweden—annual governmental appropriations or grants have diminished or disappeared, or the growth of indigenous media has been so rapid as to place heavier demands on the amount coming through appropriations, license fees, or whatever other form of government support. In either instance, stations often have sought to make up for lost revenue by initiating or increasing advertising. But because indigenous business enterprises are relatively few and often not all that prosperous, it's necessary to attempt to attract advertising from the majority economy. That in turn often means attempting to become more attractive to majority population audiences, which may mean soft-pedaling the indigenous character of the station.

The usual categories of financial support that assist (none of them cover the full costs) indigenous electronic media all have their particular drawbacks. As I've already noted, government support, usually through some form of annual appropriation, may vary from year to year, depending upon the state of the national economy. In periods of economic recession or depression, it may vanish altogether. If support comes in the form of a share of the annual license fee, as it does in New Zealand, Ireland, the United Kingdom, Sweden, Norway, and Finland, the fee itself often comes under attack from legislative bodies. They must vote to raise fees, and doing so might arouse the ire of voters. Also, as commercial stations multiply, viewers and listeners may wonder why they have to pay higher fees, or why existing fees aren't lowered, when the commercial stations provide them with news and entertainment at no readily visible cost.

Many of the independent indigenous stations attempt to get audience members to contribute through pledge drives, but few find much success, for a variety of reasons. If there's already an annual license fee, individuals may reject the idea of spending additional money to help support additional stations. If the audiences the stations hope to serve are economically deprived, as often is the case, contributions are apt to be modest, as they've been so far for Dublin's Raidio na Life, whose predominantly younger audience contains large numbers of under- or unemployed individuals.[31]

Games of chance, especially radio bingo, also have become more widespread as sources of financial support, in the face of diminishing governmental funding. Many of the Native American radio stations in Canada have introduced radio bingo over the past few years, following the virtual elimination of Canadian government support for such stations. That raises another concern: the possibility that indigenous audience members playing the games may become even more impoverished, as well as more addicted to gambling (already a problem in some indigenous communities).[32] The prizes aren't large, but they may seem tempting to listeners living well below the poverty line. Yet many of the stations claim that this is their only viable major source of revenue. Mohawk-operated CKRK radio, in Kahnawake, Quebec (just outside Montreal), draws from a relatively prosperous and heavily populated area and enjoys an average weekly income of several thousand dollars (Canadian) from radio bingo,[33] but most stations fare far less well, although CKAU-FM, Sept-Iles, Quebec, makes enough from radio bingo to award yearly grants of about CAN $46,000 to the recreation committees of the two major Native American communities it serves.[34]

Some of the gambling casinos established by Native American tribes in the United States have begun to contribute to the support of stations on their own reservations, such as station WOJB-FM, on the reservation of the Lac Court Oreilles band of the Anishinabe, near Hayward, Wisconsin. A few contribute to stations farther away—station KILI-FM, on the Pine Ridge Lakota reservation, receives support from the Mdewakanton Sioux (Lakota), who operate the Mystic Lake Casino, just outside Minneapolis and roughly 500 miles east of Pine Ridge.

Indigenous media operations often have advanced claims on government revenues based upon an equity argument: indigenous peoples had been subjected to majority culture media neglect and/or distortion for so long that they're entitled to receive assistance now that they finally have their own media. Some governments have responded to that argument by setting aside a portion of the annual license fee for the specific support of indigenous media (as in New Zealand) or by developing a specific media support item within the budget of a ministry or office of indigenous affairs

(Australia and Quebec). Still others offer annual grants for noncommercial stations, among which there are indigenous stations (France and United States), or for indigenous stations alone (Canada, which, however, withdrew that form of support starting in 1990).

Rarely have those governments indicated that the money was being made available *because* of past inequity, although New Zealand's license fee–disbursing agency, New Zealand on Air, based its appropriation for Maori electronic media on the minister of communications recommendation of at least 6 percent of the total fees collected—and the Maori population is somewhat over 6 percent. (In fact, New Zealand on Air generally appropriated about 14 percent for the purpose.)

With the exception of New Zealand, the amounts of governmental financial support haven't exactly been generous, and even in the case of New Zealand, the generosity is relative: the early success of Maori radio contributed to the rapid growth of stations, from six in mid-1990 to 25 in mid-1993, to the point where funding for a few of the stations had to be lowered.* Australia's Aboriginal and Torres Strait Islander Commission faces a similar situation, with an even more constrained budget: ATSIC's 1992 allocation for various forms of Aboriginal electronic media was AUS $11.3 million, but that dropped to $10.3 million for 1993, even though the number of Aboriginal media associations had grown from six to eight.[35]

The U.S. government has provided annual support for public, noncommercial radio and television stations since the passage in 1967 of the Public Broadcasting Act. Indigenous radio stations can be supported under the terms of that act; for example, Native American (Lakota) station KILI in Porcupine, South Dakota, received a Public Television Facilities Program grant of $135,000 for station construction in 1982. The Corporation for Public Broadcasting (CPB), which administers congressional appropriations made under the act, also offers a Minority Station Improvement Project Grant, and many Native American and Inuit stations have received financial support through it. The National Telecommunications and Information Administration (within the Department of Commerce) began to award Minority Station Start-up funding in 1978; again, a number of Native American and Inuit stations have been assisted by such funding.[36]

CPB funding can prove to be a mixed blessing. Annual grants to stations require that they meet a set of conditions that can be especially onerous for Native American and Inuit media, given the high poverty levels of many indigenous communities and the small sizes of those communities.

---

*A few of the Maori stations received no New Zealand on Air support, chiefly because the areas they served had fewer than the New Zealand on Air benchmark minimum of 10,000 Maori.

In many cases, they must generate funds to serve as "matches" for continued federal government funding. And if indigenous stations wish to join National Public Radio, a network service with excellent news programs such as "All Things Considered" (to which member stations often contribute items), the price is even higher: a minimum annual budget of U.S. $150,000, FM power of 3,000 (occasionally less) watts, at least one control room and separate production studio, 18 hours a day of programming, and five or more full-time staff. Even then, requirements of local matching funds (onerous for poverty-stricken areas) and heavy bureaucratic requirements, coupled with what many indigenous station managers see as a hostile attitude toward their enterprises, make CPB funding uncertain.[37]

The U.S. Department of Health, Education, and Welfare (HEW) also provided grants for the purchase of equipment during the 1960s and 1970s, through the Educational Broadcast Facilities Program. However, the department also came with a number of conditions attached, chief among them the requirement that the institution receiving the grant be a nonprofit corporation organized primarily to engage in or encourage noncommercial educational radio. Indian tribal governments did not meet that condition. The attempt of the Pueblo Council in Albuquerque, New Mexico, to qualify for HEW, as well as CPB, funding finally resulted in the creation of an ethnically mixed (Anglo, Black, Hispanic, and Indian) governing board for the council's station (KIPC-FM). The board itself fell to quarreling over proper ethnic balance in programming, and the station was off the air within roughly 18 months of its debut.[38]

The United Kingdom's Broadcasting Act of 1990 established a specific fund for the support of Gaelic language programming: the Gaelic Television Fund. While the size of the yearly budget is not set under terms of the act (it was £9.5 million for 1992–1993), there at least is a guarantee of some level of support for the activity. But the most unusual feature of the act is that an indigenous body—the Comataidh Telebhisein Gaidhlig—is to administer the fund.[39]

New Zealand has followed a similar path since the beginning of 1995. A Maori committee, Te Mangai Paho, now is responsible for disbursing license fee revenues to Maori stations and for some production of individual programs and series, and it is guaranteed 13.4 percent of net license fee income. New Zealand on Air will continue to fund programs "addressing Maori issues in a way relevant to all New Zealanders within mainstream programming."[40] Whether or not placing funding decisions in the hands of indigenous committees will improve program quality in either Scotland or New Zealand over the long run is an open question, but it *is* a way for majority culture agencies to escape criticism for culturally biased funding decisions. There is another potential drawback: that such a move will serve to take the issue of the adequacy of funding out of broader public debate.

Maori lawyer Ripeka Evans observes that it also may "reduce the political heat on Ministers."[41]

There are indications that Te Mangai Paho intends to take some different approaches to funding priorities for Maori broadcasting. Early in 1995, it released a draft report on proposed funding policies and invited discussion by interested parties. Its two major objectives, according to the draft, would be "ensuring that at least 50% of the net broadcast hours funded by Te Mangai Paho are in the Maori language" and that "at least 50% of the total available Maori audience listen to or view Maori programming funded by Te Mangai Paho in 1995/96." Some of the specific programming emphases included more TV programs for young Maori and a National Maori Radio Service, entirely in Maori. The contract for NMRS was awarded to Mai-FM in April, 1996, initially for five hours a day of informational programming. Many Maori broadcasters, especially those in iwi stations, expressed the fear that the service would threaten the local character of their operations, particularly if they were required to carry it as a condition of Te Mangai Paho funding.[42]

All of that would take a considerable increase in financial resources, and a number of the iwi (tribal) stations would have to increase their broadcast hours in Maori to varying degrees, as well as risk losing many of their Maori (and *pakeha,* or white) listeners who speak very little Maori.* Furthermore, audience research would have to be strengthened in order to obtain reliable figures on the Maori audience. And finally, nothing in the draft report speaks to assessments of program *quality,* although Te Mangai Paho's motto is "To foster Maori language through quality broadcasting."

One U.S. state (Alaska) and two Canadian provinces (Quebec and Ontario) have made small (tens of thousands of dollars) annual appropriations available to Native American stations. However, most states, provinces, departments, cities, or other subnational governmental units do not supply such funding. At most, they might help to fund a given series of programs on a specific topic, or they might help to meet the costs of operating a community radio or TV station that includes some indigenous programming as part of the overall schedule.

Several governments have helped indigenous stations to come on the air. Canada, Australia, New Zealand, and the United States all have appropriated money for station construction, as well as for training programs. Some of the latter have continued to receive such funding, which may come in more conventional forms, such as salary support for trainees and

---

*Professor Timoti Karetu, head of the Maori Language Commission, is a member of Te Mangai Paho. He has long been a strong advocate of the need for Maori radio to play a leading role in restoring the widespread use of Maori. Therefore, it isn't surprising that Te Mangai Paho should place such great emphasis on this issue.

costs associated with attending the programs, or in less conventional forms, such as a New Zealand youth training program that "paid" trainees in petrol (gas) coupons to offset their transportation costs!

There is one point that is common to most government financing of indigenous broadcasting: it goes to support *full-time station* operations. (There also is support for independent program production.) That may appear logical, since most government financing of any sort of broadcasting is for that purpose. Furthermore, the symbolic value of a station to an indigenous group appears to be great. However, urban indigenous peoples in any one location tend to be more diverse in their interests, and to be surrounded by more artifacts of mainstream culture in their daily lives, than are their small town and rural counterparts. They also come from a far wider assortment of indigenous culture backgrounds (including linguistic, although few of them speak any form of the indigenous language). Therefore, it seems far more difficult for the urbanites to organize themselves to create and sustain a full-time station.

Urbanites have enjoyed greater success in developing and sustaining given programs that take their place in the schedules of public or community stations. Some can manage an hour a week; others can fill 10, 20, or 30 hours with relative ease. They might increase those figures if there were more financial support available, but government funding rarely is available to them because they aren't full-time operations. Several indigenous radio staff members in urban areas have expressed their belief that governments deliberately favor full-time operations for two reasons. First, applications for station licenses, as well as funding, are likely to come from one dominant (and perhaps sole) indigenous group, meaning that the government won't have to decide between groups when awarding licenses or funding. Second, a full-time operation is far more likely to materialize in the country, where indigenous communities tend to be quite homogeneous, than it is in the city, and an indigenous station located far from major population centers will be far less annoying or distressing to the majority population than will an indigenous station located in their midst, thus reducing the level of complaints about government funding for such stations.[43]

Most nations also have a host of governmental and nongovernmental agencies, foundations, charitable institutions, and other organizations that make small amounts of money available to individual members of indigenous groups. For example, some of the new indigenous community radio stations in Ireland (Raidio na Life) and in Wales (Radio Ceredigion in Aberystwyth and Radio Maldwyn in Newtown) receive grants from governmental or quasi-governmental institutions such as the Bord na Gaeilge, the Development Board for Rural Wales, regional water and electricity boards, and tourist offices. The U.S.–based Northwest Area Foundation (Minnesota, private) has helped to support National Native News.[44]

The qualifying conditions associated with each source vary from highly specific to general, and sometimes it's possible to identify a large number of sources that may help to support would-be or actual indigenous electronic media activity. But it can be close to a full-time job to track down such sources, and then to discover whether media-related activities meet the conditions—not just those spelled out in print, but the many "understandings" and "subconditions" that disqualify such activities. Chris Lee, a member of the staff of the National Indigenous Media Association of Australia, showed me a roughly two-inch thick book listing such sources, often with many listings per page. He noted that the vast majority of the sources probably would have no interest in financing media activities, but rarely could he determine that without contacting them.[45]

Smaller media operations, such as indigenous recording (audio and video) studios, may face even greater difficulty in tapping sources of the sorts just noted. They are small businesses—even smaller than most indigenous stations—and indigenous small businesses have great difficulty qualifying for loans almost everywhere in the world. As certain indigenous big businesses (e.g., tourism in New Zealand and gambling casinos and mining in certain parts of North America) become prosperous, there are hopes that they may encourage the establishment of indigenous financial institutions, which hopefully would be more willing to make loans to small stations and recording studios. Even a few of the larger indigenous commercial radio stations—4AAA (Aboriginal country and western) in Brisbane and Radio Aotearoa (Maori MOR [middle of the road music] and talk) in Auckland—might be in a position someday to share a portion of their profits (when they begin to appear) with smaller stations. At present, however, indigenous investment generally goes into schools, hospitals, community centers, and housing projects. Recording studios and broadcast stations rarely appear in the list of higher priorities, perhaps for the same reasons noted earlier in connection with lack of tribal support for stations, since the same individuals are likely to be influential members of investment bodies.

Certain indigenous recording studios are able to scrape by financially if they invest carefully in good, modestly priced equipment, if they also operate training programs for sound technicians and broadcasters, and if they don't restrict themselves to dealing with indigenous groups and individuals. Mai-FM, a Maori rock station in Auckland, has developed a separate and quite sophisticated sound studio that serves Maori and pakeha alike. Its owners expect it to become profitable within a few years. It helps that the former station manager, Taura Eruera, is a professional musician with a thorough knowledge of recording technology and a keen eye and ear for bargains in equipment and has a sufficiently high reputation to attract good technicians.[46]

Facilities

Program production certainly doesn't take place in a vacuum, and production facilities available to indigenous media come in all shapes and sizes, not to mention states of repair. Facilities also help to explain why some media operations can turn out far more ambitious and varied productions than can others. And they often influence the sound or look of those productions.

Generally speaking, the indigenous media operations that are part of national, license fee–supported broadcast services have far better facilities at their disposal than do their unaffiliated colleagues. The three stations of Raidio na Gaeltachta (RNG) are purpose-built, although they didn't start off that way. They have relatively spacious and well-equipped studios and control rooms, editing booths, remote broadcast vans, and a full complement of salaried staff. The NRK's Sami radio station in Karasjok, Norway, enjoys a strikingly modern and spacious building, with a splendid sound recording studio fit for highly professional work. BBC Radio Cymru's Bangor studios (the main production center is in Cardiff, Wales) are in two older houses, on opposite sides of the road, but the equipment in them can handle highly complex sound productions.

In contrast, Mana Maori News headquarters facilities in Rotorua, until they were closed in late 1995, due to a severe cutback in financial support from Te Mangai Paho, occupied the second floor of a commercial building, featured recording booths not much larger than closets, and had barely adequate sound insulation. The equipment was quite decent, but there was little backup for it, and much of it was 10 or more years old. Its two remaining operations, in Auckland and in Wellington, are also in commercial buildings and suffer from most of the same problems, plus a lack of sound-insulated studios for Wellington.

Individual radio stations occasionally may feature much the same standards as do their majority culture counterparts, particularly if they're in large cities and if they're fully commercial. Mai-FM in Auckland and 4AAA Murri Country Radio in Brisbane both meet those standards, and Mai-FM also has a separate, but nearby, sound recording studio, in part because its former manager, Taura Eruera, wants to encourage young musicians, Maori and pakeha.

In smaller cities, the standards usually decline, although a few of the Native American stations in Canada, such as CHME in Les Escoumins, Quebec, have very adequate facilities. More often, an old house has to serve, however awkward it may be: toilets doubling as record libraries, closets as recording booths, and little or no money for sound insulation. Staff resourcefulness sometimes makes silk purses out of sows' ears, as it did when Te Upoko o te Ika, in Wellington, New Zealand, created a studio by placing a wooden car-shipping crate in a larger room, insulating it with egg cartons, and fitting it out with a door and window. (Te Upoko moved to a more spacious and modern office building in 1993 and left the carton studio behind.)

Perhaps the most amazing indigenous radio facility I've visited was Radio Redfern in Sydney. It was in a "liberated" house, meaning that station staff simply took over a temporarily abandoned building. There were no doors or glazed windows, so staff did without the latter and nailed boards together for the former, usually with large gaps at top and bottom. The single studio-control room also formed the sole passageway between the front room and the kitchen; when the station was on-air (it had roughly 30 hours a week on Radio RSR [Radio Skid Row]), people walked through, anyway. There was no warning light, but that wouldn't have mattered, since the announcers often stopped whoever was passing by, put them on mike, and asked them questions about their recent activities. All of this lent a highly informal, casual air to Redfern's broadcasts, which may have served to reassure the audience that this really was a voice of the community.

It certainly isn't the case, then, that indigenous media operations must be well equipped and housed in order to present high-quality program content and style. But the conditions under which many indigenous media staff work probably don't encourage long-term loyalty and don't do much for staff self-respect, especially when they compare themselves with most majority culture media operations. Nor do they encourage staff who would like to produce something out of the ordinary, especially when it might require much editing. Some of the operations can and do bring virtue out of necessity, by showing their audiences that they aren't very high-tech and that they are very economical. Those operations that finally have the chance to move, especially if there's money for a bit of remodeling, seem quite happy to leave virtue behind.

Research

If indigenous electronic media staff knew more about their actual and potential audiences, they might find it easier to make effective programming decisions. They also might be able to increase their revenues, whether through greater sales of advertising time, higher levels of government or foundation support, or more numerous and generous audience donations, if they could obtain more precise evidence of their effectiveness in reaching listeners and viewers. However, as I note in Chapter Three, few of the indigenous media have commissioned or conducted surveys.

The chief reason for that state of affairs doesn't appear to be financial. I have spoken with several dozen indigenous media staff about surveys, and most seem aware that they can be conducted quite inexpensively. But most lack any notion of how to go about the task, and some appear almost terrified at the prospect of attempting it; illustrations of ways to simplify surveys seem to fall on deaf ears. I suggest in Chapter Three that they may fear "the truth" or suspect that data could be used against them. But many seem to have a more fundamental fear of the unknown: since most hadn't served as respondents to surveys (recall that most of the world isn't as survey mad as the United States and that poor, remote, comparatively small groups of indigenous peoples are less likely to be involved in them), they lack much sense of how to begin.

Such survey research on indigenous audiences as we have has been conducted far more often by majority culture researchers than by indigenous researchers. Those few surveys conducted by the latter have followed majority culture models. At one level, that's not a serious problem: questions about demographics, times of listening or viewing, and perhaps favorite programs should differ little from one culture to another. But the framework of the research, the basic assumptions that guide it, and the more qualitative dimensions contained within it all can vary greatly from one indigenous culture to another, not to mention from indigenous culture to majority culture.

Take as one aspect the process of sampling. If an indigenous group is of modest size, and if its members live within a geographically compact area, its members may wonder why everyone (with the possible exception of children) isn't asked to participate. The collective spirit of many indigenous peoples may discourage participation by individuals chosen through sampling, on the grounds that no one is privileged to speak for anyone else nor should any one person's opinion be considered superior to someone else's. The USAID-financed local radio experiment in Guatemala (pp. 30–31) ran into just such a collective spirit in the Quiche Indian villages when project leaders attempted to sample opinions among farmers: "The Indians could not understand why some—and only some—farmers were being interviewed. In the future, therefore, any survey conducted will include all of the farmers in any given village."[47]

A second issue: students of survey research procedure are aware that getting one's verbal foot in the door—making and sustaining contact with respondents—isn't always easy. If researchers aren't aware of the forms of greeting and address used to and among members of indigenous communities, it may prove very difficult to get respondents to agree to participate. It may be inappropriate for men to ask women certain quite "innocent" (to majority culture) questions, and vice versa. Yet my examination of the research reports noted in Chapter Three, and my discussion of procedures actually followed by one of the researchers, Erja Ruohuoma, indicate that there was little, if any, consideration of that point.[48]

Third, there's the generally acknowledged problem of the compliant respondent: the individual who wants to be as helpful, and as supportive, as possible. That's a particularly sensitive matter where indigenous media are concerned. Most of those media services are of recent enough date that audience members sometimes wonder whether they'll vanish someday soon. Claiming to watch or listen for hours each day, and to relish every word or image, may be a way to keep them from vanishing. Therefore, it's doubly important to attempt to verify amounts and types of listening and viewing, as well as subjective reactions. Inclusion of follow-up questions on specific program content can help to separate the overcooperative individual from the individual who really has watched and listened to all that she or he claims. None of the surveys covered in Chapter Three had such a follow-up.

Fourth, as radio remains the predominant medium for indigenous peoples, it's often important to determine both the amount and nature of primary and secondary listening. That's been a practice in radio research for years, to the point where many researchers assume that their respondents have a clear and coterminous understanding of the nature of both categories. Indigenous peoples, often being asked to participate in surveys for the first time in their lives, may need a more thorough explanation of the distinction. Erja Ruohuoma of YLE told me that she wondered whether or not most of the Sami respondents in her 1992 study *did* understand it, and if this may have resulted in an inflation of figures for primary listening.[49] The station manager for YLE Sami Radio in Inari, Juhani Nousuniemi, felt quite certain that many listeners didn't understand the distinction and that the figures *were* inflated.[50] Ruohuoma will conduct further research on Sami listening but intends to spend more time considering cultural differences and taking them into account in the design and execution of the project.

That raises a fifth point. Interviewing for many survey projects concerning indigenous uses of the media is carried out by university students (at the University of Oulu, in the case of the 1992 Sami radio study) or other young people. They may speak indigenous languages fluently but may not speak with the authority necessary to command the respect of the traditional, hierarchically minded, respondent. It may be possible to vest them with authority (e.g., by preliminary telephone calls, letters, or visits from an authority figure who asks respondents to cooperate when contacted for the survey itself). But again, that underlines the need for inter- (and intra-) cultural sensitivity.

The translation of indigenous languages may be even more difficult for majority culture researchers than is most other translation, for two reasons: first, dictionaries of indigenous languages, as well as books purporting to teach those languages, usually have been prepared by majority culture individuals—and often quite badly prepared. To take one example, learning the subtleties of nomenclature for family relationships in certain indigenous societies (e.g., Aboriginal, which really isn't a single society, anyway) can take years, and even then there are likely to be mistakes and omissions. It's doubtful whether dictionaries and language instruction books will catch all of those nuances, but it often is vital for researchers to do so.

Second, indigenous peoples often have a much clearer understanding of the languages and paralanguages (nonverbal) of the majority culture population than the reverse. As anthropologist Eric Michaels notes, "Generally, subordinated classes do a better job of figuring out the languages and rules of the dominating class than the other way around. ... Aboriginals strike me as profoundly interested in understanding (as distinct from becoming) Europeans. ... Researchers, and other alien presences in remote settlements are tolerated, I suspect, partly because of what can be learned from such people."[51] He goes on to discuss what that imbalance in linguistic skills has meant in the case of his own research—among other things, the extreme difficulty of asking a rank-order or preferential question in Warlpiri—and at one point states that "If I could ask three such questions [e.g., on demographics] of three respondents after three years of fieldwork and could feel secure that I understood what was said to me, I would consider it an extraordinary achievement.*[52]

There are numerous other pitfalls to conducting audience research among indigenous peoples, some of them suggested in the few works that are available on the subject of conducting research in non-Western or minority cultures.[53] Probably none of the pitfalls is universally present, but all are worth some thought as the project is designed, executed, and interpreted. That would seem especially important for projects carried out in

---

*Michaels reiterated that sentiment when I met with him in Brisbane in September 1989. He underlined it by noting that, the more adept he became in Warlpiri, the more he was expected to not only understand such things as the finer distinctions of kinship but also to display the wisdom to ally himself with the "right" families—something that would make his life as an independent observer untenable.

rural areas, where indigenous traditions may be more powerful and where previous contact with audience research may be especially rare. It also will help to improve cooperation and accuracy if the research subjects themselves can be involved as active participants in the design, planning, and execution of the project.[54]

Working with the Audience

Audience research can help to provide media staff with a general idea of audience habits and preferences, but it usually doesn't provide the audience with much sense of contact with the media operation. It could, especially if the staff were to have an "open mike" (or camera) program shortly after completion of a survey: the survey's results could be announced, staff could note some evidence of its impact on their future practices, and listeners or viewers could call in with their reactions. "Town meetings" between staff and audience members could accomplish much the same thing, if staff have the time and money to travel around the service area to hold them. While I've rarely observed both of those practices in majority culture broadcasting, I have never come across either of them in the case of an indigenous electronic media outlet.

One practice followed by some of the indigenous operations is the appointment of an advisory council, made up of audience members from around the service area. Most Native American stations have such councils. Indigenous stations falling under national public service broadcast operations often are required to have such councils. Radio Cymru, for example, is within the purview of the BBC's National Broadcasting Council for Wales, as well as specialized advisory councils for education, religion, agriculture, and appeals (which advises the BBC on requests coming from organizations for time on the airwaves to make funding or other appeals to the public). Raidio nan Gaidheal works with a similar set of councils for Scotland.

Independent indigenous stations rarely are required to appoint advisory councils, although those stations receiving funding through the U.S.

federal government during a period running from the late 1970s to mid-1980s were required to have them. Many of the Maori and Aboriginal stations (e.g., Waringarri Radio in Kununurra) have appointed them, as well.

Most of those councils, whether advising PSB stations or independent stations, are composed of people appointed by the stations themselves. There may be recommendations from outside, and individuals may volunteer their services (many stations solicit recommendations and self-nominations in broadcast announcements). Station staff may consult with the "power elite" of their communities before making appointments. But the final word, at least in theory, is the station's.

That could lead to the councils' being stacked with "yes people," unwilling to criticize or to consider the criticisms of others. But it is unlikely to do so, for two reasons: such members would lose the respect of those in the community who found things to criticize but soon realized that council members would do nothing about them; and the council members themselves would tire of wasting time in meaningless meetings.

Not that council members see themselves as perpetual gadflies. They spend the bulk of their meeting time in deliberations on past programming and on plans for the future. They raise criticisms at times, often serving as channels for comments from audience members. They may request information on how the manager, program director, news director, or any other authority plans to see to it that a mistake won't be repeated. But they're likely to spend more time on matters of public relations: how the station can answer unjustified criticism, how its annual fund-raising drive might be improved, how it can please both factions in an intracommunity dispute. And station staff may press council members to be the station's advocate in various situations.

On the whole, advisory councils appear to serve useful roles for stations. Whether they're as useful to the public is harder to say, although they should be of some value if they help to improve program quality. One of the problems is that the audience as a whole often knows little about the work of the councils. Surprisingly, few of the stations broadcast information about their deliberations: some managers reason that, if the councils are supportive of the stations most of the time (which seems to be the case), such broadcasts would cause listeners and viewers to think that they were nothing but the lap dogs of station management. But if council members truly attempt to serve as the broader public's voice, and indicate their readiness to present that voice in council meetings (without necessarily agreeing with the sentiments expressed by the public), there should be ample material to show that criticisms are considered.

Many indigenous stations attempt to bring themselves to their audiences by broadcasting from villages and cities around the area, by visiting schools, churches, and mosques, by either taping programs for later broadcast or airing them live, by sponsoring or at least covering special outdoor events (often sports, musical, or literary contests), and by arranging for local residents, teachers, clerics, or journalists to phone in regular reports on local activities.

The better-endowed PSB indigenous stations often have vans or sound trucks to handle such broadcasts. Raidio na Gaeltachta purchased a large trailer in 1994 and takes it around the region covered by one of the three stations comprising the service. It's parked for a week in each town, and its equipment is sophisticated enough to handle broadcasts from just about any location: church, school, town hall, or village square. The entire RNG network takes the feed from the trailer for an hour or two each day. Among other things, the programs feature local talent and provide a portrait of the past and present of the community. The RNG station whose region the trailer is visiting furnishes the broadcast staff, so the programs are professionally produced.

Some of the independent stations have similar approaches, if more modest ones. Radio Xiberoko Botza, a Basque station in Mauleon, France, uses a car to accomplish its visits: there's enough room for a portable control board, microphones, and other pieces of equipment, but not for a portable transmitter, so it must record whatever is going on in the community and broadcast the tape later. The two or three station staff who go out for those broadcasts usually make public announcements, describing the station's activities and its continuing need for financial support. Quite often, someone agrees to "pass the hat," and the money collected comes back to the station.

Indigenous stations could involve the audience directly in program making, as authors such as Francis Berrigan and P. Beaud advocated in the early 1980s: they saw the encouragement of audience participation as part of the possible democratizing and empowering function of electronic media (see Chapter Two). However, my research on indigenous electronic media has revealed very few continuing instances of such activity, aside from the preschool and school broadcasts noted in Chapter Three. Many of the stations do encourage listeners and viewers to visit, and many invite local musical groups to submit tapes or do live broadcasts. Call-in shows also are a regular feature, both for music requests and for on-air participation in discussions. But programs made in their entirety by groups and individuals not usually connected with the station are scarce.

That may be due in part to the tendency of many of the indigenous stations, especially the independents, to rely heavily on volunteers from the community. Those individuals often represent many different backgrounds and interests; taken collectively, they may even represent a pretty fair cross section of the community, thus fulfilling the spirit of what Berrigan and Beaud proposed. If there's a good deal of turnover among the volunteers (and there usually is), it may be that just about everyone wishing to be involved in broadcasting will have that opportunity, sooner or later.

There remains the important question of how meaningful that involvement will be. On many of the stations, the journalistic functions are handled largely or entirely by paid staff, but on several, the news and public affairs programming is the responsibility of volunteers. Raidio na Life in Dublin has roughly 300 volunteers, many of whom work for the station as news teams, gathering and producing newscasts, "serious" discussion programs, and occasional documentaries.[55]

Publicizing programs can help in the development of ties between indigenous stations and their audiences, especially when programs have been recorded on site for later broadcasts: if listeners or viewers know that their group or town is on the schedule at a specific time and date, there's almost certain to be a large audience on hand from within that particular location. Most of the indigenous stations don't pay much attention to program promotion, however. Because there are few, if any, directly competing indigenous media services, some of them appear to feel that the indigenous audience will turn up for whatever is offered. They're quite aware that audience composition will differ according to the time of day and generally are careful to take that into account in scheduling programs. But publicity for individual programs and series is something of a rarity, aside from on-air promotional announcements. Still, cable- and satellite-delivered broadcasting are coming more within reach of many indigenous groups, and even if very few of the cable or satellite channels carry indigenous broadcasts, they are a further drain on available listening and viewing time. Indigenous media might be well-advised to put more effort into program promotion as the sheer number of electronic media outlets increases.

Relations with Other Media

In many countries, there are a number of significant ways in which the mass media interact: through the influence of radio and TV critics writing for newspapers, through the appetite of television for movies, through journalistic competition between newspapers and the electronic media, and through cross ownership of print and broadcast media.[56]

There is little interaction of that sort where the indigenous media are concerned. Although book publishing in indigenous languages does fairly well in many countries, very few of the books deal with indigenous media. Weekly newspapers in indigenous languages are quite rare (although definitely gaining in numbers), and dailies almost nonexistent. Even papers intended for indigenous readers, but in majority culture languages, are scarce. And almost all of the print media for indigenous peoples live a precarious existence, with resources insufficient for ownership of, or even substantial investment in, the electronic media. Indigenous-made films and videos are increasing in number, but most represent the efforts of independent producers, who live from one project to the next, always short on funds. Indigenous stations provide them with airtime and occasionally can furnish a modest level of financial support, but that, too, is chancy.

The PSB-affiliated indigenous stations are somewhat better off than their independent colleagues and do manage to supply more financial support for film- and video making. Sianel Pedwar Cymru, a commercial TV service of Wales, obtains part of its programming from the BBC but also commissions a number of independent productions, some of them single programs, some serial. The Irish language TV service that is slated to come on the air in 1996 probably will do the same. But other PSB affiliates (e.g., the NRK's Sami service) will be fortunate to have the money to commission 30 minutes of independently produced TV programming a week. Those stations, and some of the independents, are better able to provide support for audiocassette and compact disc recording, and the indigenous recorded music industry is growing, but it's far from healthy in the economic sense.

Still, there are some forms of interaction, chiefly through indigenous newspaper and magazine columns about the electronic media. *Mana,* a bimonthly (but more often "occasional") magazine published by Mana Maori Media, regularly has two or three articles about the Maori electronic media in each issue. *Assu,* a weekly Sami language newspaper published in Kautokeino, Norway, regularly runs articles about Sami programs. Several Aboriginal English language newspapers (e.g., *Koori Mail,* a fortnightly published in Lismore, New South Wales) do likewise for Aboriginal radio, TV, and videos. And almost all of the indigenous print media carry broadcast schedules.

In contrast with common practice among majority culture print media, indigenous magazines and newspapers tend to treat the electronic media as allies, rather than as adversaries or competitors. Columns devoted to radio and television usually are supportive; rarely is there negative criticism, and almost never the withering blasts that sometimes appear in the majority press. It probably will be a healthy sign of maturity and stability when the indigenous press begins to treat indigenous electronic media with less gentility. But for the time being, the press seems to see its mission as one of nurturing support.

Conclusion

Clearly, there's a wide range of practices in training, administration, research, and other nonprogramming (but essential to program making) indigenous electronic media activities. Yet certain common denominators emerge: the need for a thorough understanding by media staff, and by those with whom they interact, of aims and goals. That holds for programming, training, audience research, or anything else, for *all* parties with major involvement in the activity. That will take a good deal of skill, tact, fortitude, and foresight, as well as a close knowledge of the appropriate languages, cultures, contexts, and possibilities.

That may sound almost impossible, and it certainly would be if anyone—manager, researcher, journalist, or council member—expected to be able to manage it all without making mistakes, which *is* impossible. But at least one can hope that those involved with indigenous media will consider the several elements noted here as they undertake their various tasks and will take the time, precious though it is in the mass media, to weigh possible solutions and ponder alternative goals. Training programs themselves can help to reinforce such behavior. So can understanding critics, paymasters, and others who are in a position to apply pressure to media operations, by avoiding unrealistic expectations. If politics is the art of the possible, so is media performance.

5

A Voice for Tangata Whenua: A History of the Development of Maori Electronic Media

The Maori experience with the electronic media in Aotea-
roa/New Zealand must be understood in light of a specific
historical fact: whereas a large number of broadcast
experiences of minority groups have to do with minorities who came to
various countries as immigrants, slaves, or "guest workers," the Maori situation is a case of the original inhabitants of the land—the *tangata
whenua*—becoming a minority over time, as also is true of Aborigines in
Australia and Native Americans in North America. What makes the Maori
experience a singular one is that the entry of an external culture was ef-
fected through a supposed agreement between equal parties, here the
Maori and the British. The Treaty of Waitangi (1840) is far more all-en-
compassing in that respect than is any comparable document between Na-

tive American tribes and the U.S., British, or Canadian government, and there is no comparable document stipulating Aboriginal and British or Australian relationships.

The Maori settled what was much later named Aotearoa (Land of the Long White Cloud is the preferred translation) sometime in the ninth century A.D. They came to a land that, so far as can be determined, had never known human settlement. Numerous flightless birds (e.g., moa and kiwi) had developed because they lacked natural enemies, including humans. Those settlers were the first tangata whenua. And, while this new land had a far more rugged climate than that of the South Pacific islands (probably the Marquesas and/or Cooks) from which Maori had traveled in their canoes, it did offer abundant space in comparison with those islands. Because of that, there is little indication of the inter- or intratribal warfare that characterizes early Polynesian settlements in the South Pacific.[1]

Another wave of migration from those islands took place around 1350. Although that wave once was considered to have been one large fleet of canoes, more recent scholarship argues for different landings at different times and in different places by smaller groups of canoes.[2] However, those groups have assumed considerable importance over time in terms of Maoris' ability to trace their ancestries back to one or another of the five *waka* (canoe) families. The families differed in their settlement patterns, and some are regarded as more powerful than others. The Tainui, for example, settled over much of the North Island and account for roughly a third of the present-day ethnic Maori population of about 431,000 (1991 census).

That situation has had some bearing on the development of Maori radio, particularly in terms of the government's encouragement of the development of *iwi* (tribal) radio stations. All iwi are part of one or another waka. If two or more iwi occupy a discreet geographical entity, if only one iwi station is to serve that entity, and if the two or more iwi cannot agree on a power-sharing arrangement, each is likely to evoke waka lineage as a compelling reason for its precedence. Government regulators are expected to, and themselves expect to, take this into account in allocating the frequency. A case in point: the Ngati Whatua iwi in Auckland and the Tainui argued through much of 1991 as to who had the right to operate a station that would serve the area. Ngati Whatua had been dominant in much of the area for an extended period, but Tainui were the original waka and could make a good case for themselves having been the tangata whenua, or people of the land. As such, they would be entitled to precedence, and at the least, their *mana* (power or influence) would have to be acknowledged, whoever operated the station.[3]

Dutch, French, and British explorers began to "discover" parts of Aotearoa in 1642, when the Dutch seaman Abel Tasman briefly touched land and called it *Nieu Zeeland* (New Zeeland, after the province of Zeeland in the Netherlands). Four of his men died in an encounter with Maori, and the next European contact did not come until Captain James Cook of Great Britain touched its shores in 1769. His reports of abundant seals and timber eventually led to the coming of seal hunters and timber traders, and by the beginning of the nineteenth century there were frequent contacts between Maori and Europeans, and even a few trading posts around the islands.

Rumors of a possible French colonization of the country (the limited Maori contact with the French had not been auspicious!), coupled with an increase in intertribal warfare (itself apparently stimulated by the brisk trade in firearms for provisions) and fueled to some degree by British missionaries who wanted to secure the Maori for Christianity, induced some of the Maori chiefs to ask British Resident (i.e., Counsel) James Busby to help stabilize the situation. He agreed and in consultation with the British government proposed a treaty that would accomplish the purpose: the Treaty of Waitangi (1840).[4]

As D. H. McKenzie points out, the treaty illustrates the problem of arriving at a mutual understanding of what is being negotiated when one side (here, Maori) approaches the negotiations as an oral culture while the other side (British) operates as a written culture.[5] Although the treaty is brief, its precise meaning has been debated for decades. But there is one key term that arises again and again: *rangatiratanga*.

Rangatiratanga appears in P. M. Ryan's *Revised Dictionary of Modern Maori* as "kingdom, principality," but its implications, where Maori are concerned, are far more complex and turn more on the matter of authority.[6] Using that authority in connection with "ownership" of the land and the adjacent seas, in the sense of commodities to be given or sold to others, and relinquishing ultimate authority over that land would be alien to Maori, given the strong attachment to land as the embodiment of the soul of the family and tribe.[7] "Trusteeship" comes closer to the essence of rangatiratanga, in that a trustee holds such property in trust for future generations and would not give or sell it to others for their permanent and exclusive use. (Ian Kawharu defines *rangatira* as "a trustee for his people, an entrepreneur in all their enterprises.")[8]

Yet the sale of lands and other property by Maori to *pakeha* (literally, "imaginary beings with fair skins," and the Maori nonpejorative term for Europeans) was widespread in the nineteenth century and continued to a more limited degree in the twentieth century. Some of the sales were negotiated through less than honest means, but scholars such as Claudia Orange and D. F. McKenzie wonder whether Maori, especially in earlier times, could have been expected to understand the implications of any sale of property in the pakeha sense.[9]

One of the confounding problems with the treaty is that there is one version in Maori and another five (one of them "official") in English, and there are several important respects in which the versions differ. One difference is especially important where broadcasting is concerned. Article 2 assures the chiefs of the rangatiratanga of "full possession of their lands, their homes and all their possessions" (Maori version), while four of the five English versions are far more explicit, speaking of "full, exclusive and undisturbed possession of their Lands and Estates, Forests, Fisheries and other properties which they may collectively or individually possess," but adding that the chiefs "yield to Her Majesty [Queen Victoria] the exclusive right of Pre-emption over such lands as the proprietors thereof may be disposed to alienate, at such prices as may be agreed upon." The Maori version does not use the word "Pre-emption" but states that the "chiefs yield to the Queen the right to alienate such lands which the owners desire to dispose of."[10] Furthermore, the Maori version uses the word *taonga* for "possessions," and that term can embrace just about everything conceivable, including the Maori language, the speaking of the language, and the air through which speech travels.

The treaty became a largely forgotten document by the end of the nineteenth century. The land wars that broke out soon after the signing of the treaty saw at least as many Maori victories as defeats, but the net result was the widespread loss of Maori lands. Maori now formed a small minority in their own country, and their faith in the treaty destroyed, they virtually ceased to evoke it. The dimension of mutual respect that was the cornerstone of the treaty was replaced by assimilation, and the term "brown-skinned pakeha" neatly expressed the feelings of many pakeha. Maori language and customs might continue, but as younger generations came along, they would see and adopt a pakeha way of life, with all of its benefits. Within two decades, broadcasting would be a part of that way of life.

The Birth of Broadcasting

Despite the fact that Maori were the tangata whenua, or original settlers of Aotearoa/New Zealand, and still constituted between 5 and 10 percent of the population as of the early 1920s, the broad-casting systems that developed during the decade found no place for transmissions in Maori, aside from occasional songs and chants. The private stations that evolved and operated locally starting in 1921 were the result of pakeha investment. They were staffed by and intended for pakeha audiences, although Maori were welcome to listen. The government licensed and regulated them, simply assumed that programming would be in English, and did not require or even encourage broadcasting in Maori.[11]

A national network developed in 1926. It operated alongside the individual private stations and, like them, was licensed by the government, which collected license fees from listeners and passed five-sixths of the proceeds to a private controlling entity, the Radio Broadcasting Company (RBC). But the national scale of the RBC did not bring with it any greater attention to broadcasting in or for Maori. Like the individual private stations, the RBC stations initially were limited to 500 watts. Most Maori lived in rural areas, out of reach of daytime signals, and relatively few could have afforded radio sets, in any case. Furthermore, there was no official encouragement of the use of Maori in *any* institutional setting, and even a fair measure of unofficial discouragement, particularly by schools. As Professor Ranginui Walker observes, "In 1905 the Inspector of Native Schools instructed teachers to encourage children to speak only English in school playgrounds. This instruction was translated into a general prohibition of the Maori language within school precincts. For the next five decades the prohibition was in some instances enforced by corporeal punishment."[12]

There were occasional brief broadcasts in Maori by the late 1920s, generally in the form of cultural artifacts, but in isolated instances taking the form of a "Radio Pageant of the Maori Race," or on the nature and correct pronunciation of the Maori language.[13] A special broadcast "message of goodwill" to overseas listeners in 1934 included a fragment in Maori, and a Maori princess spoke in Maori in a 1935 broadcast, but these were instances of a still-existent tendency to treat Maori culture as something quaint or curious.[14] Some of the private stations as well as the RBC began to employ Maori announcers during the early 1930s, but all of them spoke chiefly in English.

The 1936 consolidation of all broadcasting activity under one organization—the New Zealand Broadcasting Service—brought no immediate change with respect to Maori broadcasts, which remained brief and largely irregular. In 1941, the MP for the northern Maori electoral district (there are four such districts in New Zealand designated for Maori representation), Paraire Paikea, requested of the then prime minister, Peter Fraser, that there be a regular news program in Maori.[15] However, the first example of a regularly scheduled Maori language program did not appear until early 1942, and under unusual circumstances.

When New Zealand entered World War II in 1940, Maori enlisted in the armed forces in considerable numbers. As they began to appear on the battlefronts of North Africa, they attracted attention from some of the world press, and particularly from British and American reporters. Some of that attention found its way back to New Zealand, where Maori families already were asking for more information about the activities of Maori soldiers. Broadcast administrators decided to initiate a weekly Sunday night program in Maori, in which names of Maori killed in battle would be announced. That program soon evolved into a five-minute news program in Maori, in large part to ensure that Maori would be better informed about the war effort and why their support for it was essential. The announcer chosen to deliver the death announcements and then the news, Wiremu Parker, continued that activity until 1972, but the news in Maori also remained the sole regularly scheduled national program broadcast in Maori until 1964, when "The Maori Programme" (discussion, interview, and entertainment) came on air with Parker as host.[16]

There were Maori words used in many broadcasts, however. Most of the geographical features of New Zealand, as well as many towns, bore Maori names. In many instances, their pronunciations had been altered over time, in some cases almost beyond recognition. Newscasters, sportscasters, and weathercasters alike, if they were pakeha, tended to use the altered pronunciations, much to the displeasure of Maori listeners.

A few broadcast administrators and stations were more sensitive to the matter of correct pronunciation. In 1934, announcers Clive Drummond and Arch Curry were commended by a former superintendent of Maori education for their attempts at correct pronunciation. He observed that "With ever-improving speech due largely to radio, it would be absurd for Maori only to be impure."[17] The Reverend C. G. Scrimgeour, director of the National Commercial Radio Service from 1936 to 1943, took note of disagreements in the Auckland newspapers regarding proper pronunciation of Maori place names. When the Auckland commercial station came on the air in 1937, it ran a series of broadcasts on correct use of Maori. Scrimgeour also appointed a Maori vocalist, Uramo Paora, as announcer for the Auckland station, and as further stations opened in Wellington, Christchurch, and Dunedin, they also employed Maori announcers. Scrimgeour commented that he wished "to develop Maori sessions [programs] not alone as entertainment, but also to contribute something of permanent benefit to the Maori race. ... Recordings have been made of chants and songs that were in danger of becoming lost."[18]

But Scrimgeour's policy did not ensure correct pronunciation. In part that was because some of the pakeha staff felt the need to respond to criticism from listeners who preferred the mispronounced place names with which they had grown up and to which they were accustomed. Pakeha poet Denis Glover gave sarcastic expression to their discontent in his poem "Prayers in Prejudice":

> From cinesound and the reducer's ounces,
> From the meticulous Maori of announcers,
> ... The Lord preserve us.[19]

Sportscasters in particular were quite stubborn in their adherence to pakeha pronunciations.[20] Similar problems continued through the 1960s (indeed, they continue to this day), and in 1967 a New Zealand Broadcasting Corporation (NZBC—the retitled [1962] New Zealand Broadcasting Service) policy that allowed the anglicization of some Maori place names to correspond with "local usage" drew strong opposition from certain Maori leaders.[21] In addition, there was a readiness to shield Maori listeners from controversial items, as with the South African tour of New Zealand's All Blacks rugby squad in 1960, from which Maori players were to be excluded in deference to the South African policy of apartheid. The minister for broadcasting, R. Boord, defended the decision to not refer to the controversy over the tour in the Maori newscast.[22]

The Rise of Maori Activism

The period of the late 1960s to the early 1970s was one of considerable turmoil in New Zealand, first over the issue of New Zealand's involvement in the Vietnam War, and then over pakeha society's treatment of minority groups.[23] Although South Pacific islanders were included in the latter, Maori clearly predominated. And, while a number of pakeha became involved in minority group causes, the main thrust of activity came from within the groups themselves. Media coverage of their activities tended to emphasize more "militant" aspects: stone throwing, occupancy of vacant housing, verbal threats, and calls for restoration of property rights over what were held to be Maori lands. Some of the individuals and groups were inspired by the examples of Black Power leaders in the United States.[24] Several groups bore vivid names, for example, Nga Tamatoa (the Young Warriors), or the Stormtroopers, making it easier for the media to play up the more confrontational aspects of the situation.

Maori society had changed greatly over the period since the beginning of broadcasting. In the early 1920s, some 85 percent of all Maori lived in rural areas, and the majority of pakeha society had little or no contact with them. By the early 1970s, the figures were nearly the opposite, although many pakeha still had little personal daily contact with Maori. The media formed a surrogate level of contact, however, and provided pakeha society with images of poverty, ignorance, disease, and violence.[25] Maori media were almost nonexistent: two newsletters of modest nationwide circulation, *Te Hokioi* (the War Bird) and *MOOHR* (published by the Maori Organization on Human Rights).[26]

Maori did consider the possibility of utilizing radio, and in the early 1970s perceived a window of opportunity. The government had decided to review the performance of the again-retitled national service, the Broadcasting Corporation of New Zealand (BCNZ), and in 1973 the committee appointed to carry out the review (the Adam Committee, so named for its chair, Kenneth Adam, of BBC Television) made its report. Where Maori and South Pacific Islander services were concerned—and considerable numbers of each group had testified before the committee[27]—it recommended that a commercial station be established in Auckland to serve those communities of listeners.[28] The station would operate within the framework of BCNZ but raise its own revenue—a financing source of doubtful utility, given the depressed economic situation of its primary audience.

BCNZ professed some interest in the project, even to the point of ordering a transmitter,[29] and some members of the Labour government then in power worked to prepare legislation to authorize initial financing of the station; but it did not appear to be a high priority for either entity.[30] Labor was voted out of office in the 1975 election, and the incoming National (Conservative) government halted the project as a waste of public funds.[31] However, a commercial station, Radio Pacific, came on the air in Auckland in 1979 and began offering programs intended for Maori and Pacific Islanders (e.g., Tongans), some of them presented in the indigenous languages.[32]

If any pakeha had been unaware of Maori activism during that period, the Land March of 1975 almost certainly altered their perception. Whina Cooper, an 80-year-old Maori woman, led a march of several hundred, and at times a few thousand, Maori from Te Hapua in the far north to the nation's capital, Wellington—a distance of roughly 600 miles. The march was intended to call the public's attention to Maori claims for better housing and for restoration of land rights, and Whina Cooper proved to be a vivid symbolic presentation of those grievances. (Photographs of her leading the march continue to this day to appear as posters and in historical anthologies.) However, the presentation continued to come almost entirely through pakeha-run media.

In 1978, Radio New Zealand (RNZ—BCNZ's radio and television operations were separated in 1975, although BCNZ remained in charge of both) created a Maori and Pacific Islander unit, Te Reo o Aotearoa (the Voice of Aotearoa) and placed the unit in Auckland, which has the country's largest concentration of Maori and Pacific islanders. By mid-1985, the unit was producing several programs in Maori: two daily news broadcasts of 4 and 5 minutes, a Sunday news program of 12 minutes, a Sunday 18-minute feature program on events in Maoridom, and a Wednesday 10-minute background program on current events. It also prepared four programs (about Maori news, background to Maori events, and Maori culture) weekly in English.[33] While that effort represented a notable quantitative increase in airtime devoted to programs about and in Maori, it also represented a quantitative drop in the bucket compared with programming by and for the pakeha audience—perhaps 1 percent of the total radio broadcast hours per week.

Maori activism continued through the late 1970s and early 1980s, as did generally negative coverage of it by the media. A Maori group occupied the Takaparawhe (Bastion Point) area of Auckland during over 500 days in 1977–1978, claiming that it was Maori land and protesting the government's decision to subdivide and sell it. The group was removed by force in May 1978, with television cameras recording the expulsion and subsequent crushing of the occupants' temporary housing by bulldozers. In 1979, there was a clash between a group of young Maori (He Taua, or "War Party") and some Auckland University engineering students over the latter's staging of another of its annual *haka* parties, in which the students dressed as mock Maori warriors and defiled Maori custom. The media generally transformed the clash into an attack by an organized Maori gang, held the engineers largely blameless, and accused Maori of being overly sensitive to the alleged mockery.[34]

The early 1980s saw several manifestations of interest on the part of Radio New Zealand in encouraging Maori broadcasting.[35] RNZ and its parent corporation, BCNZ, commissioned an in-depth survey of Maori attitudes toward Te Reo o Aotearoa and toward the concept of Maori radio. With the appointment of Beverly Wakem as director general of RNZ in

1984, Maori acquired a strong advocate. Wakem, herself of Lebanese ancestry, was ready to push for an expansion of Maori involvement within RNZ's programming units and for RNZ assistance to Maori groups that wished to establish separate stations.

However, she and other like-minded RNZ staff faced considerable opposition within RNZ, where many colleagues, junior and senior alike, did not relish the prospect of change.[36] There also was opposition from above, particularly in the late 1970s and early 1980s, from a member and sometime deputy chairman of BCNZ's governing board, Jim Freeman. Freeman enjoyed close ties with the then ruling National party and was reportedly a strong supporter of full assimilation of Maori in pakeha society: the "brown-skinned pakeha." He also was reported to have told several of his friends that he would never countenance the formation of a separate Maori radio service, within or outside of RNZ.[37]

In 1984, a number of leading Maori assembled in a *hui taumata,* or Maori "economic summit conference." One outcome of the meeting was an investigation by a Maori committee of the possibility of establishing a Maori-operated radio station. The committee's report appeared in June 1985; it saw such a station as both feasible and desirable. The station would be financed through a government appropriation and would be separate from Radio New Zealand, although it would maintain a close working relationship with RNZ. It also would maintain close ties with what was hoped would be a number of private Maori stations around the country, although it would eventually create a network of its own, with stations in Auckland, Wellington, and Christchurch. Above all, it would seek to involve Maori directly in the broadcasts, to lead Maori tribal groups and organizations to "feel that they are participants in shaping the destiny for the network."[38] The station would broadcast in both English and Maori.

The proposal was welcomed by some Maori, but certainly not all. There was criticism of the network system, on the grounds that iwi (tribes) throughout the country had sufficiently different needs, customs, accents, and other cultural differences that a system based on individual stations, with some network programming to occupy a minority of airtime, would be preferable. Others felt that the most important role of Maori radio would be to restore or strengthen the everyday use of Maori by young and old alike; while it was true that most young Maori spoke English with greater fluency than they did Maori (if they could speak the latter at all, which many could not), regular usage of the language would be promoted far more quickly and efficiently if broadcasts were in Maori alone.[39]

While discussions of the proposal continued, some Maori were taking matters into their own hands. In 1981, Radio New Zealand created an access radio station in Wellington by taking the broadcast time that was not used for the transmission of parliamentary sessions, freeing up some studio and office space in the RNZ building, and making a few hundred thousand dollars available to the access station for staff salaries and equipment. Community groups could apply for the use of airtime, generally for ongoing broadcasts rather than for single appearances. A number of Maori groups in and around Wellington took advantage of the opportunity and began to broadcast, generally in English.

A more significant harbinger of things to come was the use made by one Maori organization of the provision in the Broadcasting Act of 1976 authorizing short-term broadcasting by virtually any group that could show that it had a specific purpose in mind and the financing and staff necessary to execute it. A number of student groups at universities quickly took advantage of the provision, but they did not broadcast for the entire calendar year. A Maori organization in Wellington, Nga Kaiwhakapumau i te Reo (Wellington Maori Language Board), arranged with the student radio service at Victoria University, Radio Active, to have the use of its studios for the period August 4–8, 1983. Radio New Zealand provided further technical help, some studio space of its own, and the services of a producer. As a result, the experiment cost only NZ $1,300 (about U.S. $800). While English was permitted, especially to reach younger listeners, Maori predominated. A few veteran Maori broadcasters, including Wiremu Parker, took program slots. The broadcasts coincided with the annual Maori Language Week; one of the station staff stated that "Our aim is that Maori language week last the whole year."[40]

It was some time before that aim could be realized. The "on loan" producer for RNZ's Continuing Education Unit, Piripi Walker, reported in testimony to the Waitangi Tribunal in October 1990 that the staff was exhausted by the end of the five-day period. Furthermore, it had proven difficult to raise even the modest sum necessary to operate the short-term service.[41] Inspired by the success of the Wellington venture, Walker organized short-term experimental services in 1985 and 1986 in his own tribal area through Te Reo o Raukawa, or "the Voice of Raukawa." He succeeded in developing a great deal of enthusiasm among the young people who formed the mainstay of the staff, but some of them became critical of the reluctance of tribal officials and elders to raise money for a proper bid on an FM frequency.[42]

The Wellington experiment, now called Te Upoko o te Ika,* received another permit to broadcast short-term in May and June of 1987. The two-month experiment again was supported in part by loans of staff and equip-

* "The head of the fish," which Maui caught in Maori legend; the head is the site of present-day Wellington.

ment from RNZ, and again was volunteer-staffed and exhausting. However, the length of time it was on the air and its access to a more powerful transmitter brought it to the attention of a wider listenership: 25 percent of the Maori population and 5 percent of the overall population in the listening area, according to an unofficial survey conducted through a BCNZ commercial station.[43] Nga Kaiwhakapumau i te Reo conducted a survey of its own through a newspaper questionnaire and received nearly 250 replies, almost all of them from Maori, who indicated strong support for the station and who felt that it was helpful in encouraging Maori to speak their own language. One respondent wrote, "It made me feel at home at last," while another said "I wasn't a stranger in my own country."[44]

The station staff took stock of their accomplishments and problems, engaged in fund-raising (churches, tribal organizations, and prominent Maori entertainers proved to be the best sources), and came on the air in April 1988, this time to stay. The Maori Access Employment Training Programme helped the station to pay small stipends to volunteers—important because unemployment among Maori, according to some estimates, was running as high as 40 percent, and even a small stipend helped to encourage maximum staff effort and reliability.

The Third Television Channel

In 1985, the Labour government announced that it would accept bids on a third nationwide television service. There were several interested parties; most were associated with private industry, but there was one major exception: a Maori group, the Aotearoa Broadcasting Trust. The trust was founded by the Maori Council, which had been developed with the passage of the Maori Welfare Act in 1962.[45] The trust claimed several unique characteristics: it was the only bidder to offer a real programming alternative to the two existing services; it would pose less of a threat of competition for the funds (largely advertising) that supported the two existing channels than would the other, more commercially minded, bidders; and it would be one way in which New Zealand's pakeha society could show some sense of fairness in providing Maori with access to a medium that had been pakeha-dominated.

The BCNZ decided to join with the trust in making the bid and agreed to help finance the service, should the license be granted to the two partners. But BCNZ later backed out of the arrangement and bid for the license on its own. The trust had been able to secure pledges of financial support, largely from various Maori individuals and organizations, but it could not obtain the sum necessary to show that it would be a viable operation, and its bid was not accepted.

In the meantime, and perhaps because of embarrassment over its withdrawal from the Channel 3 application,[46] BCNZ managed to rearrange its budget so that several hundred thousand dollars could be put into the establishment of a Maori radio station in Auckland, perhaps as the flagship station of a national Maori radio network. That station, Radio Aotearoa, came on the air in fall 1988 for a six-week trial period, and then permanently in June 1989, with an eight-hour daily service in Maori and English and a largely pop music format. The station was advised by a Maori Radio Board, which had been appointed by BCNZ; it transformed itself into the Aotearoa Maori Radio Trust in 1989, following a restructuring of public broadcasting.[47]

The Development of the Iwi Stations

There had been some disagreement among Maori as to the best way to establish a Maori radio service. The Maori Economic Development Commission report argues for a national network with a flagship station, while an independent report ("A Global Approach to Maori Radio Development," May 1987), by a Maori group that included Piripi Walker, opts for a locally based system.[48] The report does not reject the idea of a national service but sees it in terms of RNZ's modestly scaled Te Reo o Aotearoa and feels that its major role would be to retain a Maori perspective within RNZ.[49] The local stations would reflect the views of individual *hapu* (subtribes) and iwi, with some sharing of material as appropriate.

Money would come from a 5 percent share of the audience license fee, which Maori and pakeha alike paid, and also from advertising and from the governmentally appointed Board of Maori Affairs (the last-named would fund capital expenditures). Station staff would receive salaries roughly equivalent to those in commercial radio and RNZ. Frequencies would be allotted to the new stations on the principle of fair shares between Maori and pakeha. Finally, the stations would be separate from RNZ and fully under Maori control.

Both forms of broadcasting—tribal and national—were on the scene by 1988. Radio Aotearoa was drawing criticism from some quarters because it programmed too little in Maori (only one staff member was fluent in the language) and appeared to be competing for audience with several Auckland pop music stations.[50] The station justified the approach on the grounds that it particularly hoped to reach young urban Maori.[51] Te Upoko o te Ika technically was iwi, with two tribes as major supporters and others as minor supporters, but it was Wellington-based, and thus hardly represented a typical tribal situation. A number of iwi had conducted short-term experiments with radio, but monetary and staffing problems kept them from establishing themselves more permanently.

However, in 1989 a few of the short-term operations pulled together enough resources to secure full-time temporary broadcast licenses (the last stage before requesting a permanent, or 20-year, license). Two of them were interesting demonstrations of a will to succeed in the face of adverse circumstances. Radio Ngati Porou, based in Ruatoria on the east coast, was in the heart of a major Maori area and faced little competition from any other radio stations because of the area's remoteness. It came into being in part because of several acts of arson in the area and received assistance from a private commercial station (Radio Waikato) and, later, BCNZ. The area also was economically depressed, and the station's founders had to be exceptionally imaginative in scraping together old equipment and housing. Thanks to its enlistment of a large number of volunteers (including the local pub owner, who would leave his post behind the bar each day to walk over to the station for his air shift) and wide variety of Maori-oriented and -generated material it broadcast, it soon ingratiated itself with its community and in September 1991 received a permanent (20-year) license—the first to be granted to an iwi station.[52]

Tautoko-FM radio in Mangamuka Bridge (population about 150) was almost as remotely located as was Radio Ngati Porou, and the area was nearly as poor. But the impulse came from a much narrower group—several Rastafarians who loved to play and sing Rasta music, especially reggae. They felt that having a radio outlet might bring them to the attention of others, which might lead to employment (all were unemployed). By saving money from their unemployment checks and borrowing equipment or buying used equipment at low cost (sometimes with BCNZ's assistance), as well as taking over an unused shack, they managed to get themselves on the air for a short-term experiment. People from the region, in the far north, took to the station's amateur but entertaining programming and began to provide small amounts of money and their own time as volunteers. Tautoko finally secured a temporary license in 1989 and moved into a better facility in fall 1991, and an even better one two years later.[53]

The Broadcasting Act of 1989

As more Maori broadcasting became available, Maori themselves gained increasing confidence in their cause. In May 1989, the Labour government won passage of a new broadcasting act, which replaced the Broadcasting Act of 1976. The major change was in the creation of a Broadcasting Standards Authority (responsible for maintaining advertising and programmatic standards and hearing complaints about either) and a Broadcasting Commission (responsible for encouraging programming that would enhance development of a New Zealand identity). Both bodies would be financed through shares of the Public Broadcasting Fee revenue. The authority had no specific mandate where Maori interests were concerned, but the commission (also known as New Zealand on Air) was given specific responsibility for "Promoting Maori language and culture" and "Consult[ing] from time to time with [r]epresentatives of Maori interests."[54] Furthermore, the commission had real power at its disposal: it was the disbursal agent for the roughly NZ $80 million (1990 figure) collected through the Public Broadcasting Fee. Where Maori broadcasting was concerned, there was a further stipulation by the government that at least 6 percent of the fee money be devoted to that activity.[55] Radio Aotearoa would now be supported through funding provided by the commission—roughly NZ $1.45 million a year. Te Upoko o te Ika would receive just over NZ $400,000. But there was money available for other initiatives, and they soon appeared.

One of the concerns expressed by Maori was lack of access to topical information about Maori life throughout the country. The Broadcasting Commission retained the services of Derek Fox, the first Maori to deliver the news in Maori on television,[56] and Piripi Whaanga, another Maori broadcaster, to study and make recommendations on the creation of a national Maori news service. It was the commission's intention to finance such a service, if at all possible. Fox and Whaanga's recommendations led to the creation of Mana Maori Media in May 1990. Roughly NZ $650,000 was made available for its operation, and it also received financing from RNZ for providing a daily newsmagazine to RNZ. Fox and Whaanga were its cofounders; it soon developed bureaus in Rotorua (the headquarters), Papatoetoe (a suburb of Auckland), and Wellington. The various iwi stations were invited to contribute items to its daily Maori and English newscasts, although Whaanga noted in a 1993 interview that he felt that the iwi stations hadn't really received all that much encouragement from Mana Maori Media.[57]

The Broadcasting Commission still had some NZ $1.4 million to disburse on specific projects. (It chose to place just under NZ $600,000 in a Maori Broadcasting Fund for future disbursal.) Just over half of that sum went into a networking system (StarLink) that would provide electronic linkages between iwi stations. The remainder went into iwi capital development for radio in general, and specific allotments of NZ $65,000 each to the four smaller iwi stations then on the air. That sum was not large, but the commission's annual report for 1989–1990 held promise of better things to come when it noted that stations would be eligible for as much as NZ $200,000 in annual operating costs and as much as NZ $100,000 in capital grants for transmission and studio facilities.[58] However, those figures were far below the projected operating costs for iwi stations as set forth in the 1987 report "A Global Approach to Maori Radio Development," and clearly other funding sources were assumed, as well as considerable volunteer support. The commission made this explicit in its *New Zealand on Air Newsletter* in mid-1991: "One of the factors that we will take into account is the broadcaster's ability to generate revenue from sources other than New Zealand on Air. We will expect broadcasters to supplement our funding from the community or from advertising revenues. Our aim is that over time broadcasters will be able to generate an increasing portion of the funds required to maintain the service themselves."[59]

The National Party and Maori Radio

The need for other sources of support seemed about to become even more urgent after October 1990, when the National party defeated Labour and took over the reins of government. Labour tradition-ally had been seen by Maori as friendlier to their interests than was National, although the party recently had begun to dismantle many of the social support programs that had contributed to its image as the party of the people. Also, to the extent that it chose to exercise power to influence broadcasting policy during its most recent turn at governing New Zealand (1984–1990), that influence appeared to have gone only a limited distance in answering Maori demands for a major budgetary commitment to Maori broadcasting.[60] Labour was moving increasingly in the direction of a private enterprise approach, where most broadcast operations would be expected to pay their own way.[61]

The National party victory led to an acceleration of the Labour-initi-ated "free market/user pays" approach. It was described by some New Zealanders as "leaner and meaner Reaganomics," with most of the remaining elements of Labor's social support system now marked for extinction. Derek Fox already had commented that Labor seemed to be telling the Maori, "We've deregulated the market, go get 'em!" But the traditional policy of excluding or limiting Maori involvement in broadcasting meant that Maori generally lacked the expertise and financial support to get 'em.[62] Now the National government seemed ready to tighten the purse strings even more.

But the National government, sensing Maori disenchantment with Labour, decided not to pull back on commitments made through the Broad-casting Commission. It sought to gain favor with Maori by making a number of public declarations of support for Maori broadcasting services, most notably in calling a series of *hui* (conferences) on radio and on television.[63] The levels of funding made available for Maori radio through the Broad-casting Commission actually increased from NZ $4.6 million to $6.3 million, and the commission projected an expenditure of $7.8 million for fiscal year 1992.[64] Still more iwi stations came on the air, and by September 1991 there were 16 of them plus Radio Aotearoa, with two or three more likely over the next several months. All qualified for at least some Broadcasting Commission support.

In January 1991, the minister of communications, Maurice Williamson, had set forth a major policy statement on "Broadcasting, Te Reo [the Maori language], and the Future." In it, he reaffirms the National party–led government's commitment to the further development of Maori broadcasting. He also notes that he had provisionally approved certain policy guidelines for use by the Ministry of Commerce in allocating radio frequencies for Maori stations. The guidelines indicate that

> a. long-term licenses would be issued only where there has been at least some prior use of the reserved frequency on a short-term basis;
> b. long-term licenses will be issued with the condition that the broadcaster using the frequency must have as its principal objective the promotion of Maori language and culture, and the programming of the radio station must be directed primarily at a Maori audience;
> c. the holder of any long-term license issued in respect of such reserved frequencies must be a recognized iwi organization in the area concerned; and
> d. no restrictions concerning advertising or sponsorship will be attached to licenses.[65]

Two aspects of those guidelines are particularly noteworthy. The lack of restrictions on advertising or sponsorship stemmed from a National party philosophy, shared to a considerable degree by Labour, that broadcasting should pay its own way. Whether or not there was a reasonable expectation of such support for Maori broadcasting—and indications were that there was not—wasn't the issue. Rather, it served as a reminder that Maori radio should not expect to be a continuing recipient of government funding.*

The second aspect, involving iwi retention of broadcast licenses, stemmed from a more nonpartisan political philosophy that saw great wis-

---

*However, interviews with Department of Commerce official David Harcourt (senior adviser) in Wellington in September 1991 and October 1993 indicated a continuing commitment on the part of the government to make available at least 6 percent of the license fee revenue for the support of Maori radio, with a further 5 percent (approximately) for television. In fact, New Zealand on Air funding of all types of Maori broadcast activities came to roughly 14 percent of license fee revenues each year from 1989 through 1994. Time will tell whether or not that figure will change, now that a Maori funding agency (Te Mangai Paho) has taken charge (as of January 1, 1995) of funding of Maori electronic media activities, but a drastic change seems unlikely.

dom in working through iwi as a way to avoid controversy. Politicians from all parties were well aware that there were differences of opinion within iwi.[66] If a license were to be awarded to what turned out to be one side in an intratribal dispute, the government itself well might be accused of taking sides.[67] However, several of the Maori broadcasters with whom I spoke suggested that the government saw most iwi governing structures (usually tribal trusts) as generally more conservative than most Maori, and thus perhaps a useful check on the use of radio to express more extreme political views.[68]

The Treaty
of Waitangi
and
Broadcasting

The campaign for Maori broadcasting rights throughout the 1970s and 1980s often was based upon the rights guaranteed to Maori under the terms of the jointly negotiated Treaty of Waitangi. When Maori first began to seriously challenge pakeha domination of broadcasting back in the early 1970s, they claimed that the treaty gave them rights to use of the airwaves, even though broadcasting had not existed in 1840. (The claim has been made that Maori with powerful voices used the airwaves to communicate over considerable distances, in some cases well before 1840.)[69] Whether the airwaves were taonga or not was only one part of the overall question: was the treaty a partnership, or was it not?* In 1975, the Labor government, moved in part by its allegedly greater sympathy with Maori causes, established the Waitangi Tribunal; its task was to adjudicate claims made by Maori under the terms of the treaty, and then to make recommendations to Parliament for their settlement.[70]

Shortly after the tribunal was established, Labour was voted out of office, and the tribunal remained essentially inactive until Labour returned to

---

*Wilson describes an instance of Maori-pakeha cooperation that backfired on the Maori. In 1979, the Taranaki iwi made a *koha* (gift or donation) of the sacred Mount Taranaki to the nation, Maori and pakeha alike. But when the iwi began to broadcast, the government charged it for the installation and annual costs of a transmitter located on the mountain! Wilson, Helen, "Whakarongo mai e nga iwi: Maori Radio," in Wilson, Helen, ed., *The Radio Book, 1994,* Christchurch: New Zealand Broadcasting School/Christchurch Polytechnic, 1994, 100–101.

power in 1984, although a 1983 tribunal decision on the likely pollution of traditional Maori fishing grounds by a proposed synthetic fuels plant supported the Maori claim and held the promise that something might come of the tribunal's decisions, after all.[71] The primary barrier to the tribunal's effectiveness was the provision that the only cases that could be considered were the ones occurring after passage of the act authorizing the tribunal. Labour erased that barrier in 1985, spurred by what Ranginui Walker feels were its diminishing "colonial ethos" and by the possibility that Maori might form their own political party.[72]

The first case involving broadcasting, Te Reo Maori (the Maori language), came to the tribunal in 1986 as part of a larger case involving a request for official standing for the Maori language. The tribunal did not make specific recommendations on broadcasting, but it did note that "it is consistent with the principles of the Treaty that the language and matters of Maori interest should have a secure place in broadcasting; and (d) in the formulation of broadcasting policy regard must be had to the finding that the Treaty of Waitangi obliges the Crown to recognise and protect the Maori language."[73]

The tribunal withheld a more specific recommendation on broadcasting because the Royal Commission on Broadcasting was already meeting to consider recommendations for future policy on broadcasting. The commission released its report in September 1986 and argued for a larger place for Maori programming as part of mainstream broadcasting, but especially public broadcasting. At one point, the report states "There is no doubt in our minds as to the validity of the demands for a greater share of the resources of broadcasting and the benefits of bi-culturalism."[74]

The Maori Assets Case

Shortly after release of its recommendations on Te Reo Maori, the tribunal was asked to reopen a portion of that case, specifically to consider as one issue the failure of BCNZ to carry out its financial agreement with the Aotearoa Broadcasting Trust (discussed earlier in this chapter), which the claimant (Nga Kaiwhakapumau i te Reo) held to be an action of the Crown contrary to the principles of the treaty. In the initial stages of inquiry on this claim (Wai 26), the tribunal received another claim on June 6, 1990, related to broadcasting (Wai 150), from the same source. It combined the two claims and dealt with them as one.

In 1989, the Labour government had proposed and won passage of the Radiocommunications Act of 1989. That act said very little about Maori broadcasting,[75] aside from possible use of a portion of airtime on Wellington Access Radio channel 2YB and a minimum level (52 hours a year by third year of operation) of Maori programming for TV3.[76] The claimants objected to the act on the grounds that it assumed Crown jurisdiction over a resource that was part of rangatiratanga. More specifically, "(iii) where any property or part of the universe has value as a cultural asset ... the Crown has an obligation under the Treaty of Waitangi to recognise and guarantee Maori rangatiratanga over its allocation and use for that purpose; (b) the sale of frequency management licenses under the [act] without negotiating an agreement with Maori would be in breach of the Treaty ... and prejudicial to the interests of Maori."[77] The claimants further pressed for an urgent hearing, since the government proposed to sell licenses in August 1990. The request was granted, and 10 sessions of hearings were held between October 23 and November 12, 1990. Meanwhile, the government deferred the sale of licenses.

The tribunal made its report on November 27, 1990. It took note of the fact that the government had already reserved radio frequencies for Maori use in 28 geographical areas. However, it also observed that the Ministry of Commerce had determined the frequencies on the basis of technical considerations, which failed to take into account specific needs of iwi: whether AM or FM should be used, where the best transmitter sites would be for service to specific iwi, whether one technology might be more cost-efficient than another, among other considerations.[78] Furthermore, iwi appeared to have received mixed signals from the government as to how quickly they would need to act in order to obtain any meaningful modifications of the government's proposal.[79] The tribunal felt that the government had in effect given the impression that there was little to be negotiated: "Our view that these perceptions were valid is reinforced not only by the bringing of this claim, but by the fact that so many Maori came from distant parts to express their concerns and their frustrations to us, and to try and find out what was happening."[80] It recommended that the Crown suspend the process of taking bids on frequencies "for a period of six months ... to allow further consultation with iwi to take place," that it make experienced, independent technical advisors available to iwi, and that it make available FM frequencies in Auckland and Wellington,[81] where the existing

Maori stations were confined to AM broadcasting, which was rapidly losing listeners to FM stations.

The tribunal made one observation that endorsed the concept of iwi-based stations when it said,

> consultation must recognise (as in this case it does) that Maori are not a homogeneous group and that the Treaty talks of tribes rather than an amorphous body now called "Maoridom." The protection of tino rangatiratanga means that iwi and hapu must be able to express their autonomy in the maintenance and development of their language and their culture. This inevitably involves taking more time over the consultation process, but this may prove a refreshing experience and an opportunity to get it right the first time, in pragmatic terms. We would be surprised if the general New Zealand population considered this would be detrimental.[82]

The National Party and the Treaty

The National party took power just as the tribunal reached its decision. It agreed to delay the sale of licenses until July 1991. In the meantime, iwi had the opportunity to study options and to present their requests, and because Maori broadcasting had already spread throughout much of the North Island (only the Christchurch area in the South Island had a Maori station), more iwi seemed disposed to consider developing a radio station: over 40 expressed some interest in having one. Minister of Broadcasting Maurice Williamson drew upon the discussions arising out of the four hui on the future of Maori radio held between February 9 and March 16, 1991, as well as of three hui on Maori television during July 1991, in issuing an invitation to Maori to attend a hui on the future of Maori broadcasting, to be held in Wellington in mid-September. He noted that the pace of further progress would depend upon the outcome of a Court of Appeals hearing to be held on October 29. That appeal had been brought by Maori who were objecting to the transfer of BCNZ assets to a nongovernmental organization that would carry out the same functions.

In the meantime, the minister released a booklet entitled "Maori Broadcasting: Principles for the Future" at the end of August 1991.[83] In it he highlights the work program he was proposing for Maori broadcasting over the next year. One of its most significant elements is the inclusion of a proposal for the establishment of a Maori broadcasting funding agency, but the minister does not provide details on how it would operate or how (and how strongly) it would be funded; instead, he calls for suggestions from Maori.

The agency that eventually was created by act of Parliament,[84] Te Reo Whakapuaka Irirangi (later renamed Te Mangai Paho), featured a board composed of several distinguished Maori: businesspeople, academics, and political figures. It held hearings around the country in 1993 and 1994, inviting a number of Maori broadcasters, as well as other individuals, to discuss possible lines of approach and priorities. Some of the broadcasters expressed the fear that, since the board members were members of many other boards and councils, they might not be able to devote the time to the task that it would seem to require, with uncertain consequences for the media services themselves.[85]

As for sources of financial support, the license fee would continue to be shared, with Te Mangai Paho in charge of the portion devoted to Maori electronic media; however, the increase in such media activity, coupled with the slow growth of license fee revenues and the effects of inflation, would mean fewer dollars per operation, on average. The agency sought advice from Maori and pakeha alike: advertising, sponsorship, and several other categories were suggested, but all had the usual mix of advantages and drawbacks, and none emerged as the chief alternative source as of 1995.

At the end of 1993, a major legal issue was resolved, at least for the time being: the matter of broadcast frequencies as Maori assets. The New Zealand Court of Appeals issued its judgement on the case on April 30, 1992. It held that, although there was a great deal of evidence to support criticism of the government's restructuring policy, there also was nothing in law that could force the government to abandon the structures already in place under that policy. Therefore, the right of government to dispose of its assets in this case—control over the broadcast frequencies—was upheld, by a 3-1 vote.[86] Robin Cooke, president of the Court of Appeals, dissented, mainly on the grounds that the court could not, in his opinion, avoid judging that the policy itself was inconsistent with the principles of the Treaty of Waitangi.[87] The government earlier had offered to help fund (NZ $13 million) the development of a Maori UHF channel.

The group of Maori plaintiffs decided to take the case to the court of last resort—the British Privy Council, which was rarely used by Commonwealth members and never had been in a case involving broadcasting. That hearing finally took place in October 1993, and the council's decision appeared on December 13, 1993. It upheld the government's action but reminded the government that it *did* have some remaining control over TV New Zealand, despite its transfer of some NZ $137 million to TVNZ as a Self Operated Enterprise (SOE). That being so, should the government fail to honor its pledge to help support a separate Maori TV channel, the case could be reopened.[88]

In 1995–1996, another Marori assets case arose. The government announced in June 1995 that it was ready to sell the commercial arm of Radio New Zealand—41 stations scattered across the nation. Various Maori groups met with officials at the Treasury and the Ministry of Commerce and attempted without success to convince them to consider an approach which would involve a Maori-pakeha partnership for the use of the state's broadcasting assets. The Maori Council and other Maori groups then applied to the New Zealand High Court to stop the sale, on the grounds that the Treaty of Waitangi provisions on protecting Maori taonga had not been properly considered.[89] The Court agreed to hear the case, and it opened on March 25, 1996.

The Maori groups repeated their claims, stressing the desirability of using airtime on popular commercial stations to bring their language to the widest possible audience. The New Zealand Solicitor General rejected the challenge, on the grounds that there never had been a promise to promote the Maori language through RNZ's commercial stations; the stations were a "competitive business," and holding such assets in trust to promote Maori broadcasting was "completely contrary to any reasonable expectation or logic."[90] The High Court rejected the Maori claim, and on April 3 the government announced the sale of the stations to a consortium of interests.[91] The Maori groups then announced that they intended to challenge the ruling before the Privy Council, which might or might not accept the case. There matters stand, as of April 1996.

The Dominant Forces in the Rise of Maori Media

It is clear that several forces have been involved in the development of Maori broadcasting. In earlier years, those forces were dominated by pakeha and operated as if Maori culture, including the language, either did not exist or were irrelevant to New Zealand society. To the extent that most pakeha thought about Maori, they considered them in the light of assimilation—the "brown-skinned pakeha." Thus, a separate Maori radio service would simply delay the inevitable (and desirable). The 1930s saw little change in that approach, although the Reverend C. G. Scrimgeour acknowledged Maori presence and mana to a far greater degree than did the vast majority of his contemporaries, probably more because of his maverick nature and sympathy for the "have nots" of society than for anything connected with religious proselytizing.[92]

The Maori presence became important for very specific reasons in World War II. Younger Maori males could not very well escape military service, but they would serve more willingly if they and their families and friends were to feel that their efforts were acknowledged and appreciated by New Zealand society in general. Otherwise, it is doubtful that there would even have been the death announcements and then newscasts that came on the air in 1942. The fact that the government was led by the Labour party at the time was of no consequence, regardless of Labour's more favorable disposition toward Maori. The party held power from 1935 through 1949 but did nothing to favor Maori broadcasting.

The 1950s and 1960s brought no real changes in the situation where broadcasting was concerned, but the late 1960s saw the early manifestations of what would develop into full-blown Maori activism of the early 1970s. Yet the first substantial initiative by the government—again headed by Labor—came as the result of a committee report, and the committee was chaired by a Britisher. The Adam Committee's proposal for the creation of an Auckland-based commercial radio service for Maori and Pacific Islanders seems to have been inspired by the testimony it received from members of those groups. The Broadcasting Corporation of New Zealand showed modest interest in the proposal, but it was an issue of minor importance to the Labour party, which failed to advance legislation on the project before it was voted out of office in 1975. The National party had no interest in such a project—the four Maori seats in Parliament always had gone to Labour candidates—and it died.

The increased Maori activism of the late 1970s, which was highly visible in the media, certainly made pakeha society far more aware of Maori discontent, even if the reasons for that discontent usually were not explained and sometimes were trivialized or discounted by the media. Cathy Dewes and certain members of Te Reo Maori (Wellington) and Nga Tamatoa (Auckland) worked for the establishment of Maori media outlets as ways of extending the use of Maori and also saw such outlets as the means by which Maori could speak in their own right. Radio New Zealand began to become somewhat more supportive of Maori involvement in broadcasting starting in the late 1970s. Some of the younger senior staff, especially Beverly Wakem and John Craig, worked for change not only in the form of Te Reo o Aotearoa but also through release of staff and loans of equipment for assistance to short-term broadcasting efforts, development of access radio, and appointment of a Maori manager for Te Reo o Aotearoa, Haare Williams.

In 1982, the first Maori television news program came on the air—two minutes long, but a beginning. And, while it had nothing directly to do with Maori radio, the way in which it developed tells much about the problems encountered by Maori wishing to utilize broadcasting. The program was a demonstration of Television New Zealand's willingness to do something for Maori during Maori Language Week. When the week ended, so did the newscast. According to Derek Fox, the Maori newscaster who did the broadcast, TVNZ administrators showed no interest in continuing to present such a service and reprimanded him for trying to revive it. He feels that pakeha newspaper attention to the issue, combined with some interest in it on the part of the then minister of broadcasting, Dr. Ian Shearer, were the main reasons for its restoration as a continuing program (to be called "Te Karere" ("The Messenger") in February 1983.[93]

When the dam broke in the late 1980s, the dominant forces propelling Maori radio still were not political parties, the pakeha print and electronic media, or government officials and ministries. To be sure, there was growing support within Radio New Zealand, by Maori and pakeha staff alike, for Maori radio. The Ministry for Maori Affairs and the Maori Council had encouraged the economic summit conference that led to the proposal for a Maori-run national radio service. And, when the Labour party returned to power in 1984, its leader and prime minister designate, David Lange, seemed disposed to make greater efforts on behalf of Maori.[94]

Those efforts were in some ways crucial to the eventual success of Maori radio, but in a generalized sense; that is, Lange and the Labour party did not make major efforts on behalf of Maori broadcasting per se. They did revise the modus operandi of the Waitangi Tribunal—itself the product of an earlier Labour government—and in so doing also indicated a greater willingness to attempt to implement the decisions of the tribunal, which on the whole was strongly supportive of Maori broadcasting rights. And Lange and the Labour party prepared the legislation for the Broadcasting Act of 1989, which provided for a Broadcasting Commission to fund broadcast activities promoting New Zealand culture, including Maori culture. The then minister of broadcasting, Jonathan Hunt, issued a June 1, 1989, directive to the Broadcasting Commission that called for the active promotion of Maori broadcasting through use of license fee funds at a level of at least 6 percent of fee revenues, and he told the commission to "seek, as soon as practicable, expressions of interest in assistance from Public Broadcasting Fee revenue in relation to the establishment or maintenance of specific Maori broadcasting ventures."[95] Maori iwi radio stations were not noted as a necessary element, nor were they excluded from consideration.

That increase in activity on the part of the Labour government probably had several raisons d'être. As noted earlier, Labour traditionally had been more sympathetic to Maori concerns than National had been, but that sympathy found only limited tangible expression until the mid-1980s. Lange's own relative youth (he was 42 when he became prime minister) and social activism surely helped, but Labour's nervousness about its sometimes slim majority in Parliament made it all the more anxious to ensure that the four seats reserved for Maori be in Labour's corner. There had been a potential break in that tradition in 1979, when one of the holders of a reserved seat, Matiu Rata, left the party and founded a new party, Mana Motuhake (Separate Identity). Rata was defeated by the Labour candidate in a 1980 special election, and he and three further candidates for the four reserved seats were defeated in the 1981 election, but all did well enough to show the new party to be a potentially significant force.[96]

Mana Motuhake's relatively strong showing warned Labour that it could not take the Maori vote for granted. However, by the time of the

1984 election, the Mana Motuhake platform, which called for a true biculturalism,[97] seemed quite mild when compared with the demands being voiced by Maori writer Donna Awatere. Those demands took the form of a call for the restoration of *full* control of Aotearoa to the Maori; pakeha would be *manuhiri,* or "guests," but Maori law and language would prevail. She was joined by other writers: Syd ("Action") Jackson, Ripeka Evans, Atareta Poananga, and others.[98]

It's doubtful that most politicians, government officials, or media personnel took such demands very seriously, at least in the sense that they could foresee violent revolution occurring as a result of them. However, the politicians and others with whom I spoke did see those demands as symptomatic of an increasingly broader Maori discontent with the perceived injustices and inequalities of the past 150 years. In that sense, then, those who had held the power to maintain pakeha control and domination of the broadcast media were more ready to address specific demands regarding Maori radio. Some of them had been ready to do so much earlier, but their power and/or their critical mass was not great enough to achieve more than minor changes.

One element not previously addressed in this paper should be considered as part of the overall climate of change: the pakeha public attitude toward Maori. Of course there was and is no one public attitude, but it is possible to describe a prevailing range of attitudes.[99] That range would run from relative ignorance through relative indifference to relative hostility. Since Maori culture is part (albeit a small part) of the overall curriculum for New Zealand primary and secondary schools, total ignorance of Maori life would be very rare. Nor have I encountered evidence of the polar opposite: hatred of Maori to the point of advocating their extermination. However, there still is a quite widespread assimilationist sentiment based on the belief that Maori are "brown-skinned pakeha."

Many individuals with whom I had chance encounters in the course of my research, when they heard what I was examining, stated that they supposed that it was all right for the Maori to have their own radio stations, but after all, wasn't it something of a waste of time, money, and effort? Some looked back to halcyon days when, as children, their Maori playmates, if they had any, "weren't any different from us; we all got along just fine." Some looked to the present and said, "Why bother to learn Maori when it's English that really gets you anywhere." Some looked to the future and claimed to foresee the increasing irrelevance of a "preindustrial culture" in the technological society of the twenty-first century. Their viewpoints were reinforced in the 1961 report on the Department of Maori Affairs (the Hunn report), which clearly endorsed assimilation of Maori on

pakeha terms.[100] There also were a few, including media personnel, who
felt that Maori radio was a bad idea, since it was bound to increase a sense
of division in society.[101]

There was and still is a predominant belief in pakeha society that New
Zealand is an open, discrimination-free nation, where anyone who really
wishes to succeed can do so, regardless of her or his gender, ethnicity, or
present economic circumstances. In light of that belief, no special efforts
on behalf of Maori are necessary and may even be counterproductive. A
pakeha individual's statement contained in the 1980 report of the Human
Rights Commission sums up that sentiment: "For the future of this country
and all Kiwis, we should *all* be called New Zealanders. ... I believe that by
far the majority of Maoris consider themselves as New Zealanders and are
quite happy to live as the rest of us [do]."[102]

Politicians, government officials, and media personnel, pakeha and
Maori alike, often shared that belief with the wider public, and if they did
not, they usually kept such views to themselves. The more radical position
taken by Awatere and others in the 1980s made it possible for those *not*
sharing that belief—itself a part of the "Godzown" mind-set that saw New
Zealand as heaven on earth—to be more public in their declarations and
actions. That in turn led to support for, among other things, Maori radio.

Finally, there is the role played by Maori themselves. Although no
surveys were taken on the subject at the time, it is quite likely that, before
1970, Maori views of themselves in society and of the potential usefulness
of Maori radio would have been much like pakeha attitudes toward Maori
as noted above: some degree of ignorance of Maori achievements (which
rarely appeared in pakeha media coverage), some degree of indifference to
their future as Maori, and perhaps some hostility toward Maori who
"rocked the boat." Maori may not have welcomed the idea of assimilation,
but it is very probable that many thought it inevitable.

The rise of Maori activism in the 1970s, to the extent that Maori in
general learned about it and understood it through anything other than a
pakeha perspective (pakeha media domination remained), likely gave hope
to some. It probably disturbed others as "not the Maori way to resolve differences."[103] By the early 1980s, Maori had increasing access to more balanced accounts of events in which they were involved, partly through media coverage of Waitangi Tribunal decisions, partly through limited Maori
language material in the media, such as NZTV's "Te Karere," RNZ's Te
Reo o Aotearoa, access radio, and the first independent, short-term Maori
radio services.

However, it would be a mistake to consider the creation of Maori radio as the product of strong Maori public sentiment for such a develop-

ment. The Maori public would have had little notion of how such a service might be established or what it might do. The more traditionally minded leadership of the various tribal trusts well may have been suspicious of Maori radio, in the sense that it might allow pakeha readier access to things Maori that should not be shared with non-Maori.

The driving forces behind Maori radio were those who already had acquired some experience with it (e.g., Piripi Walker and Piripi Whaanga in Radio New Zealand, Derek Fox and Ripeka Evans in Television New Zealand). They managed to enlist the support of still other Maori active in the media, such as Ranginui Walker, who wrote for BCNZ's weekly magazine the "Listener," and Wiremu Parker, who had for so many years been the only regularly scheduled Maori language radio broadcaster. This relatively small group stimulated and in some cases enlisted still other Maori to become involved (e.g., Victoria University Professor [of accounting] Whatarangi Winiata, who became a major force in the attempt to acquire the third television channel).[104] There were several pakeha supporters, as well, some of them from within Radio New Zealand (e.g., Beverly Wakem and John Craig), some from academe (e.g., Richard Benton, a prominent sociolinguist), some from government (particularly within the Ministry of Maori Affairs), and some from Maori organizations such as Nga Kaiwhakapumau i te Reo (Wellington Maori Language Board).

There also was a notable absence: Maori politicians. Holders of the four Maori reserved seats in Parliament might have been expected to lend strong support to Maori radio, but according to the roughly 80 Maori station staff with whom I spoke, they said and did little about the issue. The general explanation was that those holding the reserved seats tended to be conservative in their views, and not on the cutting edge of change. The Labour party's pakeha leadership also may have been fearful of backlash from pakeha voters if it went too far in responding to Maori concerns. Whatever the reasons, the holders of the four seats consistently have been unable to exert much influence within the party or to provide leadership for Maori causes.[105]

As for the younger urban Maori involved in the demonstrations, marches, and occupations of the 1970s and 1980s, they seemed to have a less sophisticated sense of how to manipulate the pakeha media to their advantage and/or to develop their own media outlets than did their counterparts in various other movements in Europe and North America, such as Black Power and power to the people. Maori with whom I spoke agreed with that impression but were at a loss to explain why that should have been the case. Whatever its causes, it meant that one of the societal groups that had brought about change in media portrayal of ethnic minorities in some of the other Western nations (e.g., the United States and Great Britain) doesn't appear to have been a major player in New Zealand.[106]

Conclusion

Many radical changes have modest beginnings. Many of those beginnings are the result of the initiative of a very small but ded-
icated group of individuals. But the climate of the larger society also plays
a significant role, as it certainly appears to have done in the present case.
As discussed in this chapter, individual Maori began to enter broadcasting
in the late 1930s, and formal proposals for broadcasts in Maori date back
to 1941. There was a quite well-articulated proposal for a Maori and Pacific Islander station, with major involvement by Maori and Pacific Islanders, by the early 1970s. Yet the first independent Maori station did not
appear until 1983 and then lasted for one week. Five years would pass before a continuously operating station would come on the air.

Were the "key" individuals of the 1980s any more dedicated than their
counterparts of earlier decades? Probably not. Were they more sophisticated in their knowledge of media and their political acumen? Probably
they were. But the chief advantage they appear to have had over their forerunners was the climate of increased societal awareness not only of the injustices suffered by Maori in the past and present but also of alternatives
that were more extreme than those first sought by individuals and groups
involved in the struggle for Maori broadcasting.

Still, without the labors of their forerunners, it is doubtful that Maori
radio would be as well-developed or as (relatively) secure as it is today.
When I visited Te Reo o Aotearoa in Auckland in September 1991, I noticed a photo montage on the wall above the studios. It was made up of
photographs of several Maori, surrounded by various Maori symbols. Staff
members explained that those individuals, all now deceased, had been
broadcasters at one time or another: "We feel their sacrifices, we acknowledge their contributions, we respect their mana. We trust that all that they
did for our people will find its reflection in what we have done."

There is no doubt that majority (here meaning pakeha) control of
broadcasting in Aotearoa/New Zealand has eroded, especially over the
decade since the early 1980s. It also is evident that the relinquishing of total control was grudging, especially at first, and that the struggle is far from
over, in Maori eyes. (Maori lawyer and chairperson [1994–1996] of Te
Mangai Paho Ripeka Evans contends that mainstream media coverage of
Maori affairs actually is becoming less sympathetic.)[107] Still, the Maori
have established the principle that they are entitled to a share of the airwaves, although the size of that share is yet to be determined. It would
seem an appropriate time for a careful and thorough reconsideration of the

structure and mission of Maori broadcasting, already set in motion by Te Mangai Paho (Chapter Four) and aided by a thoughtful 1994 report prepared by Lyn Jones, then editor of BBC Radio Cymru.[108]

There remains a nagging question, which I raise in discussing "professionalism" in Chapters One and Three: given the amount of time it took before Maori involvement in broadcasting became meaningful, is there the possibility that Maori listeners and broadcasters alike have lost the ability to conceive of broadcasting in anything other than the terms and standards set by pakeha during over 60 years of almost total domination of the medium? That would constitute cultural imperialism of a far more subtle and perhaps even unconscious sort.

My own visits (7 of them multiple) to 15 Maori stations in 1991, 1993, and 1996 indicated a wide variety of practices, many of them at considerable variance with what one would hear over New Zealand public or commercial radio. While that was particularly true for programming in Maori, it also was true for much of the informational programming in English: talk shows in particular displayed a more truly discursive approach than did their counterparts in the United States and Canada, and their hosts were far more interested in showing compassion, respect, and kindness toward their guests and callers than U.S. and Canadian talk shows are prone to display. That seemed to be much appreciated by listeners, pakeha and Maori alike, with whom I spoke.

It also was evident that the presence of such stations had given a considerable boost to the Maori popular music industry and that the creation of Mana Maori Media had brought about a notable increase in coverage of activities of Maori throughout the nation and overseas. Furthermore, the news items themselves generally were more detailed than were items on pakeha newscasts, and pace and style of delivery were considerably more relaxed. Still, the usual styles of production followed in the sportscasts and in popular music recording seemed clearly to have been influenced by pakeha production standards. Whether that constitutes a form of cultural imperialism, and, if it does, whether it is harmful to the development of a Maori approach to the electronic media, is another question, but one well worth pondering.

Where Maori broadcasting goes from here is another question. As I noted several times, financing is a problem, especially as the system expands. The creation of a new Maori broadcast financing agency, Te Mangai Paho (Chapter Four), has occasioned fresh consideration of how the license fee money going into Maori broadcasting should be spent. The National Maori Radio Service is likely to be on the air by mid-1996, with five hours daily of informational programming in Maori, and the iwi stations may or may not become major contributors to it.[109] If they do *not,* that will raise interesting questions in terms of the role of indigenous broadcasting in setting a more *national* agenda—a situation that I discuss in Chapter Eight. The creation of NMRS also casts doubt on the future of Mana Maori Media, already weakened by a budget cut in 1995 (p. 120). But where the overall progress of Maori broadcasting is concerned, perhaps a Maori proverb of warning strikes the most appropriate note: *po tutata, ao pahorehore* (united at night, scattered by day).

6

Speaking in Tongues: The Place of Indigenous Minority Languages in Indigenous Electronic Media

Over the millennia, groups have been displacing other groups. In the process, languages have undergone displacement, moving along with the displacees. There also have been many instances of political displacement, where an outside force has entered an area and has left the resident population reasonably intact but has established itself as the dominant power, certainly as colonial administrator, and sometimes also as settler. Colonial administrations often have imposed a new (to the indigenous population) official language but have left existing languages intact. The coming of settlers, if they're sufficiently numerous, often has resulted in the diminution or even disappearance of existing languages.

The Romans generally functioned as colonial administrators and left "native" languages alone, although any indigene who hoped to obtain meaningful employment usually had to learn Latin. The British, starting in the seventeenth century, generally acted as colonial administrators in the less hospitable (to them) regions: much of Africa, South Asia, and the Middle East. However, they also became settlers in the more habitable lands: Ireland, North America, Australia, New Zealand, Kenya, and southern Africa. They imposed their language in both cases and often actively discouraged the use of indigenous languages when acting as settlers. They operated schools where instruction was only in English, they left indigenous languages in oral forms so that access to written material was limited to English, and they sometimes punished individuals who were guilty of using indigenous languages in public settings. (Some governments, such as Spain under Francisco Franco, even attempted to forbid the use of indigenous languages such as Basque in conversations between individuals meeting on a public street.)

Over time, some of the more restrictive language policies followed by the British, the French, and other colonial powers were modified. Where broadcasting was concerned, the advent of radio in the 1920s meant that a language existing only in oral form now could reach a larger public. However, there were very few instances of nations broadcasting in indigenous languages during the 1920s, or for that matter for some time thereafter. As Chapter Two reveals, radio remained almost exclusively the province of the majority culture, including its language(s), until the 1960s. It only began to be used for indigenous language broadcasting on a fairly widespread basis in the 1980s.

Many languages appeared to be losing a battle with time until indigenous language radio materialized. Maori, Irish, Sami, Lakota, and a number of others had reached the point where even their ardent supporters wondered whether they would be spoken any longer as the twentieth century came to a close. Revival, preservation, or extension of indigenous languages served as the principal motivator for groups speaking those languages. Now that such use has become increasingly common, and is likely to continue on into the foreseeable future, it's appropriate to ask a fundamental question about indigenous language electronic media activities: when such activities begin to occur, what do they do to/for an indigenous language? Are supporters' expectations met? Are there unintended effects, and if so, are they positive or negative? My own studies of indigenous languages in the electronic media seem to show they have a fair amount in

common, and that there are some notable consequences, some of them un-
intentional, for such languages once they're introduced through the electronic media. Furthermore, that appears to be true regardless of whether the
goal was to revive, to preserve, or to extend the language.

Reviving Languages

There are very few cases of attempts to revive languages that are "dead," for all intents
and purposes. Cornish (a Celtic language,
related to Welsh and Breton) and Ainu (which bears some resemblance to
Inuit) both are on the verge of extinction but are the object of attention by
individuals and groups hoping to bring them into wider use. BBC's Radio
Cornwall has assisted in the effort to revive Cornish, by supplying a brief
daily newscast in the language, as well as "Cornish word of the week" spot
announcements, while a few Ainu are developing videocassettes for use in
teaching the language and the culture, as well.[1] It's far too early to tell
whether either effort will succeed, but each certainly has a long way to go
before reaching the level of media exposure enjoyed by even a little spoken (about 6,000 speakers) language such as Pitjantanjara (Australian Aboriginal). A once prominent Native American language, Huron, is being revived, thanks to the help of a Canadian scholar and a few Huron-Wendat
individuals who hope to see their language live once again.[2] But the Huron-
Wendat–run radio station in Wendake, Quebec, CIHW, broadcasts mainly
in French, with some material in Montagnais/ Atikamekw.[3] There are no
fluent speakers of Huron yet available, much less an audience!

There are so few records on certain long-dead languages that revival
of anything more than a few terms and phrases seems impossible. Full-
blooded Tasmanian Aboriginals were virtually wiped out in the mid- to late
nineteenth century, and their languages died with them. Attempts on the
part of various Tasmanian Aboriginal organizations (e.g., the Tasmanian
Aboriginal Center in Burnie) to uncover their linguistic pasts have led to
the discovery of little more than the names of certain utensils, foods, items
of clothing, and animals (*pileli nua,* or "Tasmanian devil"). Even that short
list of terms represents a collection from different tribes once scattered
throughout the island. But it does constitute something specifically Tasmanian and Aboriginal and is used to help instill a greater sense of pride
on the part of young people. Radio played a modest and brief role in dis-

seminating that terminology, when a few of the Tasmanian Aboriginal Center staff prepared a weekly broadcast about the center's activities. The community radio station in nearby Wynyard carried the program during the early 1990s, but within a year the center staff, already overloaded, dropped the activity.[4]

Preserving Indigenous Languages

Attempts to preserve languages through use of the electronic media are not all that numerous, either, if one takes the term *preservation* literally. Very few individuals or groups with interests in indigenous languages wish to simply preserve them as they are. That would be akin to treating them as cultural artifacts suitable for display as museum pieces, as reminders of what *was*. If preservation of languages in that restricted sense has any value, it would be in the form of oral histories and old phonograph or tape recordings, which could serve as examples of how people used the language at one time. For example, Radio New Zealand and its predecessors made a number of recordings of Maori political figures, artists, and other distinguished persons, starting in the early 1930s. Some of those individuals spoke in Maori, and were famous for their oratorical styles—a quality highly prized in Maoridom. Those recordings never were catalogued in any systematic fashion, and few people even knew that they existed.

When Maori radio stations began to come on the air in the late 1980s, some of the stations started to make recordings of elderly storytellers, educators, politicians, singers, and others who could reflect on the past and in their own language. As interest in oral history grew, some of those individuals, as well as listeners, began to wonder whether there might not be recordings of their predecessors. RNZ's Maori service, Te Reo o Aotearoa, secured a grant to hire researchers to comb through the corporation's sound archives collection, record disc material onto tape, and catalogue what was usable (as some recordings already were not). The resulting catalogue, and the recordings themselves, are available to Maori stations throughout the country.[5]

Other stations in other countries have undertaken similar projects. Raidio na Gaeltachta (RNG) has several thousand recordings of Irish language singing, poetry reading, and political speeches, as well as other recordings, from earlier times. The RNG archive is used not only by RNG itself but also by researchers examining recent Irish history. But the cost of establishing, maintaining, and cataloguing such archival collections can be high—tens of thousands of dollars a year once the collection is up and running, and a few to several hundred thousand to get it to that point. Indigenous stations without the support of national broadcasting agencies or granting institutions ordinarily couldn't begin to finance such efforts themselves.

They might not wish to do so, either. Many of the staff in indigenous stations have told me that they see radio and TV as media for moving away from the past, more than preserving it. To the extent that the past—or, more particularly, the past of the twentieth century—was marked by what those staff members regard as capitulation to the majority culture, and possibly by the use of the indigenous languages as reminders of past glory that will never come again, the effort might actually be counterproductive. That may be particularly true for younger people, who see themselves as facing very different circumstances. Under those circumstances, a station that they regard as too heavily bound to the past may strike them as irrelevant.

To some extent, that appears to have been Raidio na Gaeltachta's fate: survey data, as well as my own discussions with station staff, academic experts on the Irish language, and young people themselves, show that listenership among people in their teens and twenties is low (as is use of Irish itself).[6] The reasons seem consistent: "all that old music," "those long items about funerals," "too much talk about the past." RNG is aware of the problem and is beginning to work more closely with the schools, with pop music groups, and other organizations to make itself more visible and more attractive to younger listeners. But it faces strong counterpressures from older people who like "all that old music" (and who cannot abide the "modern stuff"), who in a sense live for the funeral announcements (funerals are a reminder and a reinforcement of community, but community may not mean much to young people who can't find work there), who relish memories of the past (a past that may strike today's youth as far too inward looking).

There is virtually no "hard" (scientific) evidence to indicate that the initiation of an indigenous language media service helps to restore or revive its usage, but all stations broadcasting substantial amounts of such languages certainly have that hope and expectation. There is some anecdotal evidence: increased interest on the part of young people (and their parents) in taking formal study courses in the languages and increased amounts of popular music, live and recorded, in the languages. It also is probable that each medium of communication through which the languages are used has its effect on every other medium. Language classes stimulate listening to indigenous media; indigenous media provide an important outlet for popular music; popular music heightens interest in learning the language. Indigenous popular music particularly benefits from radio, and that benefit can be dramatic, as it was with rock, pop, and other popular music in Basque during the 1980s when Basque stations came on the air: a roughly twentyfold increase in recorded titles within just over five years, according to record store owners and station staff with whom I spoke in Bayonne in 1989.

Extending Indigenous Languages

Most of the stations that I've visited think of themselves as extending the use of indigenous languages. I note in Chapter Four that few of them provide formal instruction in the languages, although, as indigenous use of television and videocassette recordings increases, that may change. Actually, it can be very cost-effective to teach languages through radio, but few present-day pedagogues seem to have much faith in the use of radio as a vehicle for teaching: listeners won't pay the close attention necessary for effective instruction to take place.

Most indigenous stations devote some airtime to broadcasts in indigenous languages, with several using half or more of their airtime for the purpose. A few of them, including Radio Cymru (Welsh), Raidio na Gaeltachta (Irish), Radio nan Gaidheal (Scots Gaelic), and most of the French and Spanish Basque stations, broadcast *only* in those languages. The stations differ somewhat in the uses they make of the indigenous and the majority culture languages. I record the following generalizations on the basis of my own observations:

1. Newscasts are far more apt to be delivered in majority culture languages than in indigenous ones. That's particularly true for newscasts emphasizing national and international events.

2. Music programs featuring contemporary pop music almost always are presented in majority culture languages. Those featuring older pop music are about as apt to be in the majority as in the minority language.

3. Talk shows, especially those with phone-ins, exhibit considerable variation, usually by time of day: morning and early afternoon shows are more apt to be in indigenous languages, while late afternoon and evening shows are predominantly in majority culture languages.

4. Sports programs usually are in majority culture languages.

5. Religious programs are roughly half-and-half where the languages are concerned.

6. Skits, satires, and plays are slightly more likely to be in the indigenous languages.

7. Programs for preschool and nursery school children usually are in the indigenous languages.

In many instances, choice of one or the other language is dictated by the assumed presence of audiences that either do or don't speak the indigenous language. However, it also may be dictated by audience expectations regarding specific program formats, regardless of language skills. Although I have yet to see a scientific study of the phenomenon, conversations with indigenous media staff and with audience members lead me to believe that there may be some basis to the following assumption: indigenous listeners and viewers have come to expect certain program formats, especially national and international news, sports, and DJ-moderated contemporary pop music, to be delivered in the majority culture language. A few media staff and audience members even express the feeling that the news seems more authoritative when so delivered.

If that's simply a matter of habit—there was no alternative until recently—it should be possible for the indigenous media to win audiences over to accepting such formats in the indigenous language. But if it is because audiences do find the majority language more authoritative, more believable, more appropriate, in those contexts, the task of winning acceptance for the indigenous languages will be considerably harder.

Most of those program formats offer ample scope for extending the languages, since the formats are sufficiently connected with the modern world to require the development of new terminology. In fact, a number of them pose major challenges along those lines, in that one must often start from scratch in devising appropriate vocabularies. What's more, if the indigenous language is denotative, rather than connotative, the result may be multiple-word descriptions for what the majority culture language manages in one word. A teacher of advanced Navajo at the tribal high school in Tuba City, Arizona, gave his class the exercise of translating some standard broadcast terminology (e.g., frequency modulation) into Navajo. This turned out to be largely an exercise in futility, because the necessary denotative terms in Navajo resulted in long, awkward phrases that were *not* "announcer-friendly"![7]

Sports provide another example. While some indigenous cultures retain or have revived their own sports (such as hurling, canoe racing, and wrestling), they also are quite likely to have become adept competitors in majority culture sports such as basketball, baseball, ice hockey. Majority culture sports broadcasters have developed elaborate vocabularies to describe strategies ("setting a pick" in basketball and use of a "floating linebacker" in U.S. football), to label penalties or fouls ("clipping" in U.S. football and "spiking the bat" in baseball), and to provide colorful generic titles for certain types of athletes ("goons" in ice hockey and "enforcers" in basketball). The rule books for the various sports often read more like legal manuals than the everyday prose of newspapers. When indigenous stations have chosen to cover sporting events, they've generally used majority culture terminology, simply because their own languages weren't adequate for the task.

However, realizing that sports were of great interest to many indigenous listeners, some indigenous stations have developed specialized sports minidictionaries so that, at the least, they could provide coverage featuring *some* use of indigenous terminology. The Maori Language Commission worked with sports organizations and stations to prepare such a minidictionary for the Commonwealth Games, held in New Zealand in 1987. Navajo radio station KTNN (Window Rock, Arizona) first carried a Navajo language broadcast of a professional (NBA) basketball game in 1994 and has continued to cover basketball games at various levels in Navajo.[8] Sami community radio station GLR in Kautokeino, Norway, began to carry broadcasts of the home team football (U.S. soccer) team's matches in 1994, using a mix of Sami and Norwegian terms to describe the action.[9] In each case, practicality took precedence over purity: terms that proved awkward to translate from the majority culture languages, such as "corner kick" from Norwegian into Sami, were left in their majority culture forms. Other terms proved more adaptable, although the development of appropriate terminology for sports was only a small part of a much larger, often more complex, picture.

Developing Appropriate Terminology

Many traditional languages had begun to die out by the beginning of the twentieth century, and those who continued to use them regularly didn't always see the need to develop terminology appropriate to twentieth-century society. Even the advent of indigenous minority language radio in the latter part of the century didn't automatically mean that the new services would develop new indigenous terminology that would encompass not only sports but also rock music, transnational corporations, satellite technology, AIDS, and countless other phenomena for which there may or may not have been appropriate indigenous terms.

For example, when Raidio na Gaeltachta was founded in 1972, many thought that it should function chiefly, or even solely, as a service for rural dwelling Irish speakers along the west coast. It would present storytelling, traditional Irish music, and other programs that would make it a sort of Irish pub of the air. As such, the language in its then present form was perfectly adequate. If Irish-speaking listeners wanted newscasts about national and international events, they could hear and see them on the national (Raidio Telefis Eirann [RTE]) English language radio and TV services.[10] RNG's ambitious staff members, most of them teachers, held a very different opinion: they were unwilling to regard the station as a cultural museum. After careful preparation, and some degree of opposition from their own *ceannaire* (director),[11] RNG introduced its own national and international newscasts in 1976. The staff knew that it would need far more Irish terms than existed in the Irish dictionary if it were to be successful. However, most of them were firmly convinced that the station had to serve as a leading example of the relevance of the Irish language in the contemporary world and saw RNG's origination of national and international news as of paramount importance in that regard.

Most indigenous media operations assumed from the start that they would have to develop new terms if they were to broadcast in indigenous languages. However, there were no guidebooks available to provide them with ideas as to how to do so. The sources and approaches I list here are drawn from what I've identified in my observations of station practices; no single station uses all of them.

NATIONAL LANGUAGE COMMISSIONS/COUNCILS

National language commissions/councils exist for several of the indigenous languages: Maori, Irish, Sami, Basque, and Welsh among them. Those organizations may or may not have official status as government offices or educational bodies. Their attitudes toward the languages range from pedantic to protective to expansive, meaning that some of the members of some of the organizations may want to reconstruct (purify?) the language by taking it back a few centuries; other members may wish to rid the language of foreign (which may include majority culture) influences; while still others may strive to make it as user-friendly as possible, especially for the younger speakers, who ultimately determine whether the language lives or not.

The indigenous electronic media may or may not find such councils helpful. The media usually need rapid assistance—new terms show up in the majority culture wire services, and there aren't any obvious indigenous terms available, but staff can hold back the story only so long. The council may be able to respond quickly, but staff members have told me that speed is uncommon; more often, they're told that the matter will have to wait until the next scheduled meeting or until a majority of the members can agree upon which of three or four seventeenth-century Sami, Irish, Welsh, or other language's terms would be most appropriate.

Some councils are more attuned to the needs of the media and not only can provide rapid responses but also can anticipate needs that the media might have. The Maori Language Commission does fairly well in both respects. Based in Wellington, it serves as guardian of the language, advisory body, and promoter of language education. Maori stations can reach it by telephone or computer (all of the stations have computer terminals, thanks to government grants, and can interlink through a satellite system, albeit one of limited capacity). Theoretically, they can turn to the commission for assistance in developing an appropriate word or phrase and, on rare occasions, do so. Commission staff realized in the early 1990s that they had not done as much as they might to publicize their availability to the stations or to develop the capacity to deliver rapid responses. They then began to visit some of the stations to obtain a clearer picture of actual working conditions. They seem to be making modest progress, although the common presence of Maori dialects makes it difficult for them to provide "one size (term) fits all" responses. They're particularly proud of the minidictionaries they've developed for sports and for office work, as well as their support for development of a modern Maori dictionary that is designed to be as practical as possible.[12]

SPECIALIZED ORGANIZATIONS

Specialized organizations sometimes exist to serve other purposes connected with language use but willingly cooperate with media requesting their help. For example, a few nations have policies that provide official status for indigenous languages. Sometimes this pertains to legislative action, sometimes to legal practices, sometimes to education. In such cases, legislatures, courts, schools, and related bodies will need the assistance of indigenous translators. The Irish Dail (Parliament) has an office that translates governmental terminology, such as "Single European Act" (Ionstraim Eorpach Aonair). Udaras na Gaeltachta, a board for the promotion of industrial development for Irish speakers, serves as a valuable resource for the translation of business and industrial terminology. RNG's parent corporation, RTE, developed a directory listing prominent Irish women in various occupations and professions, such as politics, medicine, sports, education, and management. Each listing also indicates whether that individual is a fluent speaker of Irish. In New Zealand there are enough of such organizations that the Maori Language Commission developed a directory that lists them, provides a brief description of their area of specialization, and notes names and titles of chief personnel, addresses, and telephone and fax numbers. UZEI (the Basque Academy) began in the 1980s to create a series of specialized dictionaries (e.g., technical and medical) of Basque terms.

INDIVIDUAL EXPERTS

Individual experts can allow indigenous media staff to take advantage of expert opinion without the burdens of administrative procedure or "groupthink." Many indigenous stations have identified such individuals, sometimes within their own communities, sometimes elsewhere. Sometimes the individuals have identified themselves, as did Sir Thomas Parry, head of the Welsh department at University College, Bangor. Professor Parry would telephone or visit a newsroom almost every Friday to complain about one or another misuse of Welsh. Sometimes his complaints were highly pedantic, but often he provided sound and practical reasons for the use of one word, rather than another.[13]

INDIVIDUAL AMATEURS

Individual amateurs are at least as variable as experts in terms of their usefulness, but true amateurs, in the sense of those who love the language, can be very helpful. Most are apt to identify themselves, as did one woman listener to Raidio na Gaeltachta: she called the Casla station in 1992 to complain about a number of RNG announcers who "couldn't even speak the language correctly." As her call came in the course of a phone-in show, the host told her that there wouldn't be time to take up such an important issue in detail but invited her to call the following week, when she could present specific instances drawn from broadcasts made during the week. She agreed, and her subsequent broadcast drew many calls from other listeners, some of whom agreed with her and added instances of their own. RNG staff then held a special internal meeting to consider the list of charges, found that they agreed with many of them, and, in fall 1993, had a course for staff that dealt with basic Irish grammar.[14]

REQUESTS TO THE AUDIENCE

Requests to the audience are closely related to the above but differ in one respect: the media operation already knows that it has a problem and asks the audience to help in resolving it. In some cases, staff members may have come up with one or more possible solutions but enlist the help of the audience to determine the best solution. Several media operations do this from time to time. For example, shortly after its foundation in 1982, Basque radio station Xiberoko Botza sought to incorporate some "genuine" (that is, untainted by French or Spanish) Basque terms in their broadcasts and asked whether listeners had any suggestions. Many came forth, and some of the terms turned out to be very usable, such as *gela* (room), an old Basque term that had been supplanted by the French-flavored *kanbera* or *sola* (*chambre* or *salle*).[15]

STRINGERS

Stringers and other sorts of occasional reporters sometimes are sources of appropriate terminology, especially if those individuals are reporting from distant places. When RNG decided to originate Irish language national and international news, it worked through Irish embassies, businesses with foreign branches or affiliates, the Catholic church, and other organizations to identify Irish speakers living or temporarily residing abroad. The stations were gratified to discover Irish-speaking entrepreneurs, missionaries, teachers, athletes, and others in most corners of the world and began to incorporate reports from Moscow, Manila, Managua, Maputo, and a host of other locations in its newscasts. Those individuals sometimes had to come up with terms to describe local phenomena that had no Irish counterparts.

Much the same situation arose if stations covered areas in which several different dialects were spoken. Here, however, it was a matter of finding the equivalent terminology in the form of the indigenous language used by the station. Rarely would the station insist that *its* term was more appropriate; that would have been insulting to the stringer, the audience in that region, and probably other audiences with their own dialect forms.

MEDIA STAFF INITIATIVES

Media staff initiatives are probably the most common of all sources of new terminology, if only because of the perceived need for immediacy in developing appropriate terminology. Many journalists and announcers spoke with me about their spur-of-the-moment searches for new terms. Helen nic Se, while a journalist at the RNG station in Baile na n'Gall, came across the term *surfboard* in a wire service item about a surfing accident that had taken place not far from the station, making the item particularly important. However, the Irish dictionary contained no listing for surfboard, so she made up a term, joining *clar* (board) and *toinne* (wave), then provided enough context that listeners would be able to follow its meaning.[16] Staff at the Sami radio station in Karasjok, Norway, had to devise an appropriate Sami term for *loudspeaker.* Using a combination of common sense and context, they employed a form of the word for *echo: skadja.*[17] Staff at Te Reo Iriraki Ki Otautahi, the Maori radio station in Christchurch, had to find a term for *computer* and came up with *roro hiko* (electric brain).[18]

Problems and Perils

No matter what methods are used to develop appropriate terminology, they all must pass one important test: audience members must find them acceptable. (It also helps if they're comfortable for announcers, as well!) A few of the indigenous stations encourage audience members to telephone, to write, or to visit the station if they have complaints about the programming, including word usage. More often, the stations assume that, if there hasn't been any significant adverse reaction, the term must be acceptable. Audience reaction certainly can be strong on occasion, but that seems to be only when listeners or viewers become very upset. Some of the

Maori stations began in 1990–1991 to revive old Maori terms for the months, with names derived from agricultural or fishing activities taking place at certain times. There were two problems: station staff themselves found it hard to break the habit of casually referring to the months in modern Maori, where their titles closely resemble the English terms. Also some listeners reacted more strongly, claiming that "even my old granny doesn't understand those terms, and she speaks perfect Maori!" As adverse reactions came in, a few stations abandoned the attempt, while others have continued on, hoping to rid the language of at least that particular bit of majority culture influence.

There are other potential perils involved in developing relevant terminology. If one of the aims of station staff is to maintain the purity of the language, insofar as possible, and if the language has a limited vocabulary to begin with, it almost certainly will be necessary to borrow from the majority culture language to discuss such subjects as AIDS. The term in Basque, *Hartutako Immuno Eskasia Sindromea,* bears a strong resemblance to the Spanish term for AIDS. It would be possible to create a more purely Basque term, but it might end up confusing Basque listeners who already were used to hearing the term in Spanish. (Because Spanish-speaking Basques outnumber their French counterparts by roughly 10 to 1, Spanish often has served as the reference point for the creation of new Basque terminology on both sides of the border.)

In fact, the term *AIDS* is a good example of how difficult it may be in certain cases to develop an appropriate indigenous term. When AIDS triggered a major media event at the beginning of the 1980s, the electronic media found it far more convenient to refer to it by its acronym than by its full title. For countries or regions where English was the dominant language, indigenous stations by and large used the term *AIDS,* since it was convenient for them, as well; also, most of their listeners already were accustomed to it, since it had established itself both rapidly and widely. Raidio na Gaeltachta considered developing an Irish term but decided not to, on the grounds that it would be fighting a losing battle: no term was likely to replace *AIDS.* Radio Cymru, however, felt that it would be worth the effort. The station worked with the Welsh Health Department and finally came up with one, which proved to be clumsy to speak if delivered in full. But the acronym *DIC* was easy to pronounce, so the station used it—for two days. The Welsh *C* is a hard *C,* and the resultant spoken acronym came out as a common English slang term for the male sex organ![19]

Even if Radio Cymru had come up with a more suitable acronym, it probably wouldn't have fared any better in terms of adoption by the indigenous public. Whether the term is *AIDS, P*(olitically) *C*(orrect), or anything else that spreads rapidly through the mass media, it's virtually impossible for the indigenous media to come up with a viable alternative quickly enough to establish it in the hearts and minds of the indigenous audience. It might be a manageable task if such audiences were monoglots in their languages, but very few in the situations under consideration here would qualify as such. Furthermore, the majority culture media are so much more prevalent than are their indigenous counterparts that the latter simply are outgunned in such instances.

And here we arrive at a dilemma: if indigenous electronic media hope to restore or preserve the purity of their languages, aren't they defeated before they begin, at least where the words of technology, medicine, perhaps sports, and possibly societal problems are concerned? Does any truly alternative term stand a chance in such circumstances? But if the media seek a compromise solution through the borrowing of majority culture terms, and "indigenizing" them with indigenous prefixes, suffixes, and pronunciations, what then? If that becomes a common practice, how much of the "true" indigenous language remains? Granted, all languages change over time, but the mass media seem to possess the capacity to bring about such change more rapidly and more comprehensively than any older media— poets, singers, or traders—ever were able to do. If French purists rail against the "franglicization" of their language, when France is a media-rich nation, what chance does Maori or Sami or Basque or Lakota stand?

Happily for speakers of those languages, enough of the "true" language has survived through the centuries that there is a solid and sizable foundation upon which to build in the twenty-first century. For all of their complaints, the French purists would have to admit that the vast majority of their native tongue remains intact, despite the incursions of "le prime time" or "le hamburger." And, after all, both *prime* and *time* came into English from Latin, while *hamburger* takes the name of the German city where something like that food item supposedly originated. There even are cases of indigenous terms being picked up by majority cultures: the Maori "hello," *kia ora,* appears to be in increasing use among New Zealand *pakeha.* Australia's famous symbols—the koala, the kookaburra, and the kangaroo—all bear Aboriginal names. The Inuit igloo is familiar to most North Americans, many of whom don't realize that they display their knowledge of at least one Inuit word when they refer to it.

Certainly there isn't anything like a two-way street in which the flow of linguistic traffic is even in both directions, but prospects for future viability *and* (relative) purity seem good for many of the indigenous languages now finding their outlets through the electronic media.

Dialects

The place of dialects in the indigenous electronic media often is a delicate issue. Many indigenous languages feature a fair amount of dialect variation. Indigenous language radio stations sometimes face difficult decisions regarding the choice of dialects, if they choose to use any at all. Recall the difficulty faced by the Maori Language Commission regarding the development of "one size fits all" terms (p. 172). And the problem isn't just a lack of common terminology: dialect variation can be a matter of intense pride. In the Tainui-dominated areas of New Zealand, most Tainui radio stations cite the superiority of the Tainui dialect form of Maori as one reason for them not to use the Maori national newscasts of Mana Maori Media. (Another reason is that there isn't enough coverage of Tainui activities.)

If linguistic areas are reasonably definable in geographic terms, *if* the indigenous language service includes local stations, and *if* the areas themselves are so configured that the station signals fit the geographical-linguistic boundaries more or less perfectly (which is rare), dialect broadcasts may present few problems. Each dialect then will have its own self-contained broadcast outlet. But a number of indigenous language services are largely or wholly national and operate from a single or limited number of locations (Ireland's RNG is such an operation). In those cases, deciding whether to broadcast in dialects at all and, if so, which ones, can be a major problem.

The problem rarely presents itself as one of comprehension. Most dialect speakers can understand other dialects at least well enough to be able to extract the basic meaning, if they're willing to make the effort. The effort may be considerable, especially with certain Sami dialects, which have evolved to the point where they might be considered as separate languages.[20] In such instances, it's doubtful that most audience members would bother to make any accommodation.

The emotional overtones connected with dialects can pose a far greater barrier. The Tainui example just cited may be extreme in its degree of exclusivity, but speakers of various dialect forms of Irish still criticize some RNG announcers for their "dreadful" Kerry accents (or Donegal or Connemara); north Welsh speakers may have similar reactions to south Welsh speakers. Like examples appear in many minority language broadcasting situations. The electronic media can help in breaking down some of the emotional barriers: staff at RNG and Radio Cymru both have told me that they hear far fewer complaints about dialects now than they once did, and even some grudging acceptance along the lines of "But I do find what she/he has to say quite interesting."* Still, no one appears to have conducted research that would help us to determine whether broadcasting in dialects reduces comprehension or turns audiences against electronic media that include them in their output.

There's yet another dimension to the dialect issue. If a minority broadcast system is based upon localized dialects, might such a system deter the minority from coalescing as a force to be reckoned with on a national level? My conversations with Aboriginal broadcasters in Australia often touched upon that issue. There are dozens of Aboriginal languages and dialects, most of them spoken by a few hundred to a few thousand individuals. While some Aboriginal broadcasters feel a commitment to providing services in those languages and dialects, there are severe limits to their ability to carry more than a half-dozen or so. Quite aside from ability, however, those broadcasters wonder how a strong Aboriginal presence could be established at a national level without working through a common language, which, willy-nilly, turns out to be English. That injures their cultural pride, but it seems to be the only practical solution to the problem of gaining access to political power—a much larger issue that forms the subject of Chapter Seven.

Reshaping Language Usage through the Electronic Media

Broadcasting follows a set of more or less universally understood practices. Programs usually start and end at hour and half-hour intervals. Voices are supposed to be "on mike" and clearly audible to the audience. Pauses between sentences within discourse or between speakers

---

*Davies makes a similar observation about earlier BBC broadcasts in Welsh dialects. He notes that many individuals, some of them quite sensitive regarding the purity of the language, were both surprised and pleased to see listener acceptance of the southern dialect in the north, and vice versa. Davies, John, *Broadcasting and the BBC in Wales,* Cardiff: University Press of Wales, 1994, 187–188.

in interviews or discussions should be brief. Announcers speak the broadcast languages correctly (or at least according to majority culture standards of correctness). In general, those practices coincide more or less closely with practices in everyday life. But some indigenous cultures follow quite different practices. Discussions among Native Americans in North America and among Aborigines in Australia often are characterized by long pauses. Formal discussions in Maori culture are held according to a strict protocol, in which the sometimes random give and take of a formal discussion in North America or Europe would be out of place. But when radio becomes a part of indigenous culture, does it bring with it a set of expectations as to practices that might be at variance with minority group custom?

Take the matter of pauses. Will indigenous listeners consciously or unconsciously reshape such practices as having long pauses and pick up the pace in order to meet what they already know to be the practices of majority culture radio? If they do not, will they face pressure from listeners who are accustomed to majority culture radio and who place similar expectations on the new stations? And if the traditional leaders within minority cultures are accustomed to providing deliberative, detailed statements in responding to questions, how will they fare if indigenous radio chooses to follow the predilection of majority culture broadcasting for sound bites, or at least relatively concise, compact statements?

There is some evidence to indicate that Aboriginal groups already have experienced some changes in notions of how leadership is communicated. City dwellers, many of them unable to speak Aboriginal languages, appear from my observations to be readier to ascribe leadership to individuals who are more ready and able to accommodate themselves to media demands. Rural dwellers may be less inclined to do so, although younger individuals seem more open to the possibility that leadership may come through something other than ancestry, longevity, or some of the other more traditional hallmarks. Michael Manley, a Tasmanian Aboriginal with blond hair and blue eyes, has become a prominent national Aboriginal figure, in part because both Aboriginal (but especially city-based) and white Australian media have provided him with considerable exposure. He is eloquent, dramatic, and controversial and seems highly adept at presenting himself (in English) through the media, sound bites and all.[21]

Raidio na Gaeltachta's daily broadcasts of discussions and disc jockey patter have featured a discursive approach: speakers take plenty of time to say whatever it is they have to say, just as they would in everyday life. But the national English language radio services of Radio Telefis Eirann have picked up their pace and reduced the amount of talk, partly in competitive response to the "more music, less talk" approach of the newer local commercial radio stations in Ireland. RNG staff also have moved in the direction of reducing the amount of talk but are divided over the degree of reduction needed. Part of that division stems from concern over the effect of such a reduction on what some staff members regard as an essential element of Irish: its discursive quality. In fact, it is perfectly possible to speak briefly in Irish, even if it isn't what Irish speakers are usually presumed to do. And there is the heart of the problem: should RNG take upon itself the role of "change agent" where style of discourse is concerned? But if it remains faithful to custom, does it risk losing listenership, particularly among the younger people who will be vital to the future of the station itself?

Speaking languages correctly on the air might seem easy enough, until one realizes that there may be a real shortage of individuals capable of doing so in indigenous languages. The task will be especially difficult when a number of indigenous media outlets appear within a short time span, as they've done in Aboriginal, Maori, and Native American (especially Canada) media. There often aren't enough *fluent* speakers of the language available to meet the demand for their services. At the same time, many of those who have struggled to keep the language alive are almost certain to press for high standards of performance through the media. However, most of the individuals who themselves have struggled to develop indigenous media realize the importance of involving younger people, both as audiences and as performers. Yet the younger generation is apt to be sorely lacking in indigenous language skills. When the media use them as announcers, DJs, and journalists—as most media operations do—there's very likely to be an outcry from skilled language speakers, as Welsh community radio station Radio Maldwyn, for one, discovered when its English-speaking announcers attempted to pronounce Welsh place names.[22]

That's a risk that most media managers seem willing to take. Still, even if younger speakers improve their command of the indigenous language, they are likely to be less respectful of its purity. They are also likely to be readier to include majority culture influences not only in choice of terminology but also in styles of presentation. Ole Henrik Magga, president of the Sami Parliament, observed that, in his opinion, Sami radio did not always serve older listeners as well as it should. He was concerned that the newscasts in Sami were prepared and delivered more in the manner of majority culture newscasts: fast-paced and abbreviated. Older Sami listeners, he contended, associate newslike items delivered in Sami with a slower and more discursive approach and sometimes find Sami radio's presentations hard to follow.[23]

Whether younger Sami listeners would welcome a slower, more discursive style is another question. At least one indigenous service, Radio Cymru, decided in 1994 that its Welsh newscasts were too discursive: a major self-study, supported by the work of an outside consultant, led the station's newsroom to conclude that its newswriting style needed a bit of slimming.[24] Part of the assumption guiding the decision was that younger (including middle-aged) Welsh speakers, whether they realized it or not, were using the language less discursively than did their forebears.[25]

Interviews could pose similar dilemmas. Indigenous electronic media can stimulate language learners to use the languages, especially in the course of interviews. If those media were to follow rigid policies of correctness of speech, the numbers of potential interviewees would shrink dramatically, especially among younger people. Very few media *are* that rigid, but some of them don't make much effort to seek out and to encourage less-than-fully fluent speakers to serve as interviewees. However, as most of the indigenous media operations have at least some staff who themselves aren't very fluent, there often is some degree of encouragement by example.

The media services also have begun to take more initiative in developing programs that require the participation of language learners. Radio Cymru has a Saturday morning program in which teenagers talk about events of special importance to them. The range of levels of fluency is apparent even to a non-Welsh speaker. The program's producers encourage just about everyone to "have a go" and seem to make a deliberate effort to display a wide range of language skills in each broadcast.[26] Raidio na Gaeltachta, one of the more "purist" of the indigenous language services, nevertheless is working harder with schools, sports clubs, and other organizations to bring language learners to the microphone. The station began in 1993 to offer secondary school Irish language learners the opportunity to prepare and present minidocumentaries about their own lives and concerns. They were to tape a roughly 20-minute program, then send it to RNG. The station broadcast the winning entries, which didn't always feature perfect Irish. And when Ireland's football (soccer) team played in the 1994 World Cup, the RNG sports announcers who were covering the event sought out Irish-speaking players (not that many, and not that fluent) on the team, encouraged them to speak in Irish, coached them where necessary, and came out with several very effective, if less than word perfect, interviews.[27]

The advantages to such practices seem obvious enough. Whether the disadvantage of sanctioning incorrect use of the language through such presentations is outweighed by the encouragement it seems to give to language learners is, of course, a matter of opinion. But the very presentation

of such "models" certainly has the potential to reshape use of the indigenous language by a wider audience.

Indigenous Visual Languages

Visual languages form a part of communication styles, as well. Because there have been
so few opportunities for indigenous peoples
to become directly involved in displaying and seeing themselves through
television, few scholars have considered the possibility that those peoples
might face problems of visual comprehension, that there might be more
and less appropriate visual expressions. Eric Michaels is one of the few researchers to have examined the visual aspect of indigenous electronic communication. Building upon the work of Sol Worth and John Adair,[28] he was
able to determine that the central Australian Aboriginal tribes with whom
he worked for several years in the 1980s did have differing concepts of
how to display themselves through video recordings.[29]

Michaels did not attempt to determine whether the comprehension of
visual communication varied within or between the groups he studied. (He
was aware that their oral languages had enough in common to permit varying degrees of mutual comprehension.) His interests lay more in identify-
ing *what* and *how* various subgroups chose to show to themselves, other
subgroups, or larger aggregations. He also noted that the Aboriginal individuals he observed seemed able to comprehend the visual dimensions of
European (white Australian) TV, although he didn't know how much or
how well they comprehended it.[30] Steven Leuthold has examined the work
of two Native American videographers, George Burdeau and Victor
Masayesva. He makes an interesting case for the use of different (from majority culture) approaches to cutting and editing by Burdeau and
Masayesva. However, his consideration of *what* they choose to show (the
land itself, certain objects within the household, children, and elderly people), and *why* they choose to show it, strikes me as more convincing and to
a certain degree coincides with the observations made by Michaels.[31]

As various studies by Ien Ang and others have shown, there are many
ways in which viewers in different western societies interpret (read) "Dallas" and other TV programs, and not all of those readings will be the ones

the production team had in mind.[32] We might assume that the same would hold true among indigenous peoples, as well as between indigenous peoples and their majority culture counterparts. At present, we may do nothing more than assume, but some of the observations that I've made about discursiveness, pauses, and other aspects of oral communication could well be relevant in the visual realm.

Using Indigenous Languages to Establish a Separate Identity

Some indigenous groups inclined toward separatism may see the indigenous language as an ally in their quest. If an indigenous minority language is very different from the majority language—say a Polynesian language such as Maori in contrast with a European language such as English, or a non-Latin or non-Germanic root European language such as Irish or Basque in contrast with English, French, or Spanish—it may be quite possible to consider using it to share a sense of identity among the speakers *and* to exclude the majority culture. Carried to extremes, that could lead to development of an entirely separate culture, possibly living as an enclave within the larger nation and perhaps even seeking total independence. The breakup of the former Soviet Union seems to have been driven in part by the desire for cultural, including linguistic, independence. Activities of Basque, Corsican, Breton, and other independence movements often display a linguistic dimension through use of their languages in graffiti, banners, leaflets, speeches, books, radio, and cassettes.

Just how the presence of indigenous language electronic media affects such developments is hard to say, but supporters of independence movements are willing to go to considerable effort to establish and maintain a linguistic presence. Spanish Basques in exile broadcast to Spain in Basque

from 1941 to 1977, in hopes of keeping the Basque independence movement alive. French authorities appear to have become nervous over Basque
language broadcasts in France for much the same reason, although the
Basque independence movement in France is almost nonexistent.[33] One alleged (by supporters of community radio) reason for the delay in licensing
community radio stations in Great Britain in the late 1980s was Conservative party Chair Norman Tebbitts' fear that South Asian and West Indian
stations operating in the large cities could foment unrest in languages that
the British authorities would not understand.[34]

Rarely would such fears seem valid. Most of the radio stations broadcasting in indigenous languages are careful to maintain distance between
themselves and the various independence groups. Aside from their concern
to maintain their licenses (which, after all, are awarded through the majority language-dominated system), most station staff are not particularly
sympathetic to such groups, although they often will include proindepen-
dence group members in broadcast discussions and may carry news items
(not always favorable) about their activities.[35] Staff appear to see such
groups as out of touch with reality in their most extreme (total independence) demands. Whether audience members agree or disagree is difficult
to say. But access to radio can be very symbolic, and politically motivated
groups sometimes have attempted to commandeer indigenous stations, as
did two Mohawk groups with a Mohawk station in Akwesasne, Quebec,
during a 1990 confrontation with law enforcement officials. The same
event led to high tension at the Mohawk reservation in Kahnawake, Quebec, but the two rival Mohawk groups there were willing to cooperate to
the extent of ensuring that the Kahnawake station's transmitter be kept in
working order, since both wanted to broadcast over it.[36] Interestingly, none
of the three Mohawk stations broadcast much material in Mohawk!

There's an interesting point of connection between the issue of creating appropriate terminologies and the issue of total, or near-total, indigenous independence. If indigenous media develop terminologies to meet
current situations and needs, whether in sports, business, technology, international affairs, or whatever, might that also help to reinforce the feeling that the minority can and even should operate independently? Once one
possesses the requisite business vocabulary, to take one example, it becomes that much easier to consider operating a business on one's own,
without the need for reference to the majority culture. As seeds of independence multiply, still broader independence becomes more imaginable.
Consider the fate of the Soviet Union in that regard. Minority languages by
and large were left in place after the 1917 Russian Revolution. They were
taught in the schools, used in daily life, and employed widely in broadcasting.[37] If the Soviet leadership had decided to eradicate or at least to ig-

nore such languages in favor of Russian (already highly favored), which is something that it certainly could have done with broadcasting, would the independence movements have been as ready or as able to seize power in the early 1990s?

My tentative conclusion is that indigenous language broadcasts very rarely encourage independence movements in any direct sense. However, they may have a certain amount of indirect, and probably unintended, influence in the form of simply bringing people to think more independently, to lead them to consider more independent actions. In most cases, that is not going to lead to declarations of independence, but it could encourage audiences to at least daydream about the possibility.

Using Indigenous Languages to Maintain Subordination

Generally speaking, indigenous media staff with whom I've spoken don't feel that their services have been licensed as part of some sort of master plan of the majority culture to relegate the indigenous language/culture to second-class status, but such a plan is not inconceivable. That line of reasoning works as follows: if indigenous media are created to serve minority populations in their own languages, speakers of those languages will have one less reason to master the language of the majority culture. Mastery of the majority culture language usually is a prerequisite to the attainment of power, whether economic, political, or military, within the nation as a whole. Thus, minorities lacking that mastery are doomed to subordination.

The Republic of South Africa's Nguni and Sotho Radio Group, broadcasting in nine Bantu languages and English (Radio Metro), may have been created with subordination in mind. A product of the white South African government, it was designed to discourage listening to "hostile" (to the South African government) broadcasts in Bantu languages and in English coming from the Black African frontline states surrounding the republic: their radio signals were beamed for the most part over shortwave, while Radio Group was an FM system (Radio Metro also had an AM signal). Also, some of the programming over Radio Group stations would appear to have been of little utility to a Black South African seeking to move up the economic, political, military, or any other power ladder. There was heavy emphasis on Christianity and on sports (segregated until shortly before Black majority rule), and the African National Congress and other opposition groups were treated negatively, when they were mentioned at all, up until the early 1990s.* In any event, if the white South African government had expected the Radio Group to keep the Black population in a state of quiescence, the enterprise wasn't successful.

Conclusion

While the indigenous electronic media may see themselves as crucial elements in the struggle to revive and expand indigenous languages, the paths leading to success are many, diverse, and of generally uncertain merit. Earlier assumptions that the mere presence of indigenous languages on the airwaves would lead to their strengthening in society are being replaced by the lessons of experience. The chief lesson so far appears to be that whatever is done along those lines will be almost certain to upset or antagonize someone, and sometimes a very influential someone. That hasn't stopped the electronic media from carrying indigenous language material, but it has ended speculation that there could be a massive and rapid resurrection in the use of Maori, Sami, or any other indigenous language.

When the educational system and the electronic media make indigenous languages available on a daily basis, that should help to increase the use of the languages. In the two cases where that situation holds—Ireland and Wales—the latter seems to be faring better than does the former, although precise figures to support that conclusion aren't available. Radio Cymru does seem to be more sensitive to the needs of the language learner than does Raidio na Gaeltachta: Radio Cymru appears to work harder to encourage such individuals to serve as interviewees; it offers a wider range

---

*Wilkins and Strydom refer to a plan by the Broederband to ensure that Blacks live and work in separate (from white South Africa) homelands, with Radio Bantu and a Black TV service as key elements in implementing the plan. Wilkins, Ivor, and Hans Strydom, *The Super Afrikaaners,* Johannesburg, Republic of South Africa: Ball, 1978, 1.

of programming; and it seeks to attract younger listeners through provision of a wide range of popular music, including music with English lyrics.

However, Radio Cymru does not escape criticism for distorting the language, any more than does any of the indigenous language media services. That criticism seems to come with the territory. Perhaps it's heightened because those who grew up speaking the languages had to fight so hard to maintain them and came to see the new indigenous media as powerful allies in the struggle. Now that sobering reality has settled in, those early combatants may feel somewhat betrayed. But the electronic media are at the forefront of language (re)formation. They serve as agents of change whether their leaders intend it or not. Those leaders can influence that change, but they will have to learn much more about which practices seem to work in which circumstances before they can expect their influence to be effective. Even then, there are bound to be a host of unexpected, and sometimes unwelcome (to the leaders), influences. That is the very nature of the electronic media.

7

The Politics of Broadcasting/ The Broadcasting of Politics

The revival, preservation, and extension of indigenous languages has been an obvious top priority for indigenous electronic media. One would expect that the strengthening of indigenous political activity would be just as important. After all, the mere existence of indigenous languages won't ensure that their speakers will address the many social problems faced by indigenous peoples. The communication of political power won't guarantee political progress, either, but the absence of communication will almost certainly guarantee the lack of progress.

However, as noted in Chapter Three, any outsider looking at or listening to indigenous electronic media soon would notice an apparent lack of political material. It may be that, once an outsider has come to understand the multifaceted and sometimes indirect or even implicit nature of indigenous political messages, the lack won't seem as great, but even then the quantity of such material often is modest. Music, the mainstay of most indigenous radio stations, certainly can carry political messages, but the vast majority of what those stations play and what indigenous listeners purchase on disc or cassette is majority culture material,* indigenous traditional, or indigenous nonpolitical (e.g., love songs). Newscasts often consist largely of relays of majority culture newscasts and/or readings from majority culture wire services. There are few equivalents of Mana Maori News in the world of indigenous electronic media, although more are emerging. Yet indigenous media managers and staff readily agree that the coverage of politics is extremely important.

Does this represent a contradiction? I would say yes and no. Media staff usually want to do more along those lines, although their vision of how to go about the task may be limited: some appear unaware of the political role that music can play, not to mention satire, drama, quiz shows, and other "entertainment" formats. Also, they often appear to find themselves between the proverbial rock and hard place.

Indigenous communities or groups may appear monolithic at first glance but often come through as highly diverse upon further acquaintance. That holds for all sorts of practices—cultural, social, economic, and political.¹ Diversity in any of those settings is potentially controversial, but political diversity appears to head the list. The already existing tribal, local, or other indigenous governing structures often are responsible for bringing the indigenous electronic media (radio in particular) into being. They also usually have the responsibility for financing the operations, in two ways: as conduits for money from majority culture government (e.g., New Zealand, Australia, Canada, and the United States, although not in every instance in any of those countries) and as a direct allocation from tribal or other forms of local funding (rare, although some tribes, municipalities, universities, and other organizations offer support through goods and services, such as buildings, utilities, furniture, and secretarial staff). Sometimes the two are combined.

If the tribal (or nontribal) government is not particularly democratic, dissenting voices are likely to find little time on the media outlets. Even if it *is* democratic, radical voices on the left and the right may be excluded.² That accounts for the order posed in the chapter title: it's necessary to examine the politics of the electronic media, and broadcast media in particular, before considering what the media outlets do and do not make available by way of political content.

Here I must enter a caveat of sorts. When I considered which subjects

---

*Some of which has generalized or specifically indigenous political implications, as anyone even vaguely familiar with Australian Aboriginal problems can recognize upon hearing Peter Garrett of the white Australian rock group Midnight Oil sing "Beds Are Burning."

to cover in this book, I hesitated to include this chapter, for one major reason: if there is one aspect of indigenous media where extended (and, hopefully, follow-up) exposure and the ability to speak indigenous languages would seem invaluable, this is it. My firsthand observation of any one of the dozens of media outlets listed in Appendix One has been brief—rarely more than two or three days at a time, sometimes less, and roughly two-thirds of the list on the basis of one visit. Furthermore, the little that has been written about indigenous electronic media rarely includes a consideration of the political dimension, aside from some treatment of how the services came into being.[3] Books on indigenous politics and government, including those cited in a number of the endnotes, are almost universally silent on the political role of the indigenous, or any other, media.[4]

Still, making allowances for the impressionistic nature of much that I present here, I do feel that it can serve as a starting point for those with the time, access, and language skills to pursue such investigations in depth and thus quite possibly to prove me wrong in some respects and certain specific instances. But the subject itself simply is too important to ignore, and it has been ignored for long enough.

The Politics of the Electronic Media

I indicate in Chapter Four that there are several external forces of influence on the indigenous media. Not all are directly political, although those that are not may have indirect effects on how the indigenous media are expected (by those having political influence) to treat political and other issues. For example, an indigenous media service might be "persuaded" by power holders to handle political interviews with it in the same deferential manner observed by majority culture media, should that be the case. The service might not even have to be persuaded; it may unconsciously imitate the majority culture practice. Here, however, I concentrate on the directly political forces.

TRIBAL AUTHORITIES

Tribal authorities exist in many countries around the world. In Chapter Three I refer to the "divide and conquer" approach, through which colonial powers sometimes strengthened such authorities in order to prevent coalitions of opposition. Those authorities often experienced a reduction in power when settlers from the colonial homelands came into their regions, but the past few decades have seen something of an increase in tribal self-government, particularly in Australia, New Zealand, and North America. In some of those cases, the self-governing structures have little in common with any precolonial forms of tribal government; in others, there may be some structural resemblance. However, whether there is or not, the older tribal hierarchies, and their accompanying hallmarks of who is to hold power, may prevail.[5]

How the exercise of power will affect indigenous media varies within countries, as well as from one country to another. The formal linkage to the tribal structure appears most clearly in New Zealand, where radio licenses are issued by the Department of Commerce to the *iwi* (tribes). Maori also may apply for licenses outside tribal structures, although they then must compete with other, largely commercial, license seekers, whereas certain frequencies are reserved for the iwi stations.

As of 1996, there were 21 iwi stations and four non-iwi stations; all of the former received government funding through New Zealand on Air; only one of the latter (Radio Aotearoa, a national service) did so. While the government would be quite happy to see non-iwi stations grow in number (indeed, according to a Ministry of Commerce official, the government would see such a development as an indication of the "maturity" of Maori radio, because it adds diversity) the iwi stations are the only ones that qualify for government funding.[6] This helps the government to avoid becoming involved in arguments over whether it favors one iwi political faction over another. It also provides the iwi tribal councils with considerable leverage where stations are concerned.

The clearest demonstration of exercise of tribal power came in 1992, when the Tuwharetoa Maori Trust Board (council) in Turangi decided that the then present iwi radio station, Te Reo Irirangi O Tuwharetoa, should be operated on a more commercial basis, so as to bring added revenue to the iwi. Some board members also were unhappy because the station's manager, Dickson Chapman, sometimes ignored or went against their wishes. The board then notified New Zealand on Air that it was establishing a new radio station and would be using New Zealand on Air–disbursed funding from license fees (NZ $200,000, or about U.S. $125,000) to support the new station.

Chapman refused to give up. He and many of his staff continued to operate the original station (now named Te Tahi, meaning "the one"), with equipment that, strictly speaking, belonged to the iwi. (The building housing the station belonged to Waiariki Polytechnic, and not to the iwi; the school allowed the station to remain there.) As Chapman had a good deal of support (including financial) from within the iwi itself, and even from certain board members, the new board-supported station faced established competition from the moment of its birth. As of 1995, the older station seemed to enjoy a substantial lead in terms of listenership.[7]

The main point here is not the rights or wrongs of the board's exercise of power. Rather, it's that the principal licensing and financing structure itself encourages the abuse of financial power by placing it in a limited number of hands and operates within a framework lacking formal checks and balances. In this case, listeners appear to have chosen a balancing mechanism by favoring the older station with their attention, but money generated through license fees continues to flow exclusively to the newer, board-created station. One could argue that, if enough listeners are upset about the situation, they will place pressure on the board to reconsider its action, and a form of democratic participation will have proven itself to be effective. But it does seem potentially wasteful of limited financial resources and talent and works against the idea that a given electronic media outlet can serve as a forum for differing views and approaches.

LICENSING AND REGULATION

There is another respect in which the iwi-based licensing and financing system gives rise to political problems. There are many parts of New Zealand where several iwi live in close proximity and enjoy a rough overall parity in population. If one iwi is granted a license, it's likely to be difficult for others to receive licenses, as well. It might be possible for the various iwi to cooperate, but many of them have long histories of mutual distrust and/or disrespect. There is no set mechanism whereby the Ministry of Commerce can compel the iwi to cooperate, although it can (and does) try to bring them together to negotiate their differences.

There are three iwi in the South Island city of Invercargill: Nga Haue e Wha, Nga Tai Tamariki A Tirahau, and Nga Tahu.* The last named has held the iwi broadcast license since 1992 but didn't come on the air until mid-1994. The first two are closely related iwi that don't get along with one another; each had airtime of the Invercargill Access Radio service, South-

---

*Nga Tahu is the dominant iwi on the South Island and operates a radio station in Christchurch.

land Community Radio. None of the three could readily fill and entire program week (iwi stations receiving funding through license fees are supposed to broadcast for 72 hours a week, although waivers are possible), so cooperation would have been sensible in economic terms.

The Department of Commerce attempted to get the three iwi to work out a cooperative arrangement, but the mutual animosities, coupled with something of a "dog in the manger" attitude on the part of Nga Tahu, prevented that.[8] Nga Haue e Wha, which had broadcast several hours of programming daily over Access Radio since May 1993, attempted to obtain a separate, non-iwi license. It converted space in its school-cum-office building into radio and studios, control rooms, and production booths but then ceased broadcasting in September 1994. Nga Tahu had finally come on the air a few months before but failed to receive financing from Te Mangai Paho and ceased operation in May 1995. Nga Tai Tamariki A Tirahau has continued on Access Radio.[9]

There's general agreement that all three groups could have been on-air with a jointly operated iwi station as early as 1992,[10] and the license fee money—all but certain at the time—would have helped to ensure a reasonable standard of programming. The one remaining station has rudimentary equipment (the "studio" for Nga Tai Tamariki A Tirahau's broadcasts over Access Radio is a 40-by-40-foot room with high ceilings, no acoustical treatment, a rudimentary board, a cheap microphone, a turntable, and a tape recorder-playback machine),[11] and Nga Haue e Wha and Nga Tahu both are off the air. Again, the system constrains the situation, although the three iwi must bear responsibility for the impasse itself.

In other parts of the world, indigenous tribal groups usually have slightly less formal power over the electronic media, at least in terms of budgetary power. Several Aboriginal media associations have been established in Australia over the past five years. The associations carry out a number of communications activities, including the production (and sometimes sale) of audio- and videocassettes, operation of radio stations, and preparation of video material for use by majority culture stations. Here, support funds come from general tax revenues and are disbursed by the Aboriginal and Torres Strait Islander Commission (ATSIC), a federal government agency. The associations draw up articles of incorporation and mission statements, present their funding applications to ATSIC, present their licensing applications (for radio stations) to the Department of Communications and the Arts, and, in most cases, eventually receive funding and licenses. Tribes certainly are involved with the associations: tribal members work with them, are on the boards of directors, and may contribute financial support on their own. But they don't actually hold the licenses or receive the funding.

That doesn't necessarily mean that association media operations are free from tribal influence, nor do association directors and staff think they should be: to the extent that the lives of Aboriginal community members are linked with the tribes, there should be influence. The key word here is *extent*. Associations located in the larger towns and cities, such as the Western Australia Media Association in Perth and the Townsville Aboriginal and Islander Media Association in Townsville, serve areas with several tribes, and tribes of differing strength, unity, and size. They also serve a number of Aboriginals who have little or no sense of tribal loyalty. In addition, they're in a good position to reach, or to try to reach, majority culture audiences. Under those circumstances, it would be difficult for the leadership of any single tribe to exercise strong and constant influence. Smaller associations, such as Wankiyupurnapurru (Fitzroy Crossing, Western Australia), are likely to contain a higher proportion of tribal members, and the tribes may be more closely associated (although sometimes they're exactly the opposite).

In either situation, the exercise of power is likely to be more subtle and quite often will take the form of hierarchies within kinship structures, rather than tribal governance structures. Individuals with higher kinship status may use it to "persuade" lower-status kin working in the associations to do or not do something specific, such as making casual mention on-air of the former's noteworthy activities, or seeing to it that a musical request gets on the air even when there isn't enough time to honor existing requests (see Chapter Six), or requesting the loan of some of the station's discs for a house party.

Most of that pressure isn't overtly political. Those who do hold political power are more apt to exercise it by such devices as withholding interviews when they feel that the association's actions have slighted them, perhaps by not clearing a news item on local events even when the item wasn't political in the sense of dealing with governance but did have implications for the community. Similarly, power holders may request last-minute clearance of airtime for coverage of something nonpolitical in which they're involved, perhaps simply to display that they have the power to do so.

The community power structures may have one further effect. Because of the sense of hierarchy, it's very difficult for any centralized (whether regionally or nationally) news gathering and disseminating operation, such as the 8KIN newsroom in Alice Springs, to develop a network of community correspondents who could report in regularly from the smaller towns around the region. Radio seems to be viewed as a high-status object, in the sense that appearances on the medium are a sign of one's importance. People may be unwilling to serve as community reporters because they don't wish to appear to be claiming higher status for themselves, and community leaders may not wish them to do so, either. Also, there are so many ways in which community residents can take offense at seemingly innocuous items that community reporters soon can find themselves ostracized. It's hardly surprising that attempts to set up correspondent networks may not succeed.[12]

Native American electronic media function along somewhat the same lines, although funding is in far shorter supply than is the case in Australia and New Zealand. Licenses for radio and television stations are issued by the U.S. FCC and the Canadian Radio-Television and Telecommunications Commission (CRTC); funding has come from a number of agencies, including the U.S. Department of Education and the Corporation for Public Broadcasting, as well as some of the Canadian provincial government departments of indigenous affairs. The Catholic church also has supported a few stations, although that is more common in Central and South America. The stations receive the funding and the licenses; the latter usually are held by a station board, which may or may not be part of the tribal governance structure, but occasionally are held by schools. Because federal government funding is so meager and uncertain, the stations often have to rely quite heavily on advertising revenue and radio bingo or other games of chance for their financial support.

In those instances, tribal pressure is most likely to come in the form of attempts to increase revenues through advertising, to the point of reducing the tribe's contribution, if any, and making the station profitable—for the tribe, not the station. Thus, stations are sometimes pushed to cut their operating costs, emphasizing DJ-hosted music programs and "rip and read" newscasts, if any news at all. Such stations not only aren't political; they may not even be very indigenous, particularly if there's a larger majority culture audience in the service area, and if that audience is more prosperous than its indigenous counterpart. That audience then may become the primary target for the station.

Money and political pressure interact more directly in certain cases. Lakota station KILI-FM (Porcupine, South Dakota) became the target of a blockade in May 1992, when those two elements collided with a third: environmental-cum-spiritual-cum-personal concerns. One faction of the local Oglala Lakota tribe was willing to consider projects that would allow experimental testing of a vaccine and a pesticide on the reservation, as well as the mining of zeolite—a potential source of carcinogenic dust. That faction included a majority of tribal council members and made its case primarily on the grounds that the ventures would ease the reservation's severe unemployment (well over 50 percent).

The opponents, who took the title Lakotas for Open Communications, expressed concern about projects they felt would result in some sacrifice of land or sovereignty or would desecrate the earth. They also felt that the white station manager, who was married to a Lakota, had reduced the station's emphasis on Lakota language broadcasts and had unfairly discharged some station staff members. He also seemed willing, in their view, to favor programs that the treaty people regarded as endorsing the development project. And finally, they claimed that pressure from the president of a bank that had loaned money to the station had led the manager to suppress coverage of the shooting death of a Lakota by a white police officer in Gordon, Nebraska (about 30 miles south of the station, and home of the bank that made the loan).[13]

The group blocked the only road leading to the station and posted signs stating "Free KILI" and, with daily updates, "__ days (of blockade)." It demanded that the manager be fired, and one member of the group threatened him with bodily harm if he tried to enter the station. The manager soon had to manage the station by telephone from his home on the reservation, but he retained the support of the station board and staff throughout the blockade. Restraining orders issued by the tribal court to limit the movement of the manager and the activities of the group did little good where the latter was concerned. Mediation attempts by a federal government official and by the American Indian Movement also failed to produce a resolution, in part because members of the group rarely appeared for meetings. The tribal president, sometimes speaking through his administrative assistant (who was one of the station staff members who had been fired), seemed to side with the protesters. The group finally left the scene in late November 1992 without formally calling off the protest.[14]

There is yet another hierarchy worth mentioning: age. Some tribes are very age-conscious and may prefer older but less well-qualified station managers over younger, better-qualified individuals. Where young people are heavily involved with an indigenous station, as is the case with a Navajo radio station at Tuba City (Arizona) High School or as was the case at Navajo Community College (Chinle, Arizona), it can be difficult for older people to accept the possibility that the students might be able to take responsibility for most of the decision making. When the college station KNCC-FM lost its faculty supervisor in the mid-1980s, no one stepped forward to take his place. The college then shut the station down, rather than trust the students to work under minimal faculty supervision, with more responsibility for their own decisions.[15] The Tuba City High School station has had adult managers who actually encourage the students to engage in administrative decision making, but who haven't advertised the fact.[16]

The examples just provided all come from rural settings. Indigenous electronic media operations located in urban areas face other sorts of problems. First, the media facility (community radio or TV service or video club) very often must be shared with other groups, some of them ethnic minorities, some not. Many such facilities are operated by a "collective" management, with representation for the groups using the facility. The politics of power usually center around issues such as who gets the largest numbers of hours of airtime or studio facilities or the best times of broadcast. They also may take the form of shutting out points of view that could make the media outlet seem more, or less, controversial than it wishes to be, thus placing license and/or financial support at risk.

The particular problem for an indigenous group (although it isn't the only group to face such a problem) is that urban centers tend to have very diverse indigenous populations: in tribal affiliation (if any), in economic status and nature of employment, in indigenous language skills (usually poor to nonexistent), and in political goals. If airtime or studio time is limited (it usually is), and if the maintenance of a continuous commitment to the media service is essential (it often is), indigenous users may have to pool their efforts and accept a measure of managerial control. That may bring with it some political control in which one group is favored over others.

Some of the Aboriginals attempting to work through community radio stations in Sydney, Melbourne, and Brisbane mentioned difficulties along those lines,[17] although that also could be a result of their not possessing the talent or the commitment to warrant airtime. Their feelings were that "_____'s mob got there first and won't let go." There could be some substance to the allegation, since it often has been tightly knit groups of friends or kinfolk who have taken the initiative to make programs when the facilities first became available; furthermore, the managers (usually nonindigenous) of such facilities don't care to become embroiled in indigenous intergroup conflict, nor do they wish to take air- or studio time away from a group that has been reliable in order to provide opportunities for one that may or may not be. While this may reduce the level of diversity within indigenous media programming, it certainly avoids a number of potential headaches for managerial staff.

Indigenous electronic media activity in urban areas has another interesting political dimension. If an indigenous group chooses to present material in the indigenous language, it's more than likely that the manager of the media outlet won't understand it; political material then can sometimes bypass the frequent restrictions imposed by such outlets on its dissemination. I have never heard of an actual situation along those lines, although there have been similar occurrences involving community or access radio station broadcasts in Farsi, Tamil, or other "exotic" (for Wellington or Sydney, at any rate!) languages. The absence of such a situation may be due to the relative scarcity of indigenous language speakers in urban areas.

In short, tribal influence in urban media operations seems almost nonexistent. The sorts of "favored groups" referred to above may or may not be made up of members of a single tribe—those I have met with generally are not—but the focus of their program content almost always is urban, and overt expressions of tribal affiliation usually are limited to reminiscences or descriptions of brief visits back to the villages, which may or may not be referred to as "home." The problems presented are more urban than rural, involving high incarceration rates for indigenous peoples and lack of access to some of the better health or educational facilities available in the cities, for example. Political campaigning by indigenous individuals is uncommon, if only because those living in urban areas rarely have the opportunity to elect one of their own to local political office.

Such opportunities do arise in rural communities. However, that does not mean that indigenous candidates will regard the electronic media as relevant. When the Mohawks living on the Canadian side of the border running through the Akwesasne reservation in New York and Quebec held elections in 1994, the reservation radio station (CKON-FM) carried roundtable discussions and interviews with several candidates. Elections on the U.S. side, held a few months later, saw almost no use of radio by candidates, even though station staff attempted to interest them in presenting their views.[18]

There is one potential form of political influence on the part of the majority culture. Radio and television stations, indigenous and otherwise, are licensed by national governments. Most governments place technical and programming restrictions on stations; in the political arena, they usually take the form of requiring airtime for political candidates. (The U.S. Communications Act of 1934, Section 315, requires any station that provides airtime for one candidate for a given office to provide it for all such candidates, and on a similar basis.)[19] There also are laws pertaining to libel and slander that apply to media operations. The majority culture in any country almost certainly will apply its own standards when interpreting such laws; although I have never encountered any instances of it, those standards could clash with indigenous practices and interpretations.

Certain indigenous peoples would regard that as irrelevant, anyway, because they claim full sovereignty over their land. When the government of Canada called a constitutional conference to identify and define aboriginal (Inuit, Métis, and Native American) rights in 1982, a number of tribes refused to participate, on the grounds that participation would have been an admission that they were subject to Canadian governmental jurisdiction.[20] However, many indigenous groups don't claim total and absolute jurisdiction over preserves, reservations, or other lands they hold. The issuance of currency, operation of the postal service, maintenance of military services, and conduct of foreign policy are almost always regarded as the broader national responsibility. Yet many reservations in North America have their own police forces, health services, schools, highway systems, courts, and other like services.

Some of the individuals living there, as well as certain of their Aboriginal, Maori, and other indigenous counterparts, feel that radio and TV should be under their full jurisdiction, as well. They do accept the need for technical regulation on a national scale, so that broadcast signals won't interfere with one another. They do not accept a similar need for restrictions on program content, including what and how much they advertise. Most of the indigenous stations are located far from major urban areas, and their signals aren't very likely to interfere with anyone else's. The regulatory agencies for the electronic media appear willing to leave the stations alone so long as interference is absent. Regulation of program content—a touchy issue in indigenous *and* majority cultures—seems virtually nonexistent, according to indigenous station staff with whom I've spoken.

National broadcast services such as the United Kingdom's BBC, Ireland's Raidio Telefis Eirann (RTE), the Finnish Yleisradio (YLE), Norwegian Norsk Rikskringskasting (NRK), and Swedish Sveriges Radio (SR) accord a fair degree of autonomy to their indigenous stations. The national services operate within the framework of codes or statutes that guarantee broadcast time to political parties during electoral campaigns and, in some cases, at other times. However, that guarantee usually applies only to parties obtaining a certain percentage of the vote in the previous election, and/or a certain number of seats in parliament. The same conditions generally hold for indigenous stations operating as part of the national service.

The national services also carry many discussion and interview programs dealing with politics and politicians; these are expected to display overall quantitative and qualitative balance in their coverage. Again, the indigenous stations are to follow suit, although there can be exceptions, particularly when opinion among the indigenous population runs heavily in one direction: staff at BBC Radio Cymru and NRK Sami Radio have noted the difficulty of finding Conservative party spokespersons (for Welsh-speaking Wales) and supporters of membership in the European Community (for Sami living in northern Norway) and so have carried broadcasts that are admittedly quite one-sided.[21]

Whatever the program format, mainstream voices predominate, often to the virtual exclusion of other political viewpoints. It may not be surprising that both the BBC and RTE would exclude the views of spokespersons for the Irish Republican Army (a ban lifted by both organizations in 1994), although those views sometimes found expression through the device of having actors (sounding as much like the spokespersons as possible) read their statements on-air! "Radical" organizations associated with acts of "terrorism" rarely find large media organizations open to them.

Should the same virtual ban apply to indigenous groups that don't pursue a policy of "terrorism" but do come into conflict with (majority culture) law enforcement agencies from time to time, as did the American Indian Movement (AIM) at Wounded Knee, South Dakota, in 1973, or the Mohawk Nation at Oka, Quebec, in 1990? To some degree, those groups did and still do have access to the airwaves, but only over the small-scale "reservation radio" stations and, occasionally, through National Native News.

Majority culture stations and networks, whether public or commercial, seem interested in providing coverage of the groups' activities only during periods of active conflict, when the more visual elements of conflict take center stage and underlying causes receive brief treatment. The U.S. National Public Radio and Canadian Broadcasting Corporation (CBC) Radio, both of them noncommercial services, have provided more extensive treatment of causes during such periods, although James Winter criticizes the CBC for what he regards as biased interviewing in the case of the Oka confrontation.[22]

NATIONAL GOVERNMENT AGENCIES

National government agencies holding some responsibility for indigenous peoples, such as Australia's ATSIC and the U.S. Bureau of Indian Affairs, could attempt to exercise control or influence over indigenous stations. They disburse funding, and they exercise certain forms of jurisdiction. Actual instances of control or influence are rare. However, the Aboriginal group operating Radio Redfern in Sydney claimed that its building, which was on land controlled by ATSIC, was demolished in 1992 by ATSIC's order, because (again, the group's claim) some of the station's broadcasts had been critical of ATSIC policies.[23] The station continued on-air as Radio Koori, but staff now had to work at the headquarters of its community radio outlet, Radio 2RSR (Radio Skid Row), some distance removed from the heart of the Aboriginal community in the Redfern district.

NATIONAL AND SUPRANATIONAL INDIGENOUS ORGANIZATIONS

National and supranational indigenous organizations such as AIM, the Maori National Congress (MNC), the Sami Parliament, or the Inuit Circumpolar Conference sometimes make declarations concerning the importance of establishing indigenous electronic media, and AIM has helped to start and otherwise assist a few Native American stations. However, they usually lack the ability to furnish financial support for those activities. Whether they would provide it if they had it is another question. Many of the Maori, Native American, Aboriginal, Sami, and other indigenous people with whom I've spoken continue to think mainly in tribal or other more narrowly defined terms. They appear wary of media activities that might stress a national agenda, to the possible detriment of tribal control over events.

An example of that attitude: Derek Fox, director of Mana Maori Media, noted that he had gone to the Maori National Congress each year it convened (1989 was the first year). He always received an enthusiastic reception when he spoke to delegates about the need for national activity through national media, Maori and *pakeha* alike. The MNC passed resolutions affirming that need and pledging support. But when he met with the MNC's chief power brokers, they spoke primarily in terms of tribal loyalties, with national efforts a very distant second. The MNC has yet to provide tangible support for national media activity.[24]

MULTINATIONAL SITUATIONS

Finally, there are a few instances of multinational situations involving indigenous peoples: the Sami of northern Scandinavia, spread across three countries;* the Kurds, spread across five countries; the Basques of Spain and France; certain Native American and Inuit tribes living in cross-border (U.S. and Canada) situations; and likewise tribes in other parts of the world. Media services may be shared within the boundaries of a reservation (the Mohawk radio station at Akwesasne, with Canadian call letters but serving all Mohawks on the reservation) or may be located in all, many, or some of the countries where the indigenous group resides. When the national (majority culture) languages are identical or similar (English in the United States and Canada, Norwegian and Swedish, possibly Spanish and French), coordination of efforts and problems of translation into the in-

---

*Sami living in the former Soviet Union now are beginning to interact more regularly with their kinfolk in the West, although media cooperation remains very modest (the USSR did *not* encourage Sami media). Varis notes that certain Finno-Ugric countries and regions (Estonia, Udmurtia, Mordovia, Yugoria, Komi Gor, Mati El, and Tjumen) signed a Finno-Ugric program promotion and exchange agreement in October 1994. However, the Sami have not yet been included, even though they, too, are a Finno-Ugric group. Varis, Tapio, *Tiedon Ajan Media* (The media of the age of knowledge), Helsinki, 1995, 111.

digenous language may be minimized; when the national languages are quite different (Finnish compared with Norwegian or Swedish), problems can increase. Also, because different national media laws prevail, what those services are free to cover may differ considerably from one side of the border to another.

As there also may be differences in terms of relative autonomy for indigenous peoples on both sides of the border, separations can have political implications, as well. Reindeer herding, for example, is treated as a Sami monopoly in Norway, a conditional monopoly in Finland, and open to any Swede. Basque separatist groups appear to circulate with more freedom in France (where Basque separatism doesn't have much support) than they do in Spain (where there's more support for separatism).

Whether those situations actually result in different sorts of political programming on the two or more sides of the borders is another matter. My lack of linguistic competence has prevented me from making assessments of possible differences in most cases; to the extent that interviews with station staff are a reliable indication of practices, there's little difference. Basque stations in France have provided program time for separatist groups, but not to speak as they wish; instead, station staff interview group members, sometimes challenging and contradicting them.[25]

On the whole, direct political influence on indigenous electronic media isn't particularly evident, although indirect influence through tribal kinship or hierarchy also must be taken into account. If that seems surprising, one must remember that those media have become available only during the past 10 years, for the most part. In some instances, indigenous politicians seem uncertain as to how the media might serve their purposes, while media staff seem at least as uncertain about their roles. As uncritical cheerleaders for "their side," which certainly hasn't had much by way of favorable coverage through the majority culture media? As watchdogs, to show that they can be at least as vigilant as their majority culture counterparts? As champions of unity among the indigenous population, in support of a better life for all indigenous people throughout the land? As supporters of the tribe, which sustains them financially and spiritually?

Whatever their role, the indigenous media clearly are involved in the transmission of political material, although some of it may be in forms that aren't ordinarily considered to be political. To paraphrase an old saying, politics (like beauty) may be in the eyes, or ears, of the beholder, or hearer.

The Indigenous Electronic Media as Channels of Politics

In many respects, indigenous electronic media and their majority culture counterparts are very much alike. Certainly that holds true for a number of program formats: newscasts, sports, and DJ-hosted pop music programs characterize much of radio, while television features the first two, plus comedies and dramas (comedies and dramas are in short supply on most indigenous TV stations). Specific content differs, but length of stories or programs and style of presentation ordinarily are very similar. That may be due to an almost innate conservatism on the part of many program decision makers. Radical departures from the tried-and-true can prove unsettling to audiences, who, as Vladimir Lenin said of the Czarist army, then may vote with their feet (or hands or remote control devices) and transfer their loyalties elsewhere.

Where political material is concerned, there may be another important likeness. The majority culture electronic media often are the targets of criticism from politicians, government officials, religious leaders, and their supposed media brethren, the press: too liberal, out of touch with the mainstream, "nattering nabobs of negativism" (according to then vice president of the United States Spiro Agnew).

Most of that criticism is directed at electronic media operating on a national level—the commercial and noncommercial networks in particular. Local stations present a quite different image in most countries. I have visited local broadcast outlets in over three dozen countries, and they tend, on the whole, to be quite conservative. Aside from the community radio services in New Zealand, Australia, France, Canada, and the United States, most local stations cover political activity in much the same manner as does the press, with relatively uncritical treatment of more or less mainstream political figures. "Radical" voices at either end of the political spectrum are rare; even the predominantly conservative talk radio shows common in the United States usually stop short of the political agendas of the John Birch Society, the Ku Klux Klan,* America Nation, and other white dominance and no-tax groups.

Much the same is true of the indigenous media. The exceptions, as with the majority culture, usually appear through community radio stations, especially in larger cities, although even here they are rare, in my experience. I suggest in Chapter Three why most indigenous stations are "light" (if even that) on overt coverage of indigenous political matters, especially through newscasts. What, then, *is* political about their programming?

INFORMATIONAL FORMATS

Newscasts originated by indigenous stations and news services (e.g., National Native News and Mana Maori Media) contain large numbers of personal success stories. Most of them are not about politicians, although National Native News broadcast a number of "personal portrait" (as opposed to "political agenda") items before and after the 1994 election victory of Native American congressional candidate Ben Nighthorse Campbell of Colorado.[26] Rather, they concern Maori, Sami, Aboriginal, and other indigenous men and women who have become bankers, doctors, professors, and crew members on America's Cup yachting teams. Are such stories political? In one sense, yes. They contribute to a heightening of indigenous self-esteem, which helps to reinforce the feeling that indigenous people can improve their lot in life by taking responsibility. That means, among other things, becoming active in election campaigns, voting, and pressing elected officials for specific responses and actions.

Indigenous newscasts also highlight stories that point out injustices and wrongs experienced by indigenous individuals and groups. Aboriginal radio stations devoted considerable attention to the death of a young Aboriginal man while in police custody (Brisbane, October 1993). His death touched off a number of demonstrations by Aboriginal and non-Aboriginal groups and individuals; the stations were careful to note the presence of non-Aboriginals and interviewed them to learn why they participated. That was not a common feature of majority culture media coverage at the time, and it served to underscore an important political message: our (indigenous) grievances are picking up support from members of the majority culture.[27]

---

*However, the Klan has had some success through cable TV, by preparing and distributing a program of items about the "positive" things it supports and avoiding the more negative issues such as racial "purity" and "superiority."

Finally, indigenous newscasts often include stories of efforts being undertaken to seek justice, as well as the fruits of those efforts. Maori radio, and Mana Maori Media in particular, provided continuing coverage of a Maori-originated legal case against the government of New Zealand. The case concerned the nature and extent of Maori rights to a fair share of the frequency spectrum for television broadcasting, and the government's responsibility to observe and implement those rights (see Chapter Five). The case went to the British Privy Council in London, which was hearing arguments on the case during fall 1993. The Maori radio reports highlighted the testimony of the Maori legal team, which received generally modest attention in the majority culture media. Although the council ultimately upheld the government's action, it reminded the government of its continuing responsibilities regarding Maori television. The political message of Maori media coverage certainly appears to have been "We're not giving up, and we're arguing our case soundly." (A number of Maori broadcast reports noted the success of the team in getting the Privy Council to request further detail, as well as to fault the government of New Zealand for inadequate responses to certain issues raised by the Maori team.)[28]

Sports and weather ordinarily wouldn't be expected to contain political messages, and for most audience members, they probably don't. However, emphasis on the specific successes of indigenous athletes, especially in countries (e.g., South Africa) where their athletic prowess had been underplayed by majority culture media may provide a feeling of empowerment. In November 1993, Umeewarra Radio (Port Augusta, South Australia) staff member Welsley (Woody) Smith produced a documentary on two Aboriginal athletes, one male, one female. The documentary noted their successes but spent far more time on their motivations for excelling, as well as the work necessary to do so. The message again and again was "I want to show the Europeans [white Australians] that a black [Aboriginal] can do as well or better" and "Once I got started, I couldn't fail my people."[29]

Weather reporting, which would seem to be the least likely of media formats to have political implications, actually displayed that characteristic on one occasion: a storm threatened to move ashore along the Frisian coast of the Netherlands. Radio Fryslan was broadcasting in Frisian but decided that it should break its policy of not speaking in Dutch for the sake of carrying a warning on this event. It attracted a number of complaints from Frisian listeners, who felt that (1) anyone who spoke Dutch could listen to other stations for news of the event and (2) maybe a good soaking would encourage them to learn Frisian![30]

Talk shows and discussion programs are available on most indigenous stations, and they cover a wide range of subjects. Overtly political issues don't seem to lead the list—health issues (including alcoholism) and family concerns (disciplining children, problems of single parents, and roles of grandparents) appear to be more prevalent—but political issues certainly air with some regularity. Subjects may range from consideration of political party platforms (with emphasis on items that are of particular interest to the indigenous, such as reforms of educational or criminal justice systems) to how to get more indigenous people to vote.

Both Australia and New Zealand held elections in fall 1993, and there were indigenous candidates in each case. However, the main topic on talk shows and discussion programs in New Zealand appeared to be a possible change in the electoral system, and its likely effect on Maori representation in the national legislature. The then present system provided for four guaranteed Maori seats, with additional seats possible but not likely; the proposed system offered no guaranteed seats but made it seem more likely that Maori could win at least some places, and quite possibly more than under the other system.

Stations carried many spot announcements, some in Maori and some in English, that explained various facets of the two plans and provided numbers to call for further information, but discussion programs and talk shows often centered around the question "Does either option really offer the Maori a fair chance?" Many of the talk show hosts, guest experts, and discussants were guardedly optimistic, even when they found it difficult to favor one plan or the other. Their callers seemed more skeptical throughout the campaign but usually indicated that they would vote, nonetheless. It's possible that they were encouraged to do so in part because the issue was so thoroughly discussed over radio: they couldn't claim lack of information or of encouragement as a reason for *not* doing so.[31]

The Australian election was specifically for Aboriginal officials at the local level, and here the major effort was on getting people informed as to why they should vote and how to go about doing so. Many of the discussion programs included one or two individuals who would ask a number of procedural questions, which someone else (usually speaking in an identifiable Aboriginal English accent) would answer. The discussants would then summarize major points, and one or another would conclude with a phrase something like, "Well, that all sounds easy enough. I can't think why any Koori [a regional designation for Aboriginal] would have any excuse for not voting." Discussants sometimes suggested that a large turnout would show the majority culture that Aboriginals were serious about voting. Questions and statements phoned in to talk shows frequently were procedural; rarely did they emphasize the "get out the vote" theme. Whether the programs had any impact on the size of the Aboriginal vote is unknown, since there was no survey of reasons for voting.[32]

Such programs also may serve as vehicles for addressing one of the most delicate of all political issues: the sharing of power. Many indigenous peoples have achieved some degree of sovereignty in recent years, including greater control over land, water, taxation, and other elements of power once held exclusively by majority cultures. Discussion programs and talk shows on indigenous stations in Australia, New Zealand, Canada, and other countries have served as town hall forums for the discussion of the 1993 Mabo decision in Australia, which recognized oral tradition as valid evidence in Aboriginal land claims; the application of the Treaty of Waitangi to Maori rights in New Zealand (Chapter 5); and the contemporary validity of rights guaranteed to Native Americans in treaties concluded in the nineteenth century.

Station WOJB in Hayward, Wisconsin, served a particularly important function during the 1992 fishing rights conflict between majority culture residents and Native American members of the Lac Court Oreilles Band of Anishinabe (Ojibwe). The band had won a court case over its right, under a nineteenth-century treaty, to spear fish in certain lakes. When members attempted to exercise that right, they were sometimes met by majority culture protesters, some carrying clubs or guns. Individuals on both sides were injured, and the situation seemed to be worsening. The station broadcast a number of discussions that included indigenous and majority culture conciliators, as well as strict advocates and opponents of indigenous rights. While there is no empirical evidence to show that the programs had a calming effect, tensions did appear to ease somewhat following the broadcasts.[33] The Salish Kootenai College low-power TV station (SKC-TV) on the Flathead Reservation in northwestern Montana is credited with having played a similar role in easing tensions between tribal members and non-Native Americans living on the reservation.[34]

Talk shows and discussions sometimes exhibit another dimension of politics: individuals participating in them seem to feel very free to express alternative views that stem from traditional political-cultural practices. As one example, in September 1991, a Maori radio station in Wellington held a two-hour discussion-talk show on the issue of how to deal with a Maori political figure accused of improper financial activities. Both discussion participants and callers raised questions about double standards of judgement and about the facts of the case, but there also were a number of comments along the lines of "Assuming he's guilty, I think that he should be punished in the Maori way. He would have disgraced his tribe. That's where he should go, and that's who should decide the nature of his punishment." Such callers clearly seemed to feel that the Maori political-judicial system was superior in this instance to the pakeha system.[35]

Some of the broadcasts of tribal council meetings that I've heard exhibit this same wide open quality. When KILI-FM broadcast a tribal coun-

cil meeting from the Pine Ridge Reservation on March 22, 1995, it was evident that a number of spectators were ready to participate. They called for
clarification of a number of points and pressed until satisfied. They chal-
lenged certain proposed actions on the grounds that the council hadn't
dealt with similar past issues in the same way. They questioned the arith-
metic used by the council in calculating the cost of wear and tear on a new
road. And at times, the council members appeared to find it difficult to get
a word in edgewise![36]

Such viewpoints don't emerge all that often in the more formal newscasts or, for that matter, in most other indigenous media formats, but I have
heard discussions and talk shows over many indigenous stations that give
voice to it. Perhaps the anonymity helps (over radio, at least); perhaps the
format itself is recognized as welcoming such expressions.

Documentaries are relatively rare on indigenous stations; when they
do appear, they often deal with political issues such as empowerment, relations with the majority culture, and indigenous history. During the cele-
bration of the bicentennial of Captain Cook's landing at Botany Bay in
1789, Station 8KIN (Alice Springs) broadcast a series of minidocumentaries on Aboriginal views of the bicentennial. Most of the incidents illustrated through the documentaries called into question just how much Aboriginals had to celebrate. The mission schools, where Aboriginal children
were taught to be white? The slaughter of Aboriginals in Tasmania? Dis-
possession from the land? Dramatic sketches were mixed with commen-
tary and recorded observations by Aboriginals, resulting in a quite richly
documented portrayal.[37]

In November 1993, Radio Koori (Sydney) produced a documentary
on Aboriginal deaths in prison, which was unusual both because of its mixture of elements (interviews, narration, and popular music featuring lyrics
appropriate to the subject) and its producers—two young women who were
interns with the operation.[38] Production quality was excellent, which illustrates that dedicated but relatively inexperienced staff are capable of producing high-quality documentaries. Many indigenous stations seem to regard the format as beyond the creative power of all but seasoned
professionals.

Videocassette recordings, on the other hand, frequently serve as vehicles for documentaries, many of them political. They're often shown to
small groups, which then discuss them; in that respect, they resemble talk
shows, although the potential for simultaneous interaction throughout a
given geographical area isn't possible, nor is anonymity on the part of the
participant. That may make them more useful for galvanizing opinion and
deciding upon specific courses of action than for assessing a range of opinions.

Some of the documentary subjects don't appear to be political at first glance. A number of Inuit women, working with two whites, produced a documentary on traditional midwifery skills. It was intended to help revive midwifery by presenting the knowledge of those few women who still possessed it. However, interest in such a revival had been sparked by the feeling among women that they had lost considerable power and prestige in their society when the practice was replaced by Euro-American methods, which also meant that women had to travel to distant hospitals. As the video shows a birth accomplished through midwifery, the narrator states, "The baby is coming out from its mother to its own surrounding. It feels it is in its own world. The baby goes out to the father, being there surrounded by loved ones. One can feel its feeling. But when they come out down south, no one we know is there. Only strangers. We used to have to come out to the world as if with no home. This one here was born free."[39]

Not only was the video used to reinforce a sense of community and to restore one element of female pride and dignity but also it was used to prompt discussion of other female social roles and responsibilities that had diminished or disappeared over time. The Inuit women's association, Pauktuutit, also used the video in its representations to government officials.[40]

A group of Aymara women in El Alto, Bolivia, began to make video recordings in 1986. A number of them developed sufficient interest and skill in video making that they committed themselves to producing a 10-minute program each week. The program was shown by local TV stations and also was used to generate discussion in small groups. Topics included women and the legal system, coping with poverty, and problems of adapting to urban culture. Perhaps the most interesting feature of the project was the development of an ongoing commitment on the part of the women: many video projects begin with a flourish but quickly fade away, especially when they concern political subjects. Perhaps the key here is that almost all of the participants were already active in community affairs and were accustomed to speaking out. Also, although it isn't noted in Carmen Ruiz's report on the project, the participants almost certainly had had a great deal of personal experience with the need for patience coupled with perseverance where political action was concerned, and were in the video project for the long haul.[41]

Aboriginal groups and individuals have made a number of videos and TV films on land rights issues. "Our Land Is Our Life," "One Mob, One Voice, One Land," and "Land Bilong Islanders" are three that have had wide distribution in Australia, including a number of showings over ABC-TV. The last deals with the Eddie Mabo case: a landmark in the annals of land rights jurisprudence, since the final decision upholding Aboriginal claims to land drew heavily on acceptance of oral tradition as valid testimony. The video was made in 1989, several years after the courts began to hear the case, and three years before the High (Supreme) Court's decision. It was intended to strengthen the resolve of Aborigines to press on with the case, and at the same time to inform white Australians of the nature and validity of the Aboriginal claim. Here, the financial and distributional support of a number of organizations—the Aboriginal and Torres Strait Commission (federal government), the Northern Territory Land Councils (state), Community Aid Abroad (despite its name, a domestically oriented nongovernmental organization), the Australian Council of Churches, and Greenpeace—was crucial to wide public exposure.[42]

Coordinators of video projects also must address a number of questions surrounding the issue of how to maximize the effectiveness of such projects. Jennifer Kawaja provides a particularly thoughtful account of what she calls "process [participatory] video" production and distribution. Empowerment usually is regarded as a major objective, but Kawaja indicates that anyone assuming a central role in either production or distribution must try to answer a number of difficult questions, such as who is ultimately responsible for the accuracy and balance of a video production and whose criteria define those terms? If the production is meant for *local* use, might the technology of video production and distribution by its very nature make the work more generalized, less local? (In other words, are people so used to seeing television productions as several steps removed from themselves that a video's very localness may be lost?) To the extent that viewers do see it as local, might it seem to them to constitute action in and of itself, making further action, toward lasting change, appear to be unnecessary?[43]

All of those questions contain political dimensions, but it is the last of them that I find especially relevant in the context of the indigenous media. The question itself resembles questions asked about the role of talk radio in the U.S. electoral process: do callers feel that talking about what's wrong is sufficient demonstration of their involvement to make further action (e.g., seeking out more information or voting) seem unnecessary? Talk radio has been a part of the U.S. media scene since the 1960s, although the heavy use of it for political discussion (or destruction?) is more recent. Subject matter and style (not least of all that of the program host) have been predominantly majority culture—often featuring views of the disaffected.

Indigenous media outlets are quite recent. Might it be that indigenous audience members, now able to express themselves through their own media channels, are particularly prone to see that level of involvement as sufficient and fail to follow up with more tangible forms of action? The use of videos as stimulators of discussion among small groups should create the necessary conditions for action, and a skillful group leader can move the group in that direction. Still, the very presence of indigenously produced messages coming through media channels that, until recently, were dominated by the majority culture can make it seem as if indigenous groups have truly entered the corridors of power.[44] And the electronic media indeed may be in those corridors, but the legislative, executive, and judicial decisions continue to be made behind the doors to which those corridors lead.

ENTERTAINMENT FORMATS

I note in Chapter Two that entertainment formats haven't been thought of as primary vehicles for political material. It often requires a stretching of definitions of *political* to see how entertainment could play a role. Still, there is value in doing so, for two reasons: entertainment programs usually are more popular than information programs (although major newscasts and minidocumentaries along the lines of the U.S. "60 Minutes" often do well), and people's defenses may be down when attending to entertainment, so material they would reject when presented in a newscast might at least receive their attention when presented through entertainment.[45] A consideration of three formats, satire, drama, and music, indicates how the process works.

Satire is quite rare in all electronic media, although it was used quite extensively by international radio stations during World War II and in the early years of the cold war.[46] It also enjoyed a fair degree of popularity on British and U.S. television during the 1960s ("That Was the Week That Was," "The Monty Python Show," "Rowan and Martin's Laugh-In"). It is very rare in the indigenous media, perhaps because indigenous groups wouldn't want the majority public to listen to or watch them criticize or mock themselves.*

However, there is an example that provides some idea of what indigenous media can manage by way of satire. Mana Maori Media produced a series of satires under the title "Reta Ki a Mama" (letter to Mama); it ran from 1991 to 1993, although not on a regular schedule: its two producer-writer-actors, Waihoroi Shortland and Rereata Makiha, also were full-time reporter-editors in Mana Maori's Auckland (Papatoetoe) studios and could manage only one production a month, if that. They developed various characters: an old woman, often representing common sense; a young, rather

---

*As I have spent more time with indigenous groups, I have become much more aware of the individuality and keenness of their senses of humor, including satire. However, it's something that they usually keep to themselves, in part because it serves as an important means of maintaining a specific sense of identity and uniqueness.

impulsive, "modern" male; an older, more traditional male; and others, as the need arose.

The characters commented on various current events, most of them political; many of the characters displayed various human foibles, such as prejudice (usually anti-Maori), stupidity, narrow-mindedness, and greed. Maori and pakeha alike formed the subjects of their portraits. Publicly prominent individuals received appropriate nicknames, usually reflecting a negative trait, at least in terms of the specific event with which they were associated. Prime Minister Jim Bolger became Potato Bolger, which represented both his former occupation as a potato farmer and his tendency to oversimplify complex issues that he didn't seem to understand. The program was very popular, judging from the mail it generated and the extent to which Maori talked about it, but it was exhausting to produce, and its originators finally dropped it.[47]

Indigenous **drama** with political themes is somewhat more common, especially where there's a longstanding tradition of dramatic writing in the indigenous language, as with Welsh and Irish. Radio Cymru, Raidio na Gaeltachta, Radio nan Gaedhael, and the Irish, Welsh, and Scots Gaelic television services all produce dramas; many of those dramas deal with political personalities and events, especially from the past, and often with considerable attention to elements not featured in majority culture accounts.

For example, Welsh TV carried a drama, "Sul y Blodau" (Palm Sunday), which dealt with an incident in the late 1980s when police conducted a predawn raid on dozens of homes in Wales, allegedly in order to determine whether their occupants had any responsibility for the burning of a number of vacation homes in Wales. Several individuals were arrested and held, but all were set free without charges. Playwright Mike Povey set this as a drama, and it provoked a great deal of discussion. It was rebroadcast during the Easter season in 1995 but excited little attention.[48]

Indigenous groups lacking traditions of political drama occasionally have produced such programs for radio, TV, or videocassette. An Aboriginal example noted earlier contained political dimensions, in that the high school students producing a series of radio plays presented their views on various authority figures—parents, but also school officials and police.

A number of Aymara women in the Bolivian city of El Alto began to produce radio dramas on an occasional basis. By 1989, they had committed themselves to more regular (and more "professional") production and produced a number of soap operas, based on their own daily experiences. Most of those experiences weren't specifically political, but they often underlined the discomfort women felt when confronted by authority figures: shopkeepers, priests, and government officials. As the characters in the series spoke out sooner or later, that seemed to give women listeners a greater sense of self-confidence and readiness to speak out—certainly a key part of political involvement.[49]

Music is easily the most prevalent of all radio formats, indigenous and otherwise, and enjoys considerable popularity as a TV format, especially MTV and its imitators. Its political dimensions are quite familiar: street musicians have sung political ballads for centuries, and composers such as Mozart, Verdi, and Shostakovich have written operas with contemporary political themes. In a Dublin High Court case involving Christy Moore's song "They Never Came Home," Justice Frank Murphy stated: "There is no reason why a song should not be as much in contempt [of court] as a leading article in a newspaper or an academic study. The method of communicating the information is irrelevant."[50]

Rap music in the United States, reggae in the Caribbean, and a variety of other musical forms have been employed to carry political messages. Some of their messages are generalized: don't trust police, teachers, or other authority figures; take pride in yourself and your people, and act on it. Some are highly specific, taking up such subjects as the riots that followed the first Rodney King–Los Angeles Police trial in 1992.

As noted earlier, indigenous peoples around the world have adapted western musical forms such as rap, rock, and country. It is truly amazing to see the numbers of indigenous music groups that have come into existence over the past few decades, assisted by the development of indigenous electronic media. That increased activity has an interesting cultural dimension: it's one of the few ways in which the more traditional rural dwellers and the urban indigenous residents share a common bond. Vocal and instrumental (especially percussion and flutelike instruments) music have long had important roles in indigenous traditions, and the men and women who were and are especially skilled have enjoyed great honor. As Brunton notes, "The status of Aboriginal musicians among their own people is high. ... They are often among the leaders of the community and have a deep commitment to improving the lot of Aboriginal people as a whole." He then goes on to make this observation: "music is one of the few areas in which non-tribal Aboriginal men, as well as women, are able to fulfill a similar function today as they did in their former tribal societies."[51]

That shared experience has a potentially important influence on "political music." Urban musicians don't appear to be all that interested in depicting their specific tribal origins but instead sing of the general problems and triumphs of the indigenous, usually within the country, occasionally on subjects as specific as resentment over majority culture (mis)appropriation of indigenous symbols (in the first of the following examples, Indian names for sports teams).

I can't believe we're still on the sporting line,
On the news each and every night.
A Redskin massacre, A Braves scalping,
Whose image do you think that's helping?

WITHOUT REZERVATIONS (Native American Rap Group),
"Mascot"

Today's life is so unreal;
White man taught us to drink and steal.
To understand why, we're really not sure,
But it's hard living under white man's law.
If you agree that this story's right,
Join together to win the fight.
Our father's dreamtime will come true;
Now it's up to me and you.

HARD TIMES (Aboriginal),
"Only a Few"[52]

Bury my heart at Wounded Knee
Deep in the earth. Cover me
With pretty lies ...
They got these energy companies who want the land
And they got churches by the dozens want to guide our hand
And sign our Mother Earth over to pollution, war and greed.

BUFFY SAINT MARIE (Native American),
"Bury My Heart at Wounded Knee"

Think you've crossed the line/for the final time?
Lift it up again!
We got lots to do
And we're comin' through
To express ourselves.
Here we are where we can call our home
This is us now and we're not alone.
(*Chorus*)
It's time to A-a-a-kona te reo [learn the language].

MOANA AND THE MOA HUNTERS (Maori),
"Akona Te Reo"

Songs expressing self-confidence as an indigenous people seem to be the most common form of indigenous "musical politics." They usually take the form of exhortation, as well: we've arrived (or we're arriving), but we need to continue the struggle in order to consolidate our gains. Songs expressing mistrust of majority culture also are frequent and often (as in the case of "Bury My Heart at Wounded Knee") offer specific examples of reasons for mistrust. The Welsh rock group Anhrefn (Chaos) warns of the incursions of culture-destroying forms of tourism in its song *"Croeso an Cymru"* (Welcome to Wales):

> Welcome to Wales ...
> But whose Wales *is* it?
> Do we want another Disneyland?
> Mickey Mouse?[53]

It usually is the work of urban indigenous musicians that gets recorded, since lack of identification with a specific tribe will probably help to attract a broader audience, indigenous or not. Also, it avoids the potential intertribal jealousy that seems to have discouraged the exchange of recordings of local groups in some instances: several managers and program directors at Maori radio stations told me that they wanted to exchange such material, because it would bring additional variety to their output, but others doubted that their listeners would want to hear music from their traditional enemies or tribes less worthy than themselves. Therefore, if music has the potential to influence political attitudes, they're likely to be attitudes on *national* issues—issues that may serve to unite indigenous peoples of different tribes and geographical locations.

Eric Rothenbuhler, discussing U.S. radio, contends that "contemporary *commercial* [italics mine] radio's influence on popular music *must* [italics Rothenbuhler's] be limiting and conservative."[54] Most indigenous stations are noncommercial, or just slightly commercial, and their freedom of choice of music seems to be broad. But if playlists become more common, and if commercialization increases, political music may find itself with less airtime. If it's rare to have an alternative rock station featuring majority culture political music in all but the largest U.S. cities, consider the likelihood of an indigenous alternative rock station!

Indigenous Media, Indigenous Women: The Politics of Gender

When I began my study of indigenous electronic media, I expected to discover a mixture of influences and approaches and was not surprised when I did. I was far more surprised to discover the place of indigenous women in the indigenous electronic media. After all, the majority culture electronic media tend to be male-dominated, especially in the executive, production, and journalistic ranks. Since many of the indigenous electronic media operations either originated as part of the majority culture media, or had no other source of trained staff for independent indigenous stations, why should the pattern of male dominance be any different? Furthermore, politically active indigenous women often have stated that their voices are heard only up to a point, after which they're told, in essence, that they shouldn't forget their "traditional" female roles—a situation described vividly by Maori lawyer Ripeka Evans.[55]

Yet my visits to several dozen indigenous electronic media operations, including training programs, have revealed that women play major roles in several capacities, chief among them as journalists (including editors) and as hosts for morning talk and entertainment shows. Many women also serve as station managers and as heads of indigenous media organizations.[56] That is particularly the case with stations and organizations that are independent of the national broadcasting corporations; the latter usually are managed by males.

Why this major involvement by women? There seem to be several answers, beginning with the very fact that, like Mount Everest, the electronic media "are there" and present a challenge and a valid opportunity. Increasing numbers of indigenous women are entering the workplace, and the very newness of the indigenous electronic media appears to have attracted many women who may perceive the media as more gender bias–free than older establishments. Second, women (and particularly female teachers) have played a major role in the creation of indigenous media. Whether or not they remained active following the initiation of services, they served as clear examples of the ability of women to work with the electronic media.

Third, the low rates of pay that characterize the independent indigenous media (indigenous stations within national media organizations feature better salary structures) may have discouraged males more than females. Fourth, according to several indigenous media trainers with whom I've spoken, females are more prone than are males to identify electronic media work, and journalism in particular, as interesting and significant. If there's a strong association of "maleness" with outdoor work—and several station managers and staff in Sami and Native American stations have told me that there often is—that also can serve to discourage male participation in radio.[57] Furthermore, females often appear to have greater aptitude for program production (again, for journalism in particular) than do males. Speculation as to why that should be the case runs along several lines but often includes the observation that indigenous females seem to be more comfortable in social interaction, especially oral interaction, than are males.[58]

But numbers alone do not lead to control, and my overall impression of indigenous electronic media *content* is that it is almost as male-dominated as that of the majority culture media. Women's voices and faces may be more prevalent, the numbers of women managers may be considerable, yet the performers whose recordings are played and the newsmakers whose activities are covered are heavily male. Marjorie Ferguson addresses the issue of whether female leadership in the media translates into increased and/or more favorable coverage of women and tentatively concludes that it doesn't necessarily make a difference.[59] The few dozen indigenous female journalists with whom I've spoken feel that they command respect among male and female interviewees alike. However, many of them have added that they often have difficulty contacting indigenous female spokespersons for various issues and organizations, both because organizations may be unable to readily identify them and because those who can be identified sometimes seem hesitant to speak on what they consider "male" subjects or roles.

Perhaps it's simply too early to tell whether the major involvement of women in indigenous electronic media will alter the balance in presentation of gender. And there already is considerable evidence to indicate that women have been very successful in employing audio- and videocassette recordings, as well as broadcast programming, to bring female political viewpoints and experiences to wider audiences.[60] The passage of time, coupled with persistence on the part of female (and, hopefully, male) journalists, managers, and program producers, may result in more equitable gender representation in the future.

Conclusion

The indigenous electronic media clearly have important roles to play in the realm of indigenous political life. If they appear to be playing those roles minimally, spasmodically, or selectively, that may not be surprising: those media are comparatively young. Also, indigenous politicians, who aren't the only important players in indigenous politics, often seem to have been slow to realize the merits of working with the indigenous media. That may be particularly true where those politicians already have reasonably solid relationships with majority culture media and may discount their indigenous counterparts as too small or insufficiently "professional." That also may be true where tribal leaders have had little media contact of any sort and feel uneasy before microphones and cameras, where words and gestures, once recorded, can return to haunt them.

But if the movement toward indigenous media "sophistication" where political coverage is concerned seems slow, there are figures who stand as examples (good or bad) of the "mediated" indigenous politician. Tasmanian Aboriginal Michael Manley, Maori Winston Peters, Canadian First Nations leader Ovid Mercredi have helped themselves and their causes to gain attention through their understanding of how to use the media. Groups such as the Maori Te Toi tu Tanga (The Upstarts) have taken over broadcast facilities when they failed to get an indigenous station to cover their opposing point of view (in this case, opposition to a land claims agreement about to be signed by Tainui tribal officials). Indigenous stations such as WOJB in Hayward, Wisconsin, or Koori Radio in Sydney have dealt with political crises and problems in meaningful and powerful ways. Women such as Carmen Ruiz and Dorothy Kidd have worked successfully with Aymara and Inuit women's groups in the production of politically oriented videocassettes. In short, there are numerous examples of how indigenous media have approached, and therefore might approach, the political uses of radio, television, and cassettes. The wider sharing of such examples should help to further the development of such programming. Changes in attitudes and practices among indigenous leaders, particularly in favoring and in working to improve the financial support of such media, also will play crucial roles.

The Past,
the Present,
and the
Likely
Future

What can we say, with some confidence, that we know
about the indigenous electronic media, recent though their
development may be? That their numbers are growing. That
very few radio stations, once on the air, have failed. That new technologies
are beginning to play some valuable roles as program distributors and also
as outlets for groups (particularly women using videocassettes) within indigenous communities. And that they've greatly encouraged the growth of
indigenous popular music. That's a considerable list of accomplishments
for such relatively young and often low-budget media ventures.

There are several other observations that must be more tentative, either because of their complexity or because of inadequate grounds for
firmer conclusions. They include the following:

1. While language revival or revitalization has been a major reason
for establishing indigenous broadcast stations, very few of them broadcast
exclusively in indigenous languages, and most of them broadcast primarily in the majority culture languages. Based on my visits to several dozen

stations, I can support that conclusion, but there remain a few hundred that I have *not* visited. Such data as I have, quite complete for Native American and Inuit stations in North America, indicate that the as yet unvisited stations fit the same pattern. However, I also have discovered that the remotely located stations are more likely to feature broadcasting in indigenous languages than are those in or near small to large cities, where fewer indigenous people speak the languages.

2. Indigenous women appear to find the indigenous electronic media quite accessible, both as places of employment and as outlets for their messages. I have suggested why that may be so (see Chapter Seven), but that tentative conclusion needs more detailed evidence.

3. Training operations for indigenous media personnel are quite common, although their quality varies a good deal, and there's relatively little training available in the field; most trainees must come to urban areas. Sales and management training is almost nonexistent yet seems to be vital in terms of future needs.

4. The vast majority of indigenous media operations indicate that reaching young people is a top priority, but very few feel that they've been successful in doing so. Those that have either feature highly specialized formats (e.g., Mai-FM's heavy concentration on rock music) or involve young people as on-air talent for large blocks of program time.

5. Pressures on indigenous electronic media come from a wide variety of sources and are at least as heavy as they are for majority culture stations. Furthermore, some of those pressures are very culture-specific, or even tribe-specific, and difficult for outsiders (researchers, certainly, but also staff members coming from outside) to detect.

6. Political broadcasting seems to be in shorter supply than one might imagine, given the oft-expressed desire of indigenous peoples to speak in their own right, seek justice, and combat stereotypes. However, broader definitions of what constitutes political broadcasting reveal somewhat higher levels of activity, especially when popular music is included.

7. Indigenous television has been slow to develop, aside from Sianel Pedwar Cymru in Wales, but is showing signs of vitality in New Zealand, Australia, and Ireland and, to a lesser extent, in Canada and the United States. Also, videocassettes are serving the needs of increasing numbers of indigenous peoples.

There are two other very important observations featured in the preceding chapters but not appearing in the above list. They are the need for audience research and the relevance of theory to practice. Each, I feel, merits special consideration.

The Continuing Need for Research

As observed in Chapter Three, very little audience research has been conducted where indigenous media are concerned. One could suggest almost anything, and it might be useful. I have chosen four quite different activities as examples chiefly in order to illustrate the potential breadth of activity.

AUDIENCE AWARENESS

Audience awareness of the media operation's existence and nature seems often to be assumed, yet my research has indicated that there seems to be widespread ignorance on both counts. Most of the media operations generated or attracted publicity when they first began operation, but very few sought to discover whether the audiences they hoped to reach had received or acted on that publicity. In those areas where there already was a fair range of media choice, even if the media were majority culture, it's quite possible that many target audience members never heard of the new operation or heard so little that they weren't disposed to try it out.

Standard questionnaire-based survey instruments serve nicely to ask two fundamental questions: are you aware of us, and have you actually heard or seen us? If the responses are positive, a third question can be a useful guide to scheduling: which programs/presentations are your favorites? This question can also help to determine whether or not respondents really have heard or seen the operation, or whether they're simply being polite. If the response is negative on awareness, a third question (why haven't you tried us?) can generate much useful data on problems of set ownership, misconceptions about the operation (e.g., "I don't speak Maori," when the station broadcasts largely in English), and other obstacles to be overcome. If negative on actually seeing or hearing, a third question can help to inform program creation and may call attention to problems of reception: why *haven't* you tried us, or would you be interested in hearing or watching *some* sort of indigenous media, and if so, what?

I regard such research as particularly important for indigenous electronic media because I have detected a tendency on the part of many staff members to assume that audiences will know about "this first ever Basque station," simply because there's never been anything like it. That might be a safe assumption in a community such as Mangamuka Bridge (pop. 150?), New Zealand, where the Maori station is the only station for some miles around. It isn't very safe in more mature media environments, and it will be even less safe as satellite-delivered TV makes its way into more and more countries, available (at a cost, but that's dropping, too) to urban and rural viewers alike. Publicizing the operation should be a continuing concern. So should the discovery of whether the publicity is finding its mark in terms of increased target audience usage of the service, and if not, why not.

"PROFESSIONALISM"

Another potentially worthwhile area of investigation would be the question of how target audiences regard the often simpler, less "professional," programs produced by the indigenous electronic media, when compared with majority culture programming. My discussions with indigenous media staff have indicated that opinions are divided. Some individuals strive to produce material that will measure up to majority culture standards of professionalism, even when that may mean producing fewer, or shorter, programs. Others have contended that the main task is to get indigenous voices and faces on-air as much as possible, even when that means more awkward shooting or editing, more uneven voice levels, and more visible and audible performance errors, so long as the resultant material isn't horribly amateurish.

The assumptions of the two groups stem from differing definitions of the tolerance and/or sophistication of the target audience, and possibly on different definitions of audience motivation to listen or view. An indigenous program producer/performer who hopes to gain employment in the majority culture media will have a strong motivation to make programs of the highest professional standard. So will individuals who want to show that the indigenous peoples are just as capable as anyone else of producing top quality material. And so will anyone who wishes to tell the indigenous audience, "We think that you deserve the very best from us" (which presupposes that "very best" means the equal of, and perhaps imitation of, majority culture output). On the other hand, an indigenous producer/performer may reason that something is better than nothing, and that more of something is better than less, because indigenous audiences have been deprived of the opportunity to see and hear themselves and need to be shown that they've "arrived" in a substantial way. Such an individual also may feel that major involvement by the community in the preparation of programs is more important to the development of strong bonds between media operation and community than the presentation of more professionally produced programming.

There are advantages and disadvantages to each approach, but if it could be demonstrated through research that what matters most to the target audience, depending upon the nature of the program, is a high degree of production quality or frequent appearances by people more or less like themselves, that would strongly suggest how the operation should invest its resources.

The research itself would not be easy, since it would call upon respondents to come up with subjective and often sensitive judgements. At one level, a questionnaire could ask respondents to evaluate two or three different types of programs that they regularly view or hear, using a list of factors generated from interviews on what people find attractive and unattractive when they watch and listen. Respondents would evaluate the levels of importance of the factors for each type of program, either rank ordering or assigning scores of 1 to factors of major importance, 2 for minor importance, 3 for no importance.

At another level, focus groups could see or hear pairs of programs of the same type that display differing sorts of approaches to production, some very professional, some considerably less so. They would then discuss the pros and cons of each, and the factors that emerged with some frequency and prominence could form the subject of further discussion.

VIDEOCASSETTE USAGE

Yet another approach to research would involve the study of videocassette usage by indigenous viewers. Clearly, much indigenous videocassette production is meant to be seen in group settings. Examples noted in earlier chapters often were meant for audiences that would be unlikely to purchase cassettes, or even to rent them. The technology of tape duplication and the decreasing cost of blank cassettes makes it possible for indigenous groups with modest financial resources to consider cassettes as a viable means of disseminating a message to a fairly large number of people during a constricted time period. Distribution through libraries or schools also can achieve much the same effect. Audiocassettes have been passed from hand to hand in Iran and Saudi Arabia, further increasing message distribution, but we know little about videocassette sharing.

A study of videocassette retransmission could take several forms. An initial survey of an indigenous population could assess the availability of playback units, patterns of utilization (including the presence or absence of discussion of cassette material), and readiness to consider library rental or individual sharing of cassettes. A second level of study could be conducted with focus groups of videocassette users. For example, it would determine factors that encourage or discourage library borrowing or individuals' sharing, such as ease of access to libraries or confidence that someone sharing a tape has something worthwhile to share. A third level of study would involve direct observation of group viewing practices, coupled with postviewing questions that would examine a variety of issues: whether videocassettes seem to lead more often to discussion, or to sharper, deeper discussion, of a topic than do comparable programs broadcast over television; what specific visual and aural elements seem to attract the most attention; for what reasons (if at all) viewers stop videocassette recorders in order to discuss particular points.

Data gathered through such studies should help indigenous groups to identify the elements of production and distribution that would help to enhance prospects for use of recordings and help to increase their persuasive power. And if it should turn out that sharing of videocassettes is as common and natural a practice as is the sharing of many things in indigenous societies, then videocassettes may prove to be a very cost-effective substitute for broadcast TV.

MUTUAL COMPREHENSION OF DIALECTS

We also know very little about the mutual comprehension of dialects, yet many indigenous media operations use a variety of them. A common supposition among media staff is that initial listener reaction to dialects other than his or her own is negative, to the point of discounting program content. However, the negativism seems to moderate over time. Assuming that dialects continue to be important in program making, it would be worthwhile to discover (1) just how mutually unintelligible or disturbing they might be, (2) whether negative feelings moderate over time, and (3) whether broadcasters could do anything to lessen negativism.

A survey questionnaire could determine whether listeners even were aware of dialects on the air. If they were, they could be asked whether they listened to entire programs or individual items in a dialect, or whether they turned them off, physically or mentally. They also could specify whether certain types of dialects, certain kinds of speakers, or certain subjects were less or more objectionable. Finally, they could be invited to offer suggestions as to how dialects might be made more "listener-friendly," at least where they're concerned. And if listeners were to indicate how long they had been listening to the station, it would be possible to compare degrees of "objectionability" in light of the duration of listeners' exposures to the dialects.

MANAGEMENT PRACTICES

Finally, there is a nonaudience category of research that could be very helpful: management practices. As I've indicated, management training is scarce, and most managers of indigenous media operations have had to learn on the job. From my research, turnover among indigenous managers seems very high: it's rare to find a given manager in place for more than two years, and a few operations have gone through five or six managers during that time. Observation- and interview-based studies that isolate the characteristics of successful and unsuccessful management practices might help to improve the process of manager selection and certainly would play a role in management training, if such were to be offered.

In any research project, it is essential for researchers to be prepared to abandon previous conceptions regarding how the project should be carried out. As I observe in Chapter Three, we have very little information on the appropriateness of standard measures and approaches in research where indigenous media audiences are concerned. For example, scaled instruments, opposing pairs of terms, and styles of discussion may be understood far differently by indigenous respondents. Pretesting, as well as plenty of consultation with indigenous individuals, seems absolutely essential.

Theory
and
Practice

I state in Chapter One that mine is not a theoretically based study, although it is theoretically informed. I feel that cultural dependency theory came closest to helping me to understand the evolution and practices of indigenous electronic media. I was particularly interested in two aspects of that theory: whether or not indigenous media personnel absorb and follow majority culture media staff "models" of "professional" production practices and other forms of behavior and whether or not indigenous media, consciously or unconsciously, follow "models" furnished by majority culture programming, imported or domestic, and borrow the majority culture portrayals of themes, values, and depictions of society. My interest was fueled by consideration of the recent indigenous past: could a people who had lived for several generations with no alternative to the majority culture model of mass media choose to, or be able to, develop different approaches to the use of their own mass media operations? Could there still be truly alternative indigenous ways of seeing and hearing mass mediated messages?

As so often seems the case with theory testing, I cannot claim that I have conclusive results that support or reject dependency theory, at least in this particular case. However, my data, mainly as presented in Chapter Six, do indicate that there are some discernable differences in indigenous uses of the electronic media and, less clearly, that there are alternative ways of seeing and hearing.

Those differences seem to become more marked in the cases of media operations in more remote locations. That shouldn't be surprising: individuals and groups living far from urban areas often have had the opportunity and the occasion to preserve more of their indigenous culture, including verbal and nonverbal languages, than have their indigenous media counterparts. I have found such elements as use of pause, slower paces of editing for sound and vision, and less rigidly time-governed formats to be much more common in rural media operations than in urban outlets. I have occasionally seen and heard shot and sound sequences that bore little resemblance to what would make sense to Western eyes and ears, but rarely has that occurred in urban settings.

Urban stations and video workshops seem to produce material that is much more like majority culture output, with one interesting difference: the concept of "media professionalism" seems considerably less important to rural, and somewhat less important to urban, indigenous media staff at *independent* media outlets than it does to majority culture media staff in general (community radio and TV excepted).* The overall result is a more relaxed, and sometimes even laid-back, style of production. That seems especially true when the indigenous media seek to involve the broader indigenous population in their work: they place a far higher premium on displaying the voices and faces of the people than do majority culture media (aside from talk radio and TV). Many indigenous media staff met with initial resistance from the average indigenous person ("who would want to see or hear me on TV or radio? That's for important people!"), but most indigenous outlets persisted in putting them on the air or on tape, to the point where it now would seem abnormal if they weren't there.

---

*However, indigenous media staff at government- and public service broadcaster–affiliated stations seem much more like their majority culture colleagues.

At the same time, I cannot claim that the indigenous electronic media look and sound radically different from their majority culture counterparts most of the time. Both play much the same music, with disk jockeys to host the programs; phone-in discussion shows usually don't sound markedly different; news programs often feature many of the same stories, fed by the same wire services. And when the stories *are* different, the manner in which they're presented usually isn't. The few indigenous TV sitcoms, soap operas, dramas, and quiz shows bear strong production resemblances to majority culture fare, even if the themes and languages might differ.*

That tendency is neither universally present nor absent. Close examination of majority culture electronic media in non-Western nations almost certainly would lead to a similar conclusion. Japanese television contains themes and portrayals that seem remarkably similar to matching program genres in the West; it also displays production values and themes that seem far removed from anything Western.[1] My more limited viewing of Tunisian, Lebanese, and other non-Western TV brings me to the same conclusion.[2] One cannot discount the potential influence of Western production and thematic values and practices, but they are not all-pervasive. Of course, the coming decades may bring changes: if multichannel satellite-delivered services become more globally available and affordable, and if Western nations continue to be the principal program suppliers, Western influence may increase. If it does, Aboriginal, Sami, and other indigenous ways of seeing, hearing, and producing programs may diminish or vanish altogether.

However, it is also possible that, if some indigenous material finds its way into the global marketplace (a long shot, but so was karaoke singing at first), some Western electronic media product might begin to show a broader range of tolerance for "professional" practices, might relax the pace of programs a bit, and might display more interest in portraying a wider range of society.

Finally, most indigenous media operations that I've visited seem to have a genuine regard for the dignity of the individual, something that often seems to be a vanishing commodity in U.S. and Japanese news reports and talk shows. To illustrate, in March 1995, Lakota radio station KINI-FM (St. Francis, South Dakota) broadcast a conference on reconciliation between the Catholic church and a number of Lakota who had attended the local Catholic mission school before it closed in the mid-1970s. For one session, many of the Lakota were expected to express very personal feel-

---

*Indigenous TV productions made for videocassette release seem to display more apparent differences. There probably are several reasons for that, ranging from the more frequent involvement of amateurs in such productions to the greater freedom from institutional constraints enjoyed by many video producers.

ings, often negative, about their experiences. The church, which furnishes almost all of KINI's budget, was perfectly happy to have that session broadcast, but the station manager decided not to, on the grounds that he didn't wish to place people in an emotional situation where they might later regret what they had said, especially if it were to have been broadcast.[3] Contrast that with the likely behavior of producers of the "Jenny Jones Show" or other "let it all hang out" U.S. TV and radio talk shows!*

I also refer to Habermas's notion of *public sphere* in Chapter One; it's not a theory, but an interesting perspective. Certainly there are far more publicly available indigenous voices now than there were 10 or 20 years ago, and there probably will be even more in the future. But there also are far more electronic media of all sorts than there were in the past, even in previously monopolistic environments such as Great Britain, France, and the former Soviet Union.[4] Having entered a public sphere that is increasingly crowded, there is a real question in my mind as to how effective the indigenous services will be in making their voices heard, particularly if they harbor hopes that they'll attract majority culture audiences. That is why I advocate greater attention to program and station promotion in Chapter Three: without it, the indigenous services may end up "preaching to the converted."

Past to Present to Future

If we look back on the development of indigenous electronic media, we see certain elements that have accompanied their growth. Those elements may or may not be indispensable to future growth, but they would seem worth bearing in mind as more indigenous groups prepare to engage in media activities. In no necessary order, they are

---

*Annette Brown, director of SKC-TV (Salish-Kootenai College, Pablo, Mont.), noted an instance where she had taped the quarterly meeting of the Consolidated Salish and Kootenai tribes. As she was editing the tape for broadcast, she received a call from one of the participants, a woman who had spoken eloquently on the issue of tribal enrollment (standards for determining membership). The woman requested that her statement not be used on the air because she felt that, even though the emotion she displayed was genuine, she did not wish to see it displayed before the larger audience. Brown readily complied with her request, although not without some regret, since the statement would have been an excellent illustration of the depth of feeling on a sensitive issue. Personal interview, Pablo, Mont., June 1995.

1. The ability to gather enough committed individuals together so that the often difficult and prolonged work of getting a media operation up and running will be shared. Very few indigenous media organizations have been set in motion by two or three individuals; more often, it's taken the sustained efforts of 8 or 10, or sometimes more, especially if the operation is nationwide rather than local or subregional.

2. The support of at least one group or organization in majority society. That group might be a media operation, a religious institution, a political body with influence on an international organization (e.g., the World Bank or UNESCO), an educational institution, a national political party, or an influential government ministry. While financial support is of great importance, so is political influence.

3. The backing of at least a few influential individuals and organizations from within indigenous society; without such support, majority culture groups are unlikely to exert much effort.

4. Reasonably favorable publicity through majority culture media on an indigenous group's attempts to develop electronic media outlets, which will help to prepare public opinion to support those attempts and to take some initial interest in the programs themselves, if and when they materialize.

5. Support in the form of advice, training, and use of equipment by majority culture electronic media organizations, particularly during any "trial run" activities that might occur before full-time operation. (Hopefully, there would be such support after the indigenous operations commence full service.)

6. Events that call the attention of society as a whole to the magnitude of injustice, inequality, and other evidences of the discriminatory treatment of indigenous groups within society. That isn't to suggest the manufacturing of events, which could easily harm the cause. But genuine, spontaneous events do seem to stimulate the interest of indigenous peoples in having their own media outlets and to encourage the support of majority culture individuals and institutions for such ventures.

7. A reasonably sound national economy at the time the campaign for indigenous media is in progress. It isn't purely coincidental that a large number of those operations have been launched or expanded during times of national prosperity.

Different combinations of those elements have produced increasing levels of indigenous media activity over the past 20 years. Many nations now have one or more forms of electronic media activity involving indigenous languages, as well, especially through radio broadcast services operated by the national governments or public service broadcasters (PSBs) or through regional or local stations. Often, those broadcasts are controlled nationally or regionally, rather than locally; where that's the case, target audience participation in program planning and production often will be modest or even absent. Most of those stations appear to be firmly established by now. Budget cutting may lead to reductions in service but isn't likely to cause the stations' extinction.

There also are many indigenous electronic media outlets that are more or less totally controlled by indigenous groups. On the whole, those groups encourage audience participation, although, as I indicate in Chapter Seven (and to paraphrase George Orwell), some community groups are "more equal" than others when it comes to access to the airwaves. Those outlets often face severe financial problems, to the point where some may be happy (and astonished) simply to have survived for another year. There are other problems: scarcity of trained personnel; high staff turnover rates; and contradictory mandates, pressures, demands, and desires from within the communities they serve. A small but growing number of radio stations seek to support themselves through sale of airtime and/or radio bingo, feeling that these may be more stable than other sources of financial support. A few show some promise of success along those lines, for example, Maori-run Mai-FM in Auckland, Aboriginal-operated 4AAA in Brisbane, Mohawk station CKRK in Kahnawake, Quebec.

The combination of availability of less expensive equipment, nongovernmental sources of financial support, and unoccupied space on the frequency spectrum (especially for low-power radio and TV transmitters) has led to a considerable growth in numbers of non-PSB stations over the past two decades. The spread of low-cost audio- and videocassette recorders (camcorders in particular), coupled with readier access to reasonably professional recording equipment, has served to familiarize many indigenous people with various forms of program production that they can do on their own, or in small groups. Indigenous popular music is the most obvious beneficiary, but videos about indigenous cultural and political concerns and pride certainly are on the increase. Such activity has fueled the demands of various minority groups that they be given the opportunity to present themselves through the electronic media.

The spread of satellite technology, coupled with its declining costs, could mean that the indigenous electronic media will come to rely more and more heavily on it. However, the still considerable expense of satellite transmission and delivery, coupled with the difficulty of maintaining the equipment in adverse climatic circumstances and with minimal or nonexistent repair services, reduce its utility for those media. Stronger national government commitment to furnishing regularly scheduled field repair services, as the Indian government did in its Satellite Instructional Television Experiment (SITE), would help. So would training programs for technicians, as well as more generous funding for the purchase and maintenance of "package" stations, such as those developed in Canada and, to a degree, in Australia's Broadcasting for Remote Aboriginal Communities Scheme (BRACS) program.

Still, there is another possible drawback to satellites: they work most economically for large areas and may not be well-suited to the needs of those indigenous people who think of themselves primarily as members of tribes or extended families, but not as part of a nationwide collective entity. On the other hand, indigenous supporters of increased national identity would regard that as a potential benefit.

As time passes, it will be interesting to see some of the differences between rural and urban indigenous electronic media nationalism and tribalism, Western-flavored indigenous pop culture and "traditional" culture—possibly different ways of seeing and hearing will shrink or grow. It seems to me that either alternative is possible; in fact, both may occur, depending upon the nature of the media activity. Television in particular, thanks to its cost, is likely to emphasize national elements of indigenous culture and politics.

If national governments were able to completely control the financing and technical configuration of the electronic media (I regard that control as still considerable, but diminishing), we might see more of a generally ignored form of "media imperialism" (in this case, domestic) than we do: the doling out of just enough broadcast frequencies and money to indigenous groups to permit them to function minimally at a local level, preferably far from urban areas. That would help to discourage the growth of potentially troublesome indigenous nationalism.

There have been accusations (some justified, some not, in my view) that certain governments have acted in such ways and for such reasons (See Chapter Seven). However, the growth, slow though it may be, of national indigenous news services (such as National Native News and Mana Maori Media), of satellite delivery systems, and of tape exchanges indicates something of a shift in the balance of power. It now seems all but impossible for any other than the most authoritarian of governments to wall indigenous peoples within severely restricted media enclosures. (But it certainly helps to have the money to break down those walls!)

Much the same would seem to apply to a closely related form of domestic media imperialism: bread and circuses. Roman emperors sometimes sought to calm the lower classes with free bread and open admissions to combats and games in the amphitheaters. Modern rulers could be tempted to do the same thing with electronic media, parceling out just enough access to lull indigenous groups and other minorities into feeling that they had an effective means to make their voices heard.

Certainly there were, and still are, many cases of minority-produced and/or -oriented programming that is available only on Sunday mornings or late at night. And, as I've noted, many of the newer indigenous radio and TV stations operate on very low wattage, sometimes because that's all that they can afford, but sometimes because that's all that the governmental licensing authority makes available. Both are examples of the tokenism implicit in the "bread and circuses" argument.

However, as indigenous media outlets continue to expand, and with the creation of national indigenous media organizations and networks, it becomes more difficult to sustain a "bread and circuses" policy. The indigenous media are becoming more visible and more audible not only to indigenous audiences but to majority culture, as well. (It remains true that we know very little about the latter's extent of viewing and listening where indigenous media are concerned, let alone how it may change their perceptions of indigenous peoples—yet another worthwhile research project!) Some indigenous groups have invoked treaty rights in order to secure access to the frequency spectrum or to financial support. Those struggles are likely to continue, but each victory sets a precedent.

There is one potential aspect of indigenous electronic media that does *not* appear to have come into being. I note in Chapter Two that there were occasional concerns over the "separatist" influence of indigenous media, that the broadcasts would induce minorities to break away from mainstream society and perhaps even seek political independence. That doesn't seem to have happened and doesn't seem very likely to happen, nor do the nations that have permitted or encouraged the development of such media seem to fear that it will. Perhaps James Jacob and William Beer are correct when they observe that "linguistic demands even when masking more fundamental redistributive goals concerning political and economic power are more easily managed within the system than as an exogenous source of alienation and political violence against the state."[5]

The Second Wave?

Most indigenous electronic media now have attained the ripe old age of 5, 10, or more years and enjoy a fair measure of security (with some precarious exceptions). They are entering a second wave of development, if not necessarily Alvin Toffler's. This may be an appropriate time to look back on the first four programming purposes of indigenous media (Chapter Three), in order to see how important each is, how well it appears to have been met, and what remains to be done.

One major purpose is the revival and renovation of indigenous languages. Since most indigenous media outlets employ indigenous languages at least some of the time, and since there's some anecdotal evidence to suggest that they've encouraged people to acquire or improve command of such languages, that would appear to be one goal met. I suggest in Chapter Three, and again in Chapter Six, that renovation might be something of a Trojan horse, since the creation of appropriate indigenous terminology in fields such as science and medicine is based heavily on majority culture terms.

There are many examples of innovative approaches to renovation, some of them enlisting the help of the audience. But it will take even more effort on the part of the media to consolidate and to expand upon this success if the languages are to survive in the multichannel future that I foresee. Broader, closer collaboration with schools and preschools is important (and certainly the schools will have to play their part) and so is the expansion of indigenous language usage in programming involving music (off to a good start), sports, and disk jockey patter. I've noted those activities because they would help to reach young people, who are the future for the languages and yet seem most vulnerable to the blandishments of the multichannel mediascape.

Combatting the negative images of indigenous peoples held by majority populations is a purpose more common among indigenous staff at urban locations than at rural ones, and by independent media outlets more than by PSB affiliates. It's one reason for offering programs in the majority culture language, although the need to communicate with indigenous audiences in that language is a far more powerful reason.

It's also a reason for placing emphasis on *positive* images of the indigenous minority, which seems to have been taken by some of the indigenous operations I've visited as meaning no negative images of that minority. The reasons for such an attitude are understandable: after decades or more of heavily negative attention by majority culture media, it will be difficult enough to improve indigenous self-images, let alone to improve majority culture images. Therefore, why carry negative material? I have heard such a justification from indigenous managers, program directors, and journalists, although not often.

Still, while it certainly is appropriate to seek to bring out any positive aspects of a situation centered around an indigenous individual or organization, it seems very risky to ignore the negative aspects. (It also is inferior journalism.) Majority culture media are quite likely to seize upon any omission of negative coverage by indigenous media as an opportunity for criticism. Furthermore, a skillful presentation of both negative and positive aspects should provide majority culture audiences with a model of how the media can manage responsible coverage of minorities. It might even lead some of the majority media to reexamine their practices in that respect.*

Almost none of the media operations I've visited think of *any* of their content as intended primarily for a majority culture audience. The very few programmatic exceptions, popular music by request for older adults and a few "one size fits all" prerecorded religious programs, don't appear to have been conscious choices, either. They simply appear to draw more letters or phone calls from majority culture listeners or viewers. In general, staff exhibit little or no interest in creating programs that would cater to the needs and limitations of majority culture audiences. They feel that much of what they produce would be understandable at some level to indigenous and majority audiences alike; producing material that would be more accessible to the majority would require time and effort that already are in short supply.

Some staff also observe that the majority culture media have become more sensitive to the portrayal of indigenous peoples in recent years, with the one large exception of overrepresentation of indigenous criminals, alleged or convicted. They take pleasure, and some pride, in learning through letters, newspaper articles, phone calls, or the rare survey that members of the majority culture watch or listen to indigenous material. However, they appear to consider those achievements more as a bonus than as attainment of a specific goal.** Therefore, while the generalized goal remains, the tendency seems to be to let the present approach, in part exemplified in the next goal, take care of it.

----

*When an Australian Aboriginal politician was placed in the position of having to confess to petty thievery of items from his parliamentary office in mid-1993 so that he could cover his gambling debts, the Aboriginal media that I heard and read were clear about the illegality of the act but placed considerable emphasis on the man's statements of contrition regarding his self-respect and the shame he had brought upon his family and his people; he vowed to not only repay the government but also to enter a rehabilitation program. Some of the majority culture media reported the vow, but very few noted his statements on self-respect and shame.

**One of the few exceptions to that rule among the stations I visited was SKC-TV (Pablo, Mont.). Frank Tyro, the head of media services for Salish Kootenai College, noted in correspondence with me (June 30, 1995) that one of the founders of Salish Kootenai College, Michael O'Donnell, saw the station as a possible link between Indians and non-Indians living in its coverage area. (Many non-Indians live on the Flathead Reservation.) Certainly some of SKC-TV's local programming would seem both understandable and appealing to both audiences, but the station also carries certain material (e.g., on powwows) that makes no concessions to the likely ignorance of non-Indians concerning much of what occurs at a powwow, and it explains nothing for their particular benefit.

Restoration of pride through focus on past and present indigenous accomplishments also is a commonly identified programming purpose, and one that certainly has been met in terms of indigenous media effort. Very few of the media outlets fail to take it into account, and some spend a great deal of time on it. Again, anecdotal evidence suggests that a number of listeners and viewers appreciate it. Whether there should be more programming based on this goal is another question, and some outlets probably would claim that they're doing as much as they can with limited resources.

If outlets have good reason to believe that there should be more, they might consider redirecting their energies, but they'd have to deal with yet another problem: which accomplishments to emphasize. An outlet that heavily favors the past over the present might be able to count on access to archival material and might win the hearts of older audience members, but younger members might become alienated. On the other hand, heavy emphasis on the present, while it might please younger members (especially if they are well-represented in the programming), could lead older members to fear that the lessons of history are being lost. Much the same would apply to the issue of tribal and family membership. Even if one tribe or family happens to be larger or more important than others in a station's service area, there could be resentment if they seem to receive the lion's share of attention. Getting the balance right would be tricky and would require a thorough and continuing appraisal of the audience.

Another programming purpose, working for a greater degree of cohesiveness among indigenous peoples, has been mentioned by many station managers, but very few production staff have responded strongly to it when I've raised it.* As noted several times already, the issue of "tribalism and nationalism" is very complex and sometimes becomes the subject of contention between urban and rural outlets. Some of the recent legal triumphs for indigenous peoples seem to have underlined the commonality of interests among them, where certain issues (notably land rights and sovereignty) are concerned. Still, there continues to be some disagreement over other possible national issues, such as universal voting rights, women's rights, and the use of indigenous systems of justice.

The creation of indigenous national news services should help to alleviate tension, but the services won't help if local stations refuse to carry

---

*However, a volunteer producer-announcer for a Maori service carried by Southland Access Radio, in Invercargill, New Zealand, told me (October 1993) that a major reason for his involvement in radio was his desire to create programming that would break down intertribal barriers: "We've got to find a way to stop thinking about something your tribe did to mine 150 years ago." Keith notes a "lack of connectedness" among stations as a matter of concern to some of them. Keith, Michael C., *Signals in the Air: Native Broadcasting in America,* Westport, Conn.: Praeger, 1995, 125. But Churchill cautions that issues such as spirituality may not be amenable to nationalism. Churchill, Ward, *Fantasies of the Master Race,* Monroe, Maine: Common Courage Press, 1992, 205.

them, as some stations in New Zealand and North America have done. It may be that, over time, those media staff members who support increased national activity will develop a greater range of programming along those lines. Less threatening programs, such as the Aboriginal top 10 music selections of the week, might help, especially if stations are invited to submit their own nominations or if there is an eleventh selection, to be filled each time by a different local station submitting a tape of a local group. Talk shows such as "Native America Calling" also hold some promise. And if national indigenous news operations were to work more closely with the local stations than some of them appear to do, especially in the form of regularly airing reports from those stations, with full acknowledgment of their origin, that could help to reduce local suspicion of the national service. As things stand, the goal of greater national unity seems to be more and more widely shared, but progress is slow.

Given the declining cost of acquiring satellite transmission time, it may be possible for indigenous radio stations in various parts of the world to interlink through satellite, and perhaps to develop an international indigenous news service that would follow in the footsteps of WINGS (Women's International News Gathering Service), which distributes a weekly collection of short features about women, drawn from broadcast reports furnished by stations from various parts of the world. There appears to be a universal curiosity among indigenous peoples concerning each other's activities, and certainly they have much in common, such as concerns over alcohol and drugs, the criminal justice system, and indigenous business enterprises. Because such material would come from abroad, it's possible that it would help to develop a sense of national agenda for those listeners who might distrust the same sort of material if it were presented by their own indigenous media.

A
Fifth Goal
and Some
Parting Words

My original consideration of purposes, or goals, included four major entries and three of lesser importance. However, my research leads me to consider a fifth major goal, although *goal* might not be the right term: *preoccupation* might come closer! Virtually every indigenous media activity that I visited identified financial stability as a major goal. In one very limited sense, it can be regarded as roughly similar to other goals: a few radio station program directors and managers said that one of their goals was to make their services financially successful in order to show that indigenous media could compete with majority culture media.* That fits nicely with goals of increasing self-esteem and providing audible and visible symbols of indigenous society.

Most station staff are concerned about financing as a matter of survival, but not in the sense that stations would vanish in the absence of financial support. The general feeling is that a certain amount of money would continue to be available but that inflation, plus a desire to improve upon present performance, would require higher levels of support in the future. (It's widely acknowledged that national government funding per station will probably decline.) In that respect, improved financial support becomes a goal because it is seen as key to greater efforts to rescue the language, increased emphasis on self-esteem, and promotion of stronger national cohesiveness. It isn't a goal in and of itself but exists to support the other goals.

It's quite clear that many indigenous media operations have struggled to make financial ends meet. Yet I know of only a few radio stations that have gone off the air. WASG-AM (Poarch Creek Enterprises, Atmore, Alabama) came on the air as a Native American–run commercial station in 1981 and went dark in 1993. The former station manager blames its demise on suspicion on the part of the "Anglo" community, which never really accepted it.[6] FM station KIPC, All-Indian Pueblo Radio (Albuquerque, New Mexico), operated from 1976 to 1977, when it declared bankruptcy for more or less political reasons: federal government (Corporation for Public Broadcasting [CPB]) financial support was linked to opening the station to the participation of a number of ethnic groups. Too many factions from too many groups sought to establish their own agendas and ultimately exhausted the station's resources.[7] Navajo Community College FM station KNCC (Tsaile, Arizona) came on the air in 1976 and lasted until 1985, when the largely college student–run station lost its faculty manager, who moved away.[8] Lakota FM station KILI (Porcupine, South Dakota) experienced a $175,000 shortfall in 1990, and there was talk of declaring bankruptcy, but the station pulled through, thanks to a successful fund-raiser and a bank loan.[9]

Financial problems, then, rarely become severe enough to cause the demise of a media operation. Furthermore, the case for continued, and even

---

*The stations were Aboriginal country and western station 4AAA in Brisbane and rock station Mai-FM in Auckland.

increased, government support for indigenous media remains strong. There was government support for majority culture electronic media for decades, usually in the form of money or privileged situations (monopolies or duopolies). Indigenous peoples and other ethnic minorities rarely shared in those benefits, either as media operators or as audiences. Unfashionable as the observation may be, the government owes them something for that neglect. Furthermore, the nation as a whole will profit from increased diversity on the airwaves and through recordings, in that more people will have the opportunity to understand its full heritage, good and bad.

Still, government funding is under close examination. The U.S. Congress sharply reduced the FY 1996 budget for the Corporation for Public Broadcasting, and CPB funding makes up as much as 30 to 40 percent of the annual budgets of many U.S. indigenous stations.[10] Some U.S. states are proposing cuts in state support for public broadcasting: the Alaskan government, which has made major commitments to Native American and Inuit broadcasting, considered a 50 percent cut in the public broadcasting budget for FY 1996 and finally settled on a 25 percent cut for radio, 50 percent for TV.[11] An "antiequal opportunity" spirit also appears to be on the rise in the United States and in some parts of Europe. License fee–based financing, important to indigenous media in Scandinavia, Great Britain, and New Zealand, also is under pressure to shrink or to increase very little. If the overall economic picture is brightening for many Western nations, most of their indigenous citizens have yet to see many rays of sunlight.

The major worry for indigenous electronic media is not survival, but progress. It isn't surprising that so many of the operations are looking for other sources of income. This is where the parting words come in. The old adage about looking a gift horse in the mouth is worth remembering. Every source of income brings with it some potential liabilities, usually of control or of dependence, although license fees seem to be freer of these than most.[12] Many independent indigenous radio stations are seriously considering advertising; that was certainly true for most of the dozen such stations that I visited twice. Some have already adopted it.*

The greatest potential problem here is in the likely need to have to appeal more strongly and specifically to the majority culture audience. The often resultant playlists, with emphasis on majority culture music selections and closer attention to the clock, may place the indigenous character (the content and style) of the station at some risk. A number of media consultants, self-styled and otherwise, began to approach some of the Maori stations in the early 1990s, indicating how they could shift their broadcasts more in the direction of majority culture radio and reap reasonably hand-

---

*But many, especially those located in remote, thinly populated areas, lack an economic base that would make advertising possible.

some rewards. At least two Maori stations, Tuwharetoa FM in Turangi and Te Reo Irirangi o Ngati Kiwa (Tumeke-FM) in Whakatane, got rid of their original managers and adopted such a policy, with increased emphasis on majority culture appeal. In the first case, the Maori audience largely remained faithful to the core staff of the original station, which remained on-air as Te Tahi-FM; in the second, the Maori audience largely stopped listening. In neither case did majority culture listeners appear to flock to the "new, improved" versions.[13]

If there is anything approaching a guarantee of greater financial stability, and perhaps improvement, it might be illustrated by another adage: "it takes money to make money." Some indigenous media are hiring development directors and/or looking for fund-raising skills as a major component in the makeup of a manager. Lakota station KILI-FM has done both, and the combination of skills that the two individuals represent appears to be materially improving the station's financial well-being.*[,14] I note (p. 112) that the Central Australian Aboriginal Media Association had founded a recording studio and retail outlets and was enjoying a good financial return on them. Forms of financial support linked directly to audience members or under the direct control of the media outlets appear most promising in terms of return and of freedom from outside control, but it takes resourcefulness and continuous vigilance to make them work, which is why a skilled development director or manager, certainly someone with an entrepreneurial spirit, is worth a decent salary. That would seem especially true if the alternative is selling a part of a station's indigenous soul, which may require money for its sustenance but which no amount of money should be able to buy.

The future for indigenous electronic media, then, looks cautiously bright. Put another way, the media have matured to the point where they will lose their foothold only if indigenous peoples themselves neglect or abuse them. That does *not* mean that majority culture support—financial, moral, or political—no longer is needed. And I argue at several points that the indigenous media certainly merit that support, most of all because they contribute to *all* of society. But the increasingly multiple-channel nature of the electronic media world will demand resourcefulness on the part of indigenous electronic media staff, if they're to maintain and (hopefully) increase their audiences, thereby increasing the understanding and appreciation of indigenous life in its many and varied forms.

---

*One is a long-term resident in the area and knows various groups and businesses in and around the reservation well enough to secure funding from many of them. The other is very knowledgable about the music business and not only can book top attraction (such as John Denver and Bonnie Raitt) fund-raising concerts but also is planning a station-operated commercial recording studio.

APPENDIX 1: Media Operations Visited

AUSTRALIA

Aboriginal training programs in Batchelor, Sydney, and Townsville—October and November 1993

Australian Broadcasting Corporation stations in Alice Springs, Brisbane, Broome, Darwin, Hobart, Port Pirie, and Sydney—September 1987 and October–November 1993

Broome Aboriginal Media Association (Broome)—October 1993

Central Australian Aboriginal Media Association (Alice Springs)—September 1987 and October 1993

Radio 4AAA (Brisbane)—October 1993

Radio 4EB (Brisbane)—September 1987 and February 1996

Radio 4XXX (Brisbane)—September 1987

Radio Redfern (Sydney); later renamed Radio Koori—September 1987 and November 1993

Radio 7THE (Hobart)—November 1993 and March 1996

Radio 6EBA (Perth)—September 1991

Radio 3CR (Melbourne)—September 1987 and November 1993

Tasmanian Aboriginal Media Association (Hobart)—November 1993

Top End Aboriginal Media Association (Batchelor)—October 1993

Townsville Aboriginal and Islander Media Association (Townsville)—October 1993

Umeewarra Aboriginal Media Association (Port Augusta)—November 1993

Waringarri Aboriginal Media Association (Kununurra)—October 1993

CANADA

Canadian Broadcasting Corporation, Northern Service (Montreal)—June 1994

Radio CHME (Les Escoumins, Quebec)—September 1992

Radio CHRG (Maria, Quebec)—September 1992

Radio CHRQ (Restigouche, Quebec)—September 1992

Radio CIHW (Wendake, Quebec)—March 1992

Radio CKHQ (Kanesatake, Quebec)—March 1992

Radio CKON (Akwesasne, Quebec)—June 1994

Radio CKRK (Kahnawake, Quebec)—March 1992

FRANCE

Gure Irratia ("Our Radio," Bayonne)—September 1989
Irulegiko Herri Irratia (Radio Irouleguy, St. Étienne de Baigorry)—September 1989
Radio France Bretagne Ouest (Quimper)—September 1984
Radio France Inter-Nice—October 1986
Radio France Pays Basque (Bayonne)—September 1989
Radio Xiberoko Botza (Mauleon)—September 1989

IRELAND

Raidio na Gaeltachta, Baile na n'Gall—September 1990 and August 1994
Raidio na Gaeltachta, Casla—September 1990 and August 1994
Raidio na Gaeltachta, Doire Beag—September 1990
Raidio na Life (Dublin)—August 1994

NEW ZEALAND

Four Winds Radio (Invercargill—on Southland Community Broadcasters)—November 1993
Mai-FM (Auckland)—September 1991 and October 1993
Mana Maori Media (Papatoetoe, Rotorua, Wellington)—September 1991 and October 1993
Maori broadcaster training programs (Christchurch, Wellington)—October–November 1993
Maori Radio (Invercargill—on Southland Community Broadcasters)—November 1993
Nga Iwi-FM (Paeroa)—October 1993
Otago Community Broadcasters (Dunedin)—November 1993
Radio Aotearoa (Auckland)—September 1991 and October 1993
Radio Kahungunu (Taradale)—September 1991
Radio Ngati Porou (Ruatoria)—October 1993
Radio 2YB—Access Radio (Wellington)—September 1987
Southland Community Broadcasters (Invercargill)—November 1993
Tautoko-FM (Mangamuka Bridge)—October 1991
Te Reo Iriraki ki Otautahi (Christchurch)—November 1993 and March 1996
Te Reo Irirangi o Tainui (Ngaruawahia)—September 1991 and October 1993
Te Reo Irirangi o Te Arawa (Rotorua)—September 1991, October 1993, and March 1996
Te Reo o Aotearoa (Radio New Zealand, Auckland)—September 1987, September 1991, October 1993, and March 1996
Te Upoko o te Ika (Wellington)—September 1991 and October 1993
Tumeke-FM (Whakatane)—September 1991 and October 1993
Tuwharetoa (Turangi)—September 1991

SCANDINAVIA

GLR-Sami Community Radio (Kautokeino, Norway)—September 1994
NRK Sami Radio (Karasjok, Norway)—June 1993, September 1994, and November 1995
Radio Ofelas (Oslo, Norway)—November 1995
Sami College (Kautokeino, Norway)—May 1993
Sveriges Radio Sami Service (Kiruna, Sweden)—May 1993
YLE Sami Radio (Inari, Finland)—May 1993 and September 1994

UNITED KINGDOM

BBC Radio Cymru (Bangor and Cardiff, Wales)—April 1993 and September 1994
Radio Ceredigion (Aberystwyth, Wales)—April 1993 and September 1994
Radio Maldwyn (Newtown, Wales)—September 1994
Radio Moray Firth (Inverness, Scotland)—September 1986
Radio Swansea Sound (Swansea, Wales)—April 1993

UNITED STATES

KGHR (Tuba City, Ariz.)—April 1995
KILI-FM (Porcupine, S.Dak.)—March 1995
KINI (St. Francis, S.Dak.)—March 1995
KNCC (Tsaile, Ariz.)—April 1985
KNNB (Whiteriver, Ariz.)—August 1995
SKC-TV (Pablo, Mont.)—June 1995
WOJB (Hayward, Wis.)—July 1993

APPENDIX 2: A Brief Note on Sources

As EXAMINATION of any of chapter notes for the eight chapters will show, there are almost no standard, readily accessible sources for this particular body of subject matter. Therefore, I've chosen to let the chapter notes serve as bibliography and to describe sources and approaches that I found useful in gathering much of my data, in hopes that future researchers who consider indigenous peoples and their uses of the electronic media will find that account helpful.

Indigenous involvement in the electronic media is by now quite well-institutionalized in most countries. If indigenous services are available through the national public service broadcaster (e.g., the BBC), one generally can obtain addresses and even names of station or service managers through the annual *World Radio-Television Handbook.* However, many of the indigenous broadcast services are not so affiliated, in which case it becomes necessary to resort to other channels.

1. Most indigenous peoples have national organizations, and usually those can be found in telephone directories for the capital cities, with the name of the indigenous group usually listed first in its title.

2. The World Association of Community Broadcasters, operating under its French acronym, *AMARC,* has considerable information on indigenous *community* broadcasting activity at its Montreal headquarters: 3575 Blvd. St-Laurent, Suite 704, Montreal, Quebec, Canada H2X 2T7.

3. National parliaments often have debated matters relating to indigenous electronic media activities. Using indexes contained in Hansard, the Congressional Record, and their equivalents elsewhere, one can obtain material relevant to those activities.

4. Certain incidents, such as the Oka crisis (Mohawk nation, Canada), or claims of insufficient protection under the law (common enough for all indigenous peoples) often are reported through Article 19 in Great Britain or in the periodical *Index on Censorship,* especially if the incidents are accompanied by alleged attempts on the part of national, regional, or local governments to stifle media discussion of them.

5. Major universities, especially those located in an area with a larger than average concentration of indigenous peoples, often will have departments of indigenous studies, whether Native American, Maori, or whatever else. Some of those universities also have specialized library collections, as does the Department of Maori Studies at Auckland University. Contacting such departments with requests for assistance can prove rewarding. If there are institutions of higher education that specialize in working with indigenous peoples (e.g. Batchelor College [for Aborig-

ines] in Batchelor, Northern Territory, Australia), they are likely to be very helpful, as such institutions often provide education in the mass media and frequently operate their own broadcast stations.

6. Directories of newspapers and periodicals or of broadcasting for a given nation sometimes list minority media enterprises separately. National licensing agencies—less common for the press than for broadcasting—also are often able to provide information such as the location, address, and power of indigenous stations. So are the few indigenous financing agencies (e.g., Te Mangai Paho, in Wellington, New Zealand).

7. Majority culture newspapers located in cities or towns where there are indigenous media activities generally cover those activities and often will have clippings files for that coverage.

8. Video clubs or workshops are far harder to identify at a distance. If electronic media activities are grouped with one organization, as they often are in the various Aboriginal media associations (e.g., Umeewarra Media Association), the association itself could identify some of the video- or audiocassette activities. However, most video clubs operate independently, frequently through indigenous associations within large cities, and these sometimes can be identified through local telephone directories.

9. Finally, because language is so important a concern of indigenous electronic media services, a researcher should attempt to gain command of greetings, farewells, and introductions ("My name is ...") in the specific indigenous language. It usually will please media staff members and serve as a further indication of the researcher's strong interest. It may even come in handy in other settings: when I discovered that my waiter in a restaurant in Göteborg, Sweden, was Welsh, I used my few Welsh terms and wasn't charged for dessert!

All of the above are suggestions for gathering information at early stages. Some of them also will be helpful once in situ. Certainly, nothing can substitute for firsthand investigation. However, prior research can help reduce the consumption of time (and money) and also should help in gaining entry to the media services themselves: many of those media enterprises are accustomed to ignorance of their media activities on the part of the majority population and generally are delighted to cooperate with an outsider who seems both to know and to have genuine interest in their work.

GENERAL BIBLIOGRAPHIC SOURCES

CIESPAL. 1986. *La Comunicacion Popular en America Latina.* Quito, Ecuador. Contains resumes of roughly 150 studies of popular communication projects, most of them involving the electronic media, during the period 1970–1983. Most are in Spanish, with a few in Portuguese. There is a keyword indexing system, but there is no keyword for indigenous activity per se.

Frachon, Claire, and Marion Vargaftig, eds. 1995. *European Television: Immigrants and Ethnic Minorities.* London: John Libbey. Deals with minorities of various sorts. Indigenous activities receive little detailed coverage; however, the general bibliography and some of the chapters contain references to material on indigenous minorities, and the chapters themselves contain a great deal of material on national and European Union policies regarding minorities and the electronic media.

Hornik, Robert C. 1988. *Development Communication: Information, Agriculture, and the Third World.* New York: Longman. Hornik's bibliography is not specific to indigenous experiences, but many of the studies he lists do involve indigenous peoples.

Husband, Charles, ed., *A Richer Vision: The Development of Ethnic Minority Media in Western Democracies,* London: John Libbey, 1994. There are several chapters containing indigenous experiences, and many useful insights from the editor.

Moragas Spa, Miquel de, and Carmelo Garitaonandia, eds. 1995. *Decentralization in the Global Era: Television in the Regions, Nationalities, and Small Countries of the European Union.* London: John Libbey. Much of what I say about Frachon and Vargaftig applies here, although there is not as much emphasis on policy in this work.

O'Sullivan-Ryan, Jeremiah, and Mario Kaplun. n.d. (1980?). *Communication Methods to Promote Grass-roots Participation.* Paris: UNESCO, Communication and Society Series 6. The bibliographic section of this study (89–155) contains 198 listings of studies, most of them set in Latin America. There are annotated descriptions for many of the studies, but no keyword system or division by subcategories that would permit easy access to studies concerning indigenous peoples.

NOTES

CHAPTER ONE

1. Wilson, Helen, "Broadcasting and the Treaty of Waitangi," *Media Information Australia*, 67 (February 1993), 92–99.

2. François Grin presents an interesting perspective on economics in his article, "The Economic Approach to Minority Languages" (in Gorter, Dirk, et al., *Fourth International Conference on Minority Languages, Vol. 1: General Papers*, Clevedon, U.K., and Philadelphia, Pa.: Multilingual Matters, 1989, 153–174). He looks at the *personal* economics of deciding to study and use minority languages. On p. 169, he notes the influence that radio and TV programs in those languages can have on changing personal economics because they may "induce a shift away from English and toward Welsh" (he employs those languages as illustrative examples).

3. "Educating the Islanders," *COMBROAD* (journal of the Commonwealth Broadcasting Association), 103 (June 1994), 17.

4. Babe, Robert E., *Canadian Television Broadcasting: Structure, Performance, and Regulation*, Ottawa: Ministry of Supply and Services, 1979; Bagdikian, Ben H., *The Media Monopoly*, Boston: Beacon Press, 1983; Mattelart, Michele, and Armand Mattelart, *The Carnival of Images: Brazilian Television Fiction*, New York: Bergin and Garvey, 1990; Murdock, Graham, and Peter Golding, "For a Political Economy of Mass Communications," in Milliband, R., and John Saville, eds., *The Socialist Register, 1973*, 205–234; Pendakur, Manjunath, *Canadian Dreams and American Control: The Political Economy of the Canadian Film Industry*, Toronto: Garamond Press, 1990; Smythe, Dallas, *Dependency Road: Communications, Capitalism, Consciousness, and Canada*, Norwood, N.J.: Ablex, 1981. There also is a very useful colloquy that includes several scholars' (Garnham, Grossberg, Carey, and Murdock) views of the utility of political economy and cultural studies as guiding theories or perspectives. See *Critical Studies in Mass Communication*, 12, 1 (March 1995), 60–100.

5. Downing, John, *Radical Media*, Boston: South End Press, 1984.

6. Gitlin, Todd, *Inside Prime Time*, New York: Pantheon Books, 1985.

7. Lins da Silva, Carlos Eduard, "Transnational Communication and Brazilian Culture," in Atwood, Rita, and Emile McAnany, eds., *Communication and Latin American Society: Trends in Critical Research, 1960–1985*, Madison: University of Wisconsin Press, 1986, 89–111. See also Martin-Barbero, Jesus, *Communication, Culture, and Hegemony: From the Media to Mediations*, London and Newbury Park, Calif.: Sage, 1993.

8. Condit, Celeste, "Hegemony in a Mass-Mediated Society: Concordance about Reproductive Technologies," *Critical Studies in Mass Communication*, 11, 3 (September 1994), 205–230.

9. Beltran, Luis, "TV Etchings in the Minds of Latin Americans," *Gazette*, 24, 2 (1978), 65–81.

10. For summaries of impact studies, see Browne, Donald R., "The American Image Overseas—the Impact of U.S. Television Abroad," *Journalism Quarterly*, 45, 2 (Summer 1968), 307–316; and Ware, William, and Michael Dupagne. "Effects of U.S. Television Pro-

grams on Foreign Audiences: A Meta-Analysis," *Journalism Quarterly*, 71, 4 (1994), 947–959.

11. Oliveira, Omar Souk, "Satellite TV and Dependency: An Empirical Approach," *Gazette*, 38 (1986), 127–145; Palma, Gabriel, "Dependency: A Formal Theory of Underdevelopment or a Methodology for the Analysis of Concrete Situations of Underdevelopment?" *World Development*, 6 (1978), 881–924; Salinas, Raquel, and Leena Paldan, "Culture in the Process of Dependent Development: Theoretical Perspectives," in Nordenstreng, Kaarle, and Herbert Schiller, eds., *National Sovereignty and International Communications*, Norwood, N.J.: Ablex, 1979, 82–98; Sarti, Ingrid, "Communication and Cultural Dependency: A Misconception," in McAnany, Emile, Jorge Schnittman, and Noreene Janus, eds., *Communication and Social Structure—Critical Studies in Mass Media Research*, New York: Praeger, 1981, Chap. 11. Francesco Reyes Matta argues on behalf of alternative modes of communication as a counterweight to dependency; see "Alternative Communication: Solidarity and Development in the Face of Transnational Expansion," in Atwood and McAnany, *Communication and Latin American Society*, 190–214. There also is a useful review of more recent scholarship on alternative approaches to communication in Latin America; see Huesca, Robert, and Brenda Dervin, "Theory and Practice in Latin America Alternative Communication Research," *Journal of Communication*, 44, 4 (1994), 53–73. The authors bemoan the lack of theoretically grounded case studies, which is a valid point, but do not deal with the lack of research on *indigenous* uses of alternative media.

12. Oliveira, Omar Souk, "Brazilian Soaps Outshine Hollywood: Is Cultural Imperialism Fading Out?," in Nordenstreng, Kaarle, and Herbert Schiller, eds., *Beyond National Sovereignty: International Communication in the 1990s*, Norwood, N.J.: Ablex, 1993, 116–131.

13. Cruise O'Brien, Rita, "Professionalism in Broadcasting: Issues of International Dependence" and "Professionalism in Broadcasting: Case Studies of Algeria and Senegal," Brighton, U.K.: Institute of Development Studies at the University of Sussex, Discussion Papers DF 100 and DP 101, December 1976; Golding, Peter, "Media Professionalism in the Third World: The Transfer of an Ideology," in Curran, James, and Michael Gurevitch, eds., *Mass Media and Society*, London: Edward Arnold, 1991, 291–308.

14. Habermas, Jurgen, *The Structural Transformation of the Public Sphere: An Inquiry into a Category of Bourgeois Society* (trans. by T. Burger), Cambridge, Mass.: MIT Press. (Original published in 1965.)

15. Curran, James, "Mass Media and Democracy: A Reappraisal," in Curran and Gurevitch, *Mass Media and Society*, 82–117.

16. Ibid., 83.

CHAPTER TWO

1. Whitaker, Ian, "The Beginnings of Political Organization among the Swedish Lapps," *Polar Record*, 19, 118 (1978), 48.

2. Davies, John, *Broadcasting and the BBC in Wales*, Cardiff: University of Wales Press, 1994. Chaps. 1–5, provides a detailed account of this period.

3. Withers, Charles W. J., *Gaelic in Scotland, 1698–1981*, Edinburgh: John Donald Publishers, 1984, 249. See also McDowell, W. H., *The History of BBC Broadcasting in Scotland, 1923–1983*, Edinburgh: Edinburgh University Press, 1992.

4. Héatta, Odd Mathis, "NRK's Samisk Sendinger, 1946–1984," M.A. thesis, University of Tromso, Institute for Speech and Literature, 1984, provides thorough documentation of slow growth of Sami radio in Norway.

5. Program director, BBC, to David Cleghorn Thomas, April 1, 1931, Gaelic Pro-

grammes, File 1, BBC Written Archives Centre, Caversham, Reading, U.K. Cited in McBride, Sarah, "Scottish Gaelic and Welsh Language Broadcasting in the United Kingdom," unpublished M.A. thesis, School of Journalism and Mass Communication, University of North Carolina at Chapel Hill, 1995, 38.

6. Shapiro, Michael J., "A Political Approach to Language Purism," in Jernudd, Bjorn H., and Michael J. Shapiro, eds., *The Politics of Language Purism*, Berlin and New York: Mouton de Gruyter, 1989, 21–29.

7. Cheval, Jean-Jacques, "Local Radio and Regional Languages in Southwestern France," in Riggins, Steven H., ed., *Ethnic Minority Media: An International Perspective*, Newbury Park, Calif.: Sage, 1992, 165–195; Howkins, John, "Basques Use TV to Speak Their Own Language," *InterMedia*, 11, 3 (May 1983), 49–50; Soley, Lawrence C., and John Nichols, *Clandestine Radio Broadcasting: A Study of Revolutionary and Counter-Revolutionary Electronic Communication*, New York: Praeger, 1987, 158–159. The experience of Catalonia parallels that of the Basque region; see Moragas Spa, Miquel de, and Maria Corominas, "SPAIN, Catalonia: Media and Democratic Participation in Local Communication," in Jankowski, Nick, Ole Prehn, and James Stappers, eds., *The People's Voice: Local Radio and Television in Europe*, London: John Libbey, 1992, 186–197.

8. Mickiewicz, Ellen, *Split Signals: Television and Politics in the Soviet Union*, New York: Oxford University Press, 1988, Chap. 1.

9. Orlik, Peter, "South Africa," in Head, Sydney (ed.), *Broadcasting in Africa*, Philadelphia: Temple University Press, 1973, 143–144.

10. Hachten, William A., and C. Anthony Giffard, *The Press and Apartheid: Repression and Propaganda in South Africa*, Madison: University of Wisconsin Press, 1984, 202–203, 205, 220–221; Phelan, John, *Apartheid Media: Disinformation and Dissent in South Africa*, Westport, Conn.: Lawrence Hill, 1987; Tomaselli, Ruth, Keyan Tomaselli, and Johan Muller, eds., *Broadcasting in South Africa*, New York: St. Martin's Press, 1985; Van Tonder, J. W., "South Africa: Apartheid of the Airwaves Still Rules," *InterMedia* 20, 6 (November 1992), 28–29; Wilkins, Ivor, and Hans Strydom, *The Broederbond*, New York: Paddington Press, 1979, 1. Wilkins and Strydom note that the Broederbond, a group of politically powerful, hard-core Afrikaaner separatists, saw Radio Bantu and a Black TV service as important ways to ensure that Blacks remain in segregated "homelands."

11. "Radio Maritzburg Community Station Launched," *COMBROAD*, 107 (1995), 30.

12. Browne, Donald R., *International Radio Broadcasting: The Limits of the Limitless Medium*, New York: Prager, 1982, 357.

13. Mansell, Gerard, *Let Truth Be Told: 50 Years of BBC External Broadcasting*, London: Weidenfeld and Nicolson, 1982, 236.

14. Powdermaker, Hortense, *Coppertown: Changing Africa—the Human Situation on the Rhodesian Copperbelt*, New York: Harper and Row, 1962, 233–234.

15. Details on the development of indigenous broadcasting in Africa during the 1950s appear in Bebey, Francis, *La Radiodiffusion en Afrique Noire*, Issy-les-Moulineaux, France: Editions Saint-Paul, 1963; Head, Sydney, ed., *Broadcasting in Africa: A Continental Survey of Radio and Television*, Philadelphia: Temple University Press, 1974; and Voss, Harald, *Rundfunk und Fernsehen in Afrika*, Köln: Verlag Deutscher Wirtschaftsdienst GmbH, 1962.

16. Ihaddaden, Zahir, "The Postcolonial Policy of Algerian Broadcasting in Kabyle," in Riggins, *Ethnic Minority Media*, 248. See also Lazreg, Marnia, "Media and Cultural Dependency in Algeria," *Studies of Broadcasting* (NHK, Japan), 26 (1990), 45–47, for a brief discussion of postindependence policy regarding broadcasting and other media in Kabyle. Lazreg notes that Algerian President Ahmed Ben Bella halted broadcasting in Kabyle shortly after Algeria attained independence in 1963, probably to discourage any separatist tendencies. If so, the cessation did not last, and as of 1994, there were 19 hours a day of radio in Kabyle,

according to the *World Radio-Television Handbook, 1995* (where Kabyle is listed as Berber).

17. The "adviser" phenomenon was quite common during the 1960s, when I was a member of the U.S. Foreign Service in Tunisia and in Guinea. I witnessed it in the latter, and several of my foreign service colleagues, as well as Western media correspondents based in Africa, noted the same phenomenon. It had largely disappeared by the 1970s.

18. Browne, Donald R., "Radio Guinea—a Voice of Independent Africa," *Journal of Broadcasting*, 7, 2 (1963), 113–122; for sections on Francophone stations in Bebey, Head, and Voss, see note 15 above.

19. Browne, Donald R., "Do We Offer Good Instruction to Mass Communication Students from Africa?," *NAEB Journal*, 25, 2 (1966), 55–64; Head, *Broadcasting in Africa*, Chaps. 13.1.1 and 14, plus index entries for OCARA and SORAFOM; Katz, Elihu, and George Weddell, *Broadcasting in the Third World: Promise and Performance*, Cambridge, Mass.: Harvard University Press, 1977, index entries for OCARA, SORAFOM, Training; Quarmyne, Alex, and Francis Bebey, "Training for Radio and Television in Africa," Paris: UNESCO, COM/WS/64, 1964.

20. Head, *Broadcasting in Africa*, Chaps. 12, 13.

21. Katz and Weddell, *Broadcasting in the Third World*, 110–119, discuss several further aspects of dependency, particularly economic.

22. Institute of Nationality Studies, "China's Minority Nationalities in the Mass Media," in UNESCO, *Mass Media and the Minorities*, Paris, 1986, 88–91.

23. Chu, James C. Y., "People's Republic of China," in Lent, John, ed., *Broadcasting in Asia and the Pacific*, Philadelphia: Temple University Press, 1978, 27–30.

24. Aguilar, Enrique, "Radio San Gabriel: The Voice of the Aymara People," in Mowlana, Hamid, and Margaret H. Frondorf, eds., *The Media as a Forum for Community Building*, Washington, D.C.: Paul H. Nitze School of Advanced International Studies, Program on Social Change and Development, 1992, 21–26.

25. Schmelkes de Sotolo, Sylvia, "The Radio Schools of Tarahumara, Mexico: An Evaluation," in Spain, Peter, et al., eds., *Radio for Education and Development: Case Studies*, vol. 1, Washington, D.C.: World Bank, Staff Working Paper No. 266, May 1977, 33–68.

26. Encinas V., Orlando, "La Radio al Servicio de la Liberacion Indigena," 90, cited in Peppino Barele, Ana Maria, *Las Ondas Dormidas: Cronica Hidalguense de una Pasion Radiofonica*, Azcapotzalco, Mexico: Universidad Autonome Metropolitana, Division de Ciencias Sociales y Humanidades, 1989, 188.

27. Encinas V., Orlando, "Radio Mezquital: Posibilidades de communicacion popular," *Comunicacion y cultura*, 8 (1982); Peppino Barele, *Las Ondas Dormidas*, 188–194.

28. Boyd, Douglas, *Broadcasting in the Arab World*, Ames: Iowa State University Press, 1993, 120–121, 124.

29. Hedges, Chris, "Turkish Premier Outlines Reform Plan for Kurds," *New York Times*, March 26, 1995, 6.

30. Soley and Nichols, *Clandestine Radio Broadcasting*, 68, 119–124, 129.

31. Rubin, Jerry, *Do It!* New York: Simon and Schuster, 1971, 106–108.

32. Harris, Paul, *When Pirates Ruled the Waves*, Aberdeen, Scotland: Impulse Publications, 1968; Hind, John, and Steven Mosco, *Rebel Radio: The Full Story of British Pirate Radio*, London: Pluto Press, 1985.

33. Smith, Bruce L., and Jerry Brigham, "Native Radio Broadcasting in North America, *Journal of Broadcasting and Electronic Media*, 36, 2 (1992), 189.

34. Department of Secretary of State, "National Aboriginal Community Radio Inventory," Aboriginal Broadcast Programs, Native Citizen's Directorate, Ottawa, 1992.

35. Stiles, J. Mark, and associates, "Broadcasting and Canada's Aboriginal Peoples," (Report to the Task Force on Broadcast Policy), Ottawa: Canadian Radio-Television and Telecommunications Commission, 1985, 38–39.

36. Cole, Barry, and Mal Oettinger, *Reluctant Regulators: The FCC and the Broadcast Audience,* rev. ed., Reading, Mass.: Addison-Wesley, 1978, 63–82; Head, Sydney, and Christopher Sterling, *Broadcasting in America,* 6th ed., Boston: Houghton-Mifflin, 1987, 460–461; Kahn, Frank J., ed., *Documents of American Broadcasting,* 2d ed., New York: Appleton-Century-Crofts, 1973, 639–664.

37. "Broadcast Skills Bank/Career Opportunities in Broadcasting," New York: National Urban League, no date (probably 1966).

38. Brown, Les, *Television: The Business behind the Box,* New York: Harcourt-Brace-Jovanovich, 1971, Chaps. 5, 12.

39. Hindley, Reg, *The Death of the Irish Language: A Qualified Obituary,* London and New York: Routledge, 1990.

40. Browne, Donald R., "Raidio na Gaeltachta," *European Journal of Communication,* 7, 3 (1992), 415–433.

41. Browne, Donald R., "Alternatives for Local and Regional Radio: Three Nordic Solutions," *Journal of Communication,* 34, 2 (1984), 36–55; Tomlinson, Tim, "The Development of Local Religious Radio in Norway and in Sweden," unpublished Ph.D. dissertation, University of Minnesota, 1994, 119–162.

42. Ananthakrishnan, S. I., "The Development of Local Radio and Ethnic Minority Initiatives in Norway," in Husband, Charles, ed., *A Richer Vision: The Development of Ethnic Minority Media in Western Democracies,* London: John Libbey, 1994, 120–125; "Nytt samisk radioprogram i Oslo," Pa Lufta (bulletin of the Norwegian Naerradioforbund), 11, 8 (1995), 5; Varsi, Torvud (coordinator for Radio Ofelas), personal interview, Oslo, Norway, November 1995.

43. Busch, Christof, *Was sie immer schon uber freie radios wissen wollten, aber nie zu fragen wagten!* Frankfurt: Zweitausendeins Versand, 1981; Collin, Claude, *Ondes de Choc,* Paris: Editions de Harmattan, 1982; Cojean, Annick, and F. Eskanazi, *FM: La folle histoire des radios libres,* Paris: Grasset, 1986; Hind and Mosco, *Rebel Radio.*

44. Browne, Donald R., *Comparing Broadcast Systems: The Experiences of Six Industrialized Nations,* Ames: Iowa State University Press, 1989, 83–86.

45. Browne, Donald R., "Finding a Basque Radio Voice," *InterMedia,* 18, 3 (1990), 39–42; Cheval, Jean-Jacques, "Local Radio and Regional Languages in Southwestern France," in Riggins, *Ethnic Minority Media,* Chap. 8.

46. Davies, *Broadcasting and the BBC in Wales,* 288–300, 325–345, provides the most detailed account of this spectacular demonstration of linguistic loyalty and the often tumultuous events that preceded it.

47. Howell, William J., Jr., "Britain's Fourth Television Channel and the Welsh Language Controversy," *Journal of Broadcasting,* 25, 2 (1981), 123–127; Howell, William J., Jr., "Minority Language Broadcasting and the Continuation of Celtic Culture in Wales and Ireland," in Riggins, *Ethnic Minority Media,* 217–242; Griffiths, Alison, "Pobol y Cym: The Construction of a National and Cultural Identity in a Welsh Soap Opera," in Drummond, Phillip, et al., eds., *National Identity and Europe: The Television Revolution,* London: British Film Institute, 1993, 9–24.

48. Browne, Donald R., *What's Local about Local Radio? Cross-national Comparative Study,* London: International Institute of Communications, Occasional Paper No. 1, 1988, 43–44.

49. Cormack, Mike, "Problems of Minority Language Broadcasting: Gaelic in Scotland," *European Journal of Communication,* 8, 1 (1993), 106–111.

50. Browne, *What's Local about Local Radio?* 64–65, 68, 73.

51. See Moragas Spa, Miquel de, and Carmelo Garitaonandia, eds., *Decentralization in the Global Era: Television in the Regions, Nationalities, and Small Countries of the European Union,* London: John Libbey, 1995, for a broad picture of some of the television initiatives

for minorities of various sorts, including indigenous peoples, in Europe. See also Frachon, Claire, and Marion Vargaftig, eds., *European Television: Immigrants and Ethnic Minorities,* London: John Libbey, 1995, for roughly similar coverage (although several of the countries are different), but greater emphasis on evolution of policies.

52. Colle, Raymond, "A Radio for the Mapuches of Chile," in Riggins, *Ethnic Minority Media,* 127–148; Davidson, J. R., "The Basic Village Education Project in Guatemala," Washington, D.C.: USAID, Report PN-AAD-299, 1976.

53. Curiel V., Ricardo, "Lenguas Indigenas de Mexico y Radiodifusion Cultural," speech to the Seventh Annual Symposium of AMLA, Pueblo, Mexico, June 10, 1988; Valenzuela, Eduardo, "New Voices," in Girard, Bruce, ed., *A Passion for Radio,* Montreal: Black Rose Books, 1992, 150–155.

54. Cassirer, Henry R., "Radio in an African Context: A Description of Senegal's Pilot Project," in Spain et al., *Radio for Education and Development,* vol. 1, 300–337; " 'Dissoo' on Rural Education Radio: An Experiment in Rural Senegal," *Media Digest,* 3 (June), 1981; Knopps, Matthew, "Dissoo: A Voice to the Voiceless," unpublished UROP (University Research Opportunities Program) paper, University of Minnesota, September 1990.

55. Special Broadcasting Service, *Annual Report, 1993–94,* Sydney, N.S.W., Australia, 1995; Jakubowicz, Andrew, and Kerie Newell, "Which World? Whose/Who's Home? Special Broadcasting in the Australian Communication Alphabet," in Craik, Jennifer, Julia James Bailey, and Albert Moran, eds., *Public Voices, Private Interests: Australia's Media Policy.* St. Leonard's, NSW, Australia; Allen and Unwin, 1995, ch. 9.

56. Keith, op. cit., 93–95; Tyro, Frank, media center director, Salish Kootenai College, personal interview, Pablo, Mont., June 1995.

57. Crabtree, Robbin, "Democratizing Radio Broadcasting in Nicaragua: A Case Study of Regional Community Radio, 1979–1989," unpublished Ph.D. dissertation, University of Minnesota, 1992 (see p. 115 for a brief description of the Miskito station).

58. Rodriguez, Clemencia, "The Rise and Fall of the Popular Correspondents' Movement in Revolutionary Nicaragua, 1982–90," *Media Culture and Society,* 16, 3 (1994), 509–520.

59. Enzensberger, Hans M., "Constituents of a Theory of the Media," in McQuail, Denis, ed., *Sociology of Mass Communications,* Harmondsworth, U.K.: Penguin, 1972. Enzensberger contends that technology now makes it possible for "the masses" to gain direct access to the media and to formulate their own messages, rather than having to rely upon others to do so for them.

60. Berrigan, Francis, *Access: Some Western Models of Community Media,* Paris: UNESCO, 1977; Berrigan, Francis, *Community Communications: The Role of Community Media in Development,* Paris: UNESCO, 1981; O'Sullivan-Ryan, Jeremiah, and Mario Kaplun, *Communication Methods to Promote Grass-Roots Participation: A Summary of Research Findings from Latin America,* Paris: UNESCO, 1978 (also available as ERIC Reports, Doc. No. 201017).

61. A rare exception is Daley, Patrick J., and Beverly James, "Ethnic Broadcasting in Alaska: The Failure of a Participatory Model," in Riggins, *Ethnic Minority Media,* 23–43. However, their argument is that the technocratic experts become so dominant in decisions affecting the establishment of participatory media activities that technology drives the project (here, the use of communication satellites), discouraging participation at the level of "ordinary people."

62. One project that has featured such participation has been radio station XEVFS in the Mexican state of Chiapas. See del Carmen Marquez, Lucia, "The Uses of Radio by Ethnic Minorities in Mexico: A Study of a Participatory Project," unpublished Ph.D. dissertation, University of Texas at Austin, 1993. Marquez's study is the only one known to me where the

author has undertaken detailed observation– and personal interview–based data gathering among both station personnel and indigenous listeners.

63. Hein, Kurt J., *Radio Baha'i Ecuador: A Baha'i Development Project,* London: George Ronald, 1988, 35–47, 91–130 (the latter covers audience evaluation).

64. Jouet, Josiane, "La Comunicacion Participatoria en el Tercer Mundo: Una Perspective Critica," delivered at the First Latin American Seminar on Participatory Communication. Quito, Ecuador: CIESPAL, 1978. Cited in Hein, *Radio Baha'i Ecuador,* 3–4.

65. David, M. J. R., "Mahaweli Community Radio," in Girard, *A Passion for Radio,* 132–140; Valbuena, Victor, *Mahaweli Community Radio Project,* Singapore: Asian Mass Communications Research Center, 1988.

66. Karunanayake, Nandana, *Broadcasting in Sri Lanka: Potential and Performance,* Moratuwa, Sri Lanka: Center for Policy Studies, 1990, 239.

67. Lewis, Peter, and Jerry Booth, *The Invisible Medium: Public, Commercial and Community Radio,* Washington, D.C.: Howard University Press, 1992, 171–172; Mills, Jack, and James Kangwana, "Community Radio in Kenya," *COMBROAD,* 59 (1983), 20–22; Vick, David, "The Voice of Kenya: Radio in a Developing Nation," internal report to the Independent Broadcasting Authority, London, March 1985, 23–26.

68. Duran, Jane, "Message From Puno: Radio Onda Azul," *Development Communication Report,* 48 (1985), 8.

69. Berque, Pascal, "The Hard Lesson of Autonomy," in Girard, *A Passion for Radio,* 122–131; World Association of Community Radio Broadcasters (AMARC) and Inter-African Centre for Studies in Rural Radio (CIERRO), "Study on Rural and Local Radio in Africa," Montreal: AMARC and Ouagadougou, Burkina Faso: CIERRO, 1990, 34, 39–40.

70. International Program for Development of Communication (IPDC), "Annual Report," Paris: UNESCO, 1983.

71. Colle, "A Radio for the Mapuches of Chile,"; Hein, *Radio Baha'i Ecuador.*

72. Kweekeh, Florida, "Radio for Rural Development in Liberia," *InterMedia,* 15, 2 (1987), 27–29; Liberian Rural Communications Network, "Inaugural 1986," Monrovia, Liberia, 1986; *Mala Ya* (Liberian Rural Communications Network newsletter), 2 (1986).

73. Peppino Barele, *Las Ondas Dormidas,* 64–74.

74. Michaels, Eric, *The Aboriginal Invention of Television in Central Australia, 1982–1986,* Canberra, A.C.T.: Australian Institute of Aboriginal Studies, 1986, 50–78, 88–89.

75. Batty, Philip, "Singing the Electric: Aboriginal Television in Australia," in Dowmunt, Tony, ed., *Channels of Resistance: Global Television and Local Empowerment,* London: British Film Institute, 1993, 106–125; Browne, Donald R., "Aboriginal Radio in Australia: From Dreamtime to Primetime?" *Journal of Communication,* 40, 1 (1990), 111–120; Chanter, Alaine, "The Redevelopment of Aboriginal Communications," in Casmir, Fred, ed., *Communication in Development,* Norwood, N.J.: Ablex, 1991, 250–269; Molnar, Helen, "Aboriginal Broadcasting in Australia," *Howard Journal of Communication,* 2, 2 (1990), 149–169.

76. Batty, "Singing the Electric,"; CAAMA, *CAAMA Report,* Alice Springs, N.T.: Central Australian Aboriginal Media Association, June 1987, 18–20; Meadows, Michael, "A Watering Can in the Desert: Issues in Indigenous Broadcasting Policy in Australia," Brisbane, Queensland: Institute for Cultural Policy Issues, Griffith University, 1992, 23–27; Molnar, Helen, "Aboriginal Broadcasting in Australia," 158–160.

77. Hussein, Ali, "Market Forces and the Marginalization of Black Film and Video Production in the United Kingdom," in Husband, *Richer Vision,* 140–141, notes the effects of financial cutbacks and increasing commercialization of broadcasting on workshops for minority film and video producers in the United Kingdom.

78. Boyd, Douglas, Joseph Straubhaar, and John Lent, *Videocassette Recorders in the*

Third World, New York: Longman, 1989; Ganley, Gladys, and Oswald Ganley, *Global Political Fallout: The VCR's First Decade,* Norwood, N.J.: Ablex, 1987; Ganley, Gladys, *The Political Fallout from Personal Media,* Norwood, N.J.: Ablex, 1992; Zoglin, Richard, "Subversion by Cassette," *Time,* September 11, 1989, 80.

79. Ganley, Gladys, *The Political Fallout from Personal Media,* 13–24; Srebemy-Mohammadi, Annabelle, and Ali Mohammadi, *Small Media, Big Revolution: Communication, Culture, and the Iranian Revolution,* Minneapolis: University of Minnesota Press, 1994, 119–121.

80. Galloway, Joseph, "Egypt Is the Prize," *U.S. News and World Report,* July 6, 1987, 35.

81. Colle, Royal, and Suzana Fernandez de Colle, "The Communication Factor in Health and Nutrition Programs: A Case Study from Guatemala," Geneva: World Health Organization, 1977.

82. Kaplun, Mario, "Cassette-Foro: Un Sistema de Comunicacion Participativa," IPRU, Montevideo, Uruguay, 1978.

83. DePalma, Anthony, "Convention of Dissent for Mexicans," *New York Times,* August 8, 1994, 5. I saw the videocassette "Convencion des Aguascalientes, Chiapas, Agosto, 1994," produced by Canal 6 de Julio, at a screening at the University of Minnesota, Minneapolis, January 27, 1995.

84. Michaels, *The Aboriginal Invention of Television in Central Australia,* 58–59.

85. Crossette, Barbara, "In India, News Videotapes Fill a Void," *New York Times,* January 2, 1991, A6; "Video for the Political Record," *Hungarian Observer,* 2, 6 (1989), 24–25.

86. Sterngold, James, "This Man Has Dream [*sic*]: It's Downright Un-Japanese," *New York Times,* August 19, 1992, A4.

87. Personal observation, visits to Alice Springs, N.T., Australia, September 1987 and October 1993.

88. Ruby, Jay, "Introduction," in Mowlana and Frondorf, *The Media as a Forum for Community Building,* ix.

89. "Indian Leader Has Many Enemies," *Minneapolis Star-Tribune,* July 19, 1994, 3B.

90. Kuttab, Daoud, "Palestinian Diaries: Grass Roots TV Production in the Occupied Territories," in Dowmunt, *Channels of Resistance,* 138–145.

91. Mader, Roberto, "Globo Village: TV in Brazil," in Dowmunt, *Channels of Resistance,* 86–87.

92. Currie, Willie, and Michael Markovitz, "The People Shall Broadcast: The Struggle for a Post-Apartheid National Television Culture in South Africa," in Dowmunt, *Channels of Resistance,* 94–96.

93. Ranucci, Karen, "Democracy in Communication: Popular Video and Film in Latin America," in Boyd, Straubhaar, and Lent, *Videocassette Recorders in the Third World,* 213.

94. Personal observation and discussion with CAAMA staff, Alice Springs, N.T., Australia, October 1993.

95. Bercu, Joanne, "Second Mesa Students Produce Film," *Hopi Tutuveni,* March 31, 1995, 1.

96. Stuart, Sara, "Some Experiences of Video SEWA: A Grassroots Women's Video Team in Ahmedabad, India," in Mowlana and Frondorf, *The Media as a Forum for Community Building,* 27–30.

97. Hudson, Heather, "Community Use of Radio in the Canadian North," in Spain et al., *Radio for Education and Development,* vol. 2, 389.

98. Ibid., 403.

99. Mohr, Lavinia, "To Tell the People—Wawatay Radio Network," in Girard, *A Passion for Radio,* 23–38.

100. Canadian Radio-Television and Telecommunications Commission (CRTC), "Report of the Committee on the Extension of Service to Northern and Remote Communities" (a.k.a. Therrien Committee), Ottawa, 1983.

101. Department of Communication, "The Northern Broadcast Policy," Ottawa, 1983.

102. Cutler, Francis, "Political Conferences to Polar Bear Hunting for Canada's Northern Third," *InterMedia*, 20, 6 (1992), 39–40; Hudson, Heather, *Communication Satellites: Their Development and Impact*, New York: Free Press, 1990, 98–99; Hudson, Heather, "The Need for Native Broadcasting in Northern Canada: A Review of Research," Ottawa: Native Citizens Directorate, 1985; Roth, Lorna, and Gail Valaskakis, "Aboriginal Broadcasting in Canada: A Case Study in Democratization," in Bruck, P. A., and Marc Raboy, *Communication for and against Democracy*, Montreal: Black Rose Books, 1989, 221–234; Valaskakis, Gail, R. Robbins, and T. Wilson, *The Inukshuk Project: An Assessment*, Ottawa: Inuit Tapirisat of Canada, 1981.

103. Meadows, Michael, "Ideas from the Bush: Indigenous Television in Australia and Canada," *Canadian Journal of Communication*, 20, 2 (1995), 198.

104. "The Great White North," *Hollywood Reporter*, January 22, 1992, 12, 35.

105. Meadows, "Ideas from the Bush," 206.

106. Northrip, Charles M., "History of Public Radio in Alaska," in *NFCB Newsletter* (publication of National Federation of Community Broadcasters), special report on community radio in Alaska, undated, but probably 1982, 2–3.

107. Hudson, Heather, *When Telephones Reach the Village: The Role of Telecommunications in Rural Development*, Norwood, N.J.: Ablex, 1984, 76–79; Kreimer, Osvaldo, "Interactive Radio for Health Care and Education in Alaska," in Spain et al., *Radio for Education and Development*, vol. 2, 432–433.

108. Olson, Scott, "Devolution and Indigenous Mass Media: The Role of Media in Inupiat and Sami Nation-Building," unpublished Ph.D. dissertation, Northwestern University, 1984, 96–97.

109. *Public Broadcasting in Alaska: A Long-range Plan*, Juneau: Alaskan Public Broadcasting Commission, 1982, 26.

110. Olson, "Devolution and Indigenous Mass Media," 99–100.

111. Hudson, *Communication Satellites*, 53–56, 59–62; *Public Broadcasting in Alaska*, 26.

112. Statistics derived from fact sheets prepared by individual stations for the Alaska Public Radio Network, 1994.

113. Daley and James, "Ethnic Broadcasting in Alaska."

114. Emanuel, Richard, "Gary Fife's Radio Program Brings Native Oral Tradition Full Circle," *Alaskan Airways Magazine*, September 1992, 75–79.

115. Department of Aboriginal Affairs, "Out of the Silent Land," Canberra, A.C.T.: Australian Government Publishing Service, 1984, 129–152.

116. Molnar, "Aboriginal Broadcasting in Australia," 163–164.

117. Aboriginal and Torres Strait Islander Commission (ATSIC), *Aboriginal and Torres Strait Islander Broadcasting Policy: Review Report and Draft Policy Statement*, Canberra, A.C.T., January 1993, 27–31, 37–38, 40–41, 48, 50, 65–66, 95–96; Meadows, "A Watering Can in the Desert," 36–38, 50; personal interviews with Wayne Wharton, manager, Station 4K1G, Townsville, Queensland, Australia, Tony Walker, station manager, Waringarri Media, Kununurra, W.A., Australia, and BRACS Training Staff members, Batchelor College, Batchelor, N.T., Australia, all on-site, in September 1993; Molnar, Helen, "The Democratization of Communications Technology in Australia and the South Pacific: Media Participation by Indigenous Peoples," unpublished Ph.D. dissertation, Monash University, Victoria, Australia, 1993.

118. Meadows, "Ideas from the Bush," 201; Molnar, Helen, "Remote Indigenous Community Broadcasting in Australia: An Extension of Indigenous Cultural Expression," paper delivered at the Annual Conference of the International Communication Association, Sydney, N.S.W., Australia, July 1994.

119. "Huge Boost for Australian Television in Asia," *COMBROAD,* 103 (1994), 7.

120. "AUSTRALIA: Aboriginal Media Wants [*sic*] Equal Time," Inter Press Service, February 25, 1993, 3:22 PM.

121. Newberg, Julie, "Native American Radio," *Spokane Spokesman Review,* June 15, 1994.

122. Shebala, Marley, "New Radio Show Calling Your Number," *Navajo Times,* June 8, 1995, A1; "Native American Talk Show Takes to Air," *Coeur d'Alene Press,* June 6, 1995, A10; "New Talk Show Covers Issues of American Indians," *New York Times,* June 11, 1995, A13.

123. Muircheartaigh, Aogan o, manager, Raidio na Gaeltachta, personal interview, Baile na n'Gall, Ireland, August 1994.

124. Ogan, Christine, "Listserver Communication during the Gulf War: What Kind of Medium is the Electronic Bulletin Board?" *Journal of Broadcasting and Electronic Media,* 37, 2 (1993), 177–196.

125. Associated Press, "Mexican Zapatistas Find World Audience on Internet," *Minneapolis Star Tribune,* February 16, 1995, 2A.

126. Michaels, *The Aboriginal Invention of Television in Central Australia,* 201–203; Toyne, Peter, "The Tanami Network," paper delivered to the Conference on Service Delivery and Communication in the 1990s, Brisbane, Queensland, Australia, March 17–19, 1992; personal observations of Aboriginal staff at 8KIN radio, Alice Springs, N.T., Australia, October 1993.

127. "Network Will Link American Indian Communities in Great Lakes Region," *Indian Country Today,* March 9, 1995, A3.

128. "Communications Enterprises Get the Word Out," *Indian Country Today,* March 9, 1995, special section entitled "Economic—the Navajo Nation," 25; Keith, *Signals in the Air,* 93–95, mentions a few other Native American television operations, all quite modest in their output.

129. Stiles and associates, "Broadcasting and Canada's Aboriginal Peoples," 24–25.

130. Ibid., 26–35.

131. Personal interviews with Suzanne Aubin, director, and other staff at CBC Northern Services, Montreal, June 1994.

132. Hudson, Heather, "New Technologies and Aboriginal Communications: A Comparison of the Australian Outback and Canadian North," paper presented at the Annual Conference of the International Communication Association, Sydney, N.S.W, Australia, July 1994.

133. Department of Aboriginal Affairs, *Annual Report, 1985–86,* Canberra, A.C.T., Australia, 1986, 60.

134. CAAMA, *CAAMA Report,* 3.

135. ATSIC, *Aboriginal and Torres Strait Islander Broadcasting Policy,* 19–48.

136. Ibid., 65.

137. Perleeka Television, "Community Television Progress Report 12/9/93," Millers Point (Sydney), N.S.W., Australia: Perleeka Television, 1993, 1. My March 1996 visit to Australia revealed very little Aboriginal or Pacific Islander programming on community television.

138. *Sami Radio mot Ar 2000,* NRK Sami Radio, Karasjok, Norway, January 1992.

139. Ibid., 45–49. See also Salonen, Seppo Heikki, "After an Ice-Age of a Century, Radio Rescues the Language of the Lapps," *InterMedia*, 20, 6 (1992), 37–38+.

140. International Information, Finnish Broadcasting Company (YLE), "Act on Yleisradio OY (Valid from 1 January, 1994)"; copies of pp. 1, 7, and 14 of full text of the act in Finnish. Certain Maori broadcasters have sought similar inclusive language in an amendment to the New Zealand Broadcasting Act that is under consideration by Parliament in 1996. They seem likely to be successful.

141. Nousuniemi, Juhani, manager, Sami Radio, YLE, personal interview, Ivalo, Finland, September 1994.

142. See Puntel, Joana Terezinha, "The Catholic Church Searching for Democratization of Communication in Latin America," unpublished Ph.D. dissertation, Simon Fraser University, 1992. Puntel's work features two case studies of situations in Brazil.

143. "Soldiers Occupy Radio Stations in Ecuador," *Solidarity Network Action Alert*, issued by AMARC (World Association of Community Radio Broadcasters), Montreal, Quebec, no date, but distributed on June 27, 1994. There was a roughly similar occurrence in Mexico in March 1995, when Radio Huayacoatl, an indigenous radio station in the state of Veracruz, had its license revoked, on the grounds that it did not conform to technical standards. AMARC reported that roughly 3,000 indigenous people signed a petition demanding that the station be reopened. The government renewed its license and gave it 30 days to fix its technical problems. Boivin, Louise, "Stations Refuse to Be Silenced," *InterRadio* (AMARC's newsletter), 7, 2 (1995), 4.

144. Garitaonandia, Carmelo, "Regional Television in Europe," *European Journal of Communication*, 8, 3 (1993), 287–291. See also Coulmas, Florian, ed., *A Language Policy for the European Community: Prospects and Quandaries*, Berlin and New York: Mouton de Gruyter, 1991.

CHAPTER THREE

1. The literature on minority languages is vast, but I have yet to see an author argue for preservation, in the admittedly narrow sense that I have defined the term here. There are many excellent sources of material on the subject of *linguistic minorities* (the title usually used for electronic searches, e.g., in Lumina). The following were particularly useful to me in developing a better sense of how linguists (and a few individuals from other disciplines) approach the topic, even if theirs isn't my approach: Ball, Martin, with James Fife, eds., *The Celtic Languages*, London and New York: Routledge, 1993; Blom, Gunilla, ed., *Minority Languages— the Scandinavian Experience* (but covers several non-Scandinavian languages), Oslo, Norway: Nordic Language Secretariat, 1992; Haugen, Einar, et al., eds., *Minority Languages Today*, Edinburgh: Edinburgh University Press, 1990; Kalantzis, Mary, et al., *Minority Languages and Dominant Culture: Issues of Education, Assessment, and Social Equity*, New York: Falmer Press, 1989; Robins, Robert H., and Eugenius M. Uhlenbeck, eds., *Endangered Languages*, New York: Oxford University Press (but distributed by St. Martin's Press), 1991; Wardhaugh, Ronald, *Languages in Competition: Dominance, Diversity, and Decline*, New York: Oxford University Press, 1987.

2. Browne, Donald R., *Comparing Broadcast Systems*, Ames: Iowa State University Press, 1989, 66.

3. Luther, Breda, "Identity Management and Popular Representational Forms," in Drummond, Phillip, et al., eds., *National Identity and Europe: The Television Revolution*, London: British Film Institute, 1993, 48–49.

4. Duff, Alan, *Maori: The Crisis and the Challenge,* Auckland, New Zealand: Harper Collins, 1993.

5. Deutsch, Sarah, et al., "Contemporary Peoples/Contested Places," in Milner, Clyde A. II, et al., eds., *The Oxford History of the American West,* New York: Oxford University Press, 1994, 659–660.

6. I am indebted to anthropologist and media practitioner E. B. Eiselein, head of the survey research firm A&A Research (Kalispell, Mont.), for sharing a roughly similar illustrative example with me. Telephone conversation, June 20, 1995.

7. The story was related to me by several Aboriginal media staff in Broome, Kununurra, Batchelor, and Alice Springs during my site visits in October 1993.

8. I do not deal with the admittedly important, but also extensive, subject of majority culture portrayals of indigenous peoples. There are many books on the subject, among them: Bataille, Gretchen, and Charles L. P. Silet, eds., *The Pretend Indian: Images of Native Americans in the Movies,* Ames: Iowa State University Press, 1980; Berkhofer, Robert F., Jr., *The White Man's Indian: Images of the American Indian from Columbus to the Present,* New York: Knopf, 1978; Blythe, Martin, *Naming the Other: Images of the Maori in New Zealand Film and Television,* Metuchen, N.J.: Scarecrow Press, 1994; Churchill, Ward, *Fantasies of the Master Race: Literature, Cinema and the Colonization of American Indians,* Monroe, Maine: Common Courage Press, 1992; Friar, Ralph, and Natasha Friar, *The Only Good Indian ... The Hollywood Gospel,* New York: Drama Book Specialists, 1972; Hamamoto, Darrell Y., *Monitored Peril: Asian Americans and the Politics of TV Representation,* Minneapolis: University of Minnesota Press, 1994; Mackinolty, Chips, and Michael Duffy, *Guess Who's Coming to Dinner in Arnhem Land?* Darwin, N.T., Australia: Northern Land Council, 1987; Noreiga, Chon, ed., *Chicanos and Film: Representations and Resistance,* Minneapolis: University of Minnesota Press, 1992; and Woll, Allen L., and Randall M. Miller, *Ethnic and Racial Images in American Film and Television: Historical Essays and Bibliography,* New York: Garland, 1987. See also Visual Communication Study Group, *Native Americans on Film and Video,* vols. 1 and 2, New York: Museum of the American Indian and Heye Foundation, 1988. There also is an interesting video compilation of Hollywood film presentations of Native Americans entitled "Images of Indians, Part 1: The Great Movie Massacre," available through the Native American Public Broadcasting Consortium, Lincoln, Nebr.

9. As Davies and Howell both point out, the controversy over the creation of a Welsh language Channel 4 service in the United Kingdom was accompanied by demonstrations, refusals to pay the annual broadcast license fee, and the bombing of TV transmitters in Wales. Davies, John, *Broadcasting and the BBC in Wales,* Cardiff: University of Wales Press, 1994, 288–300, 325–345; Howell, William J., Jr., "Britain's Fourth Television Channel and the Welsh Language Controversy," *Journal of Broadcasting,* 25, 2 (1981), 133.

10. Walker, Tony, station manager, Waringarri Media, personal interview, Kununurra, W.A., Australia, October 1993.

11. Webber, Allison, "The Need for Change: Responsibilities of the Media," in Spoonley, Paul, and Walter Hirsh, eds., *Between the Lines: Racism and the New Zealand Media,* Auckland, New Zealand: Heinemann Reed, 1990, Chap. 22, provides an interesting account by a white news reporter of how she learned to report on Maori culture.

12. I have drawn upon the following surveys in reaching my conclusions regarding audience characteristics: Brunton, Pat, "Radio Survey for the Hamilton (New Zealand) Area," undated, but during spring 1993; Demay, Joel, "Culture and Media Use in Saskatchewan Indian Country," *Canadian Journal of Communication,* 16 (1991), 417–430; Eiselein, E. B., "Who Listens to Native American Public Radio?" Kalispell, Mont.: A&A Research, June 1992; Hein, Kurt, *Radio Baha'i Ecuador: A Baha'i Development Project,* London: George

Ronald, 1988, Chap. 5 (detailed summaries of two surveys conducted by Hein in 1981 and 1983); Karam, Robert, and Arlene Zuckernick, "A Study of Audiences for Aboriginal Community Radio: A Profile of Four Northern Ontario Communities," for the Ministry of Culture and Communications (Ottawa), April 1992; Nihoniho, Anthony, and Neville Young, "Survey for Te Reo Iriraki ki Otautahi 90.5 FM" (Christchurch, New Zealand), March 1993; "Presentation Enquete pour Xiberoko Botza," Mauleon, France, 1986; Quadrant Research New Zealand, "The 1993 Maori Radio Study: A Presentation to NZ on Air," October 1993; RAJAR (Radio Authority Joint Audience Research) figures for Wales for 1992 and 1993, reported in BBC Radio Cymru section of "BBC Wales Performance Review," 1993–1994; Ruohuomaa, Erja, "Sami Radio: Audiences in Finland, Sweden and Norway," YLE (Helsinki), Internal Report, May 1992, and "Sami Radio Programming and Audiences in Finland, Sweden, and Norway," *Audience Research Review, 1995,* Helsinki: YLE, 1995, 34–41. Also, I have used partial data in a few cases: a 1988 Market Research Bureau of Ireland study of listening to Raidio na Gaeltachta; and a 1979 University of Galway survey conducted by sociology students on the same subject.

13. Eiselein, "Who Listens to Native American Public Radio?" 15.

14. Reweti, Debra, "Absolutely Positively Maori," *Mana* (Maori newsmagazine), 4 (November–December 1993), 33; "Maiden Profit for Mai-FM," *Te Maori News,* 4, 17 (September 1995), 4.

15. Eiselein, "Who Listens to Native American Public Radio?" 12 ($N = 311$).

16. Nihoniho and Young, "Survey for Te Reo Iriraki ki Otautahi 90.5 FM." There was no separation of Maori and non-Maori respondents for this item.

17. Ruohuomaa, "Sami Radio," 23, 46.

18. Nihoniho and Young, "Survey for Te Reo Iriraki ki Otautahi 90.5 FM," 1, in a random telephone sample of 500 in Christchurch, Australia, received 101 "lack of awareness" (of the Maori station) responses and 102 "may or may not be aware of it" responses. Data were not broken out according to Maori and non-Maori identity. I have often suggested inclusion of an "awareness" question when discussing surveys with indigenous station staff, but it doesn't appear to be a high-priority issue among them, despite the potential value of indicating whether or not media operations might do well to increase their self-promotion.

19. The report itself was included as attachment 5 in a briefing book prepared by New Zealand on Air for a newly created Maori funding organization for Maori electronic media (originally titled Te Reo Whakapuaka Irirangi; now Te Mangai Paho) in September 1993.

20. McCormack, Mike, "Problems of Minority Language Broadcasting: Gaelic in Scotland," *European Journal of Communication,* 8, 1 (1993), 109–114. See also Davidson, Julie, "Gift Horse for the Scots," *Spectrum* (publication of the Independent Television Commission, U.K.), 6 (1992), 17–18, for some critical observations on present and projected programming practices.

21. Gwynfryn, Hywel, program presenter, BBC Radio Cymru, personal interview, Cardiff, Wales, September 1994.

22. Delyn, Bob, executive director, Canolfan Sian, personal interview, Llandwrog, Caernarvon, Wales, April 1993.

23. Vickery, Cheryl, director, TAPE, personal interview, Melbourne, Victoria, Australia, November 1993.

24. Wilson, Helen, "Whakarongo mae e nga iwi: Maori Radio," in Wilson, Helen, ed., *The Radio Book, 1994,* Christchurch: New Zealand Broadcasting School/Christchurch Polytechnic, 1994, 107.

25. Recorded from broadcast, September 1987.

26. Wilson, *The Radio Book, 1994.*

27. "Lagasradioi 10 cuogga" (Ten points for local radio), ASSU, September 8, 1994, 4.

28. Jones, Elwyn, deputy director, BBC Radio Cymru, personal interview, Bangor, Wales, August 1994.

29. Data reported in BBC Radio Cymru section of "BBC Wales Performance Review," 1993, 94.

30. Discussion with station staff, Radio Ceredigion, Aberystwyth, Wales, September 1994.

31. Again, I am indebted to E. B. Eiselein (see endnote 6) for this example. Telephone conversation, June 20, 1995.

32. Personal observations in Port Augusta, W.A., and Sydney, N.S.W., Australia, November 1993. Material on Aboriginal-police confrontations is relatively common in Aboriginal media, especially urban-centered operations. Many stations representing ethnic minority interests and concerns in other countries also provide such coverage. See Sakolsky, Ron, "Zoom Black Magic Liberation Radio: The Birth of the Micro-Radio Movement in the USA," in Girard, Bruce, ed., *A Passion for Radio,* Montreal: Black Rose Books, 1992, 106–113.

33. Te Ua, Henare, head, RNZ Te Reo o Aotearoa, personal interview, Auckland, New Zealand, October 1993.

34. "An Innovative Drama Serial in Maori Has Arrived on Our Screens," *Pu Kaea,* August 9, 1995, 8.

35. Chang, Clair, program assistant, Radio Goolari, personal interview, Broome, W.A., Australia, October 1993.

36. Browne, Donald R., Charles M. Firestone, and Ellen Mickiewicz, *Television/Radio News & Minorities,* Washington, D.C.: Aspen Institute, 1994, 125–127.

37. Weiland, Brad, general manager, KGHR-FM, personal interview, Tuba City, Ariz., April 1995.

38. Watson, Ross, program director, 4AAA, personal interview, Brisbane, Queensland, Australia, October 1993.

39. Griffiths, Alison, "Pobol y Cym: The Construction of National and Cultural Identity in a Welsh Soap Opera," in Drummond, et al., *National Identity and Europe,* 9–24; Howell, William J., Jr., "Minority Language Broadcasting and the Continuation of Culture in Wales and Ireland," in Riggins, Stephen H., ed., *Ethnic Minority Media: An International Perspective,* Newbury Park, Calif.: Sage, 1992, 231–233.

40. Fallow, Mike, "No, Not That Tiwai," *Southland Times,* November 1, 1993, 2; Reweti, Debra, "Radio Wha Waho—It's Not All Smiles," *Mana,* 5 (1994), 46–48. African-Americans interviewed by Johnson expressed fears that white viewers in the United States might appropriate an African-American communication game known as "SNAP!" because the game was regularly featured in the Fox TV situation comedy "In Living Color." Johnson, E. Patrick, "SNAP! Culture: A Different Kind of Reading," *Text and Performance Quarterly,* 15 (1995), 122–142.

41. Worth, Sol, and John Adair, *Through Navajo Eyes,* Bloomington: Indiana University Press, 1973.

42. Michaels, Eric, *Aboriginal Invention of Television: Central Australia, 1982–86,* Canberra, A.C.T.: Australian Institute of Aboriginal Studies, 1986.

43. Oepen, Manfred, "Scavengers Go Public: Integrated Media Support to a Development Program in Indonesia," in Mowlana, Hamid, and Margaret H. Frondorf, eds., *The Media as a Forum for Community Building,* Washington, D.C.: Paul Nitze School of Advanced International Studies, Johns Hopkins University, 1992, 31–36.

44. I learned of the first of the three videos in my visit to the Townsville Aboriginal and Islander Media Association (TAIMA), Townsville, Queensland, Australia, October 1993; the second in my visit to New Zealand on Air, Wellington, New Zealand, October 1993; and the third in my visit to the CBC Northern Service in Montreal in June 1994.

CHAPTER FOUR

1. Steele, Graham, then involved with Aboriginal media development as a staff member of ABC. Personal interview, Sydney, N.S.W., Australia, September 1987.

2. Molnar, Helen, "The Democratization of Communications Technology in Australia and the South Pacific: Media Participation by Indigenous Peoples," unpublished Ph.D. dissertation, Monash University, Victoria, Australia, 1993, 548.

3. Bostock, Lester, "Aboriginal Television Training," unpublished paper, November 1993; also personal interview, Sydney, N.S.W., Australia, November 1993.

4. Townsville Aboriginal and Islander Media Association and Australian Film, Television, and Radio School, "Accreditation of the Associate Diploma of Arts (Video Production Techniques) (A Three Year Training Program), Submission to ACT Accreditation Agency," 1990, with updates.

5. Varsi, Magne Uve, instructor, Sami College, personal interview, Kautokeino, Norway, May 1993.

6. McClear, Richard, former manager, KCAW-FM, Sitka, Alaska, personal correspondence, December 10, 1994; working schedule for the Alaska Native Youth Media Institute, Anchorage, Alaska, June 21–28, 1994.

7. Haederle, Michael, "American Indians Seek More Say in Film, TV," *Los Angeles Times,* March 27, 1991, F4–5.

8. Eruera, Taura, then manager, Mai-FM, personal interview, Auckland, New Zealand, October 1993.

9. In 1994, Vitae Systems International conducted a survey of training needs at U.S. public broadcasting stations that received financial support from the Corporation for Public Broadcasting (CPB). For the subcategory of *community stations,* which would be most likely to include indigenous stations, a slight majority of the respondents ($N = 138$) returning a mailed questionnaire felt that *quantity* of training available for chief operations officers and station managers was less than needed, while another 15 percent had *no* awareness of training available for managers, and 30 percent likewise were not aware of training for CEOs. Only six Native Americans responded, so cross-tabulations for indigenous peoples would be meaningless, but the overall pattern of response is hardly encouraging. Vitae Systems International, "Training Needs Assessment Prepared for the Corporation for Public Broadcasting, Final Report," January 31, 1995, Tables 4.4 and 5.16.

10. Davidson, J. R., "The Basic Village Education Project in Guatemala," Washington, D.C.: USAID, Report No. PN-AAD-299, 1976, 34.

11. Michaels, Eric, *Aboriginal Invention of Television: Central Australia, 1982–86,* Canberra, A.C.T.: Australian Institute for Aboriginal Studies, 1986, 23–24.

12. Scott, John Ross, "Council Slap Ban on Radio Tweed," *Southern Reporter,* Selkirk, Scotland, September 25, 1986, 1+; personal interviews with station staff, Radio Tweed, Selkirk, Scotland, September 23–24, 1985. See also Browne, Donald R., *What's Local about Local Radio? A Cross-national Comparative Study,* London: International Institute of Communication, Occasional Monograph No. 1, 1988, 84.

13. Walker, Tony, manager, Waringarri Media Radio, personal interview, Kununurra, W.A., Australia, October 1993.

14. Browne, Donald R., *Comparing Broadcast Systems: The Experiences of Six Industrialized Nations,* Ames: Iowa State University Press, 1989, 33–34.

15. ICA was founded in 1991. It has provided advice and encouragement to groups wishing to create stations, and it is coordinating member station participation in an all-Native American talk program, "Native America Calling," which began distribution through American Indian Radio on Satellite (AIROS) in June 1995. See also Keith, Michael C., *Signals in the Air: Native Broadcasting in America,* Westport, Conn.: Praeger, 1995, 29–32.

16. CHRQ, "CHRQ Policy for On-Air Policy [*sic*]," Radio CHRQ, Restigouche, Quebec, Canada, 1992.

17. Australian Broadcasting Corporation, *Code of Practice,* Sydney, N.S.W., March 17, 1993.

18. Federation of Australian Radio Broadcasters, *Commercial Radio Codes of Practice,* Sydney, N.S.W., August 1993.

19. Federation of Australian Commercial Television Stations, *Commercial Television Industry Codes of Practice,* Sydney, N.S.W., August 1993.

20. Special Broadcasting Services, *SBS Codes of Practice, 1993,* Crows Nest, Sydney, N.S.W., Australia, 1993, 6.

21. Bostock, Lester, "The Greater Perspective: A Guideline for the Production of Film and Television on Aborigines and Torres Strait Islanders," Sydney, N.S.W., Australia: Special Broadcasting Services, 1990; Eggerking, Kitty, and Diana Plater, eds., "Signposts: A Guide to Reporting Aboriginal, Torres Strait Islander, and Ethnic Affairs," Sydney, N.S.W.: Australian Centre for Independent Journalists, University of Technology, 1992; King, Michael, "Kawe Korero: A Guide to Reporting Maori Activities," Pukekohe, New Zealand: New Zealand Journalists Training Board, 1985; Langton, Marcia, "Well, I Heard It on the Radio and I Saw It on the Television," North Sydney, N.S.W.: Australian Film Commission, 1993.

22. Federation of Australian Radio Broadcasters, *Commercial Radio Codes of Practice,* "Explanatory Notes to the Guidelines on the Portrayal of Indigenous Australians on Australian Commercial Radio."

23. Browne, Donald R., Charles Firestone, and Ellen Mickiewicz, *Television/Radio News & Minorities,* Washington, D.C.: Aspen Institute, 1994, 85–98.

24. Personal interview with the station manager, on-site in New Zealand, October 1993. The manager did not wish to be identified by name, so as to avoid possible further strain on his relationship with the tribal council.

25. Chapman, Dixon, "Who's in Charge?," *Mana* (Maori newsmagazine), 2 (April–May 1993), 92.

26. Baum, Dan, "Protest Voices Displeasure with KILI Radio," *Los Angeles Times,* August 31, 1992, A5.

27. Personal interviews with BRACS trainers in Batchelor, N.T., and with station staff at 8KIN, Alice Springs, N.T., Australia, October 1993.

28. Discussions with Sami Radio staff in Kiruna, Sweden, May 1993.

29. Discussions with Sami radio staff in Inari, Finland, and in Karasjok, Norway, September 1994; personal letter from Nils Johan Héatta, Head, NRK Sami Radio, Karasjok, Norway, February 13, 1996.

30. Yaxley, Louise, news editor, Radio 8KIN, personal interview, Alice Springs, N.T., Australia, October 1993.

31. MacAoire, Sean, board member and program presenter, Raidio na Life, personal interview, Dublin, Ireland, August 1994.

32. Pasqueretta, Paul, "On the Indianness of Bingo: Gambling and the Native American Community," *Critical Inquiry,* 20 (Summer 1994), 694–714, provides an excellent summary of contrasting Native American viewpoints on bingo and other forms of gambling played and managed by Native Americans.

33. Stiles, J. Mark, and associates, "Broadcasting and Canada's Aboriginal Peoples: A Report to the Task Force on Broadcasting Policy," Ottawa, 1985, 43–44. I verified this through a personal interview with Conway Jocks, station manager, CKRK, Kahnawake, Quebec, Canada, in March 1992.

34. Chaumel, Gilles, "Uashat-Maliotenam: Mutual Support, Then and Now," *Rencontre,* 16, 5 (Spring 1995), 6.

35. ATSIC *Annual Report, 1991–92,* Canberra, A.C.T., Australia, 1992, 89–92; ATSIC *Annual Report, 1992–93,* Canberra, A.C.T., Australia, 1993, 131–132 and 228–229.

36. Keith, *Signals in the Air,* 23, 139.

37. Sprague, Donovin, station manager, KILI-FM, Bernard Whiting, station manager, KINI-FM, and Brad Weiland, station manager, KGHR-FM. Personal interviews, Porcupine and St. Francis, S.Dak., March 1995; and Tuba City, Ariz., April 1995. Several sources cited in Keith raise similar points. Keith, *Signals in the Air,* Chap. 3.

38. Rada, Stephen E., "A Survey of Native American Radio Broadcasting: Policies, Operations, and Development," unpublished manuscript, 1979, 20–22.

39. Mackay, John Angus, "Winning over the Audience," *Spectrum* (publication of the Independent Television Commission), Summer 1992, 16.

40. New Zealand on Air, *Annual Report, 1993–94,* Wellington, New Zealand, 1994, 10–13.

41. Evans, Ripeka, "The Negation of Powerlessness—Maori Feminism, a Perspective," Auckland University Winter Lecture Series, 10, August 1993, 11. Evans became Chairperson of Te Mangai Paho in 1994 and resigned in 1996. She was highly controversial among iwi station staff, who saw her as championing Maori television at their expense. Also, there were numerous accusations, mainly from Maori broadcasters, of TMP favoritism, fiscal mismanagement, and poor communication. Phare, Jane, "Crackles on the Airwaves," *New Zealand Herald* (Auckland), March 23, 1996, Sec. 7.1. Searancke, Russel, "Shambolic Process Undermines National Maori Radio Service," *Te Maori News,* 5, 3, (February, 1996), 5; "Williamson Defends Competence of Maori Agency," *New Zealand Herald* (Auckland), March 21, 1996, 3.

42. Te Mangai Paho, "Draft Funding Policies, 1995–1996," subtitled "For Discussion & Consultation with Maori Interests," Wellington, New Zealand, undated, but probably March 1995.

43. Personal interviews and discussions with Aboriginal staff at Radio Redfern, Sydney, N.S.W., Radio 3CR, Melbourne, Victoria, Radio 2XX, Canberra, A.C.T., and Radio 4XXX, Brisbane, Queensland, Australia, in September 1987; with Maori staff at Te Upoko o te Ika, Wellington, New Zealand, September 1991; with Native American staff at Radio CKRK, Kahnawake (Montreal), Quebec, Canada, March 1992; with Aboriginal staff at 4AAA, Brisbane, Queensland, Australia, and the National Indigenous Media Association of Australia (NIMAA), October 1993; with Radio 3CR, Melbourne, Victoria, Australia, November 1993.

44. Emanual, Richard, "Gary Fife's Radio Program Brings Native Oral Tradition Full Circle," *Alaska Airlines Magazine,* September 1992, 7.

45. Lee, Chris, National Indigenous Media Association of Australia, personal interview, Brisbane, Queensland, October 1993.

46. Eruera, personal interview.

47. Davidson, "The Basic Village Education Project in Guatemala," 34.

48. Ruohuoma, Erja, Audience Research, YLE, personal interview, Helsinki, Finland, September 1994.

49. Ibid.

50. Nousuniemi, Juhani, head, Sami Radio, YLE, personal interview, Inari, Finland, September 1994.

51. Michaels, Eric, "Ask a Foolish Question: On the Methodologies of Cross Cultural Media Research," *Australian Journal of Cultural Studies,* 3, 2 (1985), 49–50.

52. Ibid., 49.

53. While I have yet to discover a book that covers the full range of communication research in indigenous societies, the following have been helpful in noting problems that may arise: Awa, Njoku E., "Ethnocentric Bias in Developmental Research," in Asante, Molefi,

Eileen Newmark, and Cecil Blake, eds., *Handbook of Intercultural Communication*, Beverly Hills, Calif.: Sage, 1979, 263–281; Axinn, George, and Nancy Axinn, "The Indigenous Observer Diary-Keeper: A Methodological Note," *Human Organization*, 28, 1 (1969), 78–86; Hursh-Cesar, Gerald, and Prodipto Roy, eds., *Third World Surveys: Survey Research in Developing Nations*, Delhi: Macmillan of India, 1976; Michaels, "Ask a Foolish Question"; Narula, Uma, and W. Barnett Pierce, eds., *Culture, Politics, and Research Programs: An International Assessment of Practical Problems in Field Research*, Hillsdale, N.J.: Lawrence Erlbaum Associates, 1990; Streib, Gordon F., "The Use of Survey Methods among the Navajo," *American Anthropologist*, 54 (1952), 30–40. Also useful is Shuter, Robert, ed., *World Researchers and Research in Intercultural Communication*, Wauwatosa, Wis.: Culture Publications, 1985, which is a directory of such researchers in various parts of the world. Unfortunately, it does not appear to have been updated.

54. Tanno, Delores V., and Fred E. Jandt, "Redefining the 'Other' in Multicultural Research," *Howard Journal of Communications*, 5, 1/2 (Fall 1993 and Winter 1994), 36–45.

55. MacAoire, personal interview.

56. Browne, Donald R., *Comparing Broadcast Systems*, 118–121, 169–170, 228–230, 242–243, 296–297, 348–350.

CHAPTER FIVE

1. Sinclair, Keith, *Origins of the Maori Wars*, Wellington: University of New Zealand Press, 1957.

2. Ibid.; Te Rangi, Hiroa, *The Coming of the Maori*, Wellington, New Zealand: Whitcombe and Tombs, 1949; Houghton, Phillip, *The First New Zealanders*, Auckland, New Zealand: Hodder and Stoughton, 1980; Metge, Joan, *The Maoris of New Zealand*, 2d ed., London: Routledge and Kegan Paul, 1976.

3. Drawn from personal interviews, September 1991, with Taura Eruera, manager, and Vivian Bridgewater, program director, Te Reo Irirangi o Ngati Whatua, Auckland, New Zealand; with Rick Rapana, project manager, New Zealand on Air, Wellington, New Zealand; and with Whiti Te Ra Kaihau, manager, and Barry Bartlett, secretary, Te Reo Irirangi o Tainui, Ngaruawahia, New Zealand.

4. Kawharu, Ian Hugh, ed., *Waitangi: Maori and Pakeha Perspectives on the Treaty of Waitangi*, Auckland, New Zealand: Oxford University Press, 1990; McKenzie, D. F., *Oral Culture, Literacy & Print in Early New Zealand: The Treaty of Waitangi*, Wellington, New Zealand: Victoria University Press, 1985; Orange, Claudia, *The Treaty of Waitangi*, Wellington, New Zealand: Allen and Unwin/Port Nicholson Press, 1987; Sharp, Andrew, *Justice and the Maori: Maori Claims in New Zealand Political Argument in the 1980s*, Auckland, New Zealand: Oxford University Press, 1990.

5. McKenzie, *Oral Culture, Literacy & Print in Early New Zealand*.

6. Ryan, P. M., *Revised Dictionary of Modern Maori*, Auckland, New Zealand: Heinemann Education, 1989.

7. Sharp, *Justice and the Maori*, 53–55.

8. Kawharu, *Waitangi*, xix.

9. Orange, *The Treaty of Waitangi;* McKenzie, *Oral Culture, Literacy & Print in Early New Zealand;* Mulgan, Richard, *Maori, Pakeha and Democracy.* Auckland, New Zealand: Oxford University Press, 1989, 30–41, 91–100; Sharp, *Justice and the Maori*, 15–19.

10. McKenzie, *Oral Culture, Literacy & Print in Early New Zealand*, 43.

11. Hall, John Herbert, *The History of Broadcasting in New Zealand, 1920–1954*, Wellington: Broadcasting Corporation of New Zealand, 1980; Mackay, Ian, *Broadcasting in*

New Zealand, Wellington, New Zealand: A. H. and A. W. Reed, 1953; O'Donoghue, A. F., *The Rise and Fall of Radio Broadcasting in New Zealand,* Wellington: A. F. O'Donoghue, 1946.

12. Walker, Ranginui, *Ka Whawhai Tonu Matou/Struggle without End,* Auckland, New Zealand: Penguin Books, 1990, 147.

13. Day, Patrick, *The Radio Years: A History of Broadcasting in New Zealand,* vol. 1, Auckland, New Zealand: Auckland University Press, 1995, 123. Day also notes the existence of a series of broadcasts on the correct pronunciation of Maori in the late 1920s, hosted at first by a pakeha and later by a Maori (123–124). Lemke, Claudia, "Maori Involvement in Sound Recording and Broadcasting, 1919 to 1958," unpublished M.A. thesis, University of Auckland, 1995, provides an even more detailed account of this period and contends that programming by and about Maori largely reinforced the notion of pakeha superiority.

14. Mackay, *Broadcasting in New Zealand,* 51.

15. Lemke, "Maori Involvement," 143–144; Maori Economic Development Commission, *Report of the Maori Economic Development Commission on Maori Broadcasting in New Zealand,* Auckland, New Zealand, 1985, "History," 1.

16. Te Ua, Henare, and John Turei, staff members, Te Reo o Aotearoa, Radio New Zealand, personal interview, Auckland, New Zealand, September 1991.

17. Hall, *The History of Broadcasting in New Zealand,* 70–71; Lemke, "Maori Involvement," 146–156. Lemke also notes (167–177) local station presentation of Maori programs in the 1950s and NZBC broadcasts of Maori language lessons in the 1960s and 1970s.

18. Hall, 110–111. See also Day, *The Radio Years,* 242–243, which underlines Scrimgeour's commitment to employment of Maori at all commercial stations.

19. Glover, Denis, *Sharp Edge Up,* Auckland, New Zealand: Blackwell and Janet Paul, 1968, 44.

20. Te Ua, personal interview.

21. Gregory, R. J., *Politics and Broadcasting in New Zealand,* Palmerston North, New Zealand: Dunmore Press, 1985, 46, 78.

22. Ibid., 22.

23. Gustafson, Barry, "The National Governments and Social Change (1949–1972)," in Sinclair, Keith, ed., *The Oxford Illustrated History of New Zealand,* Auckland, New Zealand: Oxford University Press, 1990, 283–285.

24. Walker, R., *Ka Whawhai Tonu Matou/Struggle without End,* 210.

25. Ling, Peter, "TV Violence and Aggressive Behavior among Maori and European Children," *Psychology Research Series,* 6, Hamilton, New Zealand: University of Waikato, 1977; Thompson, R. H. T., "Maori Affairs and the New Zealand Press," *Journal of the Polynesian Society,* 62–64 (1953–1955); Walker, Ranginui, "The Role of the Press in Defining Pakeha Perceptions of the Maori," in Spoonley, Paul, and Walter Hirsh, eds., *Between the Lines: Racism and the New Zealand Media,* Auckland, New Zealand: Heinemann Reed, 1990, 39–40.

26. Walker, R., *Ka Whawhai Tonu Matou/Struggle without End,* 209–210.

27. Ibid., 268–269.

28. New Zealand Parliament, Committee on Broadcasting (Adam Committee), *The Broadcasting Future for New Zealand,* Wellington: Government Printer, 1973.

29. Te Ua, personal interview.

30. Ibid.; Walker, R., *Ka Whawhai Tonu Matou/Struggle without End,* 269.

31. Fox, Derek, director, Mana Maori Media, personal interview, Rotorua, New Zealand, September 1991; Te Ua, personal interview; Walker, Piripi, manager, Te Upoko o te Ika, personal interview, Wellington, New Zealand, September 1991.

32. Whaanga, Philip (Piripi), "Radio: Capable of Carrying a Bi-cultural Message?" in

Spoonley and Hirsh, *Between the Lines,* 64; Hohepa, Pat, professor, Department of Maori Studies, University of Auckland, personal interview, Auckland, New Zealand, October 1993. Professor Hohepa read news and carried out other programming functions for Radio Pacific's Maori service in its early years.

33. Maori Economic Development Commission, *Report of the Maori Economic Development Commission,* "History," 2.

34. Hazlehurst, Kayleen M., *Racial Conflict and Resolution in New Zealand,* Canberra, A.C.T.: Australian National University Peace Research Centre, 1988, 11; Walker, R., *Ka Whawhai Tonu Matou/Struggle without End,* 222–225. Butterworth observes that television in particular managed to transform much of the Maori discontent of the times into "the subject of recurrent moral panics, and the emergent young Maori leaders became the handy folk devils of an insecure society." Butterworth, Ruth, "The Media," in Novitz, David, and Bill Willmott, eds., *Culture and Identity in New Zealand,* Wellington, New Zealand: GP Books, 1989, 155. Nairn and McCreanor examine the testimony of pakeha on the incident and its aftermath, evidence gathered by the New Zealand Human Rights Commission. That testimony clearly indicates some deeply held sentiments along the lines of "These [students] are bad Maori—not like the 'good' Maori we grew up with" and "When you see something like this, you see what putting these people [Maori] on the dole has done." There also are several indications of reaction to images of the Maori students as presented on television, generally along the lines of "I'm sick of seeing a bunch of wild-eyed young Maori parading themselves on television." Nairn, Raymond G., and Timothy N. McCreanor, "Sensitivity and Hypersensitivity: An Imbalance in Pakeha Accounts of Racial Conflict," *Journal of Language and Social Psychology,* 9, 4 (1990), 293–308; Nairn, Raymond G., and Timothy N. McCreanor, "Race Talk and Common Sense: Patterns in Pakeha Discourse on Maori/Pakeha Relations in New Zealand," *Journal of Language and Social Psychology,* 10, 4 (1991), 245–262.

35. Ian Cross, chair of the BCNZ during the late 1970s to early 1980s, claims that he made real efforts to get the corporation to recruit more Maori staff but that he ran into considerable internal opposition. This followed a meeting with the Te Reo Maori Society in 1978. Cross, Ian, *The Unlikely Bureaucrat: My Years in Broadcasting,* Wellington, New Zealand: Allan and Unwin, 1988, 231–232. Other corporation executives with whom I spoke did not recall him as being quite so vigilant a proponent of Maori involvement.

36. Craig, John, general manager, New Zealand Public Radio, personal interview, Wellington, September 1991; Wakem, Beverly, former director general, Radio New Zealand, personal interview, Wellington, September 1991; Fox, personal interview; Turei, personal interview; Te Ua, personal interview; Walker, P., personal interview.

37. Craig, personal interview; Wakem, personal interview; Walker, P., personal interview. One can gain a sense of the climate surrounding the issue of the Maori presence in broadcasting through a major "future-oriented" 1981 report: Moriarty, Gerald, et al., *Network New Zealand: Communications in the Future,* Wellington, New Zealand: Commission for the Future, 1981. The report features the thoughts of several experts on such issues as communications needs and rights, but only a few of the experts mention Maori needs, and even they say very little that is specific to the subject.

38. Maori Economic Development Commission, *Report of the Maori Economic Development Commission,* "Radio Aotearoa Network Recommendations," Item 2.

39. Fox, personal interview; Kaihau, personal interview; Walker, P., personal interview.

40. Radio New Zealand, internal memo, P(iripi) Walker to Val Brooke-White, executive producer, Continuing Education Unit, Radio New Zealand, undated but probably late August 1983.

41. Walker, Piripi, testimony to the Waitangi tribunal, October 1990 (personal document), brief of evidence A36, 8–9.

42. Ibid., 9–10.

43. Ibid., 10.

44. Te Upoko o te Ika, report, "Te Irirangi Maori," May/June 1987, 12.

45. Walker, R., *Ka Whawhai Tonu Matou/Struggle without End*, 203–209.

46. Fox, Derek, "Aotearoa Broadcasting System, Inc.," in Spoonley and Hirsh, *Between the Lines*, 132–133; Kaa, Hone, program director, Radio Aotearoa, personal interview, Papatoetoe, New Zealand, September 1991; Walker, P., personal interview; Walker, Ranginui, Professor, Department of Maori Studies, University of Auckland, New Zealand, personal interview, September 1991.

47. Fox, "Aotearoa Broadcasting System," 132–133; Walker, R., *Ka Whawhai Tonu Matou/Struggle without End*, 268–273.

48. Maori Economic Development Commission, "A Global Approach to Maori Radio Development," Wellington, New Zealand, May 1987.

49. Ibid., 4.

50. Fox, "Aotearoa Broadcasting System," 133.

51. Kaa, personal interview.

52. Personal visit to Te Reo Irirangi Ngati Porou, Ruatoria, October 1993.

53. Personal visit to Tautoko-FM, Mangamuka Bridge, New Zealand, October 1993.

54. New Zealand Parliament, *Broadcasting Act of 1989*, Wellington: Government Printer, 1989, Sec. 36(a)(ii) and Sec. 37(a)(iii).

55. Ministry of Broadcasting, "Directive to the Broadcasting Commission ...," from Jonathan Hunt, Minister of Broadcasting, June 1, 1989, 2.

56. Fox, Derek, "Te Karere: The Struggle for Maori News," in Spoonley and Hirsh, *Between the Lines*, 103–107, and "Honouring the Treaty: Indigenous Television in Aotearoa," in Dowmunt, Tony, ed., *Channels of Resistance: Global Television and Empowerment*, London: British Film Institute, 1993, 126–137.

57. Whaanga, Piripi, personal interview, Wellington, New Zealand, October 1993. Whaanga soon left Mana Maori Media, partly, he told me, because of disagreements with Fox over just such issues.

58. Broadcasting Commission of New Zealand, *Annual Report for 1989–90*, Wellington, 1990, 6.

59. Broadcasting Commission of New Zealand, *New Zealand on Air Newsletter*, 3, 1991, 4–5.

60. Whaanga, P., "Radio," 65–68.

61. Whitwell, Jan L., "The Rogernomics Economic Movement," in Holland, Martin, and Jonathan Boston, eds., *The Fourth Labour Government: Politics and Party in New Zealand*, 2d ed, Auckland, New Zealand: Oxford University Press, 1990, Chap. 6.

62. Cited in Whaanga, "Radio," 67.

63. Ministry of Commerce, "Maori Broadcasting: Principles for the Future," Wellington, New Zealand, August 27, 1991.

64. Broadcasting Commission of New Zealand, *New Zealand on Air Annual Report, 1990–1991*, Wellington, New Zealand, 1991.

65. Ministry of Broadcasting, "Broadcasting, Te Reo, and the Future," Wellington, New Zealand, January 1991, 5–6.

66. Sharp, Andrew, "The Problem of Maori Affairs, 1984–1989," in Holland and Boston, *The Fourth Labour Government*, 266–267.

67. Harcourt, David, senior advisor on broadcasting policy, Ministry of Commerce, personal interview, Wellington, New Zealand, September 1991.

68. Bartlett, personal interview; Walker, P., personal interview; Kaihau, personal interview.

69. Mead, Hirini, "The Treaty of Waitangi and Maori Claims to the Spectrum," in Hawke, G. R., ed., *Access to the Airwaves: Issues in Public Sector Broadcasting,* Wellington, New Zealand: Victoria University Press, 1990, 59–62; Wilson, Helen, "Broadcasting and the Treaty of Waitangi," *Media Information Australia,* 67 (February 1993), 92–99.

70. Mulgan, Richard, *Maori, Pakeha and Democracy,* 101–108; Orange, *The Treaty of Waitangi,* 249–251; Sharp, *Justice and the Maori,* Chaps. 7, 8; Walker, R., *Ka Whawhai Tonu Matou/Struggle without End,* 212.

71. Walker, R., *Ka Whawhai Tonu Matou/Struggle without End,* 248–252.

72. Ibid., 254.

73. Waitangi Tribunal, "Report on Claims Concerning Allocation of Radio Frequencies (Wai 26 and Wai 150)," Wellington, New Zealand, 1990, Vol. 3 Waitangi Tribunal Reports (WTR), 4.

74. Royal Commission on Broadcasting, *Report, September 1986,* Wellington, New Zealand: Government Printing Office, 1986, 308.

75. New Zealand Parliament, *Radiocommunications Act of 1989,* Wellington: Government Printing Office, No. 148, December 19, 1989.

76. Ibid., Sec. 178 (2)(b); Sec. 180 (2)(b).

77. Waitangi Tribunal, "Report on Claims Concerning Allocation of Radio Frequencies," 9.

78. Ibid., 25.

79. Ibid., 27.

80. Ibid., 28.

81. Ibid., 2.

82. Ibid., 44.

83. Ministry of Commerce, "Maori Broadcasting."

84. New Zealand Parliament, *Broadcasting Amendment* (An act to amend the Broadcasting Act of 1989), Wellington: Government Printing Office, July 7, 1993, Part IVa, Te Reo Whakapuaki Irirangi.

85. Impressions of the agency's activity were gathered through discussions I held in 1993 with over a dozen Maori broadcasters in different parts of the country, as well as through reading of a form letter (1993) sent by the agency to specific invited guests for the various hearings.

86. Court of Appeal, Document C.A. 206/91, Wellington, New Zealand, April 30, 1992.

87. Cited in Wilson, H., "Broadcasting and the Treaty of Waitangi," 98. See also Robb, Andrew, "Going to the Top," *Mana* (Maori newsmagazine), 2 (April–May 1993), 58–61, for background information regarding Maori viewpoints on the legal decisions up through 1992.

88. Frewen, Tom, "Channel 2 Sale Defies New Environment," *National Business Review* (New Zealand), February 28, 1994, 3.

89. Frewen, Tom, "Maori Groups Drag a Recalcitrant Government Back to Court, "*The National Business Review* (New Zealand), March 8, 1996, 27.

90. "Decision Awaited on RNZ Sale After Claims of Treaty Breach," *The Dominion* (Wellington), March 28, 1996, 3.

91. Gamble, Warren, "$89 Million for Commercial Radio," *The New Zealand Herald* (Auckland), April 4, 1996, 1.

92. Edwards, L., *Scrim: Radio Rebel in Retrospect,* Auckland, New Zealand: Hodder and Stoughton, 1971.

93. Fox, "Te Karere," 103–104; Fox, personal interview.

94. Sharp, *Justice and the Maori,* 255–257.

95. Hunt, Jonathan, "Directive to the Broadcasting Commission," June 1, 1989, Item 2(d).

96. Sharp, *Justice and the Maori*, 252–253; Walker, R., *Ka Whawhai Tonu Matou/Struggle without End*, 227–229, 244.

97. Sorrensen, M. P. K., "Modern Maori: The Young Maori Party to Mana Motuhake," in Sinclair, *The Oxford Illustrated History of New Zealand*, 350–351; Walker, R., *Ka Whawhai Tonu Matou/Struggle without End*, 244.

98. Sharp, *Justice and the Maori*, Chap. 13.

99. Ballera, Angela, *Proud to Be White? A Survey of Pakeha Prejudice in New Zealand*, Auckland, New Zealand: Heinemann Publishers, 1986; Mulgan, *Maori, Pakeha and Democracy*.

100. Ballera, *Proud to Be White?* 133–138.

101. I particularly recall a discussion I had in 1990 with a (here anonymous) New Zealand media consultant in his forties. He had deep misgivings about Maori radio, he told me, because it would increase divisiveness by encouraging separatism. He recalled his days as a young man at school with Maori classmates who, he claimed, were "just like us whites."

102. Human Rights Commission, Race Relations Office, "Racial Harmony in New Zealand—a Statement of Issues," Wellington, New Zealand: Government Printing Office, 1980, 6.

103. Sorrensen, "Modern Maori," 347.

104. Fox, "Aotearoa Broadcasting System," 129–130; Fox, personal interview; Te Ua, personal interview; Walker, P., personal interview; Walker, R., personal interview; Walker, R., *Ka Whawhai Tonu Matou/Struggle without End*, 270–271.

105. Sorrensen, "Modern Maori," 341.

106. For the United States see Wilson, Clint, and Felix Gutierrez, *Minorities and Media: Diversity and the End of Mass Communication*, Beverly Hills, Calif.: Sage, 1985; for Great Britain see Cohen, Phil, and Carl Gardner, eds., *It Ain't Half Racist, Mum*, London: Comedia, 1982.

107. Evans, Ripeka, "The Negation of Powerlessness—Maori Feminism, a Perspective," speech delivered as part of the Auckland University Winter Lecture Series, August 10, 1993, 11.

108. Jones, Lyn, *Te Reo Aotearoa Irirangi: Maori Language Broadcasting Development in New Zealand*, report prepared for the Commonwealth Relations Trust by the author, Cardiff, Wales, March 1994.

109. Lyn Jones, in *Te Reo Aotearoa Irirangi*, strongly advocates such cooperation, likening it to the structure of a meeting house, where the main beam is the national service, and the rib of the roof the iwi stations. The national service would take a major role in training iwi staff, as well. Ibid., 91–97. Maori broadcasters with whom I spoke in a March–April 1996 visit were fearful of losing control to the national service, and questioned the wisdom of placing so much emphasis on broadcasting in Maori when, according to a 1995 survey, only 14 percent of Maori surveyed considered themselves to be in the "medium high" (and above) levels of fluency. "National Maori Language Survey," *Te Maori News*, 5, 3 (February 1996), 8.

CHAPTER SIX

1. Sterngold, James, "This Man Has Dream [*sic*]: It's Downright Un-Japanese," *New York Times*, August 19, 1992, A4; De Chicchis, Joseph, "Current State of the Ainu Language," *Journal of Multilingual and Multicultural Development*, 16, 1 and 2 (1995), 114–15.

2. Delisle, Louise Bastien, "Reviving the Huron-Wendat Language," *Rencontre*, 16, 2 (Winter 1994–1995), 20.

3. Personal observations and conversations with station staff, CIHW, Wendat, Quebec, Canada, March 1992. Station staff members began taking lessons in Huron late in 1994 and hoped to begin to use Huron words and phrases on-air within a year or so. Ridjanovich, Amra, personal correspondence, February 3, 1995.

4. Siinty, Teresa, secretary, Tasmanian Aboriginal Center, Burnie, Australia, personal interview, November 1993.

5. Te Ua, Henare, director, Te Reo o Aotearoa, personal interview, Auckland, New Zealand, October 1993.

6. Browne, Donald R., "Raidio na Gaeltachta," *European Journal of Communication,* 7 (1992), 420; Hindley, Reg, *The Death of the Irish Language: A Qualified Obituary,* London and New York: Routledge, 1990; O'Fiannachta, Father Padraig, personal interview, Dingle, Ireland, August 1994; conversations with several young Irish speakers in Dingle, Galway, Donegal, and Dublin, September 1990 and August 1994. A somewhat more optimistic view appears in Clarity, James F., "Gaelic Now Trips Off Ireland's Silver Tongues," *New York Times,* September 16, 1994, A4.

7. This story was told to me by Brad Weiland, station manager of the largely student-operated high school radio station, KGHR. Personal interview, Tuba City, Ariz., April 1995.

8. "Communication Enterprises Get the Word out," *Indian Country Today,* March 9, 1995, special section entitled "Economics—the Navajo Nation," 25.

9. "Lagasradioi 10 cuogga," *ASSU* (Sami weekly newspaper), September 8, 1994, 4; personal listening to GLR, Kautokeino, Norway, September 11, 1994.

10. Feiritear, Brendan, manager, RNG, personal interview, Casla, Ireland, September 1990.

11. Glaisne, Risteard o, *Raidio na Gaeltachta,* Indreadbhan, Galway, Ireland: Clo Chois Fharraige, 1982, 229.

12. Bertos, George, executive director, and Jenny Jacobs, staff member, Maori Language Commission, personal interview, Wellington, New Zealand, September 1991; Bertos, George, personal interview, Wellington, New Zealand, October 1993.

13. Jones, Lyn, editor-in-chief, BBC Radio Cymru, personal interview, Cardiff, Wales, September 1994.

14. RNG staff, Casla, Ireland, personal discussion with group, August 1994.

15. Bordeu, Roger, former manager, Xiberoko Botza, personal interview Mauleon, France, September 1989.

16. nic Se, Helen, reporter, RNG, personal interview, Baile na n'Gall, Ireland, September 1990.

17. Varsi, Magna Uve, Sami Institute, personal interview, Kautokeino, Norway, May 1993.

18. Hippolite, Ken, manager, Te Reo Iriraki ki Otautahi, personal interview, Christchurch, New Zealand, October 1993.

19. This story was related to me by newsroom staff at Radio Cymru's Bangor, Wales, studio, April 1993.

20. Niia, Per, Sami journalist, Sveriges Television, personal interview, Kiruna, Sweden, May 1993.

21. Personal observations, listening to broadcasts, and discussions with Aboriginal media staff and "nonmedia" individuals, September 1987, September 1991, and October–November 1993.

22. Middlehurst, Simon, "Radio Told: Mind Your Language," *Cambrian News,* July 29, 1994, 1.

23. Magga, Ole Henrik, president, Sami Parliament, personal interview, Kautokeino, Norway, September 1994.

24. Davies, Aled Glynne, "Radio Cymru Y Gwasanaeth Newyddion BBC Cymru," Caerdydd (Cardiff), Wales: BBC Radio Cymru internal report, Ebrill (April), 1994. The report also revealed some ungrammatical and incorrect uses of Welsh by announcers.

25. Jones, L., personal interview.

26. Personal observation and listening to BBC Radio Cymru, September 2–3, 1994.

27. Discussions with various staff members of RNG, Baile na n'Gall, and RNG, Casla, Ireland, August 1994.

28. Worth, Sol, and John Adair, *Through Navajo Eyes,* Bloomington: Indiana University Press, 1972.

29. Michaels, Eric, *Aboriginal Invention of Television: Central Australia, 1982–86,* Canberra, A.C.T.: Australian Institute of Aboriginal Studies, 1986, and *Bad Aboriginal Art,* Minneapolis: University of Minnesota Press, 1993.

30. Michaels, Eric, Griffith University, personal interview, Brisbane, Queensland, Australia, September 1989.

31. Leuthold, Steven, "An Indigenous Aesthetic? Two Noted Videographers: George Burdeau and Victor Masayesva," *Wicazo Sa Review* (journal of the Association for American Indian Research), 10, 1 (Spring 1994), 40–51. Leuthold's dissertation " 'Telling Our Own Story': The Aesthetic Expression of Collective Identity in Native American Documentary," unpublished Ph.D. dissertation, University of Pennsylvania, 1992, supplies considerably more detail. Also, Leuthold is revising the dissertation for publication, with the tentative title *Telling Our Own Story,* to be published by the University of New Mexico Press.

32. Ang, Ien, *Watching Dallas: Soap Opera and the Melodramatic Imagination,* London and New York: Methuen, 1985.

33. Bobin, Jean-Paul, "Les Basques, Parlent aux Basques," *Midi Media* (Toulouse, France), 22 (December 1987), 49–50; Duteil, Christian, "Faut-il Brûler les Radios Basques?" *Journal Antennes Broadcast* (Paris), 3 (September–October 1987), 35–38; Soley, Lawrence, and John Nichols, *Clandestine Radio Broadcasting,* New York: Praeger, 1987, 61, 158–159, 312, 314.

34. Jones, Simon, activist in the community radio movement in Great Britain, personal conversation, Sydney, N.S.W., Australia, September 1987.

35. Browne, Donald R., "Raidio na Gaeltachta," 427–429.

36. "Kahnawake Raided," *Akwesasne Notes,* Summer 1988, 3; Jocks, Conway, manager, CKRK, personal interview, Kahnawake, Quebec, Canada, March 1992; Roth, Lorna, "Mohawk Airwaves and Cultural Challenges," *Canadian Journal of Communication,* 18 (1993), 315–331.

37. Mickiewicz, Ellen, *Split Signals: Television and Politics in the Soviet Union,* New York: Oxford University Press, 1988, 6–7, and "Rising Voices: Minorities and the Future of Soviet and American Television," *Media Studies Journal,* 5, 4 (1991), 203–215.

CHAPTER SEVEN

1. See Critchfield, Richard, *Shahhat, an Egyptian,* Syracuse, N.Y.: Syracuse University Press, 1978; Duvignaud, Jean, *Change at Shebika: Report from a North African Village,* New York: Vintage Books, 1970; and Smith, Gavin, *Livelihood and Resistance: Peasants and the Politics of Land in Peru,* Berkeley: University of California Press, 1989, for good examples of detailed accounts of village life in all its diversity. Thomas Cooper's article, "Communion and Communication: Learning from the Shuswap," *Critical Studies in Mass Communication,* 11, 4 (1994), 327–345, provides a quite detailed account of the complexity of detail in traditional oral communication, here by the Shuswap of British Columbia. Also useful as a source

of information on customs, values, traditions, and lifestyles of countries around the world is *Culturegrams: The Nations around Us,* Provo, Utah: David M. Kennedy Center for International Studies, 1991; its two volumes (*America and Europe; Africa, Asia, and Oceania*) offer brief but helpful introductions to cultural dimensions of indigenous and other peoples.

2. When Lakota station KILI-FM (Porcupine, S.Dak.) faced a shortfall of $175,000 in 1990, the tribal government said that it would be willing to step in and support the station, under three conditions: that the station drop its radio bingo broadcasts, that it replace the acting station manager (a white man married to a Lakota), and that it refuse airtime to the Porcupine Lakota Women's Organization, which some tribal leaders regarded as radical. The station turned down the offer. Jackson, Christine, "Debt-ridden KILI Radio Fights for Survival," *Rapid City Journal,* October 1, 1990, B1. And a fringe Anishinabe (Ojibwe) political group calling itself the Mille Lacs Anishinabe People's Party staged a protest outside Minneapolis/St. Paul (Minn.) station KSTP in April 1995. The station was preparing to broadcast programming about Native Americans, as a way of apologizing for some demeaning remarks made by one of its announcers about Native Americans in an earlier broadcast. The group felt that it would be excluded from gaining access to airtime to express its views if KSTP management dealt only with tribal leaders, who would seek to exclude the group from any broadcast. "Indian Protesters Seeking Access to KSTP Programs," *Minneapolis Star-Tribune,* April 4, 1995, 5B.

3. Among the rare exceptions are Wilson, Helen, "Broadcasting and the Treaty of Waitangi," *Media Information Australia,* 67 (February 1993), 92–99; parts of Michaels, Eric, *Aboriginal Invention of Television: Central Australia, 1982–86,* Canberra, A.C.T.: Australian Institute of Aboriginal Studies, 1986; and Michaels, Eric, *Bad Aboriginal Art,* Minneapolis: University of Minnesota Press, 1993.

4. Walker, Ranginui, *Ka Whawhai Tonu Matou/Struggle without End,* Auckland, New Zealand: Penguin Books, 1990, stands out for its consideration of the media as important elements in Maori life, although even he says relatively little about its impact upon Maori *political* life.

5. There are many books that deal with the subject of authority in indigenous tribes and other groups. I have found the following very helpful: Cassidy, Frank, and Robert L. Bish, *Indian Government: Its Meaning in Practice,* Lantzville, B.C., Canada: Oolichan Books, 1989; Cox, Lindsay, *Kotahitanga: The Search for Maori Political Unity,* Auckland, New Zealand: Oxford University Press, 1993; Eiselein, E. B., *Indian Issues,* rev. ed., Browning, Mont.: Spirit Talk Press, 1994; Fletcher, Christine, *Aboriginal Politics,* Melbourne, Victoria, Australia: Melbourne University Press, 1992; Purich, Frank, *Our Land: Native Rights in Canada,* Toronto: James Lorimer and Company, 1986; Mahuika, Api, "Leadership: Inherited and Achieved," in King, Michael, ed., *Te Ao Hurihuri: Aspects of Maoritanga,* Auckland, New Zealand: Reed Publishing Group, 1992, 42–63; O'Brien, Sharon, *American Indian Tribal Governments,* Norman: University of Oklahoma Press, 1989; Olson, James S., and Raymond Wilson, *Native Americans in the Twentieth Century,* Urbana: University of Illinois Press, 1986; Richardson, Boyd, *People of Terra Nullius,* Vancouver, B.C., Canada: Douglas and McIntyre, 1993; Thornton, Russell, *We Shall Live Again,* Norman: University of Oklahoma Press, 1986; Walker, Ranginui, *Ka Whawhai Tonu Matou/Struggle Without End,* Auckland, New Zealand: Penguin Books, 1992; Winiata, Maharaia, *The Changing Role of the Leader in Maori Society,* Auckland, New Zealand: Blackwood and Janet Paul, 1967; Wright, Ronald, *Stolen Continents: The Americas through Indian Eyes since 1492,* Boston: Houghton-Mifflin, 1992 (see especially Part 3).

6. Harcourt, David, senior advisor (broadcasting policy), Ministry of Commerce, personal interview, Wellington, New Zealand, October 1993.

7. Te Ua, Henare, Derek Fox, and Piripi Walker, all present or former managers of Maori stations or broadcast services, personal interviews, October 1993; correspondence with

John Craig, former manager, Radio New Zealand Special Services, April 1995.

8. Harcourt, David, and Roger Ellis, Ministry of Commerce, personal interviews, Wellington, New Zealand, September 1991; Harcourt, personal interview, October 1993; Kawe, Gary, and Pat Newton, Nga Haue e Wha, personal interviews, Invercargill, New Zealand, October 1993; Thompson, George, Nga Tai Tamariki A Tirahau, personal interview, Invercargill, New Zealand, October 1993; Diack, Chris, manager, Southland Community Radio, personal interview, Invercargill, New Zealand, October 1993.

9. Kawe and Newton, personal interviews; personal visit to office and school, October 1993; personal correspondence from David Hay, radio adviser to the Maori Council, September 1, 1995.

10. An article in the *Southland Express* (Invercargill daily newspaper), July 23, 1992, entitled "Maori Station Looks Promising," indicates that the newly licensed (to Nga Tahu) Irirangi A Iwi should be on-air "within several months."

11. Visit to "studio," October 1993.

12. Personal interview with Louise Yaxley, news director, 8KIN, Alice Springs, N.T., Australia, October 15, 1993. Several other indigenous radio station news directors or station managers with whom I have spoken in Australia, New Zealand, Canada, France (Basque), and northern Scandinavia (Sami) have noted that they either tried but failed in attempts to establish such networks or thought about it but didn't try because they were convinced that the community power structure would make it impossible.

13. In fact, KILI had broadcast a two-hour documentary and discussion of the issue and was ready to broadcast a second program on it when the Dennis Cross (the slain Lakota) Defense Committee Board requested its cancellation. Hamilton, Candy, "KILI Staff, Board, OK AIM Mediation Offer," *Rapid City Journal*, May 17, 1992, C3; Little Eagle, Avis, "Battle for KILI Radio Getting Physical," *Lakota Times*, June 24, 1992, A3.

14. Baum, Dan, "Protest Voices Displeasure with KILI Radio," *Los Angeles Times*, August 31, 1992, A5; Associated Press, "KILI Station Protesters still at Camp," *Rapid City Journal*, September 24, 1992, B3, and "KILI Radio Protesters again Ordered to Disband," *Rapid City Journal*, November 20, 1992, C2; Hamilton, Candy, several articles for the *Rapid City Journal*, with following titles, dates, and pages: "KILI Manager Locked out," May 7, 1992, B1, "Court Bars Manager from KILI," May 9, 1992, B3, "Ruling Expected Today on KILI Shakeup Effort," May 12, 1992, C2, "Judge Orders KILI Board to Deal with Allegations," May 13, 1992, C1, "AIM Members Consider Taking Part in KILI Protest," May 15, 1992, B2, "KILI Protesters Say Court Didn't End Fight," May 15, 1992, B2, "KILI Staff, Board, OK AIM Mediation Offer," May 17, 1992, C3, "Anatomy of KILI Dispute," May 17, 1992, C3, "Means Says KILI Board Illegal," June 2, 1992, B3, "KILI Manager Arrives as Protest Continues," June 17, 1992, C2, "Means Threatens KILI Takeover," July 7, 1992, B1, "KILI Directors Seek Steele's [tribal chairman] Assistance," July 8, 1992, C2, "KILI Manager Seeks Permanent Injunction," August 12, 1992, C2, "Judge Gives KILI Protesters Deadline," August 15, 1992, B2, [Lakota] Sioux High Court Overturns Order to Ban KILI Protesters," August 26, 1992, C3, "KILI Protesters Disband Camp," September 22, 1992, B3; "KILI Static," *Lakota Times*, May 13, 1992, A1, A3; Little Eagle, Avis, three articles, all *Lakota Times:* "KILI Mediation Team Gives Recommendations," June 10, 1992, A3, "KILI Board Asks Protesters to Go," June 17, 1992, A1, A2, "Battle for KILI Radio Getting Physical," June 24, 1992, A3; Sprague, Donovin, manager, KILI, personal interview, Porcupine, S.Dak., March 20, 1995; Casey, Tom, previous manager [during protest], KILI, personal interview, Porcupine, S.Dak., March 20, 1995.

15. Discussions with students and faculty at Navajo Community College, Chinle, Ariz., April 1986. When I suggested to one of the faculty that it was possible to let students take responsibility for administrative decisions—my experience as faculty advisor to student radio stations at Boston University and the University of Minnesota had shown it time and again—

they expressed grave doubts. I suspect that the hierarchical tribal structure fueled those doubts: how could young students manage such tasks?

16. Weiland, Brad, manager, KGHR, personal interview, Tuba City, Ariz., April 6, 1995.

17. An illustrative example: a staff member of an Aboriginal station in a major urban area told me that the program director would not allow the station to carry statements made by a prominent Aboriginal politician and educator because the director regarded that individual as insufficiently "tribal," and therefore not a true Aboriginal spokesperson. Confidential interview, fall 1993.

18. Personal discussion with CKON staff, St. Regis, Quebec, June 22, 1994, which also happened to be voting day on the U.S. side. The staff even had difficulty finding anyone who could give them definitive information on when the polls were closing!

19. Head, Sydney, Christopher Sterling, and Lemuel Schofield, *Broadcasting in America,* 7th ed., Boston: Houghton-Mifflin, 1994, 520.

20. Purich, Donald, *Our Land,* 197. Mohawk station CKON-FM, on the U.S.-Canadian border, was officially established in 1982, after several months on-air as "Akwesasne Freedom Radio," a clandestine operation. The tribe did not seek a license from either the CRTC or the FCC when CKON-FM came on the air, although it used Canadian call letters. Instead, the tribe claimed its own jurisdiction. Neither licensing authority seems interested in challenging the tribe. Jacobs, L. X., and Ray Cook, "Radios autochtones," Interradio, 4, 2 (1992), 9; personal discussion with CKON-FM staff, June 1994.

21. Jones, Lyn, editor, BBC Radio Cymru, personal interview, Caerdydd (Cardiff), Wales, September 2, 1994; Heatta, Nils Johann, head, NRK Sami Radio, personal interview, Karasjok, Norway, September 12, 1994.

22. Winter, James, "Showdown at the Oka Corral," in *Common Cents: Media Portrayal of the Gulf War and Other Events,* Montreal: Black Rose Books, 1992, Chap. 5. See also Sauvageau, Florian, Pierre Trudel, and Marie-Helene Lavoie, *Les tribunes de la radio: Echos de la crise d'Oka,* Quebec: Institut quebecois du récherche sûr la culture, 1995, which contains several critical accounts, particularly regarding talk shows and the bias displayed by hosts and by many anonymous callers.

23. Joseph, Nicole, ABC Radio National Radiothon (and also volunteer at Radio Redfern), personal interview, Sydney, N.S.W., Australia, November 21, 1993; Matthew Liotta, programmer, radio station 2RSR (community radio station through which Radio Koori broadcasts), personal interview, Sydney, N.S.W., Australia, November 22, 1993.

24. Fox, Derek, director, Mana Maori Media, personal interview, Ruatoria, New Zealand, October 20, 1993.

25. Browne, Donald R., "Finding a Basque Radio Voice: The French Experience," *InterMedia,* 18, 3 (1990), 41–42.

26. Based on personal listening to National Native News before and after the 1994 election.

27. Based on personal listening, watching, and reading of Aboriginal and majority culture media coverage in October 1993, while in Townsville (Queensland), Brisbane (Queensland), Darwin (N.T.), Broome (W.A.), Alice Springs (N.T.), and Kununurra, (Western Australia).

28. Based on personal listening, viewing, and reading during late October and early November 1993, mainly in Rotorua, Auckland, Ruatoria, Wellington, Christchurch, Invercargill, and Dunedin, New Zealand; Fox, personal interview.

29. Personal listening, Port Augusta, S.A., Australia, November 1993; Smith, Woody, Umeewarra Radio, personal interview, Port Augusta, S.A., Australia, November 1993.

30. Discussion with station staff at Radio Fryslan, Leeuwarden, Netherlands, October 1986.

31. Personal listening during the period October 13 to November 4, 1993.

32. Personal listening in Australia during the period November 5–23, 1993.

33. Personal discussion with WOJB staff, Hayward, Wis., July 1994; Keller, David, "Community Radio—the USA," *pbx* (publication of the Public Broadcasting Association of Australia), February 1993, 12.

34. Harte, Paul (Harteman@AOL.COM), "Low Power TV Service," e-mail message, January 3, 1995. The station was attempting to negotiate with the University of Montana, which had received a construction permit from the Federal Communications Commission in 1992 and was proposing to broadcast within the same area covered by SKC-TV, providing much the same programming (Public Broadcasting Service). SKC-TV feared both loss of revenue and loss of viewership.

35. Personal listening in Wellington, to Te Upoka o te Ika, September 1991.

36. Personal listening, over roughly two hours of what was a four-hour broadcast. Some station managers don't care to devote such long stretches of time to meetings, fearing loss of audience. Lakota Rosebud Reservation station KINI dropped such broadcasts for that reason and replaced them with two or three weekly one-hour forums devoted to the activities of the council, as well as indigenous public safety, fishing and hunting, and other offices. The public calls in, participation seems good, and the manager feels that more listeners are better served. Personal interview with Bernard Whiting, Jr., Manager, KINI, St. Francis, S.Dak., March 21, 1995. KILI manager Donovin Sprague also worries about length of broadcast, but many listeners appear to appreciate having the full account available. He has considered taping the meeting, then presenting an edited version, with the full tape available at the station upon individual request. He does wonder whether an edited version might anger some listeners, as well as council members and attendees; someone inevitably will claim that the most important part got cut and may even accuse the station of censorship. Personal interview.

37. Personal listening in September 1989, especially in Sydney, N.S.W., Melbourne, Victoria, and Alice Springs, N.T., Australia; interviews with 8KIN staff, Alice Springs, N.T., Australia, September 1989.

38. Personal listening to Radio RSR (the channel for Radio Koori) on November 22, 1993; interviews with Radio Koori staff at Radio RSR, Sydney, November 23, 1993.

39. Kidd, Dorothy, "Shards of Remembrance: One Woman's Archeology of Community Video," in Riano, Pilar, ed., *Women in Grassroots Communication: Furthering Social Change,* Thousand Oaks, Calif.: Sage, 1994, 189.

40. Ibid., 187–189.

41. Ruiz, Carmen, "Losing Fear: Video and Radio Productions of Native Aymara Women in Bolivia," in Riano, *Women in Grassroots Communication,* 171–177.

42. Smyth, Rosaleen, " 'White Australia Has a Black Past': Promoting Aboriginal and Torres Strait Islander Land Rights on Television and Video," *Historical Journal of Film, Radio and Television,* 15, 1 (1995), 105–123.

43. Kawaja, Jennifer, "Process Video: Self-Reference and Social Change," in Riano, *Women in Grassroots Communication,* 145–147.

44. Clemencia Rodriguez conveys some of the sense of "unworthiness" that the underprivileged of society feel when first asked to appear on TV, and how video projects can dispel that image. Rodriguez, Clemencia, "A Process of Identity Deconstruction," in Riano, *Women in Grassroots Communication,* 156–157.

45. Browne, Donald R., Ellen Mickiewicz, and Charles Firestone, *Television/Radio News & Minorities,* Washington, D.C.: Aspen Institute, 1994, 127–128.

46. Browne, Donald R. *International Radio Broadcasting: the Limits of the Limitless Medium,* New York: Praeger, 1982, Chap. 3, passim, also 164; Browne, Donald R., "The History and Programming Policies of RIAS: Radio in the American Sector of Berlin," Ph.D. dissertation, University of Michigan, 1961, 207–208 and 223–225;

47. Personal discussions with Mana Maori Media staff, Papatoetoe, New Zealand, Sep-

282

NOTES TO PAGES 215–221

tember 1991 and October 1993. Shortland has since gone on to other media activities, including recording a series of traditional Maori debates and presenting edited versions of them on television. He hopes they will serve as models to elevate the quality of formal debate among Maori. "Earthy Vitality," *Mana,* 11 (1996), 9.

48. Information on this drama was furnished to me by Lyn Jones, head, drama department, BBC Cymru, in a letter dated May 19, 1995.

49. Ruiz, "Losing Fear," in Riano, *Women in Grassroots Communication,* 163, 169–171.

50. Cited in Denselow, Robin, *When the Music's Over: The Story of Political Pop,* London and Boston: Faber, 1989, 167. Many books deal with music and political messages, but rarely do they present examples drawn from indigenous cultures. Denselow has an interesting section (pp. 135–137) on the Shona musician Thomas Mapfumo's political songs during the secessionist white rule of Zimbabwe (then Southern Rhodesia) and notes the role of Zimbabwe African National Union clandestine broadcasts of Mapfumo's songs into the country. The following titles provide several interesting perspectives on popular music and politics. Beltran Fuentes, Alfredo, *La Ideologia Antiautoritaria del Roc Nacional,* Buenos Aires: Centro Editor de America Latina, 1989; Bennett, Tony, et al., eds., *Rock and Popular Music: Politics, Policies, Institutions,* London and New York: Routledge, 1993; Lipsitz, George, *Dangerous Crossroads: Popular Music, Postmodernism, and the Poetics of Place,* London and New York: Verso, 1994; Pratt, Ray, *Rhythm and Resistance: Explorations in the Political Uses of Popular Music,* New York: Praeger, 1990; Ramet, Sabrina Petra, ed. *Rocking the State: Rock Music and Politics in Eastern Europe,* Boulder, Colo.: Westview Press, 1994.

51. Brunton, M., "Western Impact on Aboriginal Music," *Media Development,* 29, 1 (1982), cited in Breen, Marcus, ed., *Our Place Our Music,* Canberra, A.C.T., Australia: Aboriginal Studies Press, 1989, 91.

52. Cited in Breen, *Our Place Our Music,* 87.

53. Translation from Welsh provided by Rhys Moen, member of Anhrefn, personal interview, Caernarfon, Wales, April 1993.

54. Rothenbuhler, Eric W., "Commercial Radio and Popular Music: Processes of Selection and Factors of Influence," in Lull, James, ed., *Popular Music and Communications,* Newbury Park, Calif.: Sage, 1987, 92.

55. See Evans, Ripeka, "The Negation of Powerlessness—Maori Feminism, A Perspective," speech in the Auckland University Winter Lecture Series, August 10, 1993. She states at one point (p. 8 of the transcript), "It is not just the debate about speaking rights on the marae [tribal meeting place] which is the issue, but more the fuel which this powerful metaphor of restricted rights adds to Maori male hegemony—how it doubly oppresses and entrenches, how it silences and vaporises, how it extinguishes the collective voice of women."

56. For example, 8 of the 25 station managers of U.S. Native American and Inuit noncommercial radio stations were women, according to the March 1995 station listing provided by American Indian Radio on Satellite (Lincoln, Nebr.).

57. See also Keith, Michael C., *Signals in the Air: Native Broadcasting in America,* Westport, Conn.: Praeger, 1995, 116.

58. However, Ripeka Evans indicates that indigenous journalists of both sexes usually are unwilling to report on the abusive (toward women) behavior of many prominent Maori males, including political figures, and adds " they have done neither Maori women nor journalism a service [by their silence]." Evans, "The Negation of Powerlessness," 13.

59. Ferguson, Marjorie, "Images of Power and the Feminist Fallacy," *Critical Studies in Mass Communication,* 7, 3 (1990), 215–230.

60. There are several collections of studies on the subject, among them Creedon,

Pamela, ed., *Women in Mass Communication: Challenging Gender Values,* Newbury Park, Calif.: Sage, 1989; Gallagher, Margaret, and Lilia Quindoza-Santiago, eds., *Women Empowering Communication: A Resource Book on Women and the Globalization of Media,* New York: International Women's Tribune Center, 1994; Rakow, Lana F., ed., *Women Making Meaning: New Feminist Directions in Communication,* New York: Routledge, 1992; Riano, *Women in Grassroots Communication,* 1994; Thede, Nancy, and Alain Ambrosi, eds., *Video the Changing World,* Montreal: Black Rose Books, 1991; and UNESCO, *Women and Media Decision-making: The Invisible Barriers,* New Delhi: Sterling Publishers, 1989.

CHAPTER EIGHT

1. Browne, Donald R., *Comparing Broadcast Systems: The Experiences of Six Industrialized Nations,* Ames: Iowa State University Press, 1989, 337–346; Powers, Richard, and Hidetoshi Kato, *Handbook of Japanese Popular Culture,* Westport, Conn.: Greenwood Press, 1989.

2. Browne, Donald R., "Tunisia," in Douglas Boyd, ed., *Broadcasting in the Arab World,* Ames: Iowa State University Press, 1993; Browne, Donald R., "Television and National Stabilization: The Lebanese Experience," *Journalism Quarterly,* 52, 4 (Summer 1975), 692–698.

3. Whiting, Bernard, manager, KINI, personal interview, St. Francis, S.Dak., March 21, 1995; personal listening to the program, March 21, 1995.

4. The present situation in Russia is sufficiently fluid that it's sometimes difficult to determine whether a given electronic media operation is independent of the government. There are indications that indigenous radio outlets continue to operate in Siberia, where they broadcast in a few of the Inuit-related languages (Chukchi, Koryak, Komi, and Yakut). However, Yakimov and Morrison indicate that the indigenous press in Siberia remains tied to the Communist party (whether it operates under that title or not), and the *World Radio-Television Handbook, 1995 Edition* indicates such language services only for the regional stations that form part of the national (government-run) broadcast services. Yakimov, Oleg D., and Joy F. Morrison, "The National Press of the Indigenous Peoples of Siberia: Origins and Future Directions," *European Journal of Communication,* 10, 1 (March 1995), 109–126.

5. Jacob, James E., and William E. Beer, eds., *Language Policy and National Unity,* Totowa, N.J.: Rowman and Allanheld, 1985, 4. It is clear from the context that the authors are describing a situation and not recommending this as a course of action!

6. Keith, *Signals in the Air,* 40–41.

7. Rada, Stephen, "A Survey of Native American Radio Broadcasting: Policies, Operations, and Development," unpublished manuscript, 1978, 21–22.

8. Personal visit to KNCC, April 1985.

9. Jackson, Christine, "Debt-ridden KILI Radio Fights for Survival," *Rapid City Journal,* October 1, 1990, B1; Jackson, Christine, "$58,000 Pledged in KILI Fund-raiser," *Rapid City Journal,* October 12, 1990, C2. KILI conducted a selective national mail fund-raising campaign early in 1995. It appeared to be doing very well when I visited the station in late March of that year. One device that may have helped was the mailing address: not the station's location (Porcupine, S.Dak.), but nearby Wounded Knee, which has both great fame and high emotional appeal: it is the site of the 1890 massacre of a few hundred Lakota, mostly women and children, by the U.S. Cavalry and also the site of the 1973 confrontation there between members of the American Indian Movement and U.S. government law enforcement officials.

10. Young, John, "Public Broadcasting Cuts Threaten Reservation Radio," *Indian Country Today* [*Lakota Times* section], February 9, 1995, B2; Sprague, Donovin, manager, KILI, personal interview, Porcupine, S.Dak., March 20, 1995.

11. "Alaska's Public Radio, a Communication Lifeline, May Be Cut," *New York Times,* April 16, 1995, 10. The headline was slightly hyperbolic, since both House and Senate proposals maintained some funding for radio, although the House bill would have sharply reduced funding for public radio in communities that have commercial radio stations. Even the lower cut for radio caused many problems for the smaller stations, and six stations along the southeast coast had to agree to take more of their programming from a central source. Mc-Clear, Rich, former manager, KCAW, Sitka, Alaska, personal interview, Minneapolis, Minn., April 25, 1996.

12. Browne, *Comparing Broadcast Systems,* 17–28, provides a review of categories and problems.

13. Personal observations and discussion with station staff, October 1993.

14. Sprague, Donovin, manager, and Tom Casey, development director, KILI-FM, personal interviews, Porcupine, S.Dak., March 20, 1995.

Index